A WRITER'S GUIDEBOOK

RISE B. AXELROD
California State University,
San Bernardino

CHARLES R. COOPER
University of California,
San Diego

St. Martin's Press
New York

Director of development: Carla Kay Samodulski
Sponsoring editor: Donna Erickson
Editorial assistant: Jason Noe
Managing editor: Erica T. Appel
Senior project editor: Diana M. Puglisi
Production supervisor: Joe Ford
Marketing manager: Karen Melton
Art director: Lucy Krikorian
Text design: Robin Hoffmann, Brand X Studios; Dorothy Bungert, EriBen Graphics
Graphics: MacArt Design
Cover design: Evelyn Horovicz

Library of Congress Catalog Card Number: 97-66122

Manufactured in the United States of America.

3 2 1 0 9 8
f e d c b a

For information, write:
St. Martin's Press, Inc.
175 Fifth Avenue
New York, NY 10010

ISBN: 0-312-16755-5

Acknowledgments

Acknowledgments and copyrights are continued at the back of the book on page 456, which constitutes an extension of the copyright page.

INTRODUCTION

A Writer's Guidebook is a brief reference handbook that offers help with the research and writing you will be asked to do in college and in your career. Keep it on the shelf with your dictionary, computer manuals, and other reference works. It includes guidelines and basic information that will help you plan, research, write, edit, and present any essay or research project. You can turn to *A Writer's Guidebook* in any writing situation, confident that it will complement the requirements for research and writing that you will be expected to follow in different college courses and on the job.

A Writer's Guidebook has been designed to give you quick access to the information you need. An easy-to-follow, well-designed guide, it will help you find answers, avoid errors, and become a more confident, effective writer.

Twenty-five frequent errors

To prepare *A Writer's Guidebook*, we carried out a nationwide study of the problems first-year college students have with the conventions of standard edited English. College writing instructors and professional editors noted the errors in over five hundred essays in nine different types of writing. (Spelling errors were not counted in our study.)

As a result of this study, *A Writer's Guidebook* offers a list of the twenty-five errors that appeared most frequently in the approximately fifteen thousand sentences we analyzed. The errors, listed on the next page in order of descending frequency, can guide you in editing your own writing. The numbers in bold following each error indicate where in *A Writer's Guidebook* you can find help with understanding and correcting each error.

1 Wordiness **34a, b**
2 Misused word **35a, b**
3 Incorrect or ambiguous pronoun reference **19**
4 Verb tense errors **23a-c**
5 Missing comma between independent clauses **37a**
6 Problems with hyphens between compound adjectives **46a**
7 Missing comma after introductory elements **37b**
8 Capitalization of proper or common nouns **47a**
9 Unnecessary comma between compound elements **38a**
10 Incorrect spacing **48**
11 Missing words **26a-d**
12 Missing comma with nonrestrictive word groups **37c**
13 Comma splice or fused sentence **16, 17**
14 Problems in using quotation marks with other punctuation **42b**
15 Missing or unnecessary hyphens in compound nouns **46b**
16 Missing comma with transitional and parenthetical expressions, absolute phrases, and contrasted elements **37d**
17 Problems of pronoun-antecedent agreement **20**
18 Incorrect preposition **35c**
19 Misuse of *who, which,* or *that* **24f**
20 Unnecessarily complex sentence structure **34c**
21 Spelling out or using figures for numbers incorrectly **49a**
22 Problems with apostrophes in possessive nouns **43a**
23 Sentence fragment **18**
24 Missing comma in items in a series **37e**
25 Unnecessary comma with restrictive word groups **38b**

This list of the top twenty-five errors can be categorized into five major patterns of errors. You may find it useful to keep these patterns in mind as you edit your work.

1 Missing or unnecessary commas **(37a, 37b, 37c, 37d, 38a, 38b)**

2 Errors in word choice **(34a, b; 35a, b)**

3 Errors in pronoun reference, agreement, or use **(19, 20, 24f)**

4 Verb tense errors **(23a-c)**

5 Errors in recognizing and punctuating sentences—comma splices, fused sentences, fragments **(16, 17, 18)**

Keeping a record of your own errors

In addition to checking your work for the errors college students usually make, you might find it useful to keep a record of the errors that *you* usually make. Recording errors in your writing can help you to discover your own most frequent errors and error patterns. You can then work toward reducing them.

To use the Record of Errors form on the next page, note the name and section number of each error in the left-hand column. (See the table of contents inside the back cover or the list of correction symbols that immediately precedes it for the names of errors.) For example, if in your first essay your instructor or another student marks a vague use of the pronoun *this* at the beginning of two of your sentences, locate the section that provides help in correcting this error (19c) and enter the error name in the left column along with the section number: Vague use of *this, that,* and *which,* 19c. Then under *Essay 1* and next to the name of the error, enter the number 2 to indicate how many times you made this error. As you edit subsequent essays, you can easily review this section in *A Writer's Guidebook* to make sure you have avoided this pronoun problem.

By your second or third essay, you should begin to see patterns in the errors you make and also begin to understand how to recognize and correct them.

RECORD OF ERRORS

Name of Error and Section Number in A Writer's Guidebook	FREQUENCY						
	Essay 1	*Essay 2*	*Essay 3*	*Essay 4*	*Essay 5*	*Essay 6*	*Essay 7*

HOW TO USE THIS BOOK

A Writer's Guidebook provides many possible routes to the practical information you need to plan, research, or edit your writing: color-coded menu, comprehensive index, list of instructor's correction symbols, table of contents, and Glossary of Usage. Each of these resources is described below, with an activity that provides a model for using the resource followed by an opportunity for you to practice using the resource yourself.

Color-coded menu

The color-coded menu on the first page of *A Writer's Guidebook* briefly outlines the book's contents. Each of the eleven parts of the book is associated with a different color and an icon. Colored tabs with icons on the outside margin of every page allow you to flip quickly to the part of the book you need to consult. After the first page of each part you will find a list of contents for that part.

Model

Is the second sentence a fragment or a complete sentence?

> Parents are focused on what they care about. Rather than their children, who are the ones they should be caring about.

To answer this question, you need to find the chapter in *A Writer's Guidebook* that covers sentence fragments. (If you cannot name the potential problem or find someone to help you name it, you can use the index, which is described in the following section.)

1. Turn to the menu on the first page of this book. Under "Part 4, Sentence Boundaries," you will find "Chapter 18, Sentence Fragments." Notice that Part 4 is identified by an icon (⇩) and the color green.
2. Find Part 4 by turning to the pages with green tabs. The first green-tabbed page provides a complete contents for Part 4 along with page numbers. The chapter on sentence fragments begins on page 234.
3. Turning to page 234, you will find the answer by looking at the first example. The phrase *rather than,* like *because* in the example, is a subordinating conjunction introducing a dependent clause. Reading further, you learn that to convert a sentence fragment like this one into a complete sentence, you need to attach the fragment to the preceding sentence.

Practice

Is a comma needed between the two independent clauses in this sentence?

> Libertarians believe that government should not intervene in the free market and they advocate maximum personal freedom for everyone.

Using the color-coded menu, find the page that gives you the information you need to edit the sentence. (The clues you need are in the question.)

Index

A comprehensive index at the back of *A Writer's Guidebook* includes terms relating to every aspect of research and writing. For example, if you are not sure whether to use *a* or *an,* you can look under "articles," or simply look under *"a, an, the."* As you can see, the index provides several routes to the information you need. This flexibility makes the index especially useful for answering nearly any writing or research question you might come up with.

Model

Can I use *this* in the second sentence to refer to the entire first sentence?

> In groups, men tend to speak not to individuals but to the group. This may indicate an attempt to establish leadership in the group.

Let's assume that you do not remember that *this* is a *pronoun,* and you have no idea that using *this* to refer to the whole sentence is called *vague pronoun reference.* To find the answer in the index, all you need is the word *this.*

1. Look for *this* in the index. You will find the entry "*this,* 240–41." You may not be sure that this entry is the right one until you turn to page 240 to see whether the example looks like your sentence.
2. Turn to page 240, where you will find section 19b: "Rewrite to eliminate vague uses of *this, that,* and *which.*" The first example answers the question: after *this* in the second sentence, you need to insert a noun such as *tendency* to make it clear that you are referring to the idea in the first sentence that "men tend to speak" in a certain way.

Practice

Is a comma needed in the following sentence to separate the introductory element from the main part of the sentence, which begins with *the choice*?

> When we have to choose between carrying out everyday activities and starting a challenging task the choice is usually to do the small stuff.

Use the index to find the information you need to answer the question. Try both of the question's two obvious clues—*introductory element* and *comma.*

Correction symbols

Your instructor may mark your errors with correction symbols like *mm* (misplaced modifier). If so, the alphabetical list of correction symbols that immediately precedes the table of contents at the back of this book will lead you to the chapter and section you need.

Model

My instructor has marked the following sentence *cs.*

> Liberals believe that federal programs are neither intrusive nor oppressive, these programs guarantee to all citizens the same rights and opportunities.

1. Turn to the list of correction symbols on the last right-hand page of this book. Find *cs*, which is followed by the name of the error and a chapter number: "Comma splice 16."
2. Flip through the book, looking at the chapter and section numbers at the top of the page, and stop at Chapter 16. After surveying the options for editing comma splices, you decide that the most appropriate editing strategy is "16d Separate the independent clauses with a semicolon or period, and add a conjunctive adverb or transition." Revise the sentence accordingly.

Practice

My instructor has marked the following sentence *num.*

> Among the 7 tabloid TV segments I viewed involving personal relationships, 5 segments represented relationships based on distrust or deception.

Using the search above as a model, find the information you need to correct the error.

Contents

Your instructor may mark your errors with chapter and section numbers.

Model

My instructor has marked the following sentence "46a."

> Not even street smart young men can protect themselves from violence.

1. Turn to the table of contents inside the back cover and locate 46a. Chapter 46 covers the use of hyphens. Section 46a, "Compound adjectives," provides information and examples about a special problem with hyphens: omitting the hyphen in compound adjectives or using it incorrectly (a high-frequency error in our research study).
2. Turn to the page number for Chapter 46, 371, or flip through the book, stopping when you see 46 at the top of the page. You will find that the explanation and examples *(after-school activities, fast-growing business)* show you how to correct the error.

Practice

My instructor has marked the following sentence "42b."

> "Most people who come here aren't homeless", Carol says.

Using the search above as a model, find the information you need to correct the error.

Glossary of Usage

The Glossary of Usage offers quick advice on words that are frequently confused or misused, the second most frequent error revealed by our research.

Model

Have I used the word *further* correctly in the following sentence?

> If we drive any further on this spare tire, we'll have two flat tires to repair.

1. Turn to the Glossary of Usage on page 439 and look for the word *further*, where you will find a cross-reference.
2. Checking the entry *farther/further*, you discover that the answer is *farther.*

Practice

In the following sentence, have I used the word *relationship* correctly?

> Some writers insist that there is a relationship between a shortage of decent-paying jobs and violence among young men.

Look up the word in question, study the explanation, and decide whether the word is correct or must be changed. If you cannot find the word you are looking for in the Glossary of Usage, look for it in your dictionary.

PREFACE TO INSTRUCTORS

The idea for *A Writer's Guidebook* came after years of trying out different ways of teaching students to edit their own writing. We developed a method in which instructors point out sentence-level problems in a portion of an essay and students use a quick-reference handbook to solve the problems themselves. Then instructors review the students' work. This focus on identifying problems, giving students initiative, and providing follow-up proved highly effective, but students sometimes had difficulty finding help even when we directed them to the relevant section in the handbook we assigned. They found too much explanation and too few examples, with too little coverage, or, in some cases, no coverage at all of the errors they were actually making.

To remedy these problems, we organized a nationwide study to find out which errors occur in typical college writing situations. Focusing on the part of each essay characteristic of its genre, our team of twelve experienced writing instructors and professional editors analyzed approximately fifteen thousand sentences in over five hundred essays in nine genres of college writing. The essays, written by students in universities, four-year colleges, and community colleges, were revised drafts completed without the benefit of advice on style and sentence-level conventions. The findings from this research gave shape to *A Writer's Guidebook.*

A Writer's Guidebook provides quick, explicit answers for students working on their own. The text relies on examples of student writing, rather than abstract and complicated explanations, to illustrate grammatical concepts. Like a trail guide, *A Writer's Guidebook* shows students what to do and how to do it—how to quickly identify and correct their own errors. In addition to providing thorough coverage of the conventions of grammar and usage, the *Guidebook* supports students' research and writing in their college courses.

FEATURES OF *A WRITER'S GUIDEBOOK*

Brief guides for six writing tasks

Condensed from the *St. Martin's Guide to Writing*, Fifth Edition, these brief guides offer specific advice on writing essays that present personal experience, explain concepts, argue positions, evaluate texts or ideas, speculate about causes, or interpret literature. Each brief guide helps students plan, draft, and revise their essays, providing a sample outline of one student's essay as well as questions students can use to evaluate one another's drafts.

Numerous examples from actual student writing

Sentences illustrating common errors and grammatical concepts are taken from actual student essays. The student sentences come from essays representing the wide range of subjects first-year students write about and the many genres they write in. The realistic examples make it easier for students to match a flawed sentence to a good model.

Sentence problems organized by frequency

Our research findings have led us to present error categories in order of their frequency, making it easier for students searching for help on their own to find what they need. For example, the section on grammatical sentences in *A Writer's Guidebook* begins with pronoun reference, the single most common grammatical error covered in that section. In Chapter 19, "Pronoun Reference," the three prominent types of errors appear in order of frequency. The organization and content of all the chapters on grammar, punctuation, and mechanics are informed by our research findings and offer students extra help where they need it most.

Detailed coverage of the writing problems and topics identified by our research

Our research revealed several types of errors that occur with some frequency but that are not covered, or not covered in enough detail, by most current handbooks. As a result, *A Writer's Guidebook* provides chapters on relative pronouns (21); noun agreement (28); and errors in spacing around punctuation marks (48). Chapter 31 offers help with integrating quotations, questions, and thoughts in addition to the advice on integrating source material in Chapter 8. *A Writer's Guidebook* also provides a chapter on dashes (41), with thorough coverage of this useful punctuation mark.

We also offer stronger coverage of the following problem areas uncovered by our research than is offered by most other brief handbooks:

- Missing prepositions, conjunctions, and other small words (26a)
- Unnecessary prepositions (34e)
- Incorrect prepositions (35c)
- Comma needed with trailing participial phrases (37c)
- Unnecessary commas with trailing adverbial clauses (38d)
- Semicolon needed to join a pair or series of independent clauses with internal punctuation (39c)

Finally, Chapter 33, "Emphasis and Clarity," includes coverage of strategies that increase readability, including using cohesive devices (33c), making sentence topics visible (33d), and putting familiar information ahead of new information (33e).

Grammar definitions highlighted in the margins

To help streamline the explanations, grammar definitions appear in the margins so that students can read them as needed or skip right to the examples.

Integrated coverage of library and online research

Reflecting the way students actually do research today, Chapter 7 integrates coverage of both traditional and online sources. It also provides guidelines for evaluating both, including a separate section on evaluating Internet sources. Abundant coverage of how to cite online sources appears in our documentation chapters. Chapter 9 includes new guidelines from the Modern Language Association for citing sources from the World Wide Web.

Attention to ESL issues

For students who have learned to write English as a second language, *A Writer's Guidebook* covers the most common problem areas in four separate chapters in Part 10. In addition, boxes throughout the text provide additional information for ESL writers or refer them to Part 10 for more help.

Full-color guidebook format

Designed to help students find what to do and how to do it, the *Guidebook* minimizes lengthy explanations and uses color icons, tabbed sections, and other quick-reference features to lead students to the information they need.

A sample student assignment

To give students a specific, realistic example of how to respond to a college assignment, Chapter 1 of the *Guidebook*, "Organizing and Managing College Writing Assignments," follows one student through the process of researching, writing, and revising an essay for a history course.

Digital Hints

Throughout the book, Digital Hint boxes provide useful tips on using technology in all stages of the writing process.

A chapter on critical reading strategies

Chapter 12 includes important strategies to help students become more active, critical readers and, consequently, better writers. Strategies covered include annotating, outlining, summarizing, reflecting on the writer's perspective, and evaluating the writer's logic.

Additional Resources

- *Interactive Handbook and Exercise CD-ROM* includes an electronic reference and interactive exercises. The exercises provide opportunities for practice and are linked directly to the handbook explanations, giving students immediate help with questions and problems.
- *Web Site <www.smpcollege.com/guidebook>* gives students and instructors information on using the World Wide Web for research as well as links to useful sites for writers.
- *Transparency Masters* include student essays and revision checklists.

- *Exercise Booklet with Answer Key* provides additional opportunities for practice and is available in print or with the handbook on CD-ROM.
- *Diagnostic Tests* help students and instructors identify the grammatical concepts that students need to work on.
- ***Who Are We? Readings on Identity, Community, Work, and Career***, by Rise Axelrod and Charles Cooper, provides twenty-six selections in a brief reader.
- ***Free Falling and Other Student Essays***, edited by Paul Sladky, Augusta College, a collection of essays by students using the *St. Martin's Guide to Writing*, makes available fine writing from students at colleges across the country.

Acknowledgments

We would like to thank the following reviewers, who provided valuable comments as we developed *A Writer's Guidebook:* Peggy F. Broder, Cleveland State University; Gina Claywell, Murray State University; J. Rocky Colavito, Northwestern State University; Mark Coley, Tarrant County Junior College; Jonathan S. Cullick, University of Kentucky; Madeline J. Dennis, Broome Community College; Diana C. Grumbles, Southern Methodist University; Michael J. Hricik, Westmoreland County Community College; Ted E. Johnston, El Paso Community College; Edwina K. Jordan, Illinois Central College; Todd Marvin, Evergreen Valley College; Lynn McDonie, Antelope Valley Community College; H. Ray McKnight, California State University–Fresno; Roark Mulligan, Christopher Newport University; Tom Nawrocki, Columbia College; Theresa Nicolay, St. John Fisher College; Sue G. Parsons, Stephen F. Austin State University; Shelby J. Pierce, Owens Community College; Ace G. Pilkington, Dixie College; Barbara C. Rhodes, Central Missouri State University; Randall Roorda, University of Missouri–Kansas City; Cheryl W. Ruggiero, Virginia Polytechnic Institute and State University; Alison Russell, Xavier University; Richard Stoner, Broome Community College; Mary Ware, Los Angeles Southwest College; Mary Jane Watkins, Butler County Community College, and Mark Wiley, California State University, Long Beach.

The following ESL instructors provided helpful comments on the chapters in Part 10: Stacy Hagen, Edmonds Community College; John M. Kopec, Boston University; Mark Picus, Houston Community College–Central; Helen H. Schmidt, Iowa State University; and Peggy A. Velis, Biola University.

We have a number of people to thank for helping us to prepare *A Writer's Guidebook.* Melissa Axelrod, Kathy Graehl, Anna M. Guthrie, Carol P. Haviland, Sandra Kamusikiri, Marcia Muth, Kathryn O'Rourke, Mary Pickering, Wendy B. Smith, and Michael Weber participated in our research study. Gary Parks of Shoreline Community College helped write the chapters on research. Kevin Wilson of Boise State University gave us the benefit of his expertise in the chapters on oral presentations and document design. Beth Castrodale, Marcia Muth, and Francine Weinberg have also provided invaluable assistance in helping to prepare various parts of *A Writer's Guidebook.* Deborah Person of the University of Wyoming Law Library provided helpful comments on Chapter 7. We also wish to thank Marino Crinella and Jeremiah Axelrod and the students in their history class at the University of California, Irvine, for helping us with Chapter 1. Nancy Etheridge of Boise State University provided the student essay in Chapter 9. We are deeply grateful to them all for their efforts.

We are especially grateful to Gloria Gutierrez, Brent Knutson, and Christina Dinh, whose essays appear in Chapters 1, 9, and 10, and to Sarah West, Drew Long, Margaret Tate, Margaret Zenk, La Donna Beaty, Scott Hyder, Kirsten Dockendorff, and Anna Pride, whose work appears in Chapter 33.

We want to express our special appreciation to our editor, Carla Samodulski, without whom we would not have ventured down this path. Thanks to everyone else at St. Martin's Press who helped with this project, including Donna Erickson, Karen Melton, Diana Puglisi, Joe Ford, Lucy Krikorian, Evelyn Horovicz, Tonya Strong, and Jason Noe. Rise wishes to thank her husband, Steven, for his enduring love and patience. Charles thanks his wife, Mary Anne, for her unwavering support, liveliness, and humor.

Rise B. Axelrod
Charles R. Cooper

PART 1

WRITING IN COLLEGE

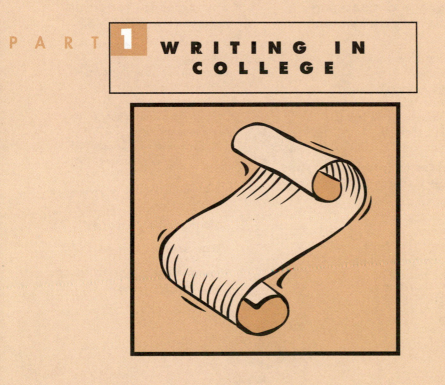

PART

1 WRITING IN COLLEGE

ORGANIZING AND MANAGING COLLEGE WRITING ASSIGNMENTS

Have you ever tried the dangerous method of writing? You begin by writing the first word of the introduction and write straight through to the last word of the conclusion. You do not plan or try out ideas before writing; add, cut, or revise as you write; or get help from friends or teachers. You do not allow yourself a second draft or second thoughts.

The dangerous method may be okay if you are expert in the subject and in the kind of writing an assignment calls for—such as arguing a position for a history course or interpreting a novel for English. But when the subject is challenging and the kind of writing is new to you, then you need a less risky, more productive writing process—one that does not take too much time but lets you use your time efficiently and helps you learn as you write.

> *Writing is easy; all you do is sit staring at a blank sheet of paper until the drops of blood form on your forehead.*
> —Gene Fowler

This chapter describes a process that makes writing productive and efficient by dividing it into a series of activities you can do over several days. Working on your writing bit by bit lets you focus on one problem at a time. Immersed in the process, you will find that even when you are driving or working out, part of your mind continues to solve problems in your essay.

> *You know when you think about writing . . . you think it is overwhelming. But, actually, you break it down into tiny little tasks any moron could do.*
> —Annie Dillard

The process described here divides into the following stages: understanding the assignment, planning, formulating a thesis, organizing and drafting, evaluating and revising, and editing and proofreading. In addition to offering practical advice for each part of the process, this chapter includes Writer at Work sections illustrating the activities of one student, Gloria Gutierrez, as she wrote an essay for her American history class. You will see the assignment (1a), some of Gutierrez's invention writings (1b), her working thesis (1c), and her scratch outline (1d). You will also see excerpts from her journal, in which she described the process of writing the essay and revising based on her instructor's advice. The revised and edited essay concludes the chapter (1g).

1a Understand the writing assignment.

Writing assignments vary widely. Some assignments are quite general, essentially requiring you to define the topic for yourself. Others are more specific, spelling out exactly what your essay should include. Whether the assignment is general or specific, you need to think about your writing situation—specifically, your audience and purpose. For most college assignments, your instructor is your reader, but you need to analyze the assignment to understand what your instructor expects before you can choose a topic (if you have that option) and decide what you want to say.

Determine what kind of writing is required and what its conventions are.

College students are assigned many different kinds of essays, for example:

For a Composition Course
Much of what happens in high school and college follows tradition. Examples of practices that have changed very little include the procedures for signing up for courses, rushing for sororities and fraternities, and trying out for sports teams. Think of a problem with an established practice in your school. Write a proposal arguing that the practice you have chosen needs improvement and that the changes you recommend will solve the problem.

For a Political Science Course
Write an essay discussing the concept of political asylum in U.S. immigration law. In the context of one particular case (such as the 14,000 Haitians who sought asylum in 1980), consider the criteria used to determine whether groups are political refugees and should be given asylum. Discuss the political debate that took place at the time and your own view on whether the group should or should not have been given political asylum.

For an American History Course
Both John Filson's popular 1780s "Adventures of Col. Daniel Boon" and the last portion of historian John Mack Faragher's acclaimed 1990s biography *Daniel Boone: The Life and Legend of an American Pioneer* deal with

what could be termed the "mythical Boone"—Filson constructs the myth and Faragher analyzes and debunks it. In the context of our study of the American frontier, think about what purposes the myth might have served for Boone's contemporaries as well as for subsequent generations. Explain the significance of some of the differences between the myth of Daniel Boone and the reality. Construct an argument that synthesizes your own ideas with material from the readings and lectures.

To understand the assignment, identify the type of writing called for, and consider the disciplinary conventions for that type of writing.

Find the Action Terms to Identify the Type of Writing. Many action terms are used in the preceding sample assignments, including *proposal, discuss, explain,* and *argument.* Action terms tell you what your instructor wants your essay to do. The actions identified by some terms, such as *explain* and *argue,* may be obvious to you, while the actions implied by other terms, such as *discuss* and *analyze,* may be less clear.

To interpret action terms, you need to consider the context both of the assignment and of the discipline. In the political science assignment, for example, the action term *discuss* can be understood in relation to the rest of the assignment, which indicates that students are expected not only to explain the issue but also to take a position in the debate and argue for it.

WRITER AT WORK

Gloria Gutierrez wrote on the American history assignment about Daniel Boone. She initially found the assignment confusing because it uses two different action terms: *explain* and *argument.* Based on her experience in other history courses, however, she understood that the assignment required an argument. She explained in her journal, "I realize that I need to stay away from an essay that merely states facts and come up with a creative way to argue my thesis."

But it took some time and help from her instructor before Gutierrez understood that in addition to showing how the myth of Daniel Boone differs from the reality, she also had to answer the second part of the assignment and suggest what purposes the myth served for different historical periods. In subsequent Writer at Work sections, you will see how her understanding of the assignment evolved as she planned, drafted, and revised the essay.

For additional help in understanding assignment action terms and the types of writing they signal, see Chapters 2 and 4.

Consider the Disciplinary Conventions. As a student, you need to learn about the general conventions of writing in college and the special requirements of each discipline you are studying. Most instructors, regardless of the subject they teach, expect students to hand in essays that have been proofread and edited according to the rules of standard written English. Because instructors usually value clear, explicit writing, they expect essays to begin with a thesis and to use topic sentences and transitions that lead the reader from one point to the next (see 3a and 3b).

In addition to these general expectations, each discipline has its own conventions regarding vocabulary, word choice, and documentation style. However, you can assume that most instructors expect your essays to be relatively formal, avoiding the kind of informal language and slang you might use with friends (see 36a and 36c). As you take courses in such subject areas as English, philosophy, and chemistry, you will learn the specialized language of each discipline and how to use it. You will also learn which style of documentation is appropriate and how to use it. (Chapters 9–11 provide guidelines for citing sources in three widely used documentation styles.)

Determine how the assignment fits into what you have been studying in the course.

Writing assignments invariably relate to the goals and subject matter of the course. Therefore, keep the course's objectives, subject matter, and modes of inquiry in mind as you consider the assignment. The following suggestions may help you connect the assignment to what you are studying.

Review Your Class Notes and the Course Reading with the Assignment in Mind. Check your notes and skim the readings to see if anything in them bears on the assignment. Look for recurring issues, questions, and ideas.

Think about the Modes of Inquiry Used in the Discipline. In many cases, writing assignments not only echo the course's themes, but also call for methods that have been used in class or that are typically used in the discipline. For example, if an English instructor continually points out how literary texts reflect or critique the cultural values and attitudes of the time in which they were written, you can expect a writing assignment that requires you to interpret a text in terms of its historical and cultural context.

WRITER AT WORK

> The American history assignment gave Gutierrez a choice of four possible topics. She chose the one shown on pages 4 and 5 because when she originally did the reading, she had noted that Faragher's image of Daniel Boone—presumably, the real Boone—differed from the image of Boone presented by Filson. Assuming that the assignment called for an explanation of the differences between the real and mythic Boone, she thought it would be easy to categorize the differences she had marked while reading Faragher and Filson and to choose quotes illustrating the differences.

1b Plan the essay.

When you are trying to understand an assignment, you are primarily concerned with your reader's expectations. When you plan your essay, your focus shifts to clarifying your own purpose for writing. During this stage, you discover what you have to say in response to the assignment.

Use systematic planning to develop your ideas.

Planning can be especially productive when it is systematic, done in an adequate amount of time, and written down.

Focus on One Part at a Time. Explore your topic systematically by dividing it into parts and exploring them one at a time. For example, if you are writing an argument to support a position, you can divide the task into these parts: define the issue, state your own position, present your argument, anticipate readers' likely questions and objections. (See the Writing Guides in Chapter 2 for advice on dividing your topic into manageable parts.)

Give Your Ideas Time to Percolate. Begin the planning process far enough ahead of the deadline so that your thinking can develop fully. Spread your planning over several days, allowing yourself time to work on the topic.

The mere process of writing is one of the most powerful tools we have for clarifying our own thinking. I am never as clear about any matter as when I have just finished writing about it.
—James Van Allen

Write as You Plan. When you put your thoughts and plans in writing, you keep a record of the information you discover as well as your ideas as they develop. Moreover, writing is itself a mode of discovery. The words you choose not only express your thoughts but also help you to think.

Use invention strategies to develop and clarify your thinking.

Every student needs a group of trusted strategies for making discoveries as well as for analyzing and synthesizing new ideas. These discovery or invention strategies can serve various purposes—for example, they may help you to find usable material in the course readings or in sources found in the library or on the Internet, to see what you already know about the topic, to make connections and forge new ideas. You may not need to use your entire repertoire of invention strategies for any single essay, but having several strategies to choose from gives you greater flexibility.

Critical Reading Strategies. Many college assignments require you to read material that has been assigned in a course or that you have found in your research. For help finding sources in the library or on the Internet, see Chapter 7. Critical reading strategies that you can use to gather information and develop ideas as you read include *annotating* a text to highlight important quotes, information, and ideas and *taking inventory* of your annotations to find patterns and connections. To learn more about these and other critical reading strategies, see Chapter 12.

WRITER AT WORK

Using the strategies of annotating and taking inventory, Gutierrez read and annotated her own copies of the two sources mentioned in the assignment: John Filson's brief pamphlet and the relevant chapter in historian John Mack Faragher's biography of Boone. She looked in both sources for material about the different images of Boone, highlighting "anything I thought would be useful for my essay." Then, she made an inventory of her annotations to see what topics these quotes could support. Here is a part of her inventory.

Boone's Role in the Development of Civilization

Who said he was responsible for settlement?

Filson: "opening the road to millions" (qtd. in Far. 322)

Faragher: Boone is known as "providential pathfinder for civilization" (322)

Masculinity

myth: Filson's heroic Indian fighter and hunter

Flint: Boone = "Achilles of the West" (qtd. in Far. 323)

"simplicity of manners, manly hardihood, and Spartan energy" (Flint, qtd. in Far. 324)

reality: women "made possible men's hunting" (Far. 49–50)

Acc. to Faragher: Flint's nostalgia for a "time when a man was a man" served "to forestall . . . rising feminine power" (324)

As you can see from her inventory, Gutierrez grouped the annotations and named each grouping. Most of her annotations contain quotations from the two readings, and she included a page reference for each quote. As she continued to plan the draft, she found that some of the material in her inventory was not as useful as she had initially thought. She then went back to her annotated texts and found other quotes that worked better.

In her journal, she explained how the process of taking inventory helped her begin to find a thesis for her essay:

> I think taking inventory helped in two ways. First, looking for quotes helped me focus on the readings and think about them in relation to the assignment. Second, having to decide on topic headings to group the quotes forced me to develop some ideas. For example, I could see that some of the quotes presented the myth of Boone's masculine qualities (hunting, exploring, fighting), while others dealt with the reality (his dependence on his wife). Taking inventory helped me develop a tentative thesis about how the mythical Boone differs from the real Boone.

Writing Strategies. The following five basic writing strategies can help you to generate ideas for most college assignments.

LISTING. Listing is an easy way to get started writing because formulating a list creates its own momentum: one idea suggests another, and so on. Use listing to discover possible writing topics or to determine what you already know and need to know about a topic.

Follow these steps when using listing for invention.

1. Give your list a title that indicates your topic or main idea.
2. Taking five to ten minutes, write your list as fast as you can, relying on short phrases, rather than complete sentences, and including anything that comes to mind about the topic or main idea. Do not try to evaluate or organize your entries at this point.
3. After you have finished listing, organize your list of ideas.
   - Identify the most promising items with an asterisk or a checkmark.
   - Number the key items in order of importance.
   - Group related items in categories.
   - Add any new items that come to mind.

WRITER AT WORK

As you saw in the preceding Writer at Work, Gutierrez's inventory of annotations led her to a tentative thesis about the differences between the mythical Boone and the real Boone. She then used listing to generate ideas about these differences.

Mythical Boone	**Real Boone**
masculinity	skilled hunter and explorer
individual/independent	dependent on wife for his lifestyle
ferocious fighter	killed only three people
prototypically American, non-European	combined Indian with American ways

Indian-hater	admired Indian culture
pursued progress	passion for hunting
led settlers	sought solitude, not civilization

BRAINSTORMING. Brainstorming is a listing activity groups can use to generate possible topics or ideas on a designated topic. When brainstorming works well, group members stimulate one another's thinking and sparks fly. A brainstorming session works best when a time limit is imposed and participants call out their contributions as quickly as possible. To organize a brainstorming session, select someone to list the group's contributions on a board that everyone can see.

TIMED EXPLORATORY WRITING. Timed exploratory writing—also called *freewriting*—allows you to put on paper or type on a computer what you know about a topic in order to explore the topic and develop a thesis. You write quickly, as the ideas come to mind, and without stopping to organize your thoughts. Exploratory writing also creates a momentum of its own—words connect to form sentences, one sentence leads to another, and soon you have filled the page or screen with ideas. The key is to write without censoring yourself.

A form of exploratory writing called *looping* can be especially helpful for finding a main idea or thesis for your essay. Sometimes you may need only two or three loops to develop a thesis; at other times, you may need more.

For timed exploratory writing or looping, do the following:

1. Begin with some aspect of the assignment that interests you. Write about what it asks you to do, what you could say about the topic, or what material you could draw on to develop an essay.
2. Write nonstop for a set length of time, usually about five minutes. Keep your pencil moving or your fingers typing. Do not reread or evaluate what you have written until after the time has elapsed.
3. When your time is up, read what you have written, looking in your initial exploratory writing for a promising insight or a pattern that emerges from the details. Restate this idea in a single sentence to start your next loop. Then write for another five minutes exploring this idea.

WRITER AT WORK

Gutierrez used timed exploratory writing to see what she could say about the topic of Boone's masculinity. As you can see in the excerpt that follows, she tried to develop the contrast between the mythical image of masculinity constructed by Boone's early biographers and the reality of his life revealed by later historians.

> Timothy Flint is one biographer largely responsible for helping to create a masculine Boone. But Faragher says that Flint was afraid that women were becoming too powerful—that's why he basically left Boone's wife out of the story. I guess the point is that historians write for their own time. For Flint, masculinity means certain "manly" characteristics like simplicity, hardihood, "Spartan energy"—isn't that warrior-like? Is that what Filson is doing too? His masculine ideal is fighting and killing. For later historians, like Faragher, Boone's masculinity is defined by activities like hunting and exploring. But he stresses that Boone couldn't have been away hunting if his wife hadn't been so good at keeping the home fires burning—farming and hunting small game to feed the family while Boone is off doing his own thing.

CLUSTERING. This strategy helps you group related ideas and information about a topic. Because clustering is fast and graphic, students often use it to try out different topics before making a choice. Clustering lets you quickly assess whether you have enough material for an essay. It also can help you focus your essay when you find that a lot of material clusters around one or two ideas or subtopics.

Clustering works as follows.

1. In the center of a piece of blank paper, write your topic in a word or phrase and circle it.
2. Also in words or phrases, write down the subtopics. Circle the subtopics and connect them with lines to the topic in the center.
3. Next, think of facts, details, examples, or ideas that are related in any way to these subtopics. Cluster these around the subtopics, and so on.

WRITER AT WORK

Gutierrez used clustering to contrast images of Daniel Boone. In the diagram below, notice that all of the ideas, facts, and examples are connected to one of the two subtopics, *the mythical Boone* or *the real Boone.*

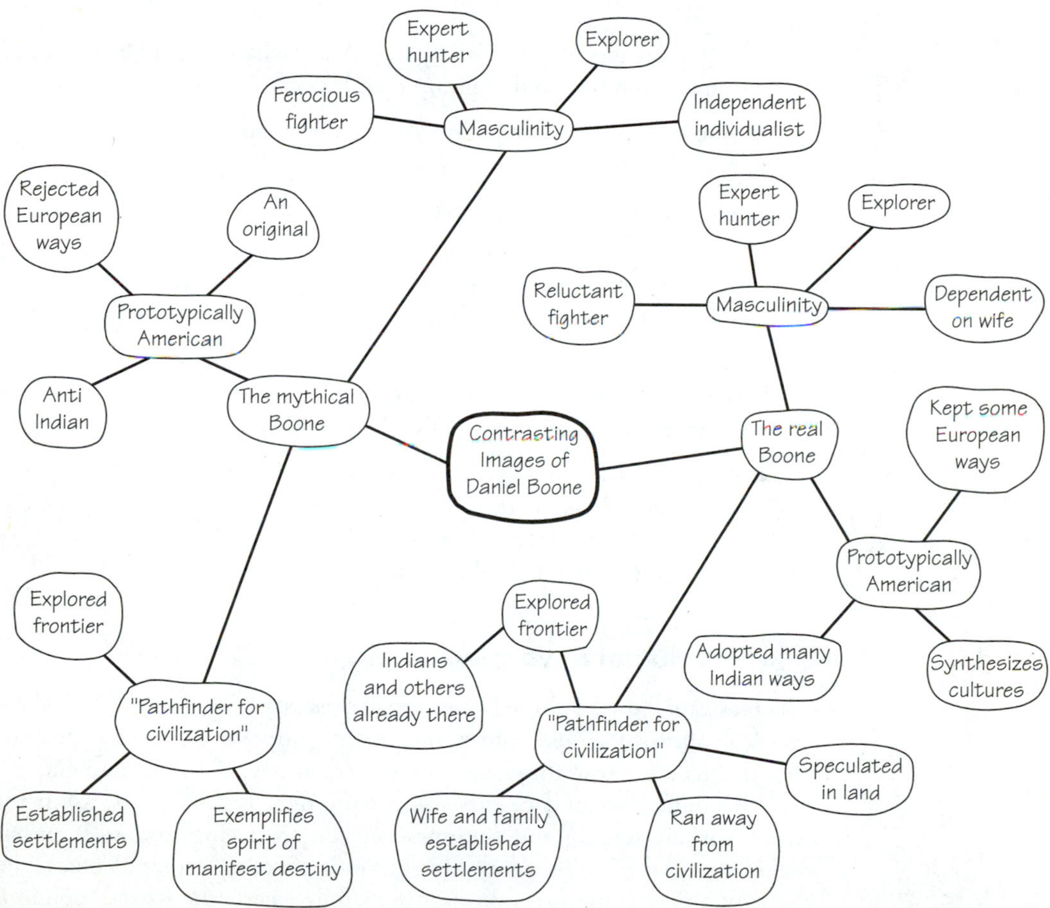

I like working collaboratively from time to time. I like fusing ideas into one vision. I like seeing that vision come to life with other people who know exactly what it took to get there.
—*Amy Tan*

WRITING COLLABORATIVELY. Like brainstorming, this strategy involves writing with a group. You may be given writing assignments that call for collaboration, most often in business or science courses but occasionally also in the humanities. Writing collaboratively can be invigorating, but it can also be frustrating if there are no ground rules to help group members to work together constructively, such as the following.

1. Set a regular meeting time and place. Also exchange email addresses or telephone numbers so that group members can contact one another.
2. Divide responsibilities equally. Make sure group members know what their duties are.
3. Set an agenda for each meeting and keep to it.
4. Treat each other with respect and consideration, but do not be surprised if disagreements and personality conflicts arise. Arguing can stimulate thinking—inspiring new ideas as well as encouraging clarity and logic.
5. As a group, schedule the deadlines and drafting responsibilities for each member. All group members should help to read and revise drafts and participate in editing and proofreading the final essay.
6. If the group will make an oral presentation, plan it carefully, giving each person a role. Rehearse the presentation as a group to make sure it satisfies the time limit and other requirements of the assignment. (See Chapter 5 for more on oral presentations.)

1c Formulate a working thesis.

The thesis may appear at the beginning of the essay or at the end, but wherever it is placed it should convey the writer's purpose. The thesis encapsulates the main point of the essay—the writer's answer to the assignment.

Obviously, the kind of thesis you write depends on the occasion for which you are writing and the question you are trying to answer. What makes a good thesis differs for different kinds of college essays. Whereas the thesis in an essay arguing a position forcefully asserts the writer's opinion, the thesis in an essay relating a personal experience may only be implied. (Consult the Writing Guides in Chapter 2 for advice on how to present a thesis in various types of college essays.)

After you have used the planning strategies in 1b to explore your topic and develop your purpose, concentrate on formulating a tentative thesis that will help you organize your ideas and write a focused draft. As you develop your ideas further, you will refine and clarify your thesis. You may even change it if you discover that you do not have enough support or that you are more interested in a different aspect of the topic.

WRITER AT WORK

Notice that Gutierrez began formulating her thesis by stating a question about her topic. Beginning in this way can be helpful because it leads you to recenter your thinking on the assignment.

> *Why was Boone portrayed mythically by different biographers?*
>
> Daniel Boone is a popular figure in American history, embodying the characteristics of the ideal American frontiersman—masculinity, independence, good fighting and hunting skills, uniquely American (not European or Indian), a "pathfinder for civilization" (Faragher or someone he quoted?). But this idealized Boone is largely a myth created by biographers because the real Boone did not live up to the ideal.

As you will see, Gutierrez's thesis evolved as she drafted and revised the essay. But she needed to articulate her main idea to begin writing the first draft.

1d Organize and draft your essay.

As you organize and draft your essay, you can expect to continue making discoveries. At this stage your primary goal changes, however, from gathering information and generating new ideas to composing a draft with a clear purpose. Now that you have clarified your purpose by formulating a working thesis, you can make an outline and write your first draft.

Develop an outline.

Most writers use some kind of outline—either an informal scratch outline or a formal multilevel outline—to organize their material and guide them as they draft the essay. When you make an outline, you arrange your material graphically so that you can see at a glance whether the sequence you are using makes sense, where additional information may be needed, and how you might separate or group your ideas to make them clearer.

You are always going back and forth between the outline and the writing, bringing them closer together, or just throwing out the outline and making a new one.
—*Annie Dillard*

Informal Scratch Outlining. Using key words, phrases, or whole sentences, list the points you want to cover in the order you plan to introduce them. It might be helpful to make several scratch outlines, trying out different ways of sequencing the material. If you are using a computer, create a new file for each outline. (See the Writing Guides in Chapter 2 for sample scratch outlines for different writing assignments.)

The items in a scratch outline do not have to coincide with the paragraphs in the essay. Sometimes two or more items may be developed in the same paragraph or one item may be covered in two or more paragraphs.

WRITER AT WORK

Below is the scratch outline Gutierrez used to organize her first draft.

> open with thesis statement (difference between myth and reality. why the myth?)
> masculinity (really a way to combat fear of women's power?)
> uniquely American (meaning anti-Indian? not really)
> "pathfinder for civilization" (really trying to get away from people)
> conclude by summarizing real Boone's virtues in contrast to the myth

Formal Outlining. Formal outlines have at least two levels and require more planning than scratch outlines. As in a scratch outline, you can use words, phrases, or sentences. But you need to think more carefully about how the items relate to each other in a formal outline. You can put items on the same level or on higher or lower levels. Here are the conventions for labeling the levels of your formal outline.

I. (Main topic)
  A. (Subtopic of I)
  B.
    1. (Subtopic of I.B)
    2.
      a. (Subtopic of I.B.2)
      b.
      c.

DIGITAL HINT

If you are using a formal outline, check to see whether your word processing program has an outlining capability. Not only can the computer make labeling the levels simple, but it also may allow you to move from outline view to normal document view and back again, making it easier to write from the outline.

Draft your essay.

Having written a thesis statement and an outline, you should be ready to write a first draft. However, remember that your working thesis and outline may change as you draft. Try to remain open and flexible, keeping in mind these suggestions.

Choose the Best Time and Place. You can write a draft at any time and in any place. Drafting is likely to go more smoothly, however, if you choose a time and place suited for sustained and thoughtful work.

Set Reasonable Goals. Divide your task into manageable portions and complete one small part—a section or paragraph—at a time. Be satisfied at this stage with less-than-perfect writing. Do not obsessively reread what you have written, cross out what you have written, or start over. Save revising and editing for later.

Do the Easy Parts First. Try not to agonize over the first sentence or paragraph. If you have trouble with the introduction or get stuck at a difficult spot, go on to an easier part. Start with the part you understand best.

Guess at Words, Facts, Spelling. As you draft, you may have trouble thinking of the right word, need to check a fact, or feel unsure about how to spell a word or where to put a comma. Do not be diverted from drafting. Make notes in the margins of the draft or on a separate list of things to check later.

Make Revision Easy. If possible, compose your draft on a word processor. If you must write out or type your draft, use only one side of the page. Write on every other line, or triple-space if you are typing, leaving wide margins and plenty of room to add, cut, and rearrange material when you revise the draft later on.

Take Short Breaks—and Reward Yourself! Drafting can be hard work, and you may need to take a break to refresh yourself. But be careful not to wander off for too long or you may lose momentum.

1e Evaluate and revise the draft.

Because of constraints on their time and energy, most students would like to call it quits as soon as they have written a draft. But experience teaches them that revising will bring them closer to the essay they really want to write.

To revise effectively, you first need to evaluate your draft—to see what works well and what does not, which ideas need to be developed, where support should be bolstered, what could be rearranged or cut. Judging how well your own draft works is difficult, however, unless you get some distance from it. Try to put the draft aside for a day or two before revising it. Another productive strategy is to ask someone—your instructor, a classmate, a tutor at the campus writing center—to read the draft and help you evaluate it.

If you are asked to read someone else's draft, you need to read with a critical eye—to evaluate but also simply to describe. By describing what you see, you help the writer see the draft more objectively.

The Writing Guides in Chapter 2 offer specific suggestions for evaluating different types of college essays. Following is some general advice on reading any draft critically.

Make a Record of Your Reading. Talking about a draft can be useful and even fun. But you can be most helpful to the writer if you put your ideas in writing, leaving a record that can be used later when the writer revises.

DIGITAL HINT

If you are using a computer to read and respond to a draft, see whether your word processing program has a revision capability that would allow you to annotate the draft and recommend changes. You might also have a program that lets you add notes to the draft.

Try Not to Be Distracted by Editing Issues. You may find errors of spelling, punctuation, grammar, or word choice in the draft. Remember that you are reading a draft that has not yet been edited or proofread. Focus instead on the overall purpose of the essay and how well it meets that purpose.

Evaluate the Draft Part by Part. Focus on individual parts of the draft, bringing to bear what you know about the kind of essay, the subject, and the discipline. Begin by considering how well the opening paragraphs introduce the essay and prepare you for what follows. Pay attention to specific writing strategies. For example, if the essay argues a position, notice whether the issue is described clearly and fairly, whether the writer provides enough support, whether other views are acknowledged and counterargued effectively.

Be Constructive. Above all, try to give constructive criticism that will help the writer solve problems. For example, if you think the support is weak, suggest what kinds of additional support would strengthen the argument or where the writer might find more support.

Evaluate and revise your own draft.

When you read your own draft thoughtfully and critically—perhaps with the advice of others in mind—you will see many opportunities for improvement. You will find ways to add, delete, rephrase, and rearrange material to say what you want to say more clearly and to develop your ideas further.

Blot out, correct,
insert, refine,
Enlarge, diminish,
interline,
Be mindful, when
invention fails,
To scratch your head,
and bite your nails.
—Jonathan Swift

Many writers find revising to be the most enjoyable part of the process. The pressure is reduced because they already have a complete draft and revising frees them to play with the draft. Following is some general advice on revising any essay.

Reconsider Your Purpose and Audience. Remind yourself of what you want to say. Reflect again on your reader's expectations and what you are trying to accomplish. If your instructor or someone else has evaluated your draft, think about how that person has interpreted your essay in relation to what you are trying to do in it. If what you now see or what your reader saw differs from your original intent, consider whether your purpose has evolved and if so, modify your thesis to accommodate your new sense of purpose.

Look at Major Problems First. Identify any major problems that are preventing the draft from achieving its purpose. Major problems that sometimes plague student writing include the following:

- Depending on sources and relying too little on your own thinking
- Repeating rather than developing your ideas
- Making assertions without support or justification
- Ignoring contradictions
- Not connecting your ideas to the themes and readings of the course
- Settling for the obvious and avoiding complexity

Focus Next on Clarity and Coherence. As you reread your essay and your readers' comments, look for places where you can state your ideas more directly and show readers how different parts of the essay are logically related.

Consider how well the beginning of your essay prepares readers for what follows. Bring your essay into sharper focus by reformulating the thesis statement to represent your main idea more clearly. Consider adding a forecasting statement that introduces the essay's main points and prepares readers for what follows. Look at each section of the essay in turn, making sure there are explicit topic sentences and appropriate transitions where they are needed to keep readers oriented. (See 3a and 3b for help in cueing readers.)

WRITER AT WORK

Gutierrez's instructor read her draft and gave her some advice on revising it. She reported his comments in her journal.

> He says it is a good draft but that he has two kinds of suggestions. One is that the point is not always clear. In paragraph 4, for example, I don't make clear what I am trying to prove until the end of the paragraph. He suggests that I rearrange the sentences so the reader will get a better understanding of the topic I am discussing and that I state more directly what each section of the essay contributes to my overall argument.
>
> Second, I need to answer the second part of the assignment better—not only to explain the differences between the mythical and real Boone, but also to explain why Americans needed the Boone myth. To answer the *why* question, he suggests I look back at the New Western Historians and their criticism of Turner's frontier thesis.

To revise her draft, Gutierrez first reread the passages she had highlighted in the texts by Filson and Faragher, but she could not find anything to help her answer the *why* question. She then reread and annotated three other assigned essays: Frederick Jackson Turner's seminal work on the frontier and responses to Turner by two New Western Historians, Michael P. Malone and Patricia Nelson Limerick. From this reading, she was able to add a Turner reference to the introduction, develop the discussion of masculinity, and write a new conclusion that explicitly answers the *why* question.

She also revised to make the essay more readable. In the opening paragraph, she added a forecast of the three areas in which the myth differs from the reality. She made the topic sentences more explicit, improved the transitions, announced more clearly the contrast between the mythical and the real Boone, and brought her main point home in the new last paragraph.

Gutierrez's revised and edited essay is reprinted in section 1g.

1f Edit and proofread your essay for problems with grammar, punctuation, and mechanics.

Once you have finished revising, edit your essay carefully to make sure that every word, phrase, and sentence is clear and follows the conventions of standard written English.

Keep a List of Your Common Errors. Keep a record of the grammatical, punctuation, and mechanical errors in your own writing. You will probably begin to recognize patterns of error you can check for as you edit your work. See page vii for advice on keeping a record for yourself.

Use Your Word Processor's Spell-Check Capability. It only takes a few minutes to check your spelling and typos with a computer. A spell check can only determine if a word is spelled correctly, however. It cannot let you know if a word is spelled correctly but is wrong for a particular context. In addition to using a spell-check, therefore, always proofread your essay with care.

Begin Proofreading with the Last Sentence. To focus your attention on sentence grammar, it may help to read the essay in reverse order, from its last sentence to its first sentence. When you do so, you will be less likely to pay attention to content and thus will recognize errors more easily.

Exchange Revised Essays with Another Student. Because it is usually easier to find errors in someone else's writing than it is in your own, consider trading essays with a classmate and proofreading one another's writing.

1g Writer at work: a final look

This section provides one final look at Gloria Gutierrez's writing process: the revised essay she handed in and her instructor's final evaluation of it.

Hero Qualifications

1 Daniel Boone is a popular figure in American history who is thought to embody the "stalwart and rugged qualities" that nineteenth-century historian Frederick Jackson Turner attributed to the ideal fron-

tiersman (34). As Americans, we look to figures like Boone to serve as an example for all of us. They show us how a "true American" should behave. However, even the real Daniel Boone did not live up to the ideal. This disparity between Turner's ideal and Boone's real life compelled many biographers and early historians to construct a mythical Boone—one who represents the qualities of masculine strength and independence Turner valued together with the pioneering spirit that, as Turner claimed, "helped to open the way for civilization" (36).

2 Masculinity is a prominent feature of the Boone mythology. From the beginning, in John Filson's 1784 "Adventures of Col. Daniel Boon," Boone is portrayed as a vigorous fighter, hunter, and adventurer. Timothy Flint's 1833 biography was largely responsible for creating the heroic image of Boone as "the Achilles of the West" (qtd. in Faragher 323). Flint admired Boone for his "simplicity of manners, manly hardihood, and Spartan energy" (qtd. in Faragher 324). It is from Flint that we get the image of Boone killing a bear with a hunting knife and "swinging Tarzan-like through the forest on a vine" (Faragher 323). The modern historian and Boone biographer John Mack Faragher argues, however, that the ideal of masculinity Flint promulgated was written for his own age, "an important metaphor in a campaign to forestall a sense of decaying masculine potency and combat a fear of rising feminine power in American culture" (324). Due to his own insecurities about the changing roles of men and women in American society, Flint uses the figure of Boone to "read a lesson to shrinking and effeminate spirits, the men of soft hands and fashionable life" (qtd. in Faragher 324). He hoped his story of the "adventures and daring of such men" would "re-inspire" Americans (qtd. in Faragher 324).

3 The historical Boone, however, does not convey such a masculine image. Although Boone did participate in such "manly" activities as hunting and exploring, "[i]t was the labor of women, in fact, that made possible men's hunting" (Faragher 49). Boone was gone for long periods of time while he was hunting, which made him very dependent on his wife, Rebecca. She carried out the necessary daily chores of running a household, including hunting small game to feed her family. Flint

would like to use the mythical Boone as a way to secure the superiority of men in society, but in reality, the historical Boone was a frontiersman who was able to pursue his passion for hunting and exploration only because of "the strength and determination of an able and intelligent woman" (Faragher 50).

4 Not only was Boone dependent on his wife, but he was also dependent on Indians, learning from them much of what made him such a successful frontiersman. Nevertheless, his early biographers, beginning with John Filson, portray Boone as ferociously anti-Indian. Filson's story of Boone's life is filled with "heroic" exploits fighting the Indians, who were supposedly responsible for all kinds of savagery. As Faragher points out, Boone's subsequent biographers embellished the many tales that made him out to be a "bragging, fighting, Indian-hating frontiersman" who had killed many Indians (333). In reality, however, Boone only killed three Indians in his entire lifetime. He was not fond of taking lives, and he was not an Indian-hater.

5 Boone, in fact, had respect for the Indian culture. As a youth, he "grew in his knowledge of the ways of the American woods and the culture of the Indians" (Faragher 23). Many biographers would like to portray Boone as a full-blooded American frontiersman who brought his own knowledge to the frontier, but according to Faragher, Boone "depended on Indian knowledge and skill" (20). Frontiersmen like Boone wore clothes that incorporated European and Indian styles. They shared cultural traits with the Indians, such as diet, medicine, and a belief in the power of omens and dreams. The Americans and Indians were, however, divided in their understanding of the world, and many Americans were confused by the Indian way of thinking. But as Faragher points out, Boone "moved quite far in the Indian direction of seeing things" (23). His settlement of the land relied heavily on his knowledge and adoption of Indian ways.

6 Daniel Boone's role in the development of civilization is another aspect of his life that causes a disparity between the mythical Boone and the historical Boone. Many biographers say Boone made a conscious effort to settle the land. For example, Judge John Coburn eulogized

Boone as "the instrument of opening the road to millions of the human family" (qtd. in Faragher 322). Boone collaborated with Filson, at least according to Faragher, "to publicize the country and thereby increase the value" of their land speculations (3). Even Turner promotes the myth of Boone as having "pioneered the way for the farmers" (36).

7 The portraits of Boone as a restless explorer who was always on the move are true. When he felt Kentucky was too crowded, he moved to Missouri. But Boone moved from place to place searching for solitude, not for a new place to settle or because as a frontiersman he was always testing the borders, looking for new adventures. As Faragher notes, Boone felt uneasy about being portrayed as "the harbinger of progress" (322). The truth is that he fell in love with solitude as a youth. It was his need for independence, not his desire to bring about civilization, that led him to search out new land.

8 The mythical Boone was created to meet the standards of an ideal American frontiersman. The mythical Boone offered a romanticized American hero, but the historical Boone gave us a practical hero with many admirable traits. He was an individual, searching for his own space, something that Americans find appealing. He was loyal to his American heritage, yet he did not dismiss the Indian's ways of living. He came to respect Indians' culture and to appreciate their knowledge and skill. He was a strong individual, but he also realized that he needed the support of his family. On several occasions, he listened to and even heeded his wife's desire not to move.

9 The mythological Boone exemplifies Turner's idea of the frontier. According to New Western Historian Michael P. Malone, Turner's frontier tends to embody all the highly esteemed qualities of America, such as "democracy, individualism, pragmatism, and a healthy nationalism" (140). The same could be said of the mythical Boone. Like Turner's frontier thesis, the Boone myth leaves out many factors that caused or sustained the westward movement. By suggesting that other factors were involved in the process of settlement, the historical Boone and New Western Historians offer an alternative to Turner. For example, as Malone argues, "Turner's heroic frontier seemed devoid of females

and . . . worked against serious consideration of the region's ethnic diversity" (144). In addition, as New Western Historian Patricia Nelson Limerick suggests, Turner's frontier represents the western expansion as all "progress" and "improvement" (86). The representation of Boone as "the harbinger of progress" obviously promotes this myth of manifest destiny (Faragher 322). The Boone myth idealizes the American frontiersman and his motives for westward exploration in a conventional Turnerian way. The historical Boone revealed by the New Western Historians, however, displays many positive images important to our understanding of American history and the frontier.

Works Cited

Faragher, John Mack. *Daniel Boone: The Life and Legend of an American Pioneer.* New York: Holt, 1992.

Filson, John. "An Appendix Containing the Adventures of Col. Daniel Boon." *The Discovery, Settlement and Present State of Kentuckey.* 1784. Ann Arbor: University Microfilms, 1966.

Flint, Timothy. *Biographical Memoir of Daniel Boone, the First Settler of Kentucky*, 1833. New Haven: College and University P, 1967.

———. *Recollections of the Last Ten Years in the Valley of the Mississippi.* 1826. Ed. George R. Brooks. Carbondale: Southern Illinois U P, 1968.

———. *Personal Narrative of James O. Pattie.* 1833. Ed. Richard Batman. Missoula, MT: Mountain P, 1988.

Limerick, Patricia Nelson. "What On Earth Is the New Western History?" *Trails: Toward a New Western History.* Ed. Patricia Nelson Limerick, Clyde A. Milner II, and Charles E. Rankin. Lawrence: U P of Kansas, 1991. 81–88.

Malone, Michael P. "Beyond the Last Frontier: Toward a New Approach to Western American History." *Trails: Toward a New Western History.* Ed. Patricia Nelson Limerick, Clyde A. Milner II, and Charles E. Rankin. Lawrence: U P of Kansas, 1991. 139–60.

Turner, Frederick Jackson. "The Significance of the Frontier in American History." 1893. *Frederick Jackson Turner: Wisconsin's Historian of the Frontier.* Ed. Martin Ridge. Madison, WI: Historical Society of Wisconsin, 1993. 26–47.

Before handing in her essay, Gutierrez ran a spell-check and read carefully for grammatical errors. Her instructor gave the essay an *A* and noted in his comments, "Your use of texts—many and varied—is subtle and skillful. Many of the paragraphs of your essay stand on their own as well-demonstrated arguments; this is a mark of a good essay."

BRIEF GUIDES TO IMPORTANT TYPES OF COLLEGE WRITING

Throughout your college years, you will encounter a wide variety of writing assignments. Among the types of writing that you are likely to be assigned are the following.

- Presenting personal experience
- Explaining concepts
- Arguing positions
- Evaluating texts, phenomena, or ideas
- Speculating about causes or effects
- Interpreting literature

This chapter provides a brief Writing Guide for each of these typical kinds of essays. Whenever you encounter these types of writing in your courses, you can refer to these guides for help. Each of the following sections includes a brief definition and examples of typical assignments, a list of basic requirements, and suggestions for planning, formulating a thesis, organizing and drafting, evaluating and revising, and editing and proofreading an essay.

Probably the most common advice given new writers is to write about what you know best—and that usually means writing about people and events in your life. Writing about personal experience for others to read can serve different purposes. Writers choose the memories and feelings they reveal to create an impression or to make a point.

Typical Assignments

Composition. Recall occasions when you exercised power over another person or were subject to someone else's power. Write about one such experience, telling what happened and conveying your feelings at the time and in retrospect.

Political Science. Voter apathy is a widespread problem, but not much is known about the origins of voting behavior. Write about the first time you became interested in an election, whether or not you were able to vote. Tell your story and reflect on how that first experience influenced your current voting behavior and attitudes.

Basic Requirements

A Well-Told Story. When writers relate a personal experience, they usually tell it as a story designed to generate suspense. You can heighten the drama by speeding up the action or by giving readers a close-up that emphasizes every action and reaction. (See 3c for more on narration.)

Vivid Description of Scenes and People. Good storytellers describe scenes vividly by naming and detailing objects readers can imaginatively see, smell, hear, taste, and touch. They may also use metaphors and similes to tap readers' associations. (See 3c for more on description and 35g for figures of speech.) Vivid portraits of people focus on a few details that show how they look, dress, or act. Snatches of reconstructed dialogue can give readers insight into character and relationships.

Significance. Most writers tell personal stories to create an impression or lead readers to think about their own experience in a certain way. You can convey significance both by telling and by showing readers what the experience means to you. To tell, intersperse into the narrative the thoughts and feelings that you had at the time the event occurred or that you have now as you look back in retrospect. To show, orchestrate your choice of words and images to create a tone or general impression that conveys your attitude.

Planning 

The following activities can help you plan your essay.

- Write for about five minutes, reconstructing what happened.
- Imagine that you are back in the scene at the time of the experience and describe what you see, hear, smell, touch, and taste as well as what you think and feel.
- To recall specific details about a person who played an important role in your story, look at photographs or letters or talk with someone else who also remembers the person.
- Re-create a conversation you had with a person who was part of the experience. How did the person usually speak to you? Recall favorite words, typical tone of voice, gestures, or mannerisms.
- Explore how you felt at the time of the experience and how you feel about it now. If you are responding to a specific question, reflect on how your experience relates to the question. Ask yourself what point you want your story to make.

Formulating a Working Thesis 

When you write an essay presenting personal experience, your readers expect to be able to see the point or significance of the experience. They do not expect you to begin your essay with the kind of thesis statement typical of argumentative or explanatory writing, but they do expect you to comment on the significance or to imply it by the way you tell the story.

Following are two excerpts from a student's personal experience essay. The first pair of sentences evaluates the experience of being arrested for shoplifting as it was happening; the second pair reflects on the experience from the writer's present perspective. Both excerpts convey the significance of the event to the reader.

> Now everyone knew I was a criminal. I was a juvenile delinquent, and thank God the cops were getting me off the street.
>
> The humiliation at that moment was overwhelming. I felt like Hester Prynne being put on public display for everyone to ridicule.

Comments such as these can be woven into the story, as these were, or presented at the end of major sections of the story or at its conclusion.

Organizing and Drafting 

To tell the story, you need to put the events in order. Most stories follow chronological order, but the judicious use of flashback or flashforward can enhance the drama and underscore the significance.

In the following example, a student used an outline to plan a narrative telling what happened when she was caught shoplifting.

> Introduce the story by describing how excited I was about going to the mall for last-minute Christmas shopping
> Describe the crowds and tell how I stole a Snoopy button
> Describe my fear then relief as I leave the store, followed by surprise when I am stopped and asked to empty my pockets
> Tell about waiting for the police and my grandmother's and sister's reactions
> Describe the drive to the police station and my confused feelings of pride in what I had done, fear of having to tell my parents, and disbelief that I had actually been arrested
> Conclude with my having to face my parents—with my mother's disappointment in me and my father's anger at the police.

The student began her story with her trip to the mall and ended it with her trip home. Along the way, she described places and people, reported conversations, and related her thoughts and feelings. Her primary strategies were narration and description. She made the story dramatic by letting readers hear what she was thinking and feeling at the time. She made the story significant by showing that her moral and emotional confusion reflected the confusion she saw in her parents and in society.

Evaluating and Revising Your Draft

To revise your draft, read it with the following questions in mind.

Story. Is there any part in which the chronology is hard to follow? Does the drama lose intensity at any point?

Scenes and People. Are any scenes vague and undefined? Are the people distinctive and their roles clear? Does any dialogue seem irrelevant?

Significance. Is the significance clear? If the essay was written for an assignment, does it address the assignment directly? Does any part of the story undermine or contradict the point?

Editing and Proofreading

Examine your essay sentence by sentence for errors in usage, punctuation, and mechanics. Because of the types of sentences typically involved in writing about past events, you should check your essay for verb tense errors. (See 23a on verb tenses and 27a on shifts in verb tense.)

Explanations inform readers. They present established information confidently and efficiently, helping readers to learn about a topic. You will find explanations in newspapers, encyclopedias, and research reports.

Explaining concepts is one type of explanatory writing that you will encounter frequently in college. Textbooks are loaded with concept explanations, and examinations and essay assignments often require you to define concepts.

Concepts abound in every field of study. Physics has "entropy," "mass," and "fission"; literature has "irony," "romanticism," and "bildungsroman"; art has "perspective" and "cubism."

Typical Assignments

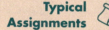

Biology. In a brief essay, explain "osmosis" and how it works. Also explain the role of osmosis in human biology.

Business. "Downsizing" is a new concept, a term that did not even enter the dictionary until 1982. Write an essay explaining what downsizing is and what it means for corporate America and for the American worker.

Basic Requirements

A Focused Concept. To write a successful but brief essay about a concept, you will need to focus on one important aspect of the concept. For example, if you were assigned to write about schizophrenia, a mental illness, you might focus on one aspect such as its symptoms, history, or treatment.

An Awareness of What Readers Know about the Concept. Readers are bored by explanations that tell them what they already know. However, if you aim too far ahead of what readers know, they are likely to be frustrated and confused.

If you must explain a concept to an instructor, you may need to include information that has been stressed in readings and lectures. In this situation, your goal is not to inform the instructor about the concept but to convince him or her that you understand the concept.

A Logical Plan. To write a successful explanation, you will need to divide the information into topics and to sequence them meaningfully. This sequence is usually forecast at the beginning, with obvious transitions and other cues to keep readers on track.

Clear Definitions. Explaining a concept requires you to write a clear extended definition. While readers will appreciate a concise definition of the concept somewhere in the essay, it may not come until near the end, where it consolidates readers' understanding. To aid understanding, define all unfamiliar terms in familiar language.

Appropriate Writing Strategies. Many strategies, in addition to definition, are useful for presenting information. The strategies you use depend on your focus, the kind of information you present, and your readers' knowledge. The following strategies are particularly useful: classification and division, process narration, comparison and contrast, illustration, and cause and effect. (See 3c.)

Careful Use of Sources. Concept explanations are nearly always based on multiple sources of information. You will need to integrate this source material smoothly into your essay by summarizing, paraphrasing, and quoting your sources appropriately. (See 8c for help with integrating quoted materials into your sentences. See 8b for guidelines for avoiding plagiarism and for summarizing and paraphrasing.)

Planning 

The following sequence of activities can help you plan your essay.

- Before researching the concept, write down what you already know about it. You may be surprised at how much you know.
- Research your concept to get an overview of it and to discover what sources are available. (See Chapter 7 for help with finding print and electronic sources and with research strategies.)
- Make notes about what aspects of the concept interest you, what your readers already know, and what they might be most interested in learning. Then choose a focus for your research.
- Return to your research with your new focus.

Formulating a Working Thesis

The thesis in an essay explaining concepts simply announces the subject and focus of the explanation, as in this example.

> The Disney conception of the perfect girl can be described, with little exception, in this way: she is always pretty, always fair, always model-thin, always endowed with a beautiful singing voice, and always at the mercy of some malevolent, often jealous, older woman. The Disney girl also has the love of a handsome, wealthy, and brave man, almost always of royal blood.

The thesis may also forecast the plan of the essay, as you can see by comparing this statement with the outline in the next section.

> What is known and agreed on, however, are the symptoms of schizophrenia—what it looks like to an observer and what it feels like to a sufferer. Schizophrenic symptoms are not attractive, but they are easy to understand. The medical manuals classify them as follows: bizarre delusions, prominent hallucinations, confusions about identity, unconnected speech, inappropriate affect, disturbances in psychomotor behavior, and impaired interpersonal functioning.

Organizing and Drafting

Before drafting, think about how you can build on your readers' knowledge. Divide your material into topics. You may need to try out several divisions and ways of sequencing them. Decide on a sequence and make a tentative scratch outline.

When you have decided on your topics, think about the best way to sequence them. Again, try out several sequences. Choose a sequence and make a tentative scratch outline.

Here is a student's scratch outline for an essay explaining the psychological concept of schizophrenia, focusing on its symptoms.

Introduction—Seriousness of this illness, history and treatments, disagreement about causes but agreement about symptoms
Patients' reports of mental imagery
    Symptom 1: Delusions
    Symptom 2: Hallucinations
    Symptom 3: Confusion about their identities

Speech characteristics
 Symptom 4: Rambling and unconnected speech
 Symptom 5: Monotonous voices
Physical characteristics and interactions
 Symptom 6: Expressionless faces
 Symptom 7: Unusual posture and movements
 Symptom 8: Difficulty interacting with others

Conclusion—The care specialists take in diagnosing schizophrenia

The student organized the essay simply as a list of primary symptoms. After deciding on the topics and naming them, she discovered a way to group the symptoms into categories. Her basic strategy was to illustrate each symptom with examples and facts from her sources. (See 3c for more on illustration.)

Evaluating and Revising Your Draft

Use the following questions to evaluate your draft:

Focus. Is the focus appropriate for the intended readers? Is there any material in the essay that is not relevant to the focus?

Readers' Knowledge. Where does the essay tell readers either more or less than they need to know?

Plan. Will the division into topics and the sequence of topics help readers comprehend the concept?

Definitions. Are all unfamiliar terms defined clearly?

Writing Strategies. Is each writing strategy used effectively? Might other strategies be helpful?

Sources. Can readers assume that all sources are reliable? Do sources support or dominate? Are quotes integrated smoothly?

Editing and Proofreading

Because of the kind of thinking required to explain a concept, sentences with adjective clauses and interrupting phrases are prominent. (See 37c and 37d for help with punctuating adjective clauses and interrupting phrases.)

Arguing a position involves controversial issues—questions about which people disagree but for which there is no obvious "right" answer, no single truth everyone accepts. As a college student, you will be asked often to consider different views on issues and to develop an argument for your own view. Learning to see an issue from different perspectives and engaging in vigorous debate that sets forth reasoned arguments and answers opposing arguments can advance everyone's thinking. Composing an argument for your position is not just a valuable intellectual exercise, however; it is also one of the primary ways we as a society build knowledge and make informed decisions. (See Chapter 1 for an expanded description and illustration of the process involved in arguing a position for a college course.)

Typical Assignments

Sociology. Many people believe that the media—particularly television and film—are the most influential socializing agents in the world today, more important than peers or parents. How would you support this position?

Health Sciences. On the issue of legalizing drugs, Gieringer describes his position as favoring "decriminalization" but "not necessarily full legalization." Present an argument for your position, using the course readings as your primary sources of evidence.

Basic Requirements

A Well-Defined Issue. Views differ on an issue partly because people understand the issue differently. Therefore, in your essay you will need to explain the issue and why it is important.

A Clear, Unequivocal Position. Because your position on the issue is the main point of your essay—the thesis you will argue—you should state it directly and unambiguously. You may need to restate the thesis to show readers exactly how each part of your argument relates to the main point.

A Well-Reasoned, Well-Supported Argument. A well-reasoned argument unfolds systematically, each point or reason following in a logical progression. To be logical, an argument should pass the ABC test: (a) all of the parts of the argument must be *appropriate* and relevant; (b) all of the assertions must be *believable*, even if they cannot be verified as true; and (c) the argument must be *complete* with all the parts working together consistently, without contradiction. (To learn more about evaluating the logic of an argument, see 12f.)

Writers support their positions by offering examples, facts, statistics, and quotes from authoritative sources. For many of the arguments you will write in college, you will need to find support in assigned readings or sources you have researched on your own. (See Chapters 8–11 and 31a for help using and citing sources.)

Good arguments also address opposing points of view, acknowledging legitimate disagreements while refuting questionable assertions and weak reasoning. (See 3c for more on counterarguing.)

A Logical Plan. To help readers follow your logic, indicate your thesis early in the essay and forecast your argument. Provide explicit topic sentences introducing each new point and transitions relating it to the point that preceded it or to the thesis of the essay. (See Chapter 3 for forecasting statements, topic sentences, transitions, and other strategies to make your argument easy to follow.)

Planning 

The following sequence of activities can help you plan your essay.

- Consider the different positions people typically take on the issue and decide on your own position.
- Research the issue, taking note of facts, statistics, examples, and quotes from authorities that you could use to support the position. (See Chapter 7 for help with finding print and electronic sources.)
- List three to five reasons why you take the position you do.
- Try to anticipate your readers' questions and objections and develop a counterargument.

Formulating a Working Thesis

A thesis for an essay arguing a position clearly and emphatically asserts the writer's position, as in this example.

> When overzealous parents and coaches impose adult standards on children's sports, the result can be activities that are neither satisfying nor beneficial to children.

The thesis statement may include qualifying language that specifies the situation to which the writer's position applies, as in these sentences that follow the one above:

> I'm concerned about all organized sports activities for children between the ages of six and twelve. The damage I see results from noncontact as well as contact sports, for sports organized locally as well as those organized nationally.

The thesis may also be followed by a statement forecasting the reasons that will be developed in the essay.

Organizing and Drafting

Before drafting, make a scratch outline of the points you will use to develop your argument.

Here is the outline a student used for her argument on whether young children should participate in competitive sports.

> Introduction—Define the issue and assert the thesis that organized competitive sports are inappropriate for young children.
>
> Reason 1: Competitive sports are inappropriate because they put young children at risk both of physical injuries and psychological damage.
>
> Reason 2: Our society values competition, and sports foster competition, but young children need to learn cooperation and sportsmanship as well as how to be competitive (acknowledges opposing argument).
>
> Conclusion—Reassert the inappropriateness of competitive sports for young children and recommend a more appropriate sports program.

The student organized the argument around two reasons, providing supporting examples, anecdotes, and quotations from authorities. She acknowledged that not all parents or coaches behave inappropriately, but cited evidence indicating that the problem is widespread. While acknowledging the economic value of teaching children to be competitive, she also emphasized the growing importance of collaboration in economic and social interactions. She concluded by supporting alternative sports programs that emphasize fitness, cooperation, sportsmanship, and individual performance. (See 3c for more on supporting a claim and counterarguing.)

Evaluating and Revising Your Draft

Use these questions to help you evaluate your draft before revising.

Issue. Is the issue explained clearly and succinctly? Is it defined in a way that sets the stage for the argument?

Position. Is the position stated explicitly? Is it clear and unambiguous? Is it stated too stridently or too timidly? Does it need to be qualified or more sharply focused?

Argument. Are the reasons clear and well supported? Does the counterargument effectively refute opposing points of view and acknowledge legitimate objections?

Plan. Are each of the reasons relevant to the thesis? Does the argument unfold logically from one point to the next, or are there gaps that need to be bridged with better transitions?

Editing and Proofreading

The type of thinking involved in making an argument leads to sentences that connect ideas with conjunctions and conjunctive adverbs. Therefore, look out for errors in punctuating compound elements linked by a conjunction and in punctuating conjunctive adverbs. (See 37 on punctuating independent clauses joined by a conjunction, 38a on punctuating other compound elements, and 39d on punctuating independent clauses that contain conjunctive adverbs.)

Evaluation involves making judgments. Friends may not ask you to support your judgment, but if you write an evaluation of something you have read, observed, or learned for an instructor or a distant audience, you must offer reasons for your judgment and support for your reasons. When you support a judgment, you use details from the subject you are evaluating and may also compare your subject to a similar subject.

Typical Assignments

Political Science. Write a research report evaluating the performances of the two major presidential candidates during one of their scheduled televised debates. If possible, videotape the debate and the postdebate television commentary so that you can analyze it and quote the candidates and commentators. Use this material together with newspaper reports and polls to support your judgment about who won the debate.

Film Studies. "Film noir" is the subject of your final. In the library, at 2 or 8 p.m. on December 6, view *The Maltese Falcon* (John Huston, 1941). You may see the film twice. Take careful notes. In your essay, explain how this film belongs to the film noir genre and evaluate it as an example of the genre, comparing it to other examples of film noir screened and discussed in class.

Basic Requirements

A Well-Presented Subject. Identify and describe the subject you are evaluating, considering what your readers know about the subject and what they need to know to understand your evaluation.

A Clear, Authoritative Judgment. Assert a judgment about your subject. Because few subjects are altogether bad or good, writers usually acknowledge some good in a subject they criticize and some bad in one they praise.

Reliance on Appropriate Standards of Judgment. Successful evaluators base their judgments on standards or criteria their readers understand. Standards need not be announced, but they must be easy to infer, and they must be standards that readers use themselves, whether they are aware of them or not. If you must rely on unfamiliar standards, you will have to describe each standard and argue for its appropriateness.

A Convincing Argument. To be convincing, an evaluation must give reasons for the judgment and support each reason with details from the subject being evaluated. Evaluative arguments nearly always make favorable or unfavorable comparisons to other similar subjects. (See 3c.)

A Logical Plan. Readers find successful evaluations easy to follow, even compelling. Each reason offered to support the judgment seems to follow naturally or logically from the previous one. Reasons may be sequenced from most obvious to least obvious, most general or familiar to most technical, least convincing to most convincing, or any other logical pattern appropriate for the subject matter and audience.

Planning 

The following sequence of activities can help you plan your essay.

- To gain confidence in your judgment and gather support for your argument, review what you already know about your subject and then learn more about it.
- Analyze your readers by drafting a quick profile of them. How much do they know about the particular subject and subjects like it? What standards of judgment would seem sensible to them? What comparisons would they recognize?
- Make a tentative list of the reasons for your judgment. Then, for each reason in your list, note specific details of your subject you could use to support your judgment of it.

Formulating a Working Thesis 

A thesis for an evaluative essay clearly and emphatically asserts the writer's judgment, as in the following examples from a student essay evaluating a film.

> At first and final glance, *Poltergeist* is simply a riveting demonstration of a movie's power to terrify. It creates honest thrills within the confines of a PG rating, reaching for shock effects and the forced suspension of disbelief throughout the movie.

An evaluative thesis may also assert a comparative judgment, as in this example comparing two environmental magazines:

> *Buzzworm* is a valuable new magazine and superior to *Sierra*.

Organizing and Drafting 

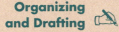

Order your reasons in a way that will lead readers step by step through your argument.

A student prepared the following scratch outline for an assignment in an environmental studies course. The essay evaluated a new environmental magazine.

> Presentation of the subject: *Buzzworm* magazine
> Assertion of judgment: *Buzzworm* is a valuable new magazine and superior to *Sierra*
> Reason 1: Visual appeal
> Reason 2: Visuals enhance the environmental reports
> Reason 3: Informative captions for all visuals
> Reason 4: Ads located in back of magazine
> Reason 5: Effective use of subfeatures
> Reason 6: Fairness in presenting issues
>
> Reservation 1: Tables and figures not as striking as the photographs
> Reservation 2: Photographs too uniform in size
>
> Conclusion: *Buzzworm* sets a new standard

The student organized the essay as a sequence of eight steps in a logical argument: six reasons followed by two reservations. In addition, notice that the student began with the most technical reasons—

visuals and captions—and moved to the most general ones—placement of ads, subfeatures (brief sections of optional information), and fairness. Although the two reservations about technical features were discussed at the end, they might have been taken up earlier in the essay, following the writer's technical reasons. (See 3c for more on supporting an argument.)

Evaluating and Revising Your Draft

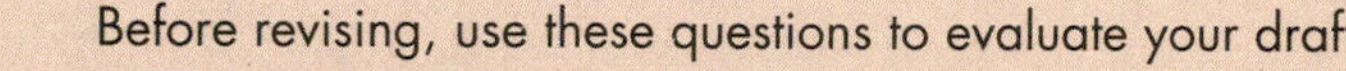

Before revising, use these questions to evaluate your draft.

Presentation of the Subject. Is the subject defined, described, and detailed clearly and interestingly? Given readers' likely knowledge and experience of the subject, is the detail appropriate?

Judgment. Is the judgment unambiguous? Might it be qualified to show that the subject is neither all good nor all bad?

Standards of Judgment. Is the judgment based on standards that readers will accept as appropriate for the subject being evaluated? Are unfamiliar standards justified?

Argument. Are there specific reasons for the judgment? Is each reason supported by details from the subject that seem well chosen, compelling, and consistent? If comparisons are used, how might they be made more relevant?

Plan. Is the evaluation easy to follow? Does each reason follow logically from the previous one?

Editing and Proofreading

When you write an evaluation, sentences of comparison become especially important. Take care to make them complete, logical, and clear. (See 22e and 26c for help with constructing comparisons.)

Speculation about causes or effects is a special type of argument. Your goal is to convince readers that your proposed causes or effects are likely or plausible, even though you cannot provide conclusive proof for them.

Typical Assignment

Psychology. Based on the readings for the course together with your personal observation and experience, write an essay speculating on the causes of racism in our society today.

Basic Requirements

A Clearly Presented Subject. Depending on how much readers know or need to know, you may have to devote a large portion of the essay to describing the subject—a mysterious or significant event (such as the abrupt resignation of a public official), a puzzling phenomenon (such as the disparity in wealth in our society), or an alarming trend (such as increasing homelessness among women). For a trend, you must always demonstrate that the trend exists.

A Logical Plan. The causes or effects must be arranged in some logical order. Background causes of a trend might precede immediate causes. Obvious causes of a phenomenon might precede less obvious or hidden causes. Immediate effects of an event might precede long-term effects. In some cases, you may be able to link your proposed causes or effects so that one leads compellingly to the next.

Convincing Support for the Plausibility of Your Proposed Causes or Effects. Because none of the causes or effects is certain, only probable, you need to support each one with statistics, facts, examples, comparisons, cases, anecdotes, or quotations from authorities. (See 3c for more on causes and effects.)

Anticipation of Readers' Objections and Preferred Causes. Assume that readers will have questions about or objections to the supporting argument for each proposed cause or effect. You must also assume that readers may have other causes or effects in mind that seem to them more likely explanations for the event, phenomenon, or trend. Therefore, anticipate and respond to possible questions and objections, and concede or refute the causes that readers may consider most likely.

Planning 

The following sequence of activities can help you plan your essay.

- Research your subject, noting any causes or effects others have proposed. (See Chapter 7 on finding library and Internet materials.)
- List the causes or effects that provide the most plausible explanation.
- Consider what facts, examples, or other support you can offer to convince readers that each cause or effect is likely.
- Analyze what your readers already know about the subject. How might they react to your speculations about its causes or effects?

Formulating a Working Thesis 

A thesis for an essay speculating about causes or effects may simply announce the subject and indicate whether the argument will focus on causes or effects, as in this example.

> While there are probably as many reasons for later childbearing as there are individual women, a few common causes contribute to the decision.

It also may specify the most plausible cause or effect, as in this thesis in the conclusion of a student essay.

> Although deinstitutionalization seems to have been the biggest factor in the increase in vagrant women, there is some evidence that the main cause is economic. . . . Together with inflation and unemployment, the loss of welfare benefits, particularly cuts in Aid to Families with Dependent Children, has effectively forced many women into homelessness.

Organizing and Drafting

With your readers and argument in mind, make a tentative plan for your speculations by sequencing your proposed causes or effects.

A student prepared the following scratch outline for an assignment in a sociology course. The essay speculated about the causes of a social trend—increasing homelessness among women.

> Presentation of the trend: One case of homelessness; statistics confirming the trend; statistics about homeless women in general
>
> Cause 1: Leaving home because of rape, incest, or other forms of abuse
>
> Cause 2: Evictions and illegal lockouts because of inability to pay rent
>
> Cause 3: Lack of inexpensive housing
>
> Refutation 1 of an alternative cause—alcoholism
>
> Cause 4: Deinstitutionalization of mentally ill women
>
> Refutation 2 of an objection that effective psychotropic drugs and expanded legal rights for deinstitutionalized, mentally ill women help them adjust
>
> Cause 5: Economic decline and poverty

The student sequenced the causes logically, beginning with immediate personal causes and moving to background social and economic causes. The student also inserted two refutations at relevant points in the essay. The primary writing strategies she used for presenting the trend included case histories, statistics, and quotations from authorities. The strategies for supporting the causes included statistics, examples, quotations from authorities, and analogies.

Evaluating and Revising Your Draft

Before revising, use these questions to evaluate your draft.

Subject. Are readers sufficiently informed about the subject? If your subject is a trend, is its existence documented conclusively?

Causes or Effects. Are there so many causes that you cannot support some of them fully? Might any of the causes seem too obvious to readers?

Plan. Are the causes or effects presented in a logical order? Would an alternative sequence have a greater impact on readers?

Support. Is each cause or effect supported so that readers will find it well argued and plausible?

Readers' Objections and Preferred Causes. Have you conceded alternative causes or effects where you can and refuted them where you must? Are your counterarguments convincingly argued and complete?

Editing and Proofreading 

Two problems often occur in speculations about causes or effects: inconsistencies in presenting numbers as evidence of a trend and mixed constructions such as *the reason is because*. (See Chapter 49 for help with presenting numbers correctly, and 30c for alternatives to *the reason is because* and other mixed constructions.)

Interpretations assert meanings and significance. In college, you may be asked to interpret a variety of literary texts—short stories and novels, plays and films, poems and songs. Whatever text you study, readers expect you to offer support for your interpretation from the text itself and possibly from other sources.

Typical Assignments

American Literature. Psychologists agree that it is important for the adult to achieve autonomy (a sense of competence and self-sufficiency) and intimacy (the ability to love and be open with another person). Analyze the representation of autonomy and intimacy in one of the texts we have read this term.

American History. Pick a scene from one of the film clips shown in class and write a brief essay interpreting the clip in light of either Frederick Jackson Turner's frontier thesis or the revisionary theory of Patricia Nelson Limerick that we discussed in class.

Basic Requirements

A Brief Description of the Subject. Most interpretive essays identify the text by title and author. When writing for class, you should not summarize the text, but you could present biographical information or quote from published essays to show where your interpretation stands in relation to other interpretations. (See Chapter 8 for help with quoting, summarizing, paraphrasing, and avoiding plagiarism, and Chapter 9 for help with citing sources.)

A Clearly Stated Interpretation. The interpretation is the main point of your essay, the thesis you will support. Writers usually state the thesis early in the essay and restate it at various stages to show readers how each part of the argument relates to the main point.

A Well-Supported Argument. Most writers argue for their interpretation not so much to convince readers to adopt it but to persuade them that the interpretation is plausible. The primary source of support comes from the text itself. You can refer specifically to the text by quoting, paraphrasing, or summarizing.

But you need to do more than just refer to a specific passage; you also need to explain the meaning of the passage and its relevance to your thesis. You cannot assume that your readers will see what you see in the text unless you show them what you see. In addition to offering textual support, you may support your interpretation with quotes, paraphrases, or summaries from outside sources. (See Chapters 8–11 for help with integrating and citing sources. See also 31a on integrating quotes into sentences.)

A Logical Plan. Interpretations usually consist of a group of ideas and insights connected to a main idea or thesis. Some students are reluctant to "give away" their argument. But instructors appreciate essays that forecast the thesis and tell where the essay is headed. Topic sentences and transitions also help keep readers on track, especially when the interpretation has twists and turns. (See Chapter 3 for more on forecasting statements, topic sentences, transitions, and other strategies for making your writing coherent and easy to follow.)

Planning 

The following activities can help you plan your essay.

- If you are working with a written text, annotate directly on the page (if the text is your own) or on a photocopy, marking anything that seems meaningful or interesting. Later, when you take inventory of your annotations, you may be able to find meaningful patterns in the details you have annotated. (See 12a and 12c for advice on annotating and taking inventory.)
- Think about the interpretive frameworks you have studied in class to see how they might help you interpret your subject. Consider how your subject resembles other subjects you have studied and how it is different as well as how some of the ideas that have been discussed in class apply to your subject.
- Reexamine your subject to find support for your ideas. As you look for support, you may need to modify your interpretation to fit the details.

- If you research outside sources, record the publication information you will need to cite the sources in your essay. (See Chapter 7 for help with finding print and electronic sources and research strategies. See Chapter 9 for guidelines on citing sources in the style of documentation advocated by the Modern Language Association [MLA].)

Formulating a Working Thesis

The thesis for an essay interpreting a work of literature must be an arguable assertion with which other readers could disagree. To be arguable, the thesis should neither state a known fact nor an obvious conclusion about the text.

Here are two thesis statements written by different students about the same story, "Araby" by James Joyce. Whereas the first student asserts that the boy in the story learns something important, the second student asserts that the boy learns nothing.

> "Araby" tells the story of an adolescent boy's initiation into adulthood . . . [by which] he realizes the parallel between his own self-delusion and the hypocrisy and vanity of the adult world.

> I believe, however, that the boy sees nothing and learns nothing—either about himself or others. He's not self-reflective; he's merely self-absorbed.

Organizing and Drafting

Before drafting, make a scratch outline of your argument.

Here is how one student used outlining to plan an essay interpreting James Joyce's story "Araby."

> Introduction—Identify the story; summarize the popular interpretation that the boy has a profound insight at the end; assert the thesis that the boy learns nothing
>
> Argue that the boy misreads other people and sees himself as the hero of romantic stories

Argue that the narrator presents the boy ironically, making fun of his chivalric quest to a suburban mall

Conclusion—Show that the story's ending should be interpreted ironically as evidence of the boy's inflated self-importance

This student's main idea emerged during a class discussion in which her classmates maintained that the boy in the story gains insight at the end. Disagreeing with this interpretation, she reread the story, annotating everything that related to sight and insight. She noticed that the images of blindness and misreading formed a pattern that would support her thesis.

Evaluating and Revising Your Draft

The following questions will help you evaluate your draft.

Subject. Is the subject adequately identified? Could background information or a review of other interpretations help situate the essay's interpretation?

Interpretation. Is the thesis stated clearly and explicitly? Is it an arguable assertion, or does it seem too simple or obvious?

Support. Is the thesis adequately supported? Are there too many quotations and is there too little explanation of what they mean and how they relate to the thesis? Are outside sources of support used effectively and cited correctly?

Plan. Are all of the ideas connected to the main idea or thesis and presented in a logical order? Are topic sentences and transitions used effectively to orient readers?

Editing and Proofreading

Because of the type of sentences usually involved in writing an interpretation, you should check your essay for errors in parallel construction and in the use of ellipsis marks. (See Chapter 32 for advice on parallelism and 44a for help with punctuating ellipsis marks.)

3 STRATEGIES FOR READABLE, COHERENT WRITING

To make your writing readable and coherent or easy to follow, you need to provide orienting cues that focus readers' attention on your main points and to use writing strategies purposefully as you develop your points in paragraphs.

3a Provide thesis and forecasting statements to orient readers.

To help readers find their way, especially in difficult and lengthy texts, you can provide two types of orienting information.

Use a thesis statement to declare your purpose.

Different kinds of essays, such as those explaining a concept, interpreting a story, or presenting personal experience, announce their purpose in different ways. (For examples, see the guides to writing these and other types of essays in Chapter 2.)

Here, we focus on a common kind of writing in college: an essay arguing a position on a controversial issue. Readers of position papers expect writers to assert their position explicitly in a clear and straightforward *thesis statement.* The following example illustrates how one student constructed a thesis statement (underlined) to assert his position on the issue of whether there should be speed limits on U.S. highways:

> In fact, there is solid reasoning to support the claim that all speed limits on rural U.S. interstate highways should be lifted. Not only are these speed limits—which currently vary from state to state—unnecessarily restrictive, they also infringe upon the personal freedom of American citizens. Although there are many urban and suburban locations where speed limits are appropriate, the vast open stretches that make up most of the

> interstate highway system do not need to be regulated. Drivers should be able to travel on interstate highways from Washington to Florida without experiencing varying state speed limits in noncongested areas. Modern automobiles are capable of traveling safely at high speeds, and despite what the auto-insurance consortium would have us believe, speed by itself does not kill. On our well-designed interstate highway system, American drivers are capable of driving at speeds over 70 miles per hour responsibly and safely. Perhaps the most compelling reason to lift the interstate speed limits is the simplest: Driving fast is enjoyable.
>
> —Brent Knutson, "Auto Liberation"

Notice, in this example, that Brent Knutson asserts his thesis in a single sentence, but that he goes on for several sentences to qualify his position by acknowledging that speed limits should be enforced under certain conditions. Like most writers, Knutson tries to satisfy readers' expectations by placing the thesis statement toward the beginning of the essay, getting quickly to the point. (To see how Knutson introduces his thesis and how he develops the rest of his essay, turn to page 143.) Whether you express the thesis in a single sentence or in several, and whether you place it at the beginning or at the end, what is most important is that the thesis be clear and explicit so that readers know exactly what your position is.

Note: The thesis statement, in addition to being an important cue for readers, is a crucial tool for writers. Formulating a thesis—however roughly—fairly early in the writing process helps writers focus their ideas and organize them as they draft their essay. The thesis, of course, can be revised and refined to accommodate new ideas and shifts in focus that arise during the writing process. (See Chapter 1 for a detailed discussion of the writing process and Chapter 2 for guides to formulating a thesis for different kinds of essays.)

Use a forecasting statement to preview points that will support the thesis.

A thesis statement may include, or be followed closely by, a *forecasting statement,* which gives an overview of the way the argument supporting the thesis will be developed. In the preceding example, notice how Brent Knutson previews the reasons for his position as well as the counterarguments he will use to answer objections to his argument.

Do not be concerned that the forecasting statement gives away the argument. Readers of position papers are not looking to be surprised but to be convinced. When considering a complicated argument, readers find it helpful to know roughly where they are going. Thesis and forecasting statements prepare them for this journey.

3b Support the thesis with paragraphs built around topic sentences.

Topic sentences assert the specific reasons and counterarguments used to support the thesis or position. A topic sentence may identify the topic of a single paragraph or a sequence of paragraphs that develop the same topic.

Here is Brent Knutson's thesis from 3a, followed by topic sentences from his essay:

> In fact, there is solid reasoning to support the claim that all speed limits on rural U.S. interstate highways should be lifted.
>
> The belief that a rural interstate system without speed limits would result in widespread carnage appears to be based more on fear than fact.
>
> Statistics related to traffic deaths can be misleading.
>
> The State of Montana offers an interesting case study of the effect of lifting speed limits on rural interstates.
>
> Driving fast in itself, however, is not a hazard; speed combined with incompetence, alcohol, or hazardous conditions is dangerous.
>
> Kohl's comment points to one of the most persuasive arguments to abolish interstate speed limits: Driving fast is pure, unadulterated, rip-snortin' fun.

In argumentative writing like Knutson's position paper, as well as in explanatory writing, topic sentences often appear at the start of the paragraph, where they give readers a sense of how the paragraph will be developed. A topic sentence that does not open a paragraph is most likely to appear at the end, where it may summarize or generalize about preceding information.

Note: Essays presenting personal experience tend to use topic sentences sparingly. Topic sentences appear in paragraphs reflecting on the significance of an event or place or commenting on relationships with people, but not in paragraphs narrating events or describing people and places. (For more on essays about personal experience and other kinds of writing, see Chapter 2.)

Be aware of topic sentence strategies.

As readers move through your essay, they will expect topic sentences to use strategies like these to keep them oriented.

Announcing the Topic. The topic sentences of explanatory writing typically introduce a topic, as in these topic sentences from Barry Lopez's book *Arctic Dreams.*

> A polar bear walks in a way all its own.
>
> What is so consistently striking about the way Eskimos used parts of an animal is the breadth of their understanding about what would work.
>
> The Mediterranean view of the Arctic, down to the time of the Elizabethan mariners, was shaped by two somewhat contradictory thoughts.

The topic sentences of argumentative writing often identify the next step in an argument or counterargument. The following topic sentences come from Richard Estrada's essay "Sticks and Stones and Sports Team Names," which argues that using ethnic groups—in particular, Native Americans—as sports mascots is offensive. Note how the first two sentences introduce opposing views to which Estrada will make a counterargument. The third topic sentence introduces Estrada's strongest defense for his position.

> The defenders of team names that use variations on the Indian theme argue that tradition should not be sacrificed at the altar of political correctness.
>
> Another argument is that ethnic group leaders are too inclined to cry wolf in alleging racial insensitivity.

> What makes naming teams after ethnic groups, particularly minorities, reprehensible is that politically impotent groups continue to be targeted, while politically powerful ones who bite back are left alone.

Making a Transition. Not all topic sentences simply point forward to what will follow. Some also refer to earlier sentences. Such sentences work both as topic sentences, stating the main point of the paragraph, and as transitions, linking that paragraph to the previous one. Here are a few topic sentences from "Quilts and Women's Culture" by Elaine Hedges that use transitional words and phrases (underlined) to tie the sentences to a previous statement.

> Within its broad traditionalism and anonymity, however, variations and distinctions developed.
>
> Regionally, too, distinctions were introduced into quilt making through the interesting process of renaming.
>
> With equal inventiveness women renamed traditional patterns to accommodate to the local landscape.
>
> Finally, out of such regional and other variations come individual, signed achievements.
>
> Quilts, then, were an outlet for creative energy, a source and emblem of sisterhood and solidarity, and a graphic response to historical and political change.

Note: Occasionally, whole paragraphs serve as transitions, linking one sequence of paragraphs with those that follow.

Stick to the point of your topic sentence.

To keep your paragraphs focused, unified, and coherent, stick to the point of your topic sentence. In the following paragraph, the writer wanders away from the main point and, thus, risks disorienting readers. Notice that the underlined sentences do not clearly support the author's main contention.

> The university's recent decision to spend $1 million to renovate the Cooley Athletic Center, while making sharp cuts in funding for the Paine Gallery, is just one example of how the administration favors athletics over the arts and other academic programs. Last year, according to the *Campus Times,* coaches' salaries rose nearly 10 percent, on average, over the previous year, while faculty salaries increased an average of 2 percent. And why is the university now planning to spend $500,000 on landscaping? The trees planted last year are already diseased, so what's the point? Is landscaping really that important?

Read your drafts closely for material that doesn't advance, clarify, or enhance the topic sentences of your paragraphs and, in turn, your thesis. You'll have to decide whether to cut such material or to broaden the scope of your topic sentence—and perhaps your thesis—to accommodate it.

3c Develop paragraphs using strategies that suit your writing purpose.

The paragraphs that support your thesis can be developed according to a variety of strategies: narrating, describing, illustrating, defining, classifying and dividing, comparing and contrasting, examining causes and effects, supporting a claim, and counterarguing. The strategy you use depends on your writing purpose. For example, an essay arguing that instructors should lower course requirements for students who work full time might include narrative paragraphs that provide examples of overburdened working students as well as paragraphs presenting research that indicates that many working students get lower grades on essays because they cannot come to campus during office hours to get extra help from their instructors. As this example illustrates, writers use these strategies flexibly, sometimes using more than one strategy in a paragraph, to support their arguments most effectively. Following is an overview of major methods of development and when they are commonly used.

1. Use narrative to present a chain of events or illustrate a process.

Narration is a basic writing strategy for presenting action. You can use narratives for a variety of purposes: to illustrate and support ideas with anecdotes, to entertain readers with suspenseful or revealing stories, to analyze causes and possible effects with scenarios, and to explain procedures with process narrative. The most common way of ordering a narrative is to present the actions chronologically, beginning with the first action and going straight through to the last. Sometimes, however, writers complicate the narrative sequence by using flashbacks or flashforwards.

Events. Sometimes a certain event—or series of events—is key to a point you want to make or a story you want to tell. For some writing tasks, such as sketching out a day of campaign events for a political science essay, your narration may be fairly straightforward. In other cases, you may want to turn a sequence of events into a dramatic story by building tension and suspense about what may happen, as in the following passage that presents a personal experience.

> One afternoon I pulled the trigger. I had been aiming at two old people, a man and a woman, who walked so slowly that by the time they turned the corner at the bottom of the hill my little store of self-control was exhausted. I had to shoot. I looked up and down the street. It was empty. Nothing moved but a pair of squirrels chasing each other back and forth on the telephone wires. I followed one in my sight. Finally it stopped for a moment and I fired. The squirrel dropped straight into the road. I pulled back into the shadows and waited for something to happen, sure that someone must have heard the shot or seen the squirrel fall. But the sound that was so loud to me probably seemed to our neighbors no more than the bang of a cupboard slammed shut. After a while I sneaked a glance into the street. The squirrel hadn't moved. It looked like a scarf someone had dropped.
>
> —Tobias Wolff, "On Being a Real Westerner"

Processes. Process narrative typically explains how something is done. Often the purpose is to point out the significance of a process rather than to help readers re-create it, as in the following passage by David Noonan, who writes about how doctors prepare for brain surgery.

Notice that the passage, like many illustrating processes, predominantly uses the present tense to create a sense of immediacy. (The present-tense verbs are underlined.) Tense is crucial to narrations of processes and events because it indicates when the actions occur and whether they are complete or in progress.

> The time the doctors must spend scrubbing their hands has been cut from ten minutes to five, but this obsessive routine is still the most striking of the doctor's preparations. Leaning over the trough-like stainless-steel sink with their masks in place and their arms lathered to the elbow, the surgeons carefully attend to each finger with the brush and work their way up each arm. It is the final pause, the last thing they do before they enter the operating room to go to work. Many . . . are markedly quiet while they scrub; they spend the familiar minutes running through the operation one more time. When they finish and their hands are too clean for anything but surgery they turn off the water with knee controls and back through the OR door, their dripping hands held high before them. They dry off with sterile towels, step into long-sleeved robes, and then plunge their hands down into their thin surgical gloves, which are held for them by the scrub nurse. The gloves snap as the nurse releases them around the doctors' wrists. Unnaturally smooth and defined, the gloved hands of the neurosurgeons are now ready; they can touch the living human brain.
>
> —David Noonan, "Inside the Brain"

2. Use descriptions to convey sensory details.

Descriptions make writing vivid. Often, they are used to create a dominant impression—a mood or an atmosphere that reinforces a writer's purpose. For example, a writer presenting personal experience might describe a room's dusty and dilapidated furniture, peeling wallpaper, and stopped clock to create a sense of neglect or gloom.

Description involves three key strategies: *naming, detailing,* and *comparing.* Writers first name things they wish to describe, whether these are people, places, or objects. They then detail what they have named with modifiers—adjectives and adverbs, phrases and clauses—that often appeal to the senses (sight, hearing, smell, touch, and taste). They may also enrich their description of one thing by comparing it to something else.

In the following passage, writer Paul Auster uses all three strategies of description to create a mood of suspense and danger.

> Then the thunder started. And after the thunder the lightning started. The storm was directly on top of us, and it turned out to be the summer storm to end all summer storms. I have never seen weather like that before or since. The rain poured down on us so hard that it actually hurt; each time the thunder exploded, you could feel the noise vibrating inside your body. When the lightning came, it danced around us like spears. It was as if weapons had materialized out of thin air—a sudden flash that turned everything a bright, ghostly white. Trees were struck, and their branches began to smolder. Then it would go dark again for a moment, there would be another crash in the sky, and the lightning would return in a different spot.
>
> —Paul Auster, "Why Write?"

3. Use examples and illustrations to provide concrete support for assertions.

Examples and illustrations are essential strategies for explanatory writing and also can provide support for arguments. They make abstract ideas concrete and generalizations specific. When readers see an example, they are more likely to understand what the writer is saying. In addition, the writer's example may remind readers of other examples that reinforce the writer's point.

You may focus on a single, vivid example or provide a number of examples to illustrate your point. In the following paragraph, Joseph Berger gives several examples of how Richard Plass, a teacher at Stuyvesant High School in New York City, helps science students achieve success.

> At Stuyvesant, Plass immerses his students in research at a tender age. Students in freshman biology take four periods of research lab a week in addition to the normal complement of six classes of biology. In short order, they are working on lengthy and distinctive experiments. Students start the year studying a number of common creatures. They study the organisms and their life cycles and then pick a substance or a physical or environmental phenomenon whose effects on the organism they will test. The projects are designed to nurture a love of research in the students. In addition to their work on experiments, students serve on student committees associated with their research projects in order to trade their lab experiences.
>
> —Joseph Berger, "What Produces Outstanding Science Students"

4. Use definitions to shed light on difficult or important concepts.

To define key words in essays, writers may draw on the dictionary or provide their own definition in a sentence or two. In certain cases, however, they may choose to use extended definitions—those of a paragraph or more—to give more emphasis to or insight into important terms and concepts. The following paragraph, in addition to defining *schizophrenia,* traces the scope and seriousness of the disease.

> Schizophrenia has been recognized for centuries, and as early as the seventeenth century its main symptoms, course of development, and outcome were described. The term *schizophrenia,* first used in 1908, refers to the disconnection or splitting of the mind that seems basic to all the various forms of the disease. It strikes both men and women, usually during adolescence or early adulthood, and is found all over the world. Treatment may include chemotherapy, electroconvulsive therapy, psychotherapy, and counseling. Hospitalization is ordinarily required, but usually not for more than a few months. It seems that about a third of patients recover completely and the rest can eventually have "a reasonable life adjustment," but some effect of the illness nearly always remains, most commonly lack of feeling and reduced drive or ambition.
>
> —Veronica Murayama, "Schizophrenia: What It Looks Like, How It Feels"

5. Use classification to sort information; use division to analyze it.

Classification and division are two related strategies for organizing and presenting complex material. They can be used for explanatory as well as argumentative purposes.

Classification. This strategy helps you sort information and ideas. When classifying, you combine items into a number of categories (or groups) and then label each one. In some cases, you tell about a classification system that already exists; in others, you lay out your own system of classification. Notice, in the following paragraph, how a sociologist classifies societies as "primitive" or "modern."

> It's hard to believe now, but for a long time the loss of community was considered to be liberating. Societies were believed to progress from closely knit, "primitive," or rural villages to unrestrictive, "modern," or urban societies. The former were depicted as based on kinship and loyalty in an age in which both were suspect; the latter, however, were seen as based on reason (or "rationality") in an era in which reason's power to illuminate was admired with little attention paid to the deep shadows it casts. The two types of social relations have often been labeled with the terms supplied by a German sociologist, Ferdinand Tonnies. One is *gemeinschaft,* the German term for community, and the other is *gesellschaft,* the German word for society, which he used to refer to people who have rather few bonds, like people in a crowd or a mass society.
>
> —Amitai Etzioni, "The New Community"

Division. This strategy helps you divide a complicated topic or concept into its various parts so that you—and your readers—can understand each part separately. In the following paragraph, the author divides and presents the various components of the "contingent" workforce.

> Every day, 1.5 million temps are dispatched from agencies like Kelly Services and Manpower—nearly three times as many as 10 years ago. But they are only the most visible part of America's enormous new temporary work force. An additional 34 million people start their day as other types

> of "contingent" workers. Some are part-timers with some benefits. Others work by the hour, the day or the duration of a project, receiving only a paycheck without benefits of any kind. The rules of their employment vary widely and so do the attempts to label them. They are called short-timers, per-diem workers, leased employees, extra workers, supplementals, contractors—or in IBM's ironic computer-generated parlance, "the peripherals." They are what you might expect: secretaries, security guards, salesclerks, assembly-line workers, analysts and CAD/CAM designers. But these days they are also what you'd never expect: doctors, high school principals, lawyers, bank officers, X-ray technicians, biochemists, engineers, managers—even chief executives.
>
> —Janice Castro, "Contingent Workers"

6. Use comparison to highlight similarities among items; use contrast to highlight differences.

Whenever you seek to understand or evaluate two or more things, it is useful to compare them. But as soon as you begin to compare two things, you usually begin to contrast them as well, for rarely are two things alike in all respects. Comparison, then, brings similar things together for examination, to see how they are alike. Contrast emphasizes how things are different.

There are two primary ways to organize comparison and contrast in writing: in chunks and in sequence. In *chunking,* each item to be compared or contrasted is presented and detailed separately. Here the writer contrasts the hairstyles of three women at a conference in order to make the point that society, often detrimentally, expects variety in women's appearance.

> One woman had dark brown hair in a classic style, a cross between Cleopatra and Plain Jane. The severity of her straight hair was softened by wavy bangs and ends that turned under. Because she was beautiful, the effect was more Cleopatra than plain.
>
> The second woman was older, full of dignity and composure. Her hair was cut in a fashionable style that left her with only one eye, thanks to a side part that let a curtain of hair fall across half her face. As she looked down to read her prepared paper, the hair robbed her of bifocal vision and

> created a barrier between her and the listeners.
>
> The third woman's hair was wild, a frosted blond avalanche falling over and beyond her shoulders. When she spoke she frequently tossed her head, calling attention to her hair and away from the lecture.
>
> —Deborah Tannen, "Marked Women"

In *sequencing,* the items are compared or contrasted point by point or one at a time, as in this example:

> A typical supermarket in 1976 had 9,000 products; today it has more than 30,000. The average produce section in 1975 carried sixty-five items; this summer it carried 285. . . . A Cosmetic Center outside Washington carries about 1,500 types and sizes of hair care products. The median household got six TV stations in 1975. Thanks to deregulation of the cable TV industry, that family now has more than thirty channels. The number of FM radio stations has doubled since 1970. A new religious denomination forms every week. . . . In 1955 only 4 percent of the adult population had left the faith of their childhood. By 1985 one-third had. In 1980, 564 mutual funds existed. This year there are 3,347.
>
> —Steven Waldman, "The Tyranny of Choice"

7. Use writing about causes to explain why something happened; use writing about possible effects to support proposals and positions on what should be done.

Writing about causes or effects can be an end in itself (see Chapter 2) or it can be used as a strategy to serve other purposes. For example, for a history class you might write an essay speculating about the causes of the Civil War. Or in a proposal to your supervisor, you might argue that a certain procedure be changed to avoid unfortunate results or effects.

When speculating about the causes or effects of a particular event (a recent football loss), phenomenon (solar eruptions), or trend (the increase in the number of "telecommuting" workers), you need to support your proposed causes or effects fully. Also, whenever there may be more than one cause, you must account for the various possibilities, as in the following paragraph tracing the causes of increased homelessness among American women.

> Why has there been such an increase in the number of vagrant American women? There are several causes of this trend. For one thing, more and more women are leaving their families because of rape, incest, and other forms of abuse. To take one example, the Christian Housing Facility, a private organization in Orange County, California, that provides food, shelter, and counseling to victims of abuse, sheltered 1,536 people in 1981, a 300 percent increase from the year before. It is unclear whether such increases are due to an actual increase of abuse in American families or whether they result from the fact that it is more socially acceptable for a woman to be on her own today. Another factor is that government social programs for battered women have been severely cut back, leaving victims of abuse no choice but to leave home.
>
> —Kim Dartnell, "Where Will They Sleep Tonight?"

8. Use support to back up your claims; use counterargument to address opposing views.

As discussed in 3a and 3b, your thesis asserts your position on an issue, and your topic sentences, ideally, provide various kinds of support for your thesis. In all essays—but especially in arguments—it is crucial to back up all the points that support your thesis with well-developed paragraphs buttressed by facts, statistics, appeals to authorities, anecdotes, or other types of evidence. In the following paragraph, the student writer supports her contention that competitive sports are damaging to children by quoting experts and providing statistics.

> Besides physical hazards and anxieties, competitive sports pose psychological dangers for children. Martin Rablovsky, a former sports editor for the *New York Times,* said that in all his years of watching young children play organized sports, he noticed very few of them smiling. "I've seen children enjoying a spontaneous pre-practice scrimmage become somber and serious when the coach's whistle blows," Rablovsky said. "The spirit of

> play suddenly disappears, and sport becomes joblike." . . . The primary goal of a professional athlete—winning—is not appropriate for children. Their goals should be having fun, learning, and being with friends. Although winning does add to the fun, too many adults lose sight of what matters and make winning the most important goal. Several studies have shown that when children are asked whether they would rather be warming the bench on a winning team or playing regularly on a losing team, 90 percent choose the latter. . . .
>
> —Jessica Statsky, "Children Need to Play, Not Compete"

Asserting a thesis and backing it with reasons and support are essential to a successful argument. Thoughtful writers go further, however, by counterarguing—anticipating and responding to their readers' objections, challenges, and questions. To anticipate readers' concerns, try to imagine other people's points of view, what they might know about the subject, and how they might feel about it.

To counterargue, writers rely on three basic strategies: *acknowledging, accommodating,* and *refuting.* Specifically, writers show they are aware of readers' objections and questions (acknowledge), modify their position to accept readers' concerns they think are legitimate (accommodate), or explicitly show why readers' objections are invalid or why their concerns are irrelevant (refute). Often, writers use more than one of these strategies in the same essay. The following paragraph, from a student paper advocating frequent brief examinations, uses all three.

> Why . . . do so few professors give frequent brief exams? Some believe that such exams take up too much of the limited class time available to cover the material in the course. Most courses meet 150 minutes a week—three times a week for 50 minutes each time. A 20-minute weekly exam might take 30 minutes to administer, and that is one-fifth of each week's class time. From the student's perspective, however, this is time well spent. Better learning and greater confidence about the course seem a good trade-off for another 30 minutes of lecture. Moreover, time lost to lecturing or discussion could easily be made up in students' learning on their

own through careful regular study for the weekly exams. If weekly exams still seem too time-consuming to some professors, their frequency could be reduced to every other week or their length to 5 or 10 minutes. In courses where multiple-choice exams are appropriate, several questions take only a few minutes to answer.

—Patrick O'Malley, "More Testing, More Learning"

In this paragraph, O'Malley acknowledges many professors' concern that frequent brief exams would take up too much time and describes how professors could accommodate such exams by curbing lectures and making other adjustments. He subtly refutes criticism of frequent exams by explaining why their benefits outweigh their drawbacks.

For more advice on argumentative writing, see Chapter 2.

3d Provide other cues to help readers follow the flow of ideas.

How you paragraph your essay, structure your sentences, and link related ideas can enhance the readability and coherence of your writing.

Use paragraphing to help readers process information.

How you group sentences into paragraphs affects your readers' ability to follow your ideas. A paragraph's length is not as important as its coherence or unity and focus. If all of the sentences in a paragraph develop the same topic, and you provide clear topic sentences and forecasting along with well-placed transitions to guide readers, your paragraphs will be easy to follow.

Writers tend to use very short paragraphs—one or two sentences long—to emphasize a point. The only writing situations in which short paragraphs are used regularly are for newspaper articles and email messages. Most instructors expect college essays to consist of well-developed paragraphs, five or more sentences long. Look, for example, at the paragraph by Patrick O'Malley on page 69. O'Malley's paragraph is from a proposal he wrote for his first-year composition course. Notice how he develops the paragraph with specifics that support and clarify his assertions. Students sometimes fail to develop their paragraphs because they do not want to belabor what seems to them to be obvious. But to understand a new idea, readers often need several sentences that restate, clarify, illustrate, and elaborate the point.

Express connections with cohesive devices.

By repeating key words and sentence patterns throughout a paragraph, and by providing transitions, you link important ideas for readers.

Repeated Words. In the following paragraph the pronouns *it* and *its* form a chain of connection with the words to which they refer (the *antecedent*): the *George Washington Bridge.*

> In New York from dawn to dusk to dawn, day after day, you can hear the steady rumble of tires against the concrete span of the George Washington Bridge. The bridge is never completely still. It trembles with traffic. It moves in the wind. Its great veins of steel swell when hot and contract when cold; its span often is ten feet closer to the Hudson River in summer than in winter.
>
> —Gay Talese, "New York"

When there are multiple pronoun-antecedent chains with references forward as well as back, careful writers make sure that readers will not mistake one pronoun's antecedent for another's. (For more advice on pronoun reference, see Chapter 19.) To avoid such confusion, writers often repeat words and phrases, as in this example:

> The first step is to realize that in our society we have permitted the kinds of vulnerability that characterize the victims of violent crime and have ignored, where we could, the hostility and alienation that enter into the making of violent criminals. No rational person condones violent crime, and I have no patience with sentimental attitudes toward violent criminals. But it is time that we open our eyes to the conditions that foster violence and that ensure the existence of easily recognizable victims.
>
> —Margaret Mead, "A Life for a Life: What That Means Today"

You can also use *synonyms,* words with identical or very similar meanings, to connect important ideas:

> I found the funeral director in the main lobby, adjacent to the reception room. Like most people, I had preconceptions about what an undertaker looked like. Mr. Deaver fulfilled my expectations entirely.
>
> —Brian Cable, "The Last Stop"

Repeated Sentence Structures. Writers occasionally repeat the same sentence structure to emphasize the connections among their ideas. Here is an example:

> But the life forms are as much part of the structure of the Earth as any inanimate portion is. It is all an inseparable part of a whole. If any animal is isolated totally from other forms of life, then death by starvation will surely follow. If isolated from water, death by dehydration will follow even faster. If isolated from air, whether free or dissolved in water, death by asphyxiation will follow still faster. If isolated from the Sun, animals will survive for a time, but plants would die, and if all plants died, all animals would starve.
>
> —Isaac Asimov, "The Case against Man"

(See 33c for further illustration of cohesive devices.)

Provide transitions within and between paragraphs.

A *transition* serves as a bridge, connecting one paragraph, sentence, clause, or word with another. Not only does a transition signal a connection, but it also identifies the kind of connection by indicating to readers how the item preceding the transition relates to the one that follows it. There are three basic groups of transitions, based on the relationships they indicate: *logical, temporal,* and *spatial.* For examples of these types of transitions, see the chart on page 73.

Logical Transitions. These words and phrases express logical relationships and help readers follow a line of reasoning. How logical transitions work is illustrated in this tightly and passionately reasoned paragraph by James Baldwin.

Transitions

Relationship	*Transition*
LOGICAL TRANSITIONS	
Addition	also; and; as well as; besides; furthermore; in addition; moreover
Comparison	also; likewise; similarly
Consequence	as a result; because; consequently; hence; since; therefore; thus
Contrast	although; but; even though; however; in contrast; nevertheless; on the contrary; yet
Illustration	for example; for instance; specifically
Order (of Ideas)	first, second; finally; for one thing, . . . for another
TEMPORAL TRANSITIONS	
Duration	briefly; during; for a long time; since
Frequency	frequently; hourly; occasionally; often; rarely
Order (of Events or Processes)	after; afterward; at first; at last; before; finally; in the beginning; in the end; late; later; next; now; subsequently; then
SPATIAL TRANSITIONS	
Direction	across; around; away; beyond; down; into; over; sideways; through; to; toward; up
Placement	along; alongside; atop; behind; below; facing; in front of; inside; on; outside
Proximity	close to; far from; here; in the distance; near; next to; there

> The black man insists, by whatever means he finds at his disposal, that the white man cease to regard him as an exotic rarity and recognize him as a human being. This is a very charged and difficult moment, for there is a great deal of will power involved in the white man's naiveté. Most people are not naturally malicious, and the white man prefers to keep the black man at a certain human remove because it is easier for him thus to preserve his simplicity and to avoid being called to account for crimes committed by his forefathers, or his neighbors. He is inescapably aware, nevertheless, that he is in a better position in the world than black men are, nor can he quite put to death the suspicion that he is hated by black men therefore. He does not wish to be hated, neither does he wish to change places, and at this point in his uneasiness he can scarcely avoid having recourse to those legends which white men have created about black men, the most unusual effect of which is that the white man finds himself enmeshed, so to speak, in his own language which describes hell, as well as the attributes which lead one to hell, as being black as night.
>
> —James Baldwin, "Stranger in the Village"

Temporal Transitions. These indicate temporal relationships—a sequence or progression in time. In the following paragraph, Annie Dillard uses temporal transitions to move readers through her childhood experiments with a microscope.

> Finally late that spring I saw an amoeba. The week before, I had gathered puddle water from Frick Park; it had been festering in a jar in the basement. This June night after dinner I figured I had waited long enough. In the basement at my microscope table I spread the scummy drop of Frick Park puddle water on a slide, peeked in, and lo, there was the famous amoeba. He was blobby and grainy as his picture; I would have known him anywhere.
>
> —Annie Dillard, *An American Childhood*

Spatial Transitions. These words and phrases orient readers to the objects in a scene. In the following passage, the writer uses spatial transitions to describe a journey through rural Georgia.

On Georgia 155, I crossed Troublesome Creek, then went through groves of pecan trees aligned one with the next like fenceposts. The pastures grew a green almost blue, and syrupy water the color of a dusty sunset filled the ponds. Around the farmhouses, from wires strung high above the ground, swayed gourds hollowed out for purple martins.

The land rose again on the other side of the Chattahoochee River, and Highway 34 went to the ridgetops where long views over the hills opened in all directions. Here was the tail of the Appalachian backbone, its gradual descent to the Gulf. Near the Alabama stateline stood a couple of LAST CHANCE! bars.

—William Least Heat-Moon, *Blue Highways*

TAKING ESSAY EXAMS

Instructors give essay exams to determine whether you understand the concepts that provide the basis for a course and whether you can use those concepts to interpret specific materials, to draw comparisons and find contrasts, and to synthesize diverse information in support of an original argument. An essay exam tests more than your memory of specific information; it requires you to use that information to demonstrate a comprehensive grasp of the topics covered in the course.

Prepare for an essay exam by reviewing notes, readings, and other materials, keeping in mind the course goals and what is likely to be tested. For example, to study for an essay exam in a history survey course, you might distinguish the primary periods and try to see relations among the periods and the works or events that define them. It is also helpful to make up questions you think the instructor might ask and then plan answers to them, perhaps with members of a study group. (Some instructors may even provide sample questions to guide your preparation.)

Once you actually get the test, make the most of your careful preparation by staying calm and plotting a course of action. Following are a few key strategies to keep in mind.

Read the exam carefully; apportion your time.

Careful time management is crucial; giving some time to each question is always better than using up your time on only a few questions and never getting to others.

Before you answer a single question, skim the entire exam so that you can divide your time realistically. Pay particular attention to how many points you may earn in different parts of the exam; notice any directions that suggest how long an answer should be. As you preview the exam, you may wish to make tentative choices about how, or in what order, you might answer questions. But before you start to complete any answers, write down an estimate of the time you expect to be working on each question or set of questions.

Determine exactly what each question requires.

Before beginning to answer a question, analyze it carefully. If you first look closely at what the question is directing you to do, you can begin to recognize the approach your answer will need to take and what information will be pertinent. Consider this question from a sociology final:

> Drawing from lectures on the contradictory aspects of American values, discussions of the "bureaucratic personality," and the type of behavior associated with social mobility, discuss the problems of bettering oneself in a relatively "open," complex, industrial society such as the United States.

The first action term, "drawing from," implies that you need to supply specific examples from lectures. "Discuss" is fairly vague, but here it probably invites you to list and explain the problems of bettering oneself. Possible sources of these problems are already identified in the opening phrases: contradictory values, bureaucratic personality, certain behavior. Therefore, you would plan to begin with an assertion (or thesis) that might include important words in the final clause (bettering oneself in an open, complex, industrial society) and then take up each type of problem in a separate paragraph.

Often, directions like "draw from" and "discuss" are cues to write one of the kinds of essays discussed in Chapter 2. For example, you might be asked to write a brief essay *explaining a concept* you have learned in the course or *interpreting a work of literature.* The action terms may also invite you to use one or more of the methods of development discussed in Chapter 3. For example, you might be asked to explain the chain of events leading up to an action or decision (*narration*); to identify important characteristics of something (*definition*); or to compare or contrast ideas, events, or people.

For a list of some typical action terms in essay exams and what they usually require of you, see the chart on page 78.

Take time to plan your answer before writing.

The amount of planning you do for an essay question will depend on how much time is allotted and how many points it is worth. For short-answer questions, a few seconds of planning will probably be sufficient. For longer answers, however, you will need to develop a much more definite plan. You have time for only one draft, so allow as much as a quarter of the time allotted the question for making notes, developing a thesis, and jotting down a quick outline.

As with planning, your strategy for writing depends on the length of your answer. When writing short answers, address the question directly and succinctly, usually in just one or two sentences. For questions that call for longer answers, begin by clearly stating your thesis and forecasting statement (see 3a), perhaps using key terms from the question. Stick to your thesis and the points of your outline, if you drafted one. Finally, proofread your answer, looking for unclear or undeveloped ideas as well as grammar errors you typically make and especially for misspellings.

If you run out of time when you are writing an answer, jot down the remaining main ideas from your outline, just to show that you know the material and with more time could have continued.

Typical Action Terms in Essay Exams

Analyze: This prompt sometimes requires you to apply a theory or concept to texts, issues, and events covered in the course. Other times, it requires you to list causes or reasons, even though this requirement may not be explicitly stated. The word *analyze* does not always appear in questions calling for analysis. Example: *Why do Maurice and Jean not succumb to the intolerable conditions of the prison camp (the Camp of Hell) as most of the others do?*

Argue: This is a call for you to take a position on an issue and to support it with evidence from lectures and readings. (Sometimes such phrases as "comment on" and "draw conclusions about" really call for argument.) Example: *Argue for or against this thesis: "In* A Clockwork Orange, *both the poetic language and the moral and political theorizing deprive the story of most of its relevance to real life."*

Compare/Contrast: This prompt requires you to explore the relations among things of importance in the course, to analyze each thing separately, and then to search out specific points of likeness or difference. Example: *Compare the views of colonialism presented in Memmi's* Colonizer and the Colonized *and Pontecorvo's* Battle of Algiers.

Explain: This prompt requires you to explain the importance or significance of something, using specific examples as the basis for a more general discussion of what has been studied. Example: *Briefly explain the last scene in* Paths of Glory *in relation to the movie as a whole.*

Discuss: Often, this prompt requires you to explain material synthesized from readings and lectures. It may also call for classification, as in this example: *On the basis of the articles read on El Salvador, Nicaragua, Peru, Chile, Argentina, and Mexico, what would you say are the major problems confronting Latin America today? Discuss the major types of problems with reference to particular countries as examples.*

Identify and Give Significance: Sometimes, this prompt requires you to write just a few sentences defining or identifying items from the course and explaining what they mean or why they're important. Example: *Identify and give the significance of "signifying" in African American literature.*

5 ORAL PRESENTATIONS

At some point in your academic career, you will probably be asked to give an oral presentation. In fact, you may give many oral presentations before you graduate, and you almost certainly will give oral presentations on the job. This chapter contains tips, techniques, and strategies for giving effective oral presentations.

Relax.

Many people are terrified at the thought of public speaking, particularly people who have little experience with it. Even experienced public speakers can become jittery before giving an oral presentation. The key to defeating nervousness and anxiety is to research and prepare. If you have researched your subject thoroughly and have planned your presentation in detail, then you should be able to relax.

Understand the kind of oral presentation you have been asked to give.

The list that follows identifies the four basic types of oral presentations.

- *Impromptu presentation:* An impromptu oral presentation is given without preparation. In a history class, for example, your instructor may call on you to explain briefly a concept you are studying such as "manifest destiny." As best you can, you would recall what you have read and summarize the information.
- *Extemporaneous presentation:* In an extemporaneous presentation, you prepare beforehand and speak from notes or an outline. For example, in your management class, you might prepare a report on a business you recently visited. In most academic and business situations extemporaneous talks are preferred, because they are informal yet well organized.

- *Scripted presentation:* Reading from a script is one way to ensure that you say exactly what you want to say—and nothing more. For example, at a conference, you might read a report you prepared ahead of time on your experience as a student teacher. Because you read to your audience, a scripted presentation can be stiff and boring unless it is carefully planned and rehearsed.
- *Memorized presentation:* This type of oral presentation is written and committed to memory beforehand. For instance, at a sales meeting, you might evaluate a new product in relation to its competition. However, since it is difficult to memorize a lengthy presentation, most people prefer scripted talks.

Assess your audience and purpose.
As with writing projects, to give effective oral presentations you need to assess your audience and your purpose. Even for an impromptu presentation, you should take a few moments to think about whom you are speaking to and why. To assess your audience, ask the same questions you would ask about readers: Why is your audience there? What do they already know about your subject?

Define your purpose by completing the following statement: "In this oral presentation, I want to. . . ." For instance, you may want to describe the recent trend of companies hiring numerous part-time and temporary workers to avoid the costs of employee benefits or argue your position on the ethics of this policy. To get an idea of the purposes you could have, see the guides to different kinds of writing in Chapter 2 and the different strategies for developing paragraphs in 3c.

Determine how much information you can present in the allotted time.
Your presentation should be exactly as long as the time allotted. Using substantially less time will make your presentation seem incomplete or superficial; using substantially more time may alienate your audience. Plan your presentation to allocate sufficient time for an introduction, concluding remarks, and follow-up questions (if a question-and-answer session is to be

part of the presentation). If you are giving a scripted presentation, each double-spaced page of text will probably take two minutes to deliver.

Use cues to orient listeners.

Listening is one of the most difficult ways to comprehend information, in part because listeners cannot look back at previous information or scan forward, as readers can. To help your audience follow your oral presentation, use the same cues you would use to orient readers. For a discussion and illustration of a variety of orienting cues, see Chapter 3. Here, we review three basic cues that are helpful for listeners.

- *Thesis and forecasting statements:* Begin your presentation with thesis and forecasting statements that announce to audience members what you intend to communicate (your thesis) and the order in which you will present your material (your forecast). For instance, if you will present an argument about deregulation in the telecommunications industry, you can begin by asserting your position and previewing the reasons you will offer to support your position.
- *Transitions:* Provide transitions when you move from one point to the next to help your audience follow the twists and turns of your presentation. For an example, when you have finished discussing your first reason, state explicitly that you are now turning to your second reason.
- *Summaries:* End your oral presentation with a summary of the main points you have made. Also look for opportunities to use summaries throughout the presentation, particularly when you have spent a long time discussing something complicated. A brief summary that indicates the point you are making and its relation to your overall thesis can help listeners see how the parts of your argument fit together to support your thesis.

Prepare effective and appropriate visuals.

For presentations that you plan ahead of time, you can use a variety of visuals—from simple lists and graphs to sophisticated computer demonstrations—to help both you and your audience. For instance, an overhead transparency listing the major points of your presentation will help you to make a forecasting statement that your listeners will pay attention to and remember. You can even leave the visual on display as you talk, referring to it to make a transition or adding to it as you answer questions. See 14d for more information about visuals.

Different technologies are available for displaying visuals. Writing on a board or flip chart has several advantages: low cost, high visibility, and the ability to compose or alter on the spot. For a long passage or detailed graphic, photocopied handouts are preferable, although they can be distracting.

As you prepare visuals, keep in mind that they must be legible to all audience members, including people seated in the back of the room. Use a large, easy-to-read font and generous amounts of space around text.

Verify that you will have the correct equipment and supplies.

Well before your presentation is scheduled to begin, verify that the presentation room contains all of the equipment and supplies you will need. For example, if you plan to use an overhead projector, make sure it is in the room, placed correctly, and working well. Anticipating your needs (bring a marker) as well as potential problems (bring a spare bulb) will make your presentation go smoothly and help reduce your anxiety.

DIGITAL HINT

If you plan to display visuals from a computer or even to run a computer-generated presentation, prepare a backup plan. Computers have a way of crashing at precisely the wrong moment, and software glitches can sabotage otherwise outstanding presentations.

Rehearse your presentation.

Rehearsing will help you to become more familiar with your material, to fit the material into the allotted time, and to feel more confident about speaking in public. If possible, rehearse in the same room in which you will give the presentation, using the same equipment, and try to rehearse before an audience of colleagues or friends who can give you constructive criticism. Rehearsing a scripted or memorized presentation will enable you to plan your delivery. For a scripted talk, mark cues very selectively on your printed text to remind yourself when to pause and what words and phrases to emphasize.

Deliver the oral presentation professionally.

Before your presentation, try to relax: Take a few deep breaths, drink some water, or step outside for some fresh air. If someone is to introduce you, give that person information about yourself and your presentation. Otherwise, begin by introducing yourself and your title or topic.

These guidelines will help you to make a professional impression:

- As you speak, try to make eye contact with everyone in the room.
- Use your hands to gesture as you would in a conversation; your hands should neither be clamped rigidly at your sides nor doing something distracting such as playing with your jewelry.
- If you are behind a lectern, avoid slouching, leaning on it, or gripping it tightly throughout the presentation.
- If you are using visuals, be careful not to block the audience's view of them. After introducing a new visual, resume making eye contact with audience members; talk to the audience, not the visual.
- Try to avoid distracting vocal mannerisms, such as repeatedly saying "uh," "like," or "you know."
- Speak loudly enough that all members of the audience can hear you, and speak clearly and distinctly. Nervousness may cause you to speak too rapidly, so watch your pace.
- Do not speak in a monotone. Instead, let the pitch of your voice rise and fall naturally, especially when giving a scripted presentation.

End your presentation graciously.

If no question-and-answer session is scheduled to follow your presentation, then end the presentation by thanking your audience for the opportunity to speak. If appropriate, offer to answer any questions in a private conversation or in follow-up correspondence.

If a question-and-answer session follows your presentation, politely and professionally invite questions by saying something like, "If you have any questions, I would be happy to try to answer them now."

6 PRESENTING A PORTFOLIO OF YOUR WORK

Assembling a portfolio, a collection of your writing, gives you an opportunity to show your most successful or rewarding work. You may have to submit a portfolio to meet the requirements of a course or an academic program, but keeping a collection of your favorite work can be rewarding for its own sake, providing you with a record of your development as a writer. Following are tips for assembling a portfolio.

Make your selections thoughtfully, using any criteria provided by your instructor.

If you are assembling a portfolio to meet a course or program requirement, your instructor or adviser usually will indicate what criteria you should use to select work. Typically for a writing course, you will be asked to include invention, drafts, critical responses, and final revisions of what you consider to be your best writing. For a science program, you might be asked to include a variety of kinds of essays you have written in different courses, such as a lab report, a review of research, or a historical survey.

To determine what work is your best, consider responses you have gotten from your instructor and other readers. Also, review your writing for passages or general approaches that are especially effective, such as a funny story, a powerful interpretation, or a compelling argument on a subject about which you feel strongly. Include work of which you are proud. In some cases, your instructor may require you to include a further revision of an essay you have selected.

Reflect on your choices.

Instructors who require portfolios typically will ask you to include an essay in which you justify your choices and explain what you have learned about writing in the course or program. Whether or not it is required, such reflection, or "thinking about your thinking," can help develop your powers of judgment, increase your satisfaction as a student and as a writer, and help you assess your strengths and weaknesses.

In your reflective essay, clearly state the reasons for your selections to show your instructor that you know precisely what makes them good. Explain how you identified and solved problems when revising and how your reading, research, or class discussion in the discipline influenced your writing. Discuss, too, how your writing can be understood in the larger context of the discipline you are studying.

Follow any specific instructions for presenting your work.

If you are assembling a portfolio for a course requirement, follow your instructor's directions for presenting your work. Typically, you should include a separate table of contents. Also number all pages and label all of your work in the upper-right corner of each page. For example, write "Draft, 1" for page 1 of a draft; "Revision, 2, 1" for page 1 of a second revision. You should also date all work. Put everything in the sequence specified by your instructor.

PART 2 RESEARCHING IN COLLEGE

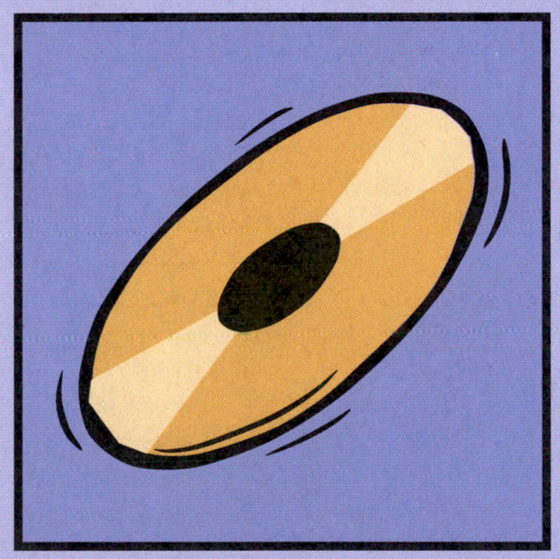

PART

2 RESEARCHING IN COLLEGE

7 FINDING SOURCES

A research assignment is an opportunity to grow intellectually. It may lead you to learn about a new topic or to alter your thinking about a familiar one. Research gives you current experience in finding and critically reading a wide variety of media, including books, journals, newsgroup postings, the World Wide Web, CD-ROMs, and many other sources. When a research project culminates in an essay, you have a chance to develop writing strategies that allow you to share your own informed perspective with other educated readers. Ultimately, research skills will help you develop intellectual curiosity, a quest for knowledge that will last for the rest of your life.

7a Understand the special challenges of research assignments.

Research assignments vary widely, from short, focused tasks to longer, more complex studies twenty pages or more. Before beginning any research project you should be aware of the following special requirements of research writing.

A good research report should reflect your informed view on the topic.

In order to use source material effectively, you must evaluate, assimilate, and reflect on a variety of views on your topic. Your sources should never "take over." Use sources as guest experts to provide background information, as authorities to lend credibility to your ideas, or as respected adversaries to represent opposing points of view.

Effective researching depends on specialized techniques.

As a researcher, you may find yourself designing a survey, searching the World Wide Web, reaching into the CD-ROM drawer, delving into book catalogs, or searching for an author's name in a periodical index. To use these resources, you will need to know how to access and interact with the information. For example, you will need to understand how your library's online catalog works in order to conduct a successful search. You will also need to understand and use the conventions for citing and documenting sources (see Chapters 8–11).

A well-researched, well-written essay requires careful planning and scheduling.

For an assignment that calls for extensive research, you should begin planning and scheduling your work early so that you will have enough time to research your topic thoroughly and complete the writing process described in Chapters 1 and 2. You need a *research strategy*, a plan that identifies the steps you have to take and when you intend to take them. The Research Paper Strategy Schedule on page 91 can help you develop and carry out your own research plan. It lists the research and writing activities with parenthetical references to the sections in *A Writer's Guidebook* where you can find help with the activity. It also includes boxes to check when you have finished each activity as well as space to schedule time for each activity and keep brief notes and reminders.

Research is a recursive process.

When researching you must constantly try to move forward, but always be ready to work recursively, moving back to earlier stages in the process when necessary. Plan ahead, but be flexible as the process unfolds. After spending time looking for sources on a particular topic, you may find you have to change topics.

When you try to integrate a source into your draft, you might find that it does not fit and that you need to look back at your annotated photocopy to find better support for the point you are trying to make. Or upon reading your draft, your instructor might suggest that you add more examples, leading you to do some further research.

Be aware of potential problems.

Finally, when embarking on a research project, watch out for the following problems that research writers often encounter:

- Underestimating the time involved in research writing, which can lead to a final essay that seems hurried or unfinished
- Neglecting to develop a thesis, which can result in an essay that reads like a patchwork of other authors' ideas, not your own informed view
- Stopping your hunt for sources too soon, or relying on only a few sources, which may limit the variety or depth of your sources and undermine the credibility of your essay
- Rushing at the end, which may leave you with no time to polish the essay and result in incorrectly formatted citations, for example, or awkwardly inserted quotations.

Research Paper Strategy Schedule

Done	*Writing/Research Activity*	*Complete by*	*Notes*
☐	**Understand the assignment (1a, 7b).**		
☐	**Browse to choose a topic (7b).**		
☐	**Find sources (7c, d, 8a).**		
☐	**Evaluate sources (7e).**		
☐	**Use reading/writing strategies to plan essay (1b, 8a, 12).**		
☐	**Organize and draft, integrating source material (1c, 8c, 14d).**		
☐	**Evaluate and revise draft, researching further if needed (1d).**		
☐	**Edit and proofread revision (viii, 1e, 16–56).**		
☐	**Recheck citations and document design (9–14).**		
☐	**Turn in the essay.**		

7b Consider your assignment and choose your topic carefully.

When your instructor announces a *research assignment,* or the term flares up in the syllabus, you may wonder how to get started. Here are some important early steps and considerations.

Understand the assignment.

Your instructor may have specifically defined the topic for you or given you a range of choices. Begin by noting what kind of writing the assignment asks for. Are you being asked, for example, to speculate about the causes of an event or to take a position on an issue and support it? (See Chapter 2 for guides to writing different kinds of essays.) Ask your instructor about the conventions or requirements for this kind of writing, such as how long the essay should be, whether certain sources, or a certain number of sources, is required, and what documentation method is expected. (See Chapters 9–10 for common documentation styles.) All of these factors will influence your choice of topic. (See 1a for additional advice on understanding writing assignments.)

Find a workable topic.

If the assignment invites you to choose a topic from a list of possibilities or to find a topic on your own, try formulating a *research question.* If you are curious about the therapeutic value of pets, for instance, you could fashion an initial research question like this: *What is the therapeutic value of pets?* This general research question would give you a direction to explore—a way of learning more about the topic so you can refine your focus. After you learn about the therapeutic value of pets, you might focus on the psychological benefits, reformulating your research question: *Do pets improve the mental health of their owners?* If you find good research information on this more specific question, the answer could become the thesis of your report.

Devising a research question helps not only when you are choosing a topic, but it can also help later as you research your topic and begin to plan your essay. The following example shows how one student's writing and researching process unfolded.

In writing a paper for a sociology class, the student started with this initial question:

> **Research Question**
> Does gender bias in math classes and science programs discourage women from pursuing careers in computer science?

This question did not work out, however, because the student found little current information on gender bias in math and science classes. As she did her preliminary browsing, though, she noticed listings and summaries for articles on female software designers' attitudes toward gaming software. Based on these resources, she arrived at a new focus:

> **Second Research Question**
> Why are so few women employed as designers of game software?

After the student selected and evaluated sources, she was able to formulate a thesis that worked well for her research paper:

> **Thesis**
> The prevalence of violent and competitive game software discourages many women from becoming software designers. This trend is especially evident in large entertainment companies such as Nintendo and Sega.

Browse to confirm your choice of topic.

Before committing to a topic, you need to make sure that you will be able to find an adequate amount of information on it.

The kind of research you need to do at this early stage in the process differs from the kind you will do later. Think of this preliminary research as *browsing*. You probably think of browsing as something you do on the World Wide Web, but browsing in the library can be an even more helpful way to locate promising sources.

If you are unfamiliar with the resources available in your college library, you might be able to take a library tour. You can also ask a reference librarian for help. Librarians are master navigators of both the library and the Web. They can help you conduct keyword searches using online book catalogs, periodical indexes, CD-ROM databases, and Internet search engines.

(See 7d for more information on using these and other tools for finding sources.)

Keep a working bibliography and accurate notes.

Even if you are still only browsing for a topic, you should begin to keep a working bibliography and take accurate notes immediately (see 8a). If you run into several promising sources right away, you will need to have an accurate record of that information. By keeping accurate records from the very beginning, you will avoid having to go back to the library to get a tiny piece of bibliographical information, or the feeling of frustration when you cannot find the perfect quotation, the only one you did not write down. Consider making photocopies of important sources so that you can quote them accurately and refer back to the source for clarification or additional material.

Keep time in mind.

Topic selection and browsing for preliminary sources should take about one-fifth of the total time given for the assignment. If you are still selecting your topic with only half of the assignment time left, you may have too little time left for further research or for writing and revising.

After you have chosen a promising topic and confirmed that you will be able to find sources on it, you may want to verify your topic choice with your instructor to make sure that it satisfies the assignment. Your instructor may want you to focus your topic even further and may be able to recommend additional sources.

7c Prepare to search for sources by subject and keyword.

To find sources on your topic in a library, you need to look under the appropriate *subject headings.* Similarly, to find sources on the Internet, you need to search by *keywords.* For most research projects, you will use a combination of subject and keyword searches.

Determine how to search for sources by subject.

Most information, especially in libraries, is referenced by subject. For example, the two major book classification systems in use in libraries today, the Library of Congress system and the Dewey decimal system, assign call numbers to books according to their specific subject. Books are then categorized by subject in the library's catalog. The print versions of periodical and newspaper indexes are also arranged by subject.

When you research a topic by subject, you will often need to determine the subject heading under which information about the topic is usually found.

Subject Heading. To locate information on your topic, it is necessary to determine the subject heading under which your topic is categorized. Searching by subject often requires imagination and persistence. For example, one student spent hours trying to find information on "subliminal advertising" under "advertising" and "psychology" before discovering that the index he was using listed it under "graphic arts."

You could ask the reference librarian to help you identify possible subject headings or you could check in the *Library of Congress Subject Headings* (LCSH) for terms related to your topic. You may also consult subject guides in periodical indexes, or use the online catalog to browse in related subject areas. These extra steps will often save you time later on.

Since holdings in libraries are generally arranged by subject, it may also be fruitful and enjoyable to browse the book shelves and the general reference area for books related to your research topic.

Subtopics. To help you focus your topic and find relevant sources, you may also need to break it down into subtopics (also known as *subdivisions* or *subheadings*). For example, a student interested in home schooling would find the following subdivisions available in the *Academic Index,* an index of magazine and journal articles.

Home Schooling

- Athletics
- Demographic aspects

- Equipment and supplies
- Finance
- History
- Laws, regulations, etc.
- Moral and ethical aspects
- Services

Related Subjects. Most subject listings in catalogs or indexes include "related terms" or "see also" subjects that you can consult for further information. For example, "Education—Parent Participation" is listed as a related term for "Home Schooling" in the *Library of Congress Subject Headings.*

Determine how to search for sources by keyword.

Search engines on the World Wide Web, online catalogs, and other specialized software allow you to use keyword searches to retrieve information. *Keywords* are words chosen by you that are likely to appear in a title, summary, full-text document, or Web page related to your subject. In a *keyword search,* you direct the software to search a database and list any resources that match your terms. On the Internet, keyword searches are more useful than subject searches because the information is not organized in any systematic way.

Some keyword search software looks for the specified terms in the whole document, whereas others search only headings, summaries, or titles. Read the instructions on the screen or ask your reference librarian or instructor for help. To launch a keyword search, type in the search terms. In most cases, logical connectors such as *and, or,* or *not* can be used to focus the search. For example, the keywords *home schooling and socialization* will retrieve references to documents that contain both of those terms. If you are researching the topic of euthanasia and want to find instances of assisted suicide other than those involving Dr. Jack Kevorkian, a doctor famous for helping terminally ill patients commit suicide, a search using the keywords "*euthanasia not Kevorkian*" will yield references to sources that contain the term *euthanasia,* excluding sources that also contain the term *Kevorkian.* Some search software allows you to search by phrases. For example, if the phrase "*working mothers*" is entered, only references that contain the phrase will be returned. Use capital letters for proper nouns and titles, and enclose phrases in quotation marks. See page 104 for more on keyword searches.

Use other search methods to locate information.

Aside from subject and keyword searches, you may be able to use other search criteria, such as author's name, title, call number, location, type of media (videotape, for example), and date. For example, you could search by name for the work of a particular author who is referred to frequently in your sources, search by library call number to determine what other sources are available in a specific subject area, or search by date in a newspaper index to research a particular event—for example, May 1980 would yield references to the eruption of Mount Saint Helens.

7d Look for library and Internet materials.

Finding specific information on research topics is a complex task because of the sheer variety and amount of information as well as the many formats in which it is stored (books, periodicals, electronic files, and so on). The following guidelines will help you to find useful source material.

- Determine the type of information available to you. For example, you will need to understand the differences between primary and secondary sources and among books, periodicals, and World Wide Web sites.
- Determine how the information is organized. If you plan to use periodical sources, for instance, find out how the periodical indexes related to your subject are organized.
- Stay focused; be selective. The amount of information available can be both daunting and fascinating, making it easy to get frustrated or sidetracked. Stay on task.
- Select a variety of material from different types of publications. Your sources should not all come from one publication or author.
- Be flexible, but keep your timeline in mind (see the Research Paper Strategy Schedule on p. 91).
- From the very beginning, keep a working bibliography of the sources you encounter and take accurate notes (see 8a).

Be aware of the difference between primary and secondary research.

Primary research is what you do yourself when you conduct interviews, surveys, and laboratory experiments. For example, a student writing about the acquisition of language might study videotapes of a child beginning to talk or survey a group of parents to determine when their children first began using sentences.

Secondary research refers to the published research you would find in the library or on the Internet. The student researching language acquisition might find useful information in the journal *TESOL Quarterly* or the book *Your Growing Child,* by Penelope Leach. These secondary sources can help the researcher fashion a new, informed view on the topic.

For many students, secondary research is the type most commonly associated with research assignments, but primary research may play an important role in the research papers you write for courses in your major.

Consult standard reference works and bibliographies.

Students commonly wonder where to start their search for source material. The most useful way to begin is by getting an overview of the topic. The instructor may provide the obvious starting point. For further background information, consult general reference works.

Standard reference works include general encyclopedias, specialized encyclopedias, disciplinary guides, almanacs, atlases, and dictionaries. A general encyclopedia such as the *Encyclopedia Americana* might help provide an overview on American education. A specialized encyclopedia such as the *Encyclopedia of Crime and Justice* or a disciplinary guide such as *Social Sciences: A Cross-Disciplinary Guide to Selected Sources* offers background on a subject and starting points for further research in related topics. Usually, these resources are found in the reference section of the library. Most reference works cannot be checked out, so budget time for library work.

Published bibliographies provide reading lists on various topics. Consult the *Bibliographic Index* for a master list of bibliographies, and if you are researching a concept or an issue in a course you are taking, check the back of your textbook for a bibliography. Note that even if you attend a large research university, your library is unlikely to hold every book or journal article a bibliography might include, so consult the library catalog and serial record (a list of the periodicals the library holds) to see whether the books or journals are available. Also, talk to a reference librarian about ordering books and articles you need through an interlibrary loan from another college library.

DIGITAL HINT

General reference resources are also available on the Internet (see pp. 102–105). Web sites have been established for the purpose of giving an overview of such topics as Tourette's syndrome, Ernesto Galarza, and Chernobyl. These sites provide background information, possible links to related Web sites, and, in some cases, bibliographies of print sources. Make sure to evaluate carefully the quality of information you find on the Web (see 7e).

Find books on your topic.

The primary resource for finding books is the library catalog. Nearly every college library offers a computerized catalog, sometimes called an online catalog. The library may also maintain a card catalog consisting of cards filed in drawers. Library catalogs organize sources by author, subject, and title. Online catalogs may be searched by keyword, call number, publication date, and media type (sometimes CD-ROMs and audiovisual material are cataloged with books). See 7c for guidelines on conducting keyword searches.

Here is one college library's online catalog display of the author entry for a recent book on home schooling. Notice the call number along the bottom line. You would need the call number to find the book on the library shelves. Most libraries provide a map showing where the various call numbers are shelved.

```
AUTHOR:         Guterson, David, 1951-
TITLE:          Family matters: Why homeschooling makes
                sense
EDITION:        1st Harvest ed.
```

```
PUBLISHER:        San Diego: Harcourt Brace & Co., c1992
PHYSICAL DESC:    x, 254 p.; 18 cm.
NOTES:            Includes bibliographical references and
                  index.
SUBJECTS:         Education—United States
                  Education—parent participation
                  Teaching methods

LOCATION /         CALL NUMBER     STATUS
UCSD Undergrad/    649.68 g 1993   Available
```

Find relevant periodical and newspaper articles.
Magazines and journals are known as *periodicals* because they are issued periodically on a regular basis. Newspapers also provide a wealth of specific information on some topics, especially on foreign affairs, economic issues, and cultural and social trends, and are useful when you research a current event.

Articles in periodicals and newspapers are usually not listed in the library catalog; to find them, you must use indexes and abstracts. *Indexes* list articles; *abstracts* summarize them as well. Indexes and abstracts are available in both print and electronic versions. Electronic versions may be either portable media, such as CD-ROMs that the library has purchased, or networked information available over the Internet or on an interlibrary network. Although the electronic resources may be more convenient to use, they may cover only a limited number of years and contain less information than print indexes.

One useful general index for periodicals that you may already be familiar with is the *Readers' Guide to Periodical Literature* (1900–; online and CD-ROM, 1983). Updated quarterly, this resource covers about two hundred popular periodicals and may help you to launch your search for sources on general and current topics. *InfoTrac,* on CD-ROM, is another index available in many libraries. It includes three indexes: (1) the *General Periodicals Index,* which covers over twelve hundred general-interest publications;

(2) the *Academic Index,* which covers four hundred scholarly and general-interest publications, including the *New York Times;* and (3) the *National Newspaper Index,* which covers the *Christian Science Monitor, Los Angeles Times, New York Times, Wall Street Journal,* and *Washington Post.* Some entries also include abstracts of articles.

Here is an example of the first two *Academic Index* listings under "home schooling."

```
Home Schooling
Mommy, what's a classroom? (the merits of home schooling are
still being debated) Bill Roorback. The New York Times
Magazine, Feb 2, 1997 p30 col1 (112 col in).
—Abstract Available—
Holdings: 10/92—present  Periodicals—1st Floor Paper
          01/66—present  Microfilm (Room #162)

Microfilm
The natural curriculum. (educating children at home) Rosie
Benson-Bunch. Times Education Supplement, Dec 27, 1996 n4200
pA25(1).
—Abstract Available—
```

Notice that the *Academic Index* provides information about which periodicals are available in the library and whether an abstract of the article is available. Examples of other periodical and newspaper indexes include *Facts on File, Editorial Research Reports, African Recorder, Public Affairs Information Service Bulletin* (PAIS), *Art Index, Sociological and Agricultural Index, Historical Abstracts,* and *Science Abstracts.*

Many periodical and newspaper indexes and abstracts use the Library of Congress subject headings, but some have their own systems. *Sociological Abstracts,* for example, has a separate volume for subject headings. Check the opening pages of the index or abstract you are using or, to see how subjects are classified, refer to the system documentation.

Periodicals are usually arranged alphabetically by title in the periodical section of the library. For previous years' collections of popular magazines and many scholarly journals, look for bound annual volumes rather than individual issues. Some older periodicals may be stored on microfilm (reels) or microfiche (cards) that must be read in viewing machines. Likewise, libraries usually store noncurrent newspapers on microfilm or microfiche.

Search computer databases for sources on your topic.
Many libraries subscribe to computer services or own CD-ROMs that list books or articles in particular subject areas. The computer services or CD-ROMs may provide abstracts or even the full text of articles, either in the database (so you can see them on-screen or print them out) or by mail or fax for a fee. These databases are generally searchable by subject, author, title, and keywords, and often you can print out the search results or download them onto your own disk. Some common databases include *ERIC (Educational Resources Information Center), Business Periodicals Ondisc, ABI/INFORM,* and *PsycBooks. Carl/UnCover,* an online document delivery service, can be visited on the Web at <http://www.carl.org>.

Your library may be connected to an interlibrary network. Known by different names in different regions, these networks allow you to search in the catalogs of colleges and universities in your area and across the country. In many cases, you can request a book or a copy of an article your library does not have through interlibrary loan. It may take from a few days to several weeks for you to receive the material, so plan accordingly.

Keep in mind that because most electronic indexes cover only the most recent years, you may need to consult print indexes and the library card or online catalog as well.

Find sources on the Internet, especially the World Wide Web.
The *Internet* is a global network of many smaller computer networks that enables users to store and share information and resources. You may be able to gain access to the Internet through your college, through a commercial Internet service provider (as long as you have an appropriate computer and modem), or through your library.

Research on the Internet is very different from library research. As you use the Internet, keep the following characteristics and guidelines in mind.

- *The Internet has no central system of organization.* On the Internet, a vast amount of information is stored on many different computers and many different networks, each with its own system of organization. There is no central catalog, reference librarian, or standard classification system for the vast resources available on the Internet.
- *It is easier to get published on the Internet than in print.* As a result, it can be difficult to determine the reliability of information. Depending on your topic, purpose, and audience, the sources you find on the Internet may not be as credible or authoritative as library sources, and for some topics most of what you find may be written by amateurs. In most cases, you will probably have to balance or supplement Internet sources with print sources. When in doubt about the reliability or acceptability of online sources for a particular assignment, be sure to check with your instructor. Also, see 7e for tips on evaluating Internet sources.
- *Sources used from the Internet must be documented.* The requirements for documenting source material found on the Internet and source material found in more traditional sources are the same, though the formats are slightly different. As with sources you locate in the library, you will need to follow appropriate conventions for quoting, paraphrasing (see 8a and 8b), and documenting the online sources you cite (see Chapter 9).

Learn How to Navigate the Web. For many academic users, an especially useful feature of the *World Wide Web* is that it allows "hypertext links" to other documents or files, so that with a simple click of the mouse a reader might find more detailed information on a subject or access a related document. Most material on the Web is available twenty-four hours a day (unless the network is slow or clogged).

A *Web browser* is a software program that allows you to display and navigate Web pages on your computer. Web browsers have evolved from basic text-driven browsers such as Lynx (still used by many people today) into graphical, point-and-click interfaces such as Netscape Navigator and Microsoft Internet Explorer, which include not only text and hypertext links but also images, sound, animation, and even video.

Most material available on the Web is stored in *Web sites,* databases of related materials (pages) made available to the public. The central or starting point for a Web site is often called its *home page.* Web sites may be sponsored by companies, institutions, government agencies, organizations, clubs, or individuals.

Each Web site has its own address, called a *uniform resource locator* (URL). The URL for the Ecology Action Centre is typical: <http://www.cfn.cs.dal.ca/Environment/EAC/EAC-Home.html>. The first part usually consists of the abbreviation *http://* that tells the sending and receiving computers the type of information being sent and how to transfer it. The second part of the URL usually includes the standard *www.* to establish that the location being accessed is on the World Wide Web, and the country, if outside of the United States, where the document is located. After a slash, the rest gives the address of the directory and file where the page is found as well as the name of the specific page itself, separated by slashes.

Many organizational and resource sites list the URLs of their home pages in print publications so that readers can access the Web sites for further information. Keep an eye out for such resources related to your research project.

Searching the Web. Keyword searches are generally the most useful way to locate sources on the Web (see page 96). *Search engines* are resources that have been developed specifically for searching the World Wide Web. The home page of a search engine is set up to allow you to enter a keyword or phrase. The search engine scans the Web for your keyword and produces a list of direct links to pages containing the keyword. The program searches both the titles of Web pages and the actual text of those pages for the keyword. Usually, the list of search results includes a brief description of each page. By clicking on one of the links in the list, you can directly access the Web page. When you find a useful page, you should create a bookmark, which records the location of the Web page on your browser and allows you to return to it easily later.

By clicking Search on the home page for both Netscape Navigator and Microsoft Internet Explorer, you can access a list of links to such popular search engines as Lycos and AltaVista. Or you can access these and other common search engines directly at their URL addresses:

AltaVista	http://www.altavista.digital.com
Excite	http://www.excite.com
Lycos	http://www.lycos.com
WebCrawler	http://www.webcrawler.com
Yahoo!	http://www.yahoo.com

Each search engine works a bit differently. Read the on-screen instructions or help information for each particular search engine, and try more than one search engine. Web browsers are available in most libraries.

The success of a Web search depends on the keywords you choose; if a search yields few sources or irrelevant ones, try rephrasing your keywords or choosing more specific ones to locate the most useful information. If your topic is ecology, for example, you may find information under the terms *ecosystem, environment, pollution,* and *endangered species,* as well as a number of other related keywords. As with library searches, however, you may need to narrow your topic to keep the number of sources manageable. For example, an AltaVista search using the keyword *speed limits* resulted in about 200,000 matches, including the ones shown on page 106. With so many possibilities, you should limit your keyword search by adding the words *and, or,* or *not* to your keyword, as illustrated on page 96. Allow yourself enough time to sort through the results of your search.

Use email for research.

Another advantage of using the Internet for research is that you can contact other researchers directly by sending email (electronic mail). Some authors include their email addresses along with their articles, so you may be able to write to them for further information. Web pages often include email links to individuals who have further information on specific topics.

Newsgroups are another important email resource for some projects. They are interest groups in which people post email messages related to a specific topic. These messages are usually posted for anyone to read and respond to, much like a public bulletin board. You can also use email for research by joining a *listserv.* Like a newsgroup, a listserv is an email interest group; however, listserv messages are sent only to members of the group. For

Results of an AltaVista Search

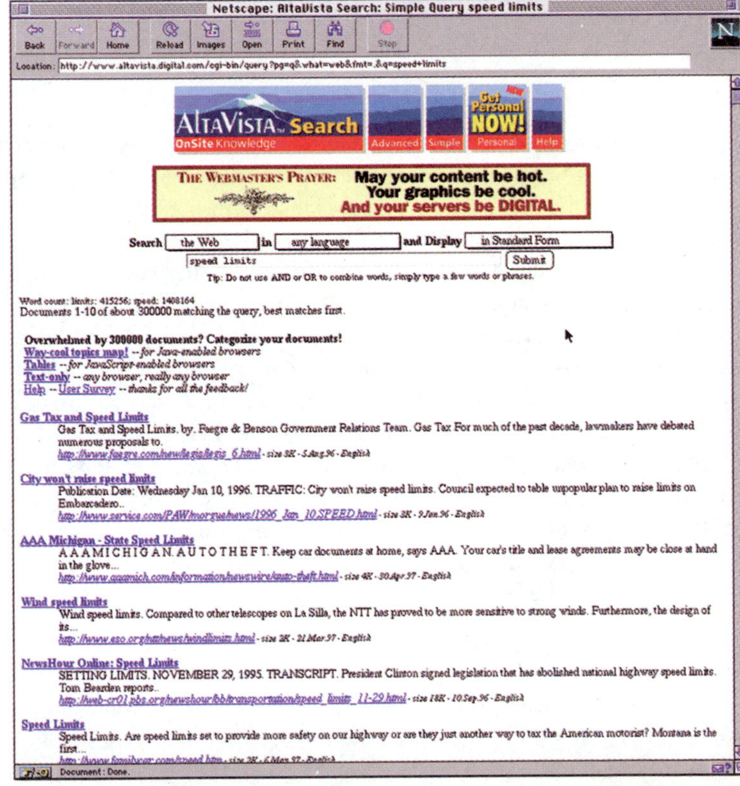

example, one student who wanted to research language acquisition joined a listserv comprising teachers of English as a second language. After reading the mail from the group for a while to determine whether her question would be appropriate, the student sent a message to the listserv group asking a question related to her research. In return, she received much useful information from professionals in the field. Finally, note that newsgroups and listservs sometimes keep searchable archives of previous postings. Contact a reference librarian for help in identifying useful email research tools, or do a keyword search for *listserv* or *newsgroup* on the Web.

DIGITAL HINT

Deja News archives postings on newsgroups and listservs and is probably the quickest way to search for previous postings. The URL is <www.dejanews.com>.

Search for sources using online library catalogs on the Internet.
Many library catalogs throughout the world can be accessed by a Web browser, *telnet,* or direct dialing via modem. Contact your local library to see whether it offers Web-based, telnet, or modem access to online catalogs. By searching the book catalogs of local and remote libraries, you may be able to find listings for valuable resources or, in some cases, complete articles. For more information, as well as a long list of links to searchable library catalogs, visit the Library of Congress site at <http://lcweb.loc.gov/z3950/gateway.html>.

Consider using MOOs and MUDs to further your research.
MUDs (derived from *multi-user dungeons*) and *MOOs* (from *MUD object oriented*) began as computer games, similar to Dungeons and Dragons, in which participants could play in real time and interact with one another. These media have now become serious tools for writing and research. Students and professionals can interact and become part of research projects. Two MUDs that are useful resources for students are the *Idea Exchange* (<http://www.imaginary.com/LPMud/IdeaExchange>) and *Diversity University* (<http://du.org>).

Use a diversity of sources.
For an academically sound research project, the sources you select and the working bibliography you compile should be comprehensive and include a variety of viewpoints. Just as you would not depend on a single author for all of your information, so you do not want to use only authors who belong to one school of thought or who publish in the same magazine or journal. Try to select from a variety of sources: books, journals, electronic databases, Web pages, and popular magazines. If appropriate, use primary research as well.

7e Evaluate library and Internet sources you find.

From the beginning of your search, you should evaluate the relevance, bias, credibility, and currency of potential sources to determine which ones to use in your essay. Use the following criteria to evaluate the usefulness of the sources you have found.

Determine the relevance of sources to your topic.
Check the title, subtitle, description, and abstract (if one is available) of each source to make sure it relates in a useful way to your topic. For a book, check the table of contents and index to see how many pages are devoted to the topic you are researching, and read the preface or introduction. For an article, read the abstract or opening paragraphs. Read any biographical information given about the author to determine the author's basic approach to the subject. In most cases, you will want an in-depth, rather than a superficial, treatment of the subject. However, extremely specialized works may be too technical. Determine whether the source offers the kind of information and level of detail you need for your project.

Determine the bias of potential sources.
The word *bias* simply refers to the fact that writing is rarely, if ever, neutral or objective. Authors come to their subjects with particular viewpoints derived from their philosophies, experiences, educational backgrounds, and affiliations. When you examine a source, you can often determine its point of view by considering the following:

- *Title:* Look closely at the title and subtitle to see if they use words that indicate a particular bias.
- *Author:* Consider how the author's professional affiliation might affect his or her perspective.
- *Editorial slant:* Notice where the selection was published. To determine the editorial slant of a newspaper, all you have to do is read some of its editorials. For periodicals, you could also check such sources as the *Gale Directory of Publications and Broadcast Media* (1990) and *Magazines for Libraries* (1992). For books, looking at the preface or introduction as well as the acknowledgments and sources cited may give you some idea of how the authors position themselves in relation to other specialists in the field.

Determine whether the sources are authoritative.

Just because a book or essay appears in print or online does not mean that an author's information or opinions are reliable. Check the author's professional credentials, background, and publication history to verify that he or she is an authoritative voice in the field. To help determine which authors are authoritative, note whether they are cited in encyclopedia articles, bibliographies, and recent works on the subject. For books, you can also look up reviews in newspapers or academic journals.

Experts will (and should) disagree on topics, and each author will naturally see the topic in his or her own way. Yet authoritative authors will explain and support, not just assert, their opinions. They will also cite their sources. Because articles published in most academic journals and books published by university presses are judged by other experts in the field, you can assume that the authors' point of view is respected even if it is controversial. Allowing for differences of viewpoint, information about the topic provided in the source should be consistent with information you have found on the topic in other sources.

Determine whether the sources are current.

Currency—or the timeliness of sources—is more important for some topics than for others. In an essay about changes in tax laws, for instance, you would need to use the most current information available to describe current laws. Although you should always consult the most up-to-date sources available on your subject, older sources often establish the principles, theories, and data on which later work is based and may provide a useful perspective for evaluating more current sources.

Use special care in evaluating Internet sources.

The same principles used to evaluate other types of sources apply to sources found on the Internet; but if you are using Internet sources in your research project, you will need to deal with some of the unique problems of evaluating Internet information.

Unlike most published print resources that have been reviewed and selected by editors in a "filtering" process to ensure their accuracy and credibility, publications on the Internet have no comparable filtering process. Anyone who can upload material to a server can publish on the Web. Web sites may be sponsored by academic institutions, government agencies, companies, organizations, clubs, or individuals—either amateur or professional. This variety makes it essential that you take extra care in evaluating the credentials of the author and the credibility of the information before you use an Internet publication as a source.

Often, the information needed to evaluate Internet sources is more difficult to locate than it is for print sources. Books, for example, display the name of their publisher on the spine and the title page, include information about the author in the beginning or at the end of the book, and often make the purpose of the work clear in a preface or introduction. Determining the publisher, the purpose, and sometimes even the author of a Web page, however, can often be more difficult because of the technical differences between print and online media. For example, Web pages that are part of a larger Web site might—when they are retrieved by a search engine—appear on your screen isolated from the rest of the site. These Web pages may carry little or no indication of who published or sponsored the site or of its overall purpose or author. In this situation, the researcher should not use the source unless more information about the Web page can be tracked down. In addition, the following specialized techniques for reading and evaluating Web pages may help.

- *Look for credible pages that provide enough information.* Look for the following information on any online articles you retrieve: the author's professional title, affiliation, and other credentials; the sponsor of the page and the Web site; a link to the site's home page; the date the site was created and last revised.

  Check the title, headers, and footers of the page for this information. If it is provided, it may indicate a willingness to publish in a professional manner, and it will help you evaluate the source according to the criteria discussed earlier. Checking the home page of the Web site will help you discover its purpose, for example, if it is a commercial site published to sell radar detectors or one established by the Highway Patrol to give information on highway safety.

- *Alter the URL in the browser's "location" box, and try to contact the sponsoring institution.* By deleting part or all of the directory and filename (the third section of the URL), you may be able to determine the sponsoring institution for the page. For example, in <*http://lcweb.loc.gov/z3950/gateway.html*>, if you take away the subdirectory *(z3950)* and filename *(gateway.html)* you will reveal the sponsoring computer's address: *http://lcweb.loc.gov* (in this case, the Library of Congress home page). Enter this address in your browser and access the site to determine where the information comes from. (For more on URLs, see page 104.)

- *Use any evaluation techniques available.* Even if you cannot discover the author's credentials, you can check his or her facts, details, and presentation. Can you verify the facts? Does the information make sense to you? You may find that, even though the author is not a recognized expert in the field, he or she may offer specific information valuable to your project. One advantage of the Web is that it is democratic. Anyone, not just recognized experts, can express views and develop topics of interest. In particular, the Internet allows individuals to relate firsthand experiences to readers. You may find yourself in the role of primary researcher, reading firsthand accounts related to your topic.

8 INTEGRATING SOURCES

When you include research sources in your writing, you show your instructor how well you read critically, analyzing and synthesizing other people's ideas as well as a diversity of information. This chapter provides guidelines for several important skills related to the use of source material: effective notetaking, summarizing, paraphrasing, and using strategies for integrating source material into your own sentences.

8a Take notes from secondary sources.

You may already have a method of notetaking you prefer. Some researchers like to use index cards for notes. Some use cards of different colors to organize their notes or lay their cards on a table or floor to make an outline. Others prefer to keep their notes in the pages of a notebook. Still others enter notes into a computer or download and save articles from electronic databases or the Internet. Selectively photocopying promising source material is an effective method for gathering information, enabling you to reread and analyze important sources as well as to highlight material and write in the margins.

Whatever method you use, keeping accurate and organized notes is essential. It is also essential to use the appropriate documentation system specified by your instructor (such as MLA or APA style—see Chapters 9 and 10) for all borrowed material, whether it is directly quoted or expressed in your own words. Establishing a systematic and accurate method for extracting information from sources will help you avoid costly errors, the loss of promising material, and unintentional plagiarism, which is the use of information or ideas from others without proper acknowledgment (see 8b).

An effective set of research notes includes the following components: a working bibliography, summaries, paraphrases, direct quotations, and personal observations on the source material. Each bibliography entry and each summary, paraphrase, or quotation should be kept as a separate note. Also, keep your comments and questions as separate notes keyed to your summaries, paraphrases, and quotations.

Keep a working bibliography.

Begin keeping a working bibliography as soon as you begin browsing (see 7b). This working bibliography becomes the draft for the list of works cited at the end of your essay. If you are using index cards, your bibliography notecard might look like one in the following example. To see how this entry would look in the list of works cited at the end of your essay, turn to page 152.

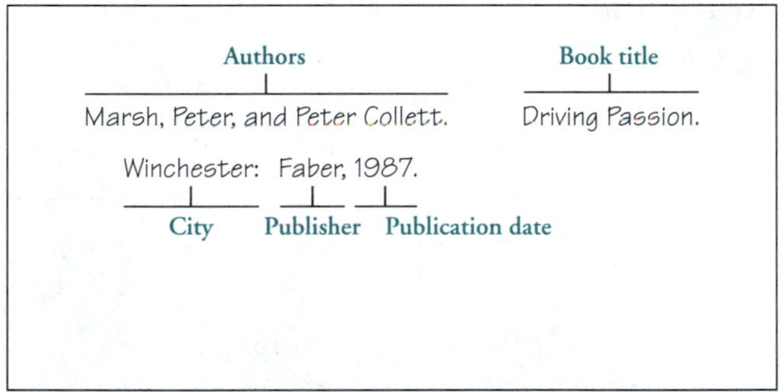

A bibliography card for a magazine article would contain slightly different information: author(s), title of article, title of magazine, date of publication, and pages of the article.

Record essential information.

Notes that contain summaries, paraphrases, or quotes should always include at least the author's name, the title of the work, the page number(s) on which the material appears in the source, and the topic covered in the note.

Note: If you photocopy or download any sources, record all of this information on your photocopy or printout.

Summarize from sources.

A *summary* encapsulates in your own words the central ideas of a source (see 12c). In deciding what to include in a summary, be sure not to distort the author's meaning. A summary should reflect the content of the passage accurately.

Here is an original passage on design improvements in automobiles:

> Air bags and antilock brakes are the most obvious advances. In addition, overall structures are much stronger, so doors don't fly open nearly as often in collisions. Computer-designed front and rear "crumple zones" soak up much of the energy of a crash before it reaches passengers. Suspensions hold the road better; steering is more precise. Better tires channel more water away to improve wet-road handling and are more supple, to stay in better contact with the road.
>
> —Steven D. Kay, "Hello 75, So Long 55"

Here is a summary of the same passage on a note card:

Kay, "Hello 75"	Auto design
Automotive design improvements in suspension, steering, tires, brakes, doors, and other key safety features have made modern cars safer. (p. 73)	

If you need to summarize several pages or a whole chapter, be sure to record the entire range of pages used: (*50–75*) or (*19, 25–27*), for example.

Paraphrase from sources.

Whereas a summary boils down the source to its main idea, a *paraphrase* restates all the relevant information from a passage, without any additional comments or elaborations. A paraphrase is useful for recording details of the passage when the order of the details is important but the source's exact wording is not. Because all the details of the passage are included, a paraphrase is often about the same length as the original passage.

Original Passage

Bruner and the discovery theorists have also illuminated conditions that apparently pave the way for learning. It is significant that these conditions are unique to each learner, so unique, in fact, that in many cases classrooms can't provide them. Bruner also contends that the more one discovers information in a great variety of circumstances, the more likely one is to develop the inner categories required to organize that information. Yet life at school, which is for the most part generic and predictable, daily keeps many children from the great variety of circumstances they need to learn well.

—David Guterson, *Family Matters: Why Homeschooling Makes Sense*

Here is a paraphrase of the Guterson passage, on a note card:

Guterson, Family Matters — Learning theory

According to the "discovery theorists," particularly Bruner, certain situations enhance learning. Because these situations are specific to each individual, many children are not able to learn in school. According to Bruner, when people explore phenomena in different settings, they learn to classify and order what they discover. The general routine of the school day, however, does not provide children with the diverse activities and situations that would allow them to acquire these skills. (p. 172)

Quote selectively from sources.

Direct quotation used thoughtfully at key points in your essay can offer powerful support for your thesis. Direct quotation is an exact, word-for-word duplication of the source's wording. Unless a quotation is long enough to be treated as a block quote (see p. 122), it should always be enclosed in quotation marks both in your notes and in your essay.

As a general rule, it is better to integrate selected words or phrases quoted from sources into your paraphrase or summary than to quote indiscriminately. If you use too many quotations from sources, you risk creating an essay that is a patchwork of other authors' voices rather than your own. Direct quotation can be effective in the following situations, however.

- When the original wording is particularly striking or expresses a point so well that you would lose some of the meaning by paraphrasing
- When the words of reliable and respected authorities would lend credibility to your position
- When you wish to highlight the author's opinions or hold them up for inspection
- When you are analyzing the author's choice of words, as in an essay interpreting a work of literature

When you are quoting directly, supply any missing information needed for understanding in brackets. If you change a letter from lowercase to uppercase, or from uppercase to lowercase, enclose the letter in brackets. (For more on using brackets, see 44d.) Here is an example of a note card that records a direct quotation:

> Fremon and Hamilton, — Placement/civil rights
> "Are Schools Failing Black Boys?"
>
> "[M]isclassifying students may effectively strip them of their civil rights by denying them access to a core curriculum. In short, a student who is unnecessarily placed in special education is not likely to get his needs met." (p. 125)

8b Take care to avoid plagiarizing your sources.

The word *plagiarism,* which derives from the Latin word for "kidnapping," refers to the unacknowledged use of another author's words, ideas, or information. Plagiarism is a serious academic offense that can lead to a failing grade on the essay, a failing grade in the course, or in some cases even expulsion from college.

Plagiarism may occur in several ways and for several reasons. In the most obvious example, plagiarism occurs when another writer's exact words are used without quotation marks or proper documentation. Students sometimes plagiarize inadvertently, however, because they mistakenly assume that only direct quotations must be documented. Keep in mind that you must indicate the source of any ideas or information from secondary sources that you use in your research essay, whether you include the information as a direct quotation, a paraphrase, or a summary.

Plagiarism may also occur when a writer substitutes synonyms and imitates the sentence structure of the original. Notice in the following example that the synonym *claims* replaces *contends* and *knowledge* replaces *information,* and that the sentences all have the same structure as the original.

Original Passage

Bruner also contends that the more one discovers information in a great variety of circumstances, the more likely one is to develop the inner categories required to organize that information. Yet life at school, which is for the most part generic and predictable, daily keeps many children from the great variety of circumstances they need to learn well.

—David Guterson, *Family Matters: Why Homeschooling Makes Sense,* p. 172

Inappropriate Paraphrase (Plagiarized)

Bruner claims that when a learner discovers knowledge in different circumstances he is more likely to develop internal categories for organizing the knowledge. However, school is generic and predictable, and every day it keeps many children from experiencing the different types of circumstances they need to learn effectively.

In this case, the writer should use his or her own words and sentence structures, quoting only important words from the source.

When an editor or friend helps a writer so much with the language of an essay that the writing is no longer the author's, another form of plagiarism occurs. It is generally advisable to get tutoring help with your writing assignments under the proper conditions, as long as you actively take part in the learning process and take full control of the writing. Ask your instructor if you have any questions about appropriate ways to get help with your writing.

Some people plagiarize simply because they do not know the conventions for using and acknowledging sources. Others plagiarize because they keep sloppy notes and thus fail to distinguish between their own and their sources' ideas. If you keep an accurate working bibliography and careful and comprehensive notes, you will avoid the serious mistake of plagiarism.

Know when *not* to document.

It is not necessary to document thoughts or observations of your own that are not derived from secondary source material. A good rule of thumb is this: If you knew the material before you began your research project, you do not have to document it. For example, if you personally observed traffic traveling at over 80 mph on the Autobahn, you do not need to document the fact that people drive at that speed on the Autobahn when you use it in your essay. Also, it is not necessary to document information that is shared "common knowledge." For example, you do not need to document the fact that there are nine justices on the U.S. Supreme Court.

8c Use appropriate strategies for integrating quotations.

Since a research report usually contains more direct quotation than other types of writing, you will need to use effective strategies for introducing and integrating quotations. Integrate quotations grammatically and smoothly, maintaining as much as possible your own writing style. See 31a for further information on integrating quotes with your own writing.

The examples that follow show in-text citations in the style recommended by the Modern Language Association (MLA). See Chapters 9, 10, and 11 for more specific information about in-text citations using MLA and other documentation styles.

Avoid awkwardly inserting quotes into your essay.

Quotes that are simply "plopped" into your essay are ineffective, especially when one or more whole sentences are inserted into a paragraph without introduction, as in this example:

> Wilde constructed a driving simulation experiment in which he changed factors such as speeds and speed limits. "Neither speed limit nor speeding fine had a significant impact on accident loss" (qtd. in Jackson and Blackman 956).

Here the quotation has been integrated effectively:

> During a driving simulation experiment in which he changed factors such as speeds and speed limits, Wilde determined that "[n]either speed limit nor speeding fine had a significant impact on accident loss" (qtd. in Jackson and Blackman 956).

One way to smoothly integrate quotations is to use *signal phrases.* These are words or phrases that signal when a quotation begins or ends.

> The token women writers authenticated the male canon without disrupting it, for *as Ruth Bleier points out,* "The last thing society desires of its women has been intellectuality and independence" (73).

> *According to Eric Peters,* who covers the automobile industry for the Washington Times, "70–75 mph is appreciably lower than the rated safe speeds for many [Interstate highways], which were conceived with speeds comparable to the European autobahn in mind when they were built" (13).

As these examples demonstrate, some signal phrases are simple verbs such as *argues, claims, rejects,* and *points out* that are useful in introducing the observations of others. Some signal phrases are general, such as *says, states,* and *writes.* Others can be used to indicate the writer's attitude toward or purpose in using the quotation.

Agreement

agrees	confirms	endorses

Disagreement

denies	disagrees	disputes
refutes	responds	

A Claim

argues	asserts	claims
contends	considers	holds
insists	maintains	predicts
suggests	thinks	

Concession

admits	acknowledges	concedes
grants	allows	

Facts

comments	concludes	describes
illustrates	observes	points out
reports	reveals	sees

A question

asks	poses the question	queries

Punctuation marks such as the comma and colon can also help you to introduce quotations.

> German Chancellor Helmut Kohl summed up the German attitude regarding speed limits quite concisely: "For millions of people, a car is part of their personal freedom" (qtd. in Cote 12).

See 31a for more information about using punctuation and other methods to introduce quotes.

It is not at all necessary to quote whole sentences at a time. In fact, it can be even more effective to insert a memorable phrase rather than the whole sentence. Note that if the quotation fits grammatically with your own words, it is not necessary to separate it with a comma.

> It is time to return control of the automobile to the driver and "free us from our speed slavery once and for all" (Csere 9).

Use ellipsis marks to omit material from quotes.

When you omit words from within a quotation, use *ellipsis marks*—three spaced periods—to signal that something has been left out. For an omission within the sentence, put a space before and after each of the three periods.

> Hermione Roddice is described in Lawrence's *Women in Love* as a "woman of the new school, full of intellectuality and . . . nerve-worn with consciousness" (17).

When the omission falls at the end of a sentence, place a sentence period directly after the last word, followed by three spaced periods (for a total of four).

> But Grimaldi's recent commentary on Aristotle contends that for Aristotle rhetoric, like dialectic, had "no limited and unique subject matter upon which it must be exercised. . . . Instead, rhetoric as an art transcends all specific disciplines and may be brought into play in them" (6).

A period plus ellipsis marks can indicate the omission of the rest of the sentence as well as whole sentences, paragraphs, or even pages. When a parenthetical reference, *6* in the example below, follows the ellipsis marks at the end of a sentence, place the three spaced periods after the quotation, and place the sentence period after the final parenthesis.

> But Grimaldi's recent commentary on Aristotle contends that for Aristotle rhetoric, like dialectic, had "no limited and unique subject matter upon which it must be exercised . . ." (6).

Note: When you quote only single words or phrases, you do not need to use ellipsis marks because it will be obvious that you have left out some of the original. See 44a for more information on using ellipses.

Use block quotations for long extracts.

Put in block form prose quotations of five or more typed lines and poetry quotations of four or more lines for MLA style. For APA style, use block form for quotations of forty words or more. If you are using MLA style, indent the quotation ten character spaces from the left margin, as shown in the student essay on page 143. If you are using APA style, indent the block quotation five spaces from the left margin, as shown in the student essay on page 170. In both MLA and APA styles, double-space between the lines of a block quotation just as you do in the text of your essay. Use a colon to introduce a block quotation, unless the context calls for another punctuation mark or none at all. Do not enclose the block quote within quotation marks.

DOCUMENTING SOURCES USING MLA STYLE

Guide to MLA in-text citation models (9a)

Guide to MLA works-cited entries (9b)

The documentation style of the Modern Language Association (MLA) is used in English, journalism, and humanities courses. The following guidelines are sufficient for most college research assignments. For additional information, see the *MLA Handbook for Writers of Research Papers,* Fourth Edition (1995).

9a Use in-text citations to indicate where you have used source material.

In-text citations mark places in the text of an essay where information, ideas, or quotations from other sources have been included. Every in-text citation has a corresponding works-cited entry in a list at the end of the essay that tells readers how to find the source (see 9b). Place the citation in parentheses as near as possible to the borrowed material without disrupting your sentence. Include a citation each time you refer to a source, except when you refer to the same page in the source more than once in a single paragraph—and no reference to another page in the source or to another source intervenes. Then, you may use a single parenthetical citation, placing the parentheses after the last sentence that includes information from that page in the source. Do not cite common knowledge or personal knowledge (see 8b).

The following examples demonstrate how to cite most of the kinds of sources you will use within the text of your college essays. (For guidelines on preparing a list of works cited, see 9b.)

1. Author indicated in a signal phrase

Signal phrase.

Page number.

```
"Despite his immense working vocabulary, Shakespeare did
not mention chocolate at all," Sokolov points out, even
though by 1569 chocolate was available in England (134).
```

See 8c for more on using signal phrases to integrate quotations into your sentences.

2. Author and page indicated in a parenthetical citation

```
Dr. James is described as a "not-too-skeletal Ichabod
Crane" (Simon 68).
```

Parenthetical citation.

```
While automotive design improvements have made American
cars safer than ever at high speeds (Kaye 73), speed
limits in many places still remain low.
```

Parentheses close to borrowed material.

3. More than one author

Names of up to 3 authors.

```
Dyal, Corning, and Willows identify several types of
students, including the "Authority-Rebel" (4).
```

```
Authority-Rebels see themselves as "superior to other
students in the class" (Dyal, Corning, and Willows 4).
```

```
AZT has been shown to reduce the risk of transmission
from HIV-positive mothers to their infants by as much as
two-thirds (Van de Perre et al. 4-5).
```

Name of first author on first or title page.

Use *et al.* for 4 or more authors.

4. Author not listed

```
However, in 1992, five years after the Symms legisla-
tion, the number of deaths from automobile accidents
reached a thirty-year low ("Highways" 51).
```

Shortened title begins with word alphabet-ized in works-cited list.

5. Corporate or government author

```
A tuition increase has been proposed for community and
technical colleges to offset budget deficits from
Initiative 601 (Washington State Board for Community and
Technical Colleges 4).
```

Organization as author.

6. Two or more works by the same author

When old paint becomes transparent, it sometimes shows the artist's original plans: "a tree will show through a woman's dress" (Hellman, Pentimento 1).

Short title indicates which work cited.

7. Two or more authors with the same last name

Full name in signal phrase.

According to Edgar V. Roberts, Chaplin's Modern Times provides a good example of montage used to make an editorial statement (246).

Chaplin's Modern Times provides a good example of montage used to make an editorial statement (E. V. Roberts 246).

Initials and last name in parentheses.

8. A work without page numbers

The average speed on Montana's interstate highways, for example, has risen by only 2 miles per hour since the repeal of the federal speed limit, with most drivers topping out at 75 (Schmid).

Reference to Web site without page numbers.

9. A quotation taken from a secondhand source

Chancellor Helmut Kohl summed up the German attitude: "For millions of people, a car is part of their personal freedom" (qtd. in Cote 12).

Abbreviation for "quoted" indicates secondhand source.

Create a works-cited entry for the source in which you found the quote, not for the original source.

10. A multivolume work

"Double meaning," according to Freud, "is one of the most fertile sources for . . . jokes" (8: 56).

Ellipsis marks indicate words left out.

Volume number.

11. A literary work

To fulfill his tribal obligation, Okonkwo strikes down Ikemefuna with his machete, "afraid of being thought weak" (Achebe 59; ch. 7).

For novels: Page number and chapter.

Regan's fawning rhetoric hides her true attitude toward Lear: "I profess / myself an enemy to all other joys . . . / And find that I am alone felicitate / In your dear highness' love" (1.1.72-73).

For plays: act, scene, and line numbers.

Whitman finds poetic details in busy urban settings, as when he describes "the blab of the pave, tires of carts . . . the driver with his interrogating thumb" (8.7-8).

For poems: line numbers as well as stanza, if available.

If the source gives only line numbers, use the term *lines* in the first citation; in subsequent citations, give only the numbers.

12. A work in an anthology

In "Six Days: Some Rememberings," Grace Paley recalls that when she was in jail for protesting the Vietnam War, her pen and paper were taken away and she felt "a terrible pain in the area of my heart--a nausea" (191).

Title of essay in anthology.

Author of essay, not editor of anthology.

Page in anthology.

If you are discussing the editor's *preface* or *introduction,* name the editor.

13. Two or more works

When two or more different sources are used in the same passage, it may be necessary to cite them in the same parentheses, separated by a semicolon.

The fact that Montana's speed limit has risen only 2 miles per hour since the federal limit was lifted proves what studies have shown: Most drivers won't travel over 75 (Schmid; Sullivan 37).

No page number for Web site.

14. An entire work

In the Structure of Scientific Revolutions, Thomas Kuhn discusses how scientists change their thinking.

Page numbers not needed.

15. Internet material

In handling livestock, "many people attempt to restrain animals with sheer force instead of using behavioral principles" (Grandin).

Author's name.

If the author is not named, give document title. Include page or paragraph numbers, if available.

9b Include all of the works you cite in a list of works cited at the end of your essay.

The works-cited list provides information that enables readers to find the sources cited in the essay. Every source referred to in your essay must have a corresponding entry in the works-cited list. Conversely, every entry in the works-cited list must correspond to at least one parenthetical citation in the essay. Although there are many varieties of works-cited entries, the information in a works-cited entry generally follows this order:

Entry for a Book

One space.
One space.

Author's last name, First name, Middle initial. Title of the Book. City of publication: Publisher's name, year published.

Entry for a Journal

One space.

Author's name. "Title of the Article." Journal Name Volume number. Issue number (Year published): Page range.

One space.

Copy the author's name and the title from the book's title page or the first page of the article. Do not worry about including information that is unavailable, such as the author's middle initial or the issue number for a periodical. See the sample works-cited list on page 152 for formatting, 47d for help in capitalizing titles and subtitles.

DIGITAL HINT

If your instructor permits, you may italicize rather than underline titles. (See 50a for more on using italics for titles.)

The following examples provide models for most documentation situations that you will encounter.

Books

1. A book by a single author

Arnold, Marion I. Women and Art in South Africa. New York: St. Martin's, 1996.

Shorten publisher's name.

2. Multiple works by the same author (or same group of authors)

Vidal, Gore. Empire. New York: Random, 1987.

---. Lincoln. New York: Random, 1984.

Entries alphabetized by title.

3 hyphens to indicate same name.

3. A book by an agency, organization, or corporation

Association for Research in Nervous and Mental Disease. The Circulation of the Brain and Spinal Cord: A Symposium on Blood Supply. New York: Hafner, 1966.

Organization in author slot.

4. A book by two or more authors

For two or three authors:

Gottfredson, Stephen G., and Sean McConville. America's Correctional Crisis. Westport: Greenwood, 1987.

Subsequent authors: first name, then last.

Subsequent authors: first name, then last.

Dyal, James A., William C. Corning, and Dale M. Willows. Readings in Psychology: The Search for Alternatives. 3rd ed. New York: McGraw, 1975.

For four or more authors:

Use *et al.* for other authors' names.

Nielsen, Niels C., Jr., et al. Religions of the World. 3rd ed. New York: St. Martin's, 1992.

5. A book with an unlisted author

Rand McNally Commercial Atlas. Skokie: Rand, 1993.

Alphabetize by title.

6. A book with one or more editors

Use *ed.* or *eds.* to indicate an edited book.

Axelrod, Steven Gould, and Helen Deese, eds. Robert Lowell: Essays on the Poetry. Cambridge: Cambridge UP, 1986.

7. A book with an author and an editor

If you refer to the work itself:

Arnold, Matthew. Culture and Anarchy. Ed. J. Dover Wilson. Cambridge: Cambridge UP, 1966.

If you discuss the editor's work in your essay:

Wilson, J. Dover, ed. Culture and Anarchy. By Matthew Arnold. Cambridge: Cambridge UP, 1966.

Standard abbreviation for University Press.

8. One volume of a multivolume work

If only one volume from a multivolume set is used, indicate the volume number after the title.

Freud, Sigmund. The Complete Psychological Works of Sigmund Freud. Vol. 6. Trans. James Strachey. London: Hogarth, 1962.

Number of volume cited.

9. Two or more volumes of a multivolume work

Sandburg, Carl. Abraham Lincoln. 6 vols. New York: Scribner's, 1939.

Total number of volumes.

10. A book that is part of a series

Photography as a Tool. Life Library of Photography. New York: Time-Life, 1970.

Series name as well as number, if available.

11. A republished book

Provide the original publication date after the title of the book, followed by normal publication information for the current edition.

Takaki, Ronald. Strangers from a Different Shore: A History of Asian Americans. 1989. New York: Penguin, 1990.

Original publication year; year of edition used.

12. A later edition of a book

Rottenberg, Annette T. The Structure of Argument. 2nd ed. Boston: Bedford, 1997.

Later (second) edition.

Year second edition was published.

13. A book with a title in its title

Kinney, Arthur F. Go Down, Moses: The Miscegenation of Time. New York: Twayne, 1996.

Title of a novel by another author.

14. A work in an anthology or a collection

Fairbairn-Dunlop, Peggy. "Women and Agriculture in Western Samoa." Different Places, Different Voices. Ed. Janet H. Momsen and Vivian Kinnaird. London: Routledge, 1993. 211-26.

Title and editors of the anthology.

Page range of the work in the anthology.

15. Two or more works from the same anthology

Atwan, Robert, and Jamaica Kincaid, eds. The Best American Essays, 1995. New York: Houghton, 1995.

A separate entry for the anthology, alphabetized by editor.

One of the works in the anthology, alphabetized by the author of the work.

Paley, Grace. "Six Days: Some Rememberings." Atwan and Kincaid 187-92.

16. A translation

If you refer to the work itself:

Tolstoy, Leo. War and Peace. Trans. Constance Garnett. London: Pan, 1972.

If you discuss the translation in your essay:

Garnett, Constance, trans. War and Peace. By Leo Tolstoy. London: Pan, 1972.

17. An article in a reference book

Suber, Howard. "Motion Picture." The Encyclopedia Americana. 1991 ed.

Volume and page numbers not needed.

18. An introduction, preface, foreword, or afterword

Part cited.

Page span.

Holt, John. Introduction. Better than School. By Nancy Wallace. Burnett: Larson, 1983. 9-14.

Articles

19. An article from a newspaper

Pages (continues after page 1).

Edition, if known.

Wilford, John Noble. "Corn in the New World: A Relative Latecomer." New York Times 7 Mar. 1995, late ed.: C1+.

20. An article from a weekly or biweekly magazine

Day and month.

Kaye, Steven D. "Hello 75, So Long 55." U.S. News and World Report 18 Dec. 1995: 71-75.

21. An article from a monthly or bimonthly magazine

Month but no day.

Spencer, Paula. "No More Whining." Parenting Apr. 1997: 151-56.

22. An article in a scholarly journal with continuous annual pagination

```
Jackson, Jeremy S. H., and Roger Blackman. "A Driving
     Simulator Test of Wilde's Risk Homeostasis Theory."
     Journal of Applied Psychology 79 (1994): 950-58.
```

Volume number.

23. An article in a scholarly journal that paginates each issue separately

```
Epstein, Alexandra. "Teen Parents: What They Need to Know."
     High/Scope Resource 1.2 (1982): 6.
```

Volume number.

Issue number.

24. An article by an unidentified author

```
"Highways Become Safer." Futurist Jan.-Feb. 1994: 51-52.
```

Alphabetize by first important word in title.

25. An editorial

```
"Meth Lab Charades." Editorial. Press-Enterprise [Riverside]
     2 Oct. 1997: A8.
```

Capitalize even if original uses lower case.

For local paper, identify city if not in title.

26. A letter to the editor

```
Rissman, Edward M. Letter. Los Angeles Times 29 June 1989:
     B5.
```

Section ("B").

27. A review

If the review is titled:

```
Anders, Jaroslaw. "Dogma and Democracy." Rev. of The Church
     and the Left, by Adam Minchik. New Republic 17 May
     1993: 42-48.
```

Abbreviation for "review."

Title of book reviewed.

Magazine in which review was published.

If the review is untitled:

```
Lane, Anthony. Rev. of The English Patient, dir. Anthony
     Minghella, New Yorker 25 Nov. 1996: 118-121.
```

Title of film reviewed.

Abbreviation for "director."

If the review has no title and no named author, start with the words *Rev. of* and the title of the work being reviewed.

Internet sources

The models for citing sources on the World Wide Web are based on guidelines on citing Web sources authorized by the MLA. These guidelines can be found at <www.mla.org>. The MLA recommends the following format for works-cited entries for the World Wide Web:

One space.
One space.
One space.
One space.

```
Author's last name, First name, Middle initial. "Title of
     Short Work." Title of Book, Periodical, or Site.
     Publication date or date of last revision. Page numbers
     or number of paragraphs. Name of sponsoring institution
     or organization. Date of access. <URL>.
```

Models for citing other kinds of Internet sources not covered by the MLA guidelines—a posting to a discussion group or newsgroup or on a listserv and a synchronous communication—are taken from Andrew Harnack and Eugene Kleppinger, *Online! A Reference Guide to Using Internet Sources* (New York: St. Martin's, 1998).

DIGITAL HINT

Wired Style (1996), by the editors of *Wired* magazine, recommends making line breaks in URLs in the following three places.

- Following the protocol abbreviation at the beginning (*http://*)
- Before a punctuation mark such as a period, a tilde (~), or a slash (the punctuation mark appears at the beginning of the next line)
- If no other option is available, between syllables (do not hyphenate).

28. A professional or personal World Wide Web site

Professional site:

Sponsoring organization.
URL.

```
Schmid, Randolph E. "Debate Continues over Danger of Higher
     Speed Limits." NETarrant.Net Community News. 10 Oct.
     1996. Fort Worth Star-Telegram. 29 Apr. 1997
     <http://www.netarrant.net/news/doc/1047/1:NATION51
     /1:NATION51101096.html>.
```

Personal site:

Johnson, Suzanne H. Home page. 5 Oct. 1997 <http://members.aol.com/suzannehi/hello.htm>.

Indicates site with no title.

29. A book or poem

Book:

Blind, Mathilde. Dramas in Miniature. London: Chatto & Windus, 1891. Victorian Women Writer's Project. Ed. Perry Willett. 3 Oct. 1997. Indiana U. 13 Oct. 1997 <http://www.indiana.edu/~letrs/vwwp/blind/dramas.html>.

Original publication information.

Indicates editor of the project.

Date site was last updated.

Poem:

Mosko, Marc. "Muir Woods." Home page. 1996. 13 Oct. 1997 <http://www.tear.com/poems/mosko/muirwoods.html>.

Indicates site with no title.

30. An article in a reference database

Atwood, Margaret. "Memento Mori--but First, Carpe Diem." Rev. of Toward the End of Time, by John Updike. New York Times Book Review 12 Oct. 1997: 9-10. The New York Times Books on the Web. 1997. The New York Times Company. 13 Oct. 1997 <http://search.nytimes.com/books/97/10/12/reviews/971012.12atwoodt.html>.

Print publication information.

Name of database.

Name of sponsoring organization.

31. An article from an online journal

Killiam, Rosemary. "Cognitive Dissonance: Should Twentieth-Century Women Composers Be Grouped with Foucault's Mad Criminals?" Music Theory Online 3.2 (1997): 30 pars. 10 May 1997 <http://smt.ucsb.edu/mto/mtohome.html>.

Indicates number of paragraphs.

32. An article from an online magazine

Keillor, Garrison. "Why Did They Ever Ban a Book This Bad?" Salon 13 Oct. 1997. 14 Oct. 1997 <http://www.salon1999.com/feature/>.

Date of publication.

Date of access.

33. A posting on a discussion group or newsgroup or on a listserv

A discussion group or newsgroup:

Author's email address.
Subject line of posting.
Name of the group.

Conrad, Ed. <edconrad@prolog.net> "Proof of Life after Death." 8 July 1996. 9 July 1996 <sci.archeology>.

A listserv:

Author's email address.
Subject line of posting.
Listserv address.

Sherman, Matthew. <mgs@vt.edu> "Writing Process and Self-Discipline." 15 Feb. 1995. 16 Feb. 1995 <engl3764@ebbs.english.vt.edu>.

34. An archived posting

Name of the discussion list.
URL for the archive.

Healy, Jack. "Intellectual Property and Fair Use." Online posting. 3 July 1997. ACW-L. 14 Oct. 1997 <http://www.ttu.edu/lists/acw-1/>.

35. Synchronous communication (MOOs, MUDs)

Name of site or speaker.
Date of event.

LambdaMOO. "Seminar Discussion on Netiquette." 28 May 1996. 28 May 1996 <telnet://lambda.parc.xerox.edu:8888>.

See 7d for more on MOOs and MUDs.

36. A scholarly project

Editor of the project.

The Ovid Project. Ed. Hope Greenberg. 13 Mar. 1996. U of Vermont. 13 Oct. 1997 <http://www.uvm.edu/~hag/ovid/index.html>.

Other electronic sources

The MLA distinguishes between two kinds of electronic publications: portable databases, such as CD-ROMs, and online databases, such as those available through a computer service or the Internet.

37. Material from a CD-ROM database

Print source.
Title of the database.
Name of distributor.
Electronic publication date.

Braus, Patricia. "Sex and the Single Spender." American Demographics 15.11 (1993): 28-34. ABI/INFORM. CD-ROM. UMI-ProQuest. 1993.

If no print version is available, include the author, title, and date (if provided) along with information about the electronic source.

38. Material published on a CD-ROM, magnetic tape, or diskette

Picasso: The Man, His Works, the Legend. CD-ROM. Danbury: Grolier Interactive, 1996.

The medium.

39. Material from an online computer service

Fineman, Howard. "A Brawl on Tobacco Road: How Bill Clinton--and the Democrats' 'Butt Man'--Is Maneuvering to Turn Joe Camel into Bob Dole's Willie Horton." Newsweek 15 July 1996: n. pag. Online. America Online. 11 July 1996.

Source of print version.

Computer service.

Date of electronic publication.

If no print version is available, include the author, title, and date (if it is provided), along with information about the electronic source.

Other sources

40. A published, personal, or broadcast interview

Lowell, Robert. "Robert Lowell." Interview with Frederick Seidel. Paris Review 25 (1975): 56-95.

Person interviewed.

Interviewer.

Harkness, Edward. Personal interview. 7 May 1996.

Date interview was conducted.

Calloway, Cab. Interview with Rich Conaty. The Big Broadcast. WFUV, New York. 10 Dec. 1990.

Title of radio or television program.

Date interview was broadcast.

41. A lecture or public address

Timothy, Kristen. "The Changing Roles of Women's Community Organizations in Sustainable Development and in the United Nations." UN Association of the United States. Seattle. 7 May 1997.

Speaker's name.

Sponsoring organization.

42. A government document

Government agency.

Title of document.

United States. Dept. of Health and Human Services. Clinical Classifications for Health Policy Research, Version 2: Hospital Inpatient Statistics. Rockville: AHCPR Publications Clearinghouse, 1996.

If the author is known, the author's name may either come first or be placed after the title and introduced with the word *By.*

43. A pamphlet

Issuing organization.

Harborview Injury Prevention and Research Center. A Decade of Injury Control. Seattle: Harborview Medical Center, 1995.

44. A published doctoral dissertation

Title underlined.

Year dissertation was accepted.

Hilfinger, Paul N. Abstraction Mechanisms and Language Design. Diss. Carnegie-Mellon U, 1981. Cambridge: MIT P, 1983.

45. An unpublished doctoral dissertation

Title in quotation marks.

Year dissertation was accepted.

Bullock, Barbara. "Basic Needs Fulfillment among Less Developed Countries: Social Progress over Two Decades of Growth." Diss. Vanderbilt U, 1986.

46. A dissertation abstract

Title of the dissertation.

Abbreviation for "*Dissertation Abstracts International.*"

Bernstein, Stephen David. "Fugitive Genre: Gothicism, Ideology, and Intertextuality." DAI 51 (1991): 3078-3079A.

47. Published proceedings of a conference

Abbreviation of "proceedings."

Name of the conference.

Duffett, John, ed. Against the Crime of Silence. Proc. of the International War Crimes Tribunal, Nov. 1967, Stockholm. New York: Clarion-Simon, 1970.

If the name of the conference is part of the title of the publication, it should not be repeated. Use the format for a work in an anthology (see 14) to cite an individual presentation.

48. A letter or email message

Hamilton, Alexander. "To William Seton." 3 Dec. 1790. The Papers of Alexander Hamilton. Vol. 7. Ed. Harold C. Syrett. New York: Columbia UP, 1969. 190.

Date of the letter.

Title of book in which it is published.

Hannah, Barry. Letter to the author. 10 May 1990.

Sender's name.

Indicates personal letter.

To cite an email message, substitute "Email to the author."

49. A map or chart

Mineral King, California. Map. Berkeley: Wilderness P, 1979.

Use title or name of location.

50. A cartoon

Wilson, Gahan. Cartoon. New Yorker 14 July 1997: 74.

Cartoonist's name.

Provide the cartoon's title (if given) in quotes.

51. An advertisement

Reliance National Employment Practices Liability. Advertisement. Wired May 1997: 196.

Product or company being advertised.

Publication source.

52. A work of art or a musical composition

De Goya, Francisco. The Sleep of Reason Produces Monsters. Norton Simon Museum, Pasadena.

Name of the artwork underlined.

Beethoven, Ludwig van. Violin Concerto in D Major, op. 61.

Musical work identified by form, number, or key is not underlined.

Gershwin, George. Porgy and Bess.

Opera, ballet, or named composition is underlined.

53. A performance

Abbreviation for "performer."

Date of performance.

Hamlet. By William Shakespeare. Dir. Jonathan Kent. Perf. Ralph Fiennes. Belasco Theatre, New York. 20 June 1995.

Include any performers or other contributors who are relevant to your essay.

54. A television or radio program

Program title.

Episode title.

Network.

Local station.

"The Universe Within." Nova. Narr. Stacy Keach. Writ. Beth Hoppe and Bill Lattanzi. Dir. Goro Koide. PBS. WNET, New York. 7 Mar. 1995.

Include any contributors who are relevant to your essay. If you are discussing the work of a particular person (for example, the director or the writer), begin the entry with that person's name.

55. A film or videotape

Distributing company.

Othello. Perf. Laurence Fishburne, Irene Jacob, and Kenneth Branagh. Castle Rock Entertainment, 1995.

Date film was originally released.

Indicates medium.

Date video was released.

Casablanca. Dir. Michael Curtiz. Perf. Humphrey Bogart 1942. Videocassette. MGM-UA Home Video, 1992.

Include any performers or other contributors who are relevant to your essay. If you are discussing the work of a particular person (for example, an actor), begin with that person's name.

Bogart, Humphrey, perf. Casablanca. Dir. Michael Curtiz. 1942. Videocassette. MGM-UA Home Video, 1992.

56. A sound recording

Title identified by form, number, and key.

Manufacturer.

Bach, Johann Sebastian. Italian Concerto in F, Partita No. 1, and Tocata in D. Dubravka Tomsic, piano. Polyband, 1987.

Jane's Addiction. "Been Caught Stealing." Ritual de lo Habitual. Audiocassette. Warner Brothers, 1990.

Song title.

Name of medium (omit if CD).

If the year of issue is not known, add n.d.

9c Use optional content and bibliographic notes if you need to include additional information.

Notes give additional information in an essay without disrupting the flow of the text. *Content notes* include information about a topic. *Bibliographic notes* refer to additional sources. If possible, however, integrate content and bibliographic references into the essay itself.

When a content or bibliographic note is needed, insert a numeral at the place in the essay where you want to refer readers to the corresponding *footnote,* which appears at the bottom of a page, or *endnote,* which appears in a separate list headed *Notes* at the end of the essay, just before the list of works cited.

Here is an example from an essay:

British Romantic poets such as Wordsworth, Shelley, Keats, and Blake[1] began to redefine notions of "delight" and secular bliss as poetic topics.

A content note might look like this:

[1] Blake's lyric works, such as Songs of Innocence and Experience, show many characteristics associated with British Romanticism. However, Blake's epics (Milton and Jerusalem) are not neatly categorized as works of Romanticism.

A bibliographic note might look like this:

[1] See Northrop Frye's Fearful Symmetry for a more complete analysis of how Blake fits within the context of the British Romantic movement.

Note: Any works referred to in content and bibliographic notes should be included in the works-cited list.

9d A sample research essay in MLA style.

In the sample student essay that follows, the writer argues that speed limits should be lifted on rural interstate highways. The author mixes personal experience with expert opinion—in quotations, paraphrases, and summaries—to support his position. The essay has been revised to illustrate a variety of sources.

Knutson 1

Brent Knutson
Professor Etheridge
English 101
2 May 1997

Auto Liberation

The driver of a late-model Japanese sports car grins as he downshifts into third gear and releases the clutch. The car's rear end abruptly swings out in the wide, sweeping corner. He cranks the wheel. The engine emits a metallic wail and barks angrily as the driver pulls the gearshift into fourth. The secondary turbocharger engages and slams the driver's cranium against the headrest. With a rush of adrenaline, he watches the needle on the speedometer sweep toward the end of the scale. The driver then flicks the turn signal and blasts onto the interstate like a guided missile launched from a fighter jet. Today, he will not be late for work.

This scenario may seem a bit exaggerated, and one might conclude that the driver is unnecessarily risking his life and the lives of other people on the road. On Germany's autobahns, however, people normally drive in excess of 80 miles per hour. Yet these German superhighways are the safest in the world, filled with German drivers who are skilled, competent, and courteous.

½″ from top, put your name and page number.

1″ from top, put your name, instructor's name, course, and date.

Double-space above and below title, centered.

Indent 1″ at left margin.

Leave at least 1″ at right margin.

Indent ½″ or 5 spaces for paragraphs.

Double-space your essay.

1″ from bottom of page.

Knutson 2

Using the autobahn system as a model, it is possible to examine whether rural interstate speed limits in the United States are necessary.

Thesis asserts the writer's position.

In fact, there is solid reasoning to support the claim that all speed limits on rural U.S. interstate highways should be lifted. Not only are these speed limits--which currently vary from state to state--unnecessarily restrictive, they also infringe upon the personal freedom of American citizens. Although there are many urban and suburban locations where speed limits are appropriate, the vast, open stretches that make up most of the interstate highway system do not need to be regulated. Drivers should be able to travel on interstate highways from Washington to Florida without experiencing varying state speed limits in noncongested areas. Modern automobiles are capable of traveling safely at high speeds, and, despite what the auto-insurance consortium would have us believe, speed by itself does not necessarily kill. On our well-designed interstate highway system, American drivers are capable of driving at speeds of over 70 miles per hour responsibly and safely. Perhaps the most compelling reason to lift the interstate speed limits is the simplest: Driving fast is enjoyable.

Qualifies position.

Gives reasons.

Summarizes the opposing arguments.

Those opposed to lifting interstate speed limits argue that removing such restrictions would result in mayhem on the freeway; they are convinced that the countryside would be littered

Knutson 3

with the carcasses of people who achieved terminal velocity only to careen off the road and explode into flames. Speed limit advocates also argue that American drivers do not possess the skill or capacity to drive at autobahn speeds. They contend that our driver-education programs do not sufficiently prepare drivers to operate vehicles, and obtaining a driver's license in most states is comically easy; therefore, lifting the speed limit would be irresponsible.

The belief that a rural interstate system without speed limits would result in widespread carnage appears to be based more on fear than fact. In 1987, Idaho Senator Steve Symms introduced legislation allowing states to raise speed limits on rural interstates to 65 miles per hour (Csere 9). Auto-insurance industry advocates responded that the accident rates would skyrocket and the number of fatalities caused by auto accidents would increase accordingly. However, in 1992, five years after the Symms legislation, the number of deaths from automobile accidents reached a thirty-year low ("Highways" 51). In 1995, the federal government gave control of speed limits to individual states, and over twenty states raised limits soon after. Although death rates rose slightly in eight states in the following year, they also dropped slightly in four states, proving that raised speed limits do not necessarily increase traffic deaths (Schmid).

Parenthetical citation: author and page.

Shortened form of title given for source with no author indicated.

Paraphrases a Web site with no page number.

Summarizes research report.

Figure introduced within the text.

Knutson 4

Statistics related to traffic deaths can be misleading. In fact, figures showing total increases in the number of deaths--statistics often cited by the insurance companies--are generally deceptive because they fail to recognize increased use of the highway systems. Over the past seventy-five years, average speeds on U.S. highways have increased steadily, but the fatality rate has declined steadily, from 25 deaths per 100 million vehicle miles traveled (VMT) in 1920, to the 1995 rate of 1.7 deaths per 100 million VMT (Peters 14). Even in the past ten years, with higher interstate speed limits, the deaths per million VMT have continued to decline because of safety improvements. Figure 1 shows the decline in death rate per million VMT from 1985 to 1995.

The state of Montana offers an interesting case study of the effect of lifting speed limits on rural interstates. When the federal speed limit was lifted in 1995, Montana altered its laws more dramatically than any other state. The new laws specified only that in the daytime drivers must travel at a "reasonable and prudent speed," making Montana's laws the closest to those governing the German autobahn system. In the year following the enactment of the new speed limit, the number of deaths on Montana highways actually declined from 165 to 152 (Schmid). Clearly, the correlation between lifted speed limits and traffic deaths has not been established.

Knutson 5

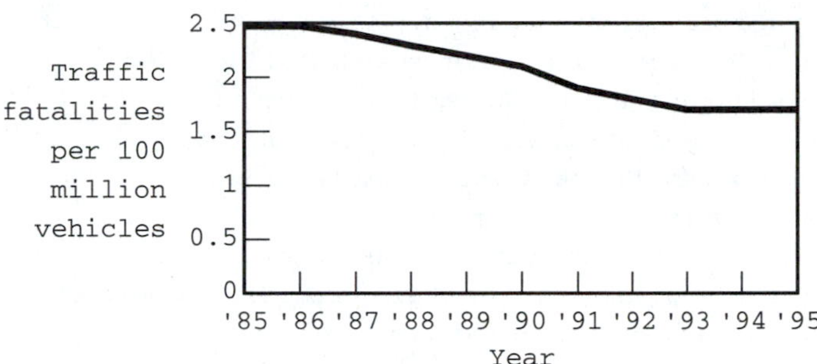

Fig. 1. Changes in U.S. Fatality Rates per 100 Million Miles Traveled, 1985 to 1995, Traffic Safety Facts 1995: Overview (Washington: United States. Dept. of Transportation, National Highway Traffic Safety Administration, 1996).

Abbreviate "figure."

Double-space title or description and source.

One of the biggest fallacies perpetrated by the auto-insurance industry and car-fearing legislators is that "speed kills." Driving fast in itself, however, is not a hazard; speed combined with incompetence, alcohol consumption, or hazardous conditions is dangerous. A skilled motor-vehicle operator traveling at 90 miles per hour on a divided rural highway does not present a significant risk. Psychologist and compensation theorist G. J. Wilde "developed the RHT (Risk Homeostasis Theory) to account for the apparent propensity of drivers to maintain a constant level of experienced accident risk" (qtd. in Jackson and Blackman 950). During a driving simulation experiment in which he changed

Indicates credentials of a source.

Quotes an indirect source.

Paraphrases a source; gives source's name in parentheses.

Introduces source with a signal phrase; page number at end of sentence.

"non-motivational factors," Wilde determined that "neither speed limit nor speeding fine had a significant impact on accident loss" (qtd. in Jackson and Blackman 956). Wilde's theory emphasizes the human tendency towards self-preservation as a motivating factor. In other words, drivers do not increase their personal risk by driving faster than their capabilities dictate, regardless of the speed limit.

In fact, according to studies, the majority of people are confident at speeds of up to 75 miles per hour, no matter what the speed limit is (Sullivan 37). The average speed on Montana's interstate highways, for example, has risen by only 2 mph since the repeal of the federal speed limit, with most drivers topping out at 75 (Schmid). And those drivers who do choose to drive 75 miles per hour or even faster are simply reaping the benefits of improved contemporary highway and automobile design, while saving time across immense, open expanses and having fun. According to Eric Peters, who covers the automobile industry for the Washington Times, interstate highways were engineered for speeds similar to the European autobahn when they were built (13). At the same time, design improvements in suspension, steering, tires, brakes, and doors have made modern cars safer than ever at high speeds (Kaye 73). Indeed, the stringent safety requirements imposed by the Department of Transportation for vehicles sold in

Knutson 7

the United States ensures that our cars and trucks are the safest in the world.

Unfortunately, the Insurance Institute for Highway Safety (IIHS) doesn't see things this way. It has been busy manipulating statistics in an attempt to convince people that raising the interstate speed limits has resulted in a veritable blood bath. A headline in a recent edition of the IIHS status report states, "For Sixth Year in a Row, Deaths on U.S. Rural Interstate Highways Are Much Higher Than before Speed Limits Were Raised to 65 MPH" (qtd. in Bedard 20). That statistic is more than a little misleading because it does not compensate for the increased number of drivers on the road. Patrick Bedard explains: "What's the real conclusion? Rural interstate fatalities over the whole United States increased 19 percent between 1982 and 1992. But driving increased 44 percent. So the fatality rate is on a definite downward trend from 1.5 to 1.2 [percent]" (21).

One might ask what the insurance industry stands to gain by misrepresenting auto-fatality statistics. The real issue is what it stands to lose if speed limits are deregulated. Lifted speed limits translate into fewer traffic citations issued by police. Fewer tickets mean fewer points assessed on Americans' driving records, which would remove the insurance industry's primary tool for raising premiums. Two speeding tickets can make annual insurance

Abbreviation in parentheses at first mention.

Parenthetical citation between the quotation marks and the period.

Encloses word not in the original quotation in brackets.

Writer reports his own experience.

Writer presents his "most compelling" reason last.

Knutson 8

premiums jump by $1,000 per year or more. Needless to say, insurance companies aren't thrilled about the prospect of lifted speed limits because it would mean less money in their coffers.

I recently returned from a four-year stay in Kaiserslautern, Germany. While there, I learned the pleasure of high-speed motoring. I was particularly impressed by the skill and discipline demonstrated by virtually all drivers traveling on the network of superhighways that make up the autobahn system. Germany's automobile regulatory laws are efficient and practical, and they serve as an example for all countries to follow. It is striking that automobiles and driving fast are such integral components of German culture. Germans possess a passion for cars that is so contagious I didn't want to leave the country. German Chancellor Helmut Kohl summed up the German attitude regarding speed limits quite concisely: "For millions of people, a car is part of their personal freedom" (qtd. in Cote 12).

Kohl's comment points to one of the most persuasive arguments to abolish interstate speed limits: Driving fast is pure, unadulterated, rip-snortin' fun. It is an expression of personal freedom, an example of the "pursuit of happiness" set forth as a basic right in the U.S. Constitution. As Peter Marsh and Peter Collett

Knutson 9

point out, my experience of high-speed driving in Germany is not unique:

> Few people can describe in words the mixture of sensations they experience, but for some the effect is so psychologically intense that no other experience can match it. . . . For some people the psychological effects are experienced as pure fear. For others, however, this basic emotional state is modified to give a sharply tingling experience which is perceived as intensely pleasurable. The fear, and the state of alertness are still there--but they have been mastered. (179)

Lifting rural interstate speed limits in all states is a proposition that every driver should carefully consider. At a time when our elected officials are striving to control virtually every aspect of our lives, it is imperative that we fight to regain our freedom behind the wheel. Like Germans, Americans have a rich automotive culture and heritage. The automobile represents our ingenuity, determination, and independence. It is time to return control of the automobile to the driver, and to "free us from our speed slavery once and for all" (Csere 9).

Block quotation indented 1″ or 10 spaces.

Four ellipsis marks indicate that part of the sentence or one or more sentences have been omitted.

Writer concludes by restating thesis.

Works-cited list begins on a new page.

Heading centered 1″ from top.

List is alphabetized by last names of authors or titles (if no author is indicated).

First line is aligned at left margin; subsequent lines are indented ½″ or 5 spaces.

Entries are double-spaced.

1″ for right margin.

At least 1″ from bottom of page.

Knutson 10

Works Cited

Bedard, Patrick. "Auto Insurance Figures Don't Lie, but Liars Figure." Editorial. Car and Driver Mar. 1994: 20-21.

Cote, Kevin. "Heartbrake on Autobahn." Advertising Age Sept. 1994: 1+.

Csere, Csaba. "Free the Speed Slaves." Editorial. Car and Driver Nov. 1993: 9.

"Highways Become Safer." Futurist Jan.-Feb. 1994: 51-52.

Jackson, Jeremy S. H., and Roger Blackman. "A Driving Simulator Test of Wilde's Risk Homeostasis Theory." Journal of Applied Psychology 79.6 (1994): 950-58.

Kaye, Steven D. "Hello 75, So Long 55." U.S. News and World Report 18 Dec. 1995: 71-75.

Marsh, Peter, and Peter Collett. Driving Passion. Winchester: Faber, 1987.

Peters, Eric. "Why Must Motorists Drive Only 55?" Consumers' Research Nov. 1995: 13-16.

Schmid, Randolph E. "Debate Continues over Danger of Higher Speed Limits." NETarrant.Net Community News. 10 Oct. 1996. Fort Worth Star-Telegram. 29 Apr. 1997 <http://www.netarrant.net/news/doc/1047/1:NATION51/1:NATION51101096.html>.

Sullivan, Lee R. "The American Autobahn." Forbes 15 July 1996: 37.

10 DOCUMENTING SOURCES USING APA STYLE

The American Psychological Association (APA) system of documentation is used in the social sciences. The following guidelines are sufficient for most college research reports that call for the APA style. For additional information, see the *Publication Manual of the American Psychological Association,* Fourth Edition (1994).

10a Use in-text citations to show where you have used material from sources.

In-text citations mark places in the essay where information from sources is included. Every in-text citation has a corresponding entry in a list of references at the end of the essay that tells readers how to find the source (see 10b).

Place the in-text citation as near as possible to the borrowed material without disrupting your sentence. Cite each time you refer to a source, except when all of the sentences in a single paragraph refer to the same source. Then, in the first reference you may cite the author's name and the year the work was published and in subsequent references omit the author and year as long as there is no mention of another source that would confuse readers. Do not cite common knowledge or personal knowledge (see 8b).

The following examples provide models for most of the documentation situations you will encounter in college. (For guidelines on preparing a list of references, see 10b.)

1. Author indicated in a signal phrase

As Allis (1990) noted about home-schooling environments, "There are no drugs in the bathroom or switchblades in the hallways" (p. 85).

Signal phrase.

Page reference.

See 8c for more on using signal phrases.

2. Author and year indicated in a parenthetical citation

"The children in my class made fun of my braids, so Sister Victoire, the principal, sent a note home to my mother asking her to comb my hair in a more 'becoming' fashion" (Lorde, 1982, pp. 59-60).

Author's last name and year source published.

Indicates more than one page cited.

While home schoolers are a diverse group--libertarians, conservatives, Christian fundamentalists, and a growing number of ethnic minorities (Wahisi, 1995)--most cite one of two reasons as their primary motive for home schooling.

Parentheses close to paraphrase.

Page reference is optional for paraphrase.

3. A work with two authors

Gallup and Elam (1988) show that lack of proper financial support ranked third on the list of the problems in public schools, while poor curriculum and poor standards ranked fifth on the list.

Use *and* between authors' names in signal phrase.

Year of publication.

In a 1988 Gallup poll, lack of proper financial support ranked third on the list of the problems in public schools; poor curriculum and poor standards ranked fifth on the list (Gallup & Elam).

Use & between authors' names in parentheses.

4. A work with three or more authors

First citation for three to five authors:

Authors' last names, following order in source.

Dyal, Corning, and Willows (1975) identify several types of students, including the "Authority-Rebel" (p. 4).

One type of student that can be identified is the "Authority-Rebel" (Dyal, Corning, & Willows, 1975, p. 4).

Subsequent citation for three to five authors:

Signal phrase.

According to Dyal et al. (1975), Authority-Rebels "see themselves as superior to other students in the class" (p. 4).

Parenthetical citation.

Authority-Rebels "see themselves as superior to other students in the class" (Dyal et al., 1975, p. 4).

For six or more authors, use the last name of the first author and *et al.* in all in-text citations.

5. Two or more works by the same author

Indicates second work in reference list by this author.

When old paint becomes transparent, it sometimes shows the artist's original plans: "a tree will show through a woman's dress" (Hellman, 1973b, p. 1).

6. Author not listed

Use shortened title in signal phrase.

As reported in the 1994 Economist article "Classless Society," estimates as late as 1993 placed the number of home-schooled children in the 350,000 to 500,000 range.

Use shortened title in parenthetical citation.

An international pollution treaty still to be ratified would prohibit all plastic garbage from being dumped at sea ("Awash," 1987).

See 47d for help capitalizing titles cited within the text. Capitalize only the first word of titles and subtitles in the list of references (see 10b).

7. Corporate author

First in-text citation, with signal phrase:

According to the Washington State Board for Community and Technical Colleges, a tuition increase has been proposed to offset budget deficits from Initiative 601 (1995).

Full name of organization in every signal phrase.

First parenthetical citation:

Tuition increases proposed for Washington Community and Technical Colleges would help offset budget deficits brought about by Initiative 601 (Washington State Board of Community and Technical Colleges [WSBCTC], 1995).

Full name of organization.

Abbreviation in brackets.

Subsequent parenthetical citation:

The tuition increases would amount to about 3 percent and would still not cover the loss of revenue (WSBCTC, 1995).

Abbreviation.

8. Authors with the same last name

"Women are more in the public world, the heretofore male world, than at any previous moment in history," transforming "the lives of women and men to an extent probably unparalleled by any other social or political movement" (W. Brown, 1988, pp. 1, 3).

Use author's first initial and last name, to avoid confusion.

Indicates pages quoted are not continuous.

9. Two or more works cited in the same parentheses

Through support organizations and programs offered by public schools, home schooled children are also able to take part in social activities outside the home, such as field trips and sports (Guterson, 1992; Hahn & Hasson, 1996).

Cited alphabetically by authors' last names.

When citing multiple works by the same author in the same parentheses, order the citations by date, with the oldest reference first: (Postman, 1979, 1986).

10. Material taken from a secondhand source

Use *as cited in* to indicate your source.

```
Forster says "the collapse of all civilization, so real-
istic for us, sounded in Matthew Arnold's ears like a
distant and harmonious cataract" (as cited in Trilling,
1955, p. 11).
```

It is not necessary to list the original source in the list of references. Give the secondhand source.

11. Internet material

Paragraph instead of page numbers, if available.

```
Each type of welfare recipient "requires specific ser-
vices or assistance to make the transition from welfare
to work" (Armato & Halpern, 1996, par. 7).
```

12. Personal communication

Name of person communicated with.

Date of communication.

```
According to Linda Jones (personal communication, May 2,
1997), some parents believe they must maximize their day
care value and leave their children at day care centers
for up to ten hours a day, even on their days off.
```

In the APA style, it is not necessary to list personal correspondence, including email, in your reference list.

10b Include all of the works you cite in a list of references at the end of your essay.

The reference list appears at the end of the essay and provides information enabling readers to find the sources cited in the essay (see 10a). Every in-text citation (except personal communication) must have a corresponding entry in the list of references. Likewise, every entry in the reference list must correspond to at least one in-text citation. If you want to list sources you consulted but did not cite in the essay, title the page *Bibliography* instead of *References.*

For books:

```
Author's last name, First initial. Middle initial. (year
     published). Title of the book. City of publication:
     Publisher's name.
```

One space.
One space.

For journal articles:

```
Author's last name, First initial. Middle initial. (publi-
     cation date). Title of the article. Journal Name,
     Volume number (issue number), page range.
```

One space.
One space.

Copy the author's name and the title from the first or title page of the source. Do not worry about including information that is unavailable, such as the author's middle initial and the issue number for a journal article. See the sample reference list on page 176 for formatting and 47d for help in capitalizing words in journal titles.

Note: The APA recommends that only the first line of each entry be indented five to seven spaces for manuscripts intended for publication. However, instructors may require students to use a *hanging indent:* The first line of the entry is not indented, but subsequent lines are indented five to seven spaces. Ask your instructor which format is preferred. The examples in this section demonstrate a hanging-indent style.

DIGITAL HINT

The APA discourages the use of italics, but your instructor may approve of or even prefer italics. The underlined titles in the models that follow can be italicized instead. (See 50a for more on using italics for titles.)

Books

1. A book by a single author

Last name, first initial.

Guterson, D. (1992). Family matters: Why homeschooling makes sense. San Diego: Harcourt.

Book title underlined.

2. A book by more than one author

Last name first for every author.

Gottfredson, S. G., & McConville, S. (1987). America's correctional crisis. Westport, CT: Greenwood.

No limit on number of authors.

Dyal, J. A., Corning, W. C., & Willows, D. M. (1975). Readings in psychology: The search for alternatives (3rd ed.). New York: McGraw-Hill.

3. A book by an agency, organization, or corporation

Organization.

Association for Research in Nervous and Mental Disease. (1966). The circulation of the brain and spinal cord: A symposium on blood supply. New York: Hafner.

4. A book with an unlisted author

Alphabetize by first word in title.

Rand McNally commercial atlas. (1993). Skokie, IL: Rand McNally.

When the word *Anonymous* appears on the title page, cite the author as *Anonymous.*

5. A later edition of a book

Lewis, I. M. (1996). Religion in context: Cults and charisma (2nd ed.). New York: Cambridge University Press.

Edition information in parentheses.

6. Multiple works by the same author (or same group of authors)

Entries ordered by year published, oldest first.

Ritzer, G. (1993). The McDonaldization of society. Newbury Park, CA: Pine Forge Press.

Ritzer, G. (1994). Sociological beginnings: On the origins of key ideas in sociology. New York: McGraw-Hill.

If the works were published in the same year, arrange them alphabetically and add a letter after the date: 1996a, 1996b.

7. A multivolume work

Sandburg, C. (1939). Abraham Lincoln: Vol. 2. The war years. New York: Scribner's.

Sandburg, C. (1939). Abraham Lincoln (Vols. 1-6). New York: Scribner's.

Colon.
To cite a single volume, give volume number.
To cite entire work, indicate total number of volumes.

8. A book with an author and an editor

Baum, L. F. (1996). Our landlady (N. T. Koupal, Ed.). Lincoln: University of Nebraska Press.

Author.
Abbreviation for "editor."

9. An edited collection

Carter, K., & Sptizack, C. (Eds.). (1989). Doing research on women's communication. Norwood, NJ: Ablex.

To cite whole collection, list work under names of editors.

10. A work in an anthology or a collection

Fairbairn-Dunlop, P. (1993). Women and agriculture in western Samoa. In J. H. Momsen & V. Kinnaird (Eds.), Different places, different voices (pp. 211-226). London: Routledge.

Name of author of work.
Title of work.
Title of the anthology.
Page range of work in the anthology.

11. A republished book

Arnold, M. (1966). Culture and anarchy (J. D. Wilson, Ed.). Cambridge: Cambridge University Press. (Original work published 1869).

Year book was republished.
Original publication year.

Note: Both the original and the republished dates are included in the in-text citation, separated by a slash: (*Arnold, 1869/1966*).

12. A translation

Abbreviation for "translator."

Tolstoy, L. (1972). War and peace (C. Garnett, Trans.). London: Pan Books. (Original work published 1869)

Note: Both the original publication date and the publication date for the translation are included in the in-text citation, separated by a slash: (*Tolstoy, 1869/1972*).

13. An article in a reference book

Indicates where article appeared.

Both volume number and page range.

Suber, H. (1991). Motion picture. In Encyclopedia Americana (Vol. 19, pp. 505-539). Danbury, CT: Grolier.

14. An introduction, preface, foreword, or afterword

Author of part cited.

Identifies part of book.

Holt, J. (1983). Introduction. In N. Wallace, Better than school (pp. 9-14). Burnett, NY: Larson.

Articles

15. An article in a scholarly journal with continuous annual pagination

Journal title underlined.

Volume number underlined.

Natale, J. A. (1993). Understanding home schooling. Education Digest, 9, 58-61.

See 47d for more on capitalizing titles.

16. An article in a scholarly journal that paginates each issue separately

Mayberry, M., & Knowles, J. G. (1989). Family unit objectives of parents who teach their children: Ideological and pedagogical orientations to home schooling. Urban Review, 21(4), 209-225.

Issue number in parentheses.

17. An article from a newspaper

Year, month, and day.

Wilford, J. N. (1995, March 7). Corn in the New World: A relative latecomer. The New York Times, pp. C1, C5.

18. An article from a magazine

Rohn, A. (1988, April). Home schooling. Atlantic Monthly, 261, 20-25.

Year and month.

19. An unsigned article

Awash in garbage. (1987, August 15). The New York Times, p. A26.

Alphabetized by title.

20. A review

Anders, J. (1993, May 17). Dogma and democracy [Review of the book The church and the left]. The New Republic, 42-48.

Author of the review.

Identifies work reviewed.

If the review is untitled, use the bracketed information as the title, retaining the brackets.

21. An editorial or a letter to the editor

Meader, Roger. (1997, May 11). Hard to see how consumers will benefit from deregulation [Letter to the editor]. Seattle Post-Intelligencer, p. E3.

Type of work, in brackets.

22. Two or more articles by the same author in the same year

Selimuddin, A. K. (1989a, March 25). The selling of America. USA Today, pp. 12-14.

Selimuddin, A. K. (1989b, September). Will America become #2? USA Today Magazine, 14-16.

Articles in alphabetical order, by first important word in title.

Internet sources

APA citation guidelines for online resources are currently being discussed and evaluated. If your source is available both in print and online, the APA prefers that you cite the print version. The following models of Internet source entries, taken from Andrew Harnack and Eugene Kleppinger, *Online!*

A Reference Guide to Using Internet Sources (New York: St. Martin's, 1998), offer more specific guidelines for citing Internet sources than the APA provides at present.

References for sources on the Internet typically follow this format:

One space.

One space.

Author's last name, First initial. Middle initial. (Publication date). Title of document. Title of Complete Work. <URL> (Date of access).

DIGITAL HINT

Wired Style (1996), by the editors of *Wired* magazine, recommends making line breaks in URLs in the following places.

- After the protocol abbreviation at the beginning (*http://*)
- Before a punctuation mark such as a hyphen, a period, or a slash
- If no other option is available, between syllables (do not hyphenate).

23. A World Wide Web site

Author of Web site.

Gibson, B. E. (1995). Still going on exhibit. Still Going On: An Exhibit Celebrating the Life and Times of William Grant Still. <http://scriptorium.lib.duke.edu/sgo/home.html> (1997, July 14).

24. Linkage data

To help readers access a file through a link to a source document:

Use *n.d.* to indicate no date given.

Means "linked from."

Introduces additional linkage information.

Gwitch'in Steering Committee. (n.d.). The Arctic wildlife refuge: America's last great wilderness. Lkd. Alaska Web Servers, at "Virtual Tourist." <http://www.tourist.com> (1996, July 11).

25. A telnet site

Earthquake report for 6/27/96. (1996, July 6). Weather Underground. telnet madlab.sprl.umich.edu:3000/Latest Earthquake Reports (1996, July 11).

Telnet address.

Date accessed.

26. An FTP (file transfer protocol) site

Date of publication, if known.

Altar, T. W. (1993, January 14). Vitamin B12 and vegans. ftp wiretap.spies.com Library/Article/Food/b12.txt (1996, May 28).

Introduces FTP address.

Greig, A. (1995, November 21). Home magazines and modernist dreams: Designing the 1950s house. <ftp://coombs .anu.edu.au/coombs papers/coombs archives /urban-research-program/working-papers/wp-047-1995.txt> (1996, July 11).

Introduces URL.

27. A gopher site

Title of publication.

Africa on the brink of a brighter future. (1997). gopher hafaus01.unicef.org Public Information/1997 Publications and Information Items/1997 Press Releases/Africa on the Brink of a Brighter Future (1997, July 11).

Introduces gopher path.

Use *n.d.* to indicate no date given.

Gipe, P. (n.d.). Tilting at windmills: Public opinion toward wind energy. <gopher://gopher.igc.apc.org:70/0/orgs /awea/faq/surv/gipe> (1997, September 11).

Introduces URL.

Date of access.

28. A posting on a discussion group or newsgroup (Usenet)

Introduces author's email address.

Conrad, E. <edconrad@prolog.net> (1996, July 8). Proof of life after death. <sci.archeology> (1996, July 9).

Subject line of posting.

Name of newsgroup.

29. A posting on a listserv

Date of posting. Listserv address. Date of access.

Sherman, M. <mgs@vt.edu> (1995, February 15). Writing process and self-discipline. <engl3764@ebbs.english.vt.edu> (1995, February 16).

For an article or a file archived at a Web site or listserv address:

Listserv address. Introduces pathway to list's archive.

Krause, S. <krause@mind.net> (1996, June 15). "Grading" without grading. <acw-1@unicorn.acs.ttu.edu> via <http://www.ttu.edu/lists/acw-1> (1997, July 11).

30. Synchronous communication (MOOs, MUDs)

Name of site or speaker. Date of communication. Date of access.

LambdaMOO. (1996, May 28). Seminar discussion on netiquette. <telnet://lambda.parc.xerox.edu:8888> (1996, May 28).

See 7d for more on MOOs and MUDs.

Other electronic sources

The following guidelines are from the *Publication Manual of the American Pyschological Association,* Fourth Edition.

31. Article from an online journal

Indicates path, directory, and filename. No final period if ending with electronic address or with path, file, or item number.

Nielsen, R. (1995, March). Radon risks [16 paragraphs]. Carcinogens [On-line serial], 4(12). Available FTP: Hostname: princeton.edu Directory: pub/carcinogens/1995 File: radon.95.3.12.radonrisks

32. Material from an online computer service

Title of journal. Indicates article number.

Reece, J. S. (1978). Measuring investment center performance. Harvard Business Review [On-line], 56(3), 28-40. Available: Dialog file 107, item 673280 047658

33. Material from a CD-ROM database or other electronic media

For information retrieved from electronic media, follow general citation models. (For date of publication, cite the year copies of the data were first made generally available.) Insert, in brackets, the type of medium from which you are citing *(CD-ROM, Data file, Database)* after the title of the work. Give the location and name of both the producer and the distributor.

Legal wear and tear of school uniforms. (1996, July 31) The Oakland Post, 33 (15). Ethnic NewsWatch [CD-ROM]. Stamford, CT: SoftLine Information [Producer and Distributor].

Indicates medium.

Include location and name of both producer and distributor, if different.

34. Computer software

Bergman, L. R., & El-Khouri, B. M. (1995). SLEIPNER. A statistical package for pattern-oriented analysis (Version 1.0) [Computer software]. Stockholm, Sweden: Stockholm University Department of Psychology.

Persons with proprietary rights to software, if listed.

Indicates medium.

Other sources

35. An interview

Do not list personal interviews in your references list. Cite the person's name in your text, and give the notation *personal communication* (see page 158). Cite a published interview like an article from a magazine (see page 163).

36. A government document

U.S. Department of Health, Education and Welfare. (1979). Healthy people: The surgeon general's report on health promotion (DHEW Publication No. 79-55071). Washington, DC: U.S. Government Printing Office.

Agency, if author unlisted.

Serial number of publication, if available.

37. A dissertation abstract

Fairhall, J. L. (1989). James Joyce, history, and the political unconscious. (Doctoral dissertation, State University of New York at Stony Brook, 1989). Dissertation Abstracts International, 51, 3582-A.

Year printed.

Year accepted.

Volume and page numbers.

38. An unpublished doctoral dissertation

Bullock, B. (1986). Basic needs fulfillment among less developed countries: Social progress over two decades of growth. Unpublished doctoral dissertation, Vanderbilt University, Nashville.

Location of university, if not part of name.

39. Published proceedings of a conference

Year proceedings published.

Bingman, C. F. (1985). The President as manager of the federal government. In C. L. Harriss (Ed.), Control of Federal Spending (pp. 146-161). New York: Proceedings of The Academy of Political Science.

40. A technical or research report

Brown, B. B., Kohrs, D., & Lazarro, C. (1991, April). The academic costs and consequences of extracurricular participation in high school. Chicago: American Education Research Association.

If given, put report number in parentheses.

Publisher's name.

41. A television program

Title of the program.

Hoppe, B., & Lattanzi, B. (Writers). (1995). The universe within (G. Koide, Director). In P. Apsell (Producer), Nova. Boston: WGBH.

Name of series.

42. A film or videotape

Name of primary person discussed in the essay.

Parker, O. (Director). (1995). Othello [Film]. New York: Castle Rock Entertainment.

Distributor.

10c Use content footnotes in APA style if you need them.

When background information is needed, it should be integrated into the essay itself if at all possible and documented according to the conventions described in 10a and 10b. When necessary information would disrupt the essay, you may add content footnotes indicated by raised numbers in the text that correspond to the raised numbers on the page headed "Footnotes" (centered).

Here is an example of how to cite a content footnote in an essay:

```
While home schoolers are a diverse group--libertarians,
conservatives, Christian fundamentalists, and a growing
number of ethnic minorities¹ (Wahisi, 1995)--most cite
one of two reasons as their primary motive for home
schooling.
```

Raised footnote.

Here is the corresponding entry on the "Footnotes" page.

```
     ¹ Wahisi (1995) points out that because of exclu-
sionary laws and policies, minority groups such as
African Americans have relied upon home schooling for
their education through most of U.S. history, and that
some of the same exclusionary dynamics are bringing
about a revival of home schooling among some ethnic
minorities.
```

10d A sample research essay in APA style.

In the following sample research essay, the student writer analyzes the causes of a national trend—the increase in home schooling. The author cites statistics, quotes authorities, and paraphrases and summarizes background information. Christina Dinh's essay has been revised to illustrate a greater variety of APA citations.

Note: For research reports that will be published, the APA requires a brief abstract (of no more than 120 words) that summarizes the content of the report. The abstract should include keywords that can be used in electronic databases for future researchers. The abstract should appear on a new page after the title page, followed by the first page of the research report. (See 12c for help in writing an abstract or summary for your essay if one is required.)

Running head: short title and page number.

[The title page appears on a separate page.]

Educating Children 1

Title.

Student's name.

College.

Educating Children at Home

Christina Dinh

University of California at San Diego

[The first page of text begins on a new page, after the title page or abstract (if there is one).]

Educating Children 2

Full title.

Paragraphs indented ½″ or 5 spaces.

Left margin should be 1½″; other margins at least 1″.

Presents the trend.

Double-space everything.

Shortened title for source without an author.

Educating Children at Home

In this era of growing concerns about the quality of public education, increasing numbers of parents across the United States are choosing to educate their children at home. These parents believe they can do a better job teaching their children than their local schools can. Home schooling, as this practice is known, has become a national trend over the past twenty years and has rapidly increased in the past three to four years. While estimates as late as 1993 placed the number of home-schooled children in the 350,000 to 500,000 range ("Classless," 1994), more recent estimates by the Department of Education (Wahisi, 1995) placed the number of children taught at home at about 1.2 million. The Home School Legal Defense Association (1995) put the estimate even higher, at up to 1.5 million, and estimated that "the ranks are currently growing at 15% to 20% each year" (p. 16).

What is home schooling, and why are so many families choosing it? In this essay I will analyze some of the reasons families become involved in home schooling. In describing their motives, I will also describe to some extent the ideology of these families and their orientation to education and to government.

Forecasts plan.

David Guterson (1992), a high school teacher whose own children are home schooled, defines home schooling as "the attempt to gain an education outside of institutions" (p. 5). Home-schooled children spend most of the conventional school day learning in or near their homes rather than in traditional schools; parents or guardians are the prime educators. Home-schooled children follow what Holtrop (1996) calls "interest-initiated activities" that help them learn the same language, thinking, mathematical, and content skills as their classroom counterparts but in a more integrated environment, so that the learning is a more natural part of their daily lives (p. xx). A lesson on how to multiply fractions, for example, can be integrated into an afternoon baking cookies, as children are challenged to triple the recipe not just for an exercise but also for a purpose: more cookies.

Author's credentials in signal phrase.

Page number for quotation.

With these kinds of activities, advocates say, children learn not only basic skills but also how to use these skills in real life, how to communicate about them, and how to relate them to their social context. Through support organizations and, in some cases, interaction with programs offered by public schools, home-schooled children can also take part in social activities outside the home, such as field trips and sports (Guterson, 1992; Hahn & Hasson, 1996).

Two sources in alphabetical order.

While home schoolers are a diverse group--libertarians, conservatives, Christian fundamentalists, and a growing number of ethnic minorities (Wahisi, 1995)--most cite one of two reasons as their primary motive for home schooling. One group is primarily concerned about the education public schools offer their children. The other group is also concerned about educational effectiveness, but particularly about the ideologies fostered in public schools. This latter group is made up mostly of families who are concerned about exposing their children to a secular education that may contradict their religious beliefs (Guterson, 1992, pp. 5-6).

Parenthetical citation close to paraphrase, no page number.

Divides home schoolers into two groups based on motivation.

The first group, those primarily concerned with educational effectiveness, generally believes that children need individual attention and the opportunity to grow at their own pace in order to learn well. Hahn and Hasson (1996) pointed out that "the typical student in [public] school receives less than eight minutes of individual attention per day" (p. 14). Parents who choose home schooling believe they can give their children greater enrichment and more specialized instruction than public schools can provide. At home, parents can work one-on-one with each child and be flexible

Describes first group of home schoolers.

Brackets used to add information within quotation.

about time. Many of these parents, like home schooler Peter Bergson, believe that

> home schooling provides more of an opportunity to continue the natural learning process that's in evidence in all children. [In school,] you change the learning process from self-directed to other-directed, from the child asking questions to the teacher asking questions. You shut down areas of potential interest. (as cited in Kohn, 1988, p. 22)

Block quotation indented ½″ or 5 spaces.

Secondhand source.

As the public educational system has continued to have problems, parents have seen academic and social standards get lower. They have mentioned several reasons for their disappointment with public schools and for their decision to do home schooling. A lack of funding, for example, leaves children without new textbooks. Many schools also cannot afford to buy laboratory equipment and other teaching materials. High school science teacher Brett Hamilton (personal communication, May 7, 1997) pointed out that it is difficult to upgrade lab and computer equipment essential for teaching subjects such as chemistry and biology.

Personal communication cited.

Parents have also cited overcrowding as a reason for taking their kids out of public school. Faced with a large group of children, a teacher cannot satisfy the needs of all the students. Thus, a teacher ends up gearing lessons to the students in the middle level, so children at both ends miss out. Gifted children and those with learning disabilities particularly suffer in this situation. At home, parents of these children say, they can tailor the material and the pace for each child, "taking into account personality differences and stages, not ages" (Holtrop, 1996, p. 75). Home-schooling methods seem to work well in preparing children academically. Home-schooled children averaged in the top 27% or higher in the Iowa Tests of Basic Skills (Wells, 1996).

Source of statistic cited.

In addition, home-schooling parents have claimed that their children are more well rounded than those in public school. Because they do not have to sit in a classroom all day, home-schooled kids can pursue their own projects, often combining crafts or technical skills with academic subjects. Some school districts invite home-schooled children to participate in sports and to use libraries (Guterson, 1992), and recent breakthroughs in educational software and Internet interactivity have made it possible for home schoolers to broaden their range of learning activities at home ("Classless," 1994; Hawkins, 1996).

Many home-schooling parents believe that these activities provide the social opportunities children need without exposing them to the peer pressure they would have to deal with in a public school. Occasionally, peer values can be good; often, however, students in today's schools face many negative peer pressures. According to Klaidman (1996), in the 1996 National Household Survey on drug abuse, "the number [of high school kids] who said they had smoked pot in the previous month rose from 4 percent in 1992 to 8.2 percent [in 1996]" (p. 37). Even more alarming, potentially, is that 4.4 million respondents identified themselves as "'binge drinkers,'--people who sometimes consume more than four drinks at one sitting" (p. 37).

Single quotation marks indicate a quotation within a quotation.

In addition to fears that peer pressure might push their children into using alcohol, marijuana, or other drugs, many parents fear violence in and near public schools. As one home-schooling parent put it, "a bullet in the wall of a [local] classroom made up our minds for us" (as cited in Wells, 1996, p. A15). Whereas the public school may be a dangerous environment in some cases, home schooling offers a more controlled environment in which the learner and teacher can experience the comfort level necessary for learning. As Allis (1990) noted about home-schooling environments, "There are no drugs in their bathrooms or switchblades in the hallways" (p. 85).

[Dinh discusses the second group of home schoolers.]

Armed with their convictions, home-schooling parents, such as those who belong to the Home School Legal Defense Association, have fought in court and lobbied for legislation that allows them the option of home schooling. In the 1970s, most states had compulsory attendance laws that made it difficult, if not illegal, to keep school-age children home from school. By 1993, thirty-two states permitted home schooling, ten allowed it with certain restrictions, and eight insisted that the home school be a legal private school (Guterson, 1992). Because of their efforts, children across the country can start the school day without leaving their houses.

Concludes by indicating movement's success.

Educating Children 8

References

List is alphabetized.

Allis, S. (1990, October 22). Schooling kids at home. Time, 136, 84-85.

Title (no author indicated).

Classless society. (1994, June 11). The Economist, 331, 24, 27.

Gatto, J. T. (1997, May 4). The nine assumptions of modern schooling. The Education Liberator. <http://www.sepschool.org> (1997, May 7).

First line is aligned at left margin; subsequent lines are indented ½″ or 5 spaces.

Guterson, D. (1992). Family matters: Why homeschooling makes sense. San Diego: Harcourt.

Hahn, K., & Hasson, M. (1996). Catholic education: Homeward bound. San Francisco: Ignatius Press.

Entries are double-spaced, with double space before and after each entry.

Hawkins, D. (1996, February 12). Homeschool battles: Clashes grow as some in the movement seek access to public schools. U.S. News & World Report, 120, 57-58.

Article from online computer service.

Holtrop, S. (1996). Individualization starts at home. Educational Leadership [On-line], 54(2), 74-77. Available Academic ASAP No. 18919600

Organization (no author indicated).

Home School Legal Defense Association. (1995, June 9). Human Events [On-line], 51(22), 16. Available Ebscohost No. 9506213940

Klaidman, D. (1996, October 21). Here's the straight dope. Newsweek, 128, 37.

Kohn, A. (1988, April). Home schooling. Atlantic, 261, 20-25.

Mayberry, M., & Knowles, J. G. (1989). Family unit objectives of parents who teach their children: Ideological and pedagogical orientations to home schooling. Urban Review, 21(4), 209-225.

Educating Children 9

Shackelford, L., & White, S. (1988). A survivor's guide to home schooling. Westchester, IL: Crossway.

Sullivan, M. R. (1995, October 15). Home-schoolers question districts' eagerness to help [Letter to the editor]. The Seattle Times, p. B5.

Wahisi, T. T. (1995, October). Making the grade: Black families. Crisis [On-line], 102(7), 14-16. Available Ebscohost No. 9510250477

Wells, T. (1996, February 11). Home-schooling movement finds legitimacy but it's still tough, despite test success. The Seattle Times, p. A15.

No period after item number.

11 DOCUMENTING SOURCES USING CHICAGO OR ALTERNATIVE STYLES

This chapter presents the *Chicago Manual of Style* documentation system and lists a variety of documentation guides used in different disciplines.

11a Use the *Chicago Manual of Style* system if your instructor requires it.

Some publications and instructors require the *Chicago Manual of Style* documentation system. For further information, consult the *Chicago Manual of Style,* Fourteenth Edition (1993).

Use superscript numbers for in-text citations.

Signal phrase.

Raised number after final punctuation.

```
Gordon points out that Mormons were continually charged
with "disloyalty to the national government . . .
Mormons were widely believed to pledge their first
loyalty to the church."2
```

The in-text citations are numbered consecutively throughout the essay and correspond to endnotes that appear in a list at the end.

Use numbered endnotes to list your sources.

Every numerical in-text citation must have a corresponding numerical endnote. Double-space endnotes, with the first line indented three spaces and subsequent lines flush with the left margin. List endnotes on a separate page at the end of the essay headed "Endnotes."

For a book:

One space.
One space.

```
   Number of citation. Author's first name Middle initial
Last name, Title of the Book (City of publication:
Publisher's name, year published), page number.
```

For a journal article:

One space.
One space.
One space.

```
   Number of citation. Author's first name Middle initial
Last name, "Title of Article," Title of Journal volume
number, no. issue number (Month year of publication): page
number.
```

The sample endnotes that follow demonstrate the Chicago format for the first entry for a source. For subsequent references to the same source, see item number 9.

DIGITAL HINT

Titles that have been underlined in the models that follow may be italicized instead, if you use a word processing program and your instructor allows you to use italics. (See 50a for more on using italics for titles.)

1. A book by a single author

11. Marion I. Arnold, Women and Art in South Africa (New York: St. Martin's Press, 1996), 111-17.

Endnote number is not raised.

2. A book by two or more authors

7. Tim Brooks and Earl Marsh, The Complete Directory to Prime Time Network TV Shows, 1946-Present (New York: Ballantine, 1985), 55.

All authors' names, as on the first or title page of the work.

3. A book with an unlisted author

4. Studies on the British Pottery Industry. (Keele, England: Keele University Library, 1969), 22.

Title of book.

City and country, if not U.S.A.

4. An article in an edited book

9. Nancy F. Cott, "Giving Character to our Whole Civil Polity: Marriage and the Public Order in the Late Nineteenth Century," in U.S. History as Women's History: New Feminist Essays, ed. Linda K. Gerber, Alice Kessler-Harris, and Kathryn Kish Sklar (Chapel Hill: University of North Carolina Press, 1995), 208-28.

Indicates book in which article appeared.

Indicates book editor or editors.

Year book published.

5. An article in a scholarly journal

1. Sarah Barringer Gordon, "The Liberty of Self-Degradation: Polygamy, Woman Suffrage, and Consent in Nineteenth-Century America," Journal of American History 83 (1996): 832.

No punctuation between journal title and volume number.

6. An article in a newspaper or magazine

8. Glenn Collins, "Trial Begins in Class-Action Suit on Secondhand Smoke," New York Times, 15 July 1997, sec. A, p. 10.

Day month year of publication.

Section number (if available) and page number.

7. Ed McEndarfer, "The Press-Molded Figure of Shiwan," Ceramics Monthly, April 1997, 63-65.

7. Audiovisual material

Title of work.

12. Easter Island, dir. Jose Gomez-Sicre, 25 min., Museum of Modern Art of Latin America, 1970, videocassette.

Indicates medium.

8. A World Wide Web page

The following model is taken from Andrew Harnack and Eugene Kleppinger, *Online! A Reference Guide to Using Internet Sources* (New York: St. Martin's, 1998).

Put title of entire work here, if given.

Indicates electronic address.

Date document accessed.

7. Rupert Austin, "The Mint Yard Gate," 2 October 1996, <http://www.hillside.co.uk/arch/mint/mint93.html> (13 May 1997).

Note: See p. 134 for guidelines on breaking electronic addresses between lines.

9. Subsequent references

For a reference that immediately follows a reference to the same source:

Refers to preceding entry.

6. Ibid., 829.

For a reference that does not immediately follow the same source:

Cite author's last name.

7. Gordon, 837.

The following sequence of entries from an endnote page demonstrates proper format for subsequent references:

1. Sarah Barringer Gordon, "The Liberty of Self Degradation: Polygamy, Woman Suffrage, and Consent in Nineteenth-Century America," Journal of American History 83 (1996): 832.

2. Ibid., 823-29.

3. Lawrence Foster, Women, Family, and Utopia: Communal Experiments of the Shakers, the Oneida Community, and the Mormons (Syracuse: Syracuse University Press, 1991), 207.

4. Gordon, 845.

Provide a bibliography in Chicago style if your instructor requires it.

A *bibliography*—a separate alphabetical listing of works used in the essay—may not be required if endnotes or footnotes are provided. Check with your instructor. Note that the first line of each entry is aligned against the left margin and subsequent lines are indented three spaces. Double-space within and between entries.

Sample Bibliography Format

Arnold, Marion I. Women and Art in South Africa. New York: St. Martin's Press, 1996.

Punctuation followed by one space.

Gordon, Sarah Barringer. "The Liberty of Self-Degradation: Polygamy, Woman Suffrage, and Consent in Nineteenth-Century America." Journal of American History 83 (1996): 815-47.

Page range for journal articles or works in a collection.

McEndarter, Ed. "The Press-Molded Figure of Shiwan." Ceramics Monthly, April 1997, 63-65.

Studies on the British Pottery Industry. Keele, England: Keele University Library, 1969.

Alphabetized by first word of title if author not named.

11b Depending on the requirements of a particular course, use the style manual that is required in the discipline you are studying.

Guidelines for three commonly used documentation styles are provided in *A Writer's Guidebook,* but you may find that a particular instructor requires you to use a style not covered in this book. One of the style manuals listed here may provide the help you need.

Biology, the Physical Sciences, Mathematics

Council of Biology Editors. *Scientific Style and Format: The CBE Manual for Authors, Editors, and Publishers.* 6th ed. Cambridge: Cambridge UP, 1994.

Chemistry

Dodd, Janet S., ed. *The ACS Style Guide: A Manual for Authors and Editors.* Washington: American Chemical Society, 1986.

Engineering

Information for IEEE Transactions and Journal Authors. New York: Institute of Electrical and Electronics Engineers, 1989.

Geology

Cochran, Wendell, Peter Fenner, and Mary Hills, eds. *Geowriting: A Guide to Writing, Editing, and Printing in Earth Science.* Alexandria, VA: American Geological Institute, 1984.

Journalism

Goldstein, Norm. *Associated Press Stylebook and Libel Manual.* Reading, MA: Addison, 1994.

Law

The Bluebook: A Uniform System of Citation. Comp. Editors of *Columbia Law Review* et al. 16th ed. Cambridge: Harvard Law Review, 1996.

Linguistics

Linguistic Society of America. LSA style sheet. *LSA Bulletin* Dec. 1996. (Published each year in the December issue.)

Mathematics

American Mathematical Society. *A Manual for Authors of Mathematical Papers.* Rev. ed. Providence: AMS, 1990.

Medicine

Iverson, Cheryl, et al. *American Medical Association Manual of Style.* 8th ed. Baltimore: Williams and Williams, 1989.

Music

Holoman, D. Kern, ed. *Writing about Music: A Style Sheet from the Editors of* Nineteenth-Century Music. Berkeley: U of California P, 1988.

Physics

American Institute of Physics. *AIP Style Manual.* 4th ed. New York: AIP, 1990.

12 STRATEGIES FOR ACTIVE, CRITICAL READING

Reading critically means not just comprehending and remembering what you read but also analyzing and evaluating it. When you read critically, you alternate between striving to understand the text on its own terms and taking care to question its ideas and authority.

Critical reading is also crucial for effective writing. By noting and reacting to the ideas in a reading, and the way they are expressed, you can begin to frame a thoughtful response in your own essay. You can also learn from the writers you are reading writing strategies you may be able to apply to your own writing situations.

Following are six major strategies for critical reading—strategies that you can learn quickly and use productively throughout your college career.

12a Annotate to become more involved.

To *annotate* means to mark a text as you read it, highlighting important information and noting questions, comments, and other reactions. Annotating increases your involvement with the text and gives you a valuable record of your reactions, a record that you may want to return to later to get ideas for writing. (If you borrowed the text, annotate a photocopy.)

Most readers annotate in layers, adding further annotations on second and third readings. Annotations can be light or heavy, depending on the reader's purpose and the difficulty of the material. Here are some tips.

Come up with a system for marking the text.

Before you start to read, decide on a system for marking the text. For example, you could underline important sentences, circle unfamiliar words, and bracket anything you question. You might connect ideas with lines and number related points in a sequence. Whatever system you use, you will want to jot down comments, questions, and other reactions in the margins.

Try to identify the main ideas.

To aid your understanding, try to express the main point of each paragraph by jotting a few words in the margin. If you can find the *thesis,* which states the main point of the essay, and topic sentences, which state the main ideas of individual paragraphs, mark or paraphrase them (see 3a and 3b). If you cannot find the thesis or topic sentences, try to infer the main point of the essay and each paragraph by asking yourself questions like these: "What is the point of this paragraph?" "What role does it play in furthering the essay's overall purpose?"

Do not be afraid to challenge what you read.

Do not think that, just because something is in print, it has special authority. If your own observations lead you to question an assertion or you find an explanation confusing, make a note of your questions and comments.

Following is an example of how a writer might annotate the Declaration of Independence. Since other strategies often are based on annotating, these annotations are referred to later. Add your own annotations, if you like.

Thomas Jefferson *(1743-1826), an accomplished lawyer, statesman, and revolutionary, became the third president of the United States in 1801. He may be best known, however, for writing the Declaration of Independence, the famous document* *that put forth the American colonies' reasons for forming an independent nation, free from the oppressive rule of Britain's King George III. In truth, the Declaration of Independence was a collaborative effort, based on Jefferson's consultation with Benjamin Franklin, John Adams, and the Continental Congress.*

An Annotated Sample from the Declaration of Independence

THOMAS JEFFERSON

IN CONGRESS, JULY 4, 1776
THE UNANIMOUS DECLARATION OF
THE THIRTEEN UNITED STATES OF AMERICA

1 When in the Course of human events, it becomes necessary for one people to dissolve the political bands which have connected them with another, and to assume among the Powers of the earth, the separate and equal station to which the Laws of Nature and of Nature's God entitle them, a decent respect to the opinions of mankind requires that they should declare the cause which impel them to the separation.

> **Like wedding bands or shackles**
>
> **Invokes God, but why Nature?**
>
> **Reasons must be declared—explained, justified?**

2 We hold these truths to be self-evident, that all men are created equal, that they are endowed by their Creator with certain unalienable Rights, that among these are Life, Liberty and the pursuit of Happiness. That to secure these rights, Governments are instituted among Men, deriving their just powers from the consent of the governed. That whenever any Form of Government becomes destructive of these ends, it is the Right of the People to alter or to abolish it, and to institute new Government, laying its foundation on such principles and organizing its powers in such form, as to them shall seem most likely to effect their Safety and Happiness. Prudence, indeed, will dictate that Governments long established should not be

> **If a government interferes with basic human rights, people have a right to abolish it and set up a new government.**
>
> **Is happiness really a right?**
>
> **"Men" supposed to include women.**
>
> **Why are so many words capitalized?**
>
> **Good judgment/ caution**

Quickly changing

demonstrates

to take what belongs to another

People are willing to put up with a lot, but king has pushed too far.

King has shown a history of repeated abuses, including
—refusal/neglect to pass laws that help colonists (3–4)
—obstruction of legislative representation (5–8)
—obstruction of colonial systems of justice (10–11)
—use of officers who harass people (12)
—unjust use of military power (13–14)

changed for light and transient causes; and accordingly all experience hath shown, that mankind are more disposed to suffer, while evils are sufferable, than to right themselves by abolishing the forms to which they are accustomed. But when a long train of abuses and usurpations pursuing invariably the same Object evinces a design to reduce them under absolute Despotism, it is their right, it is their duty, to throw off such Government, and to provide new Guards for their future security.—Such has been the patient sufferance of these Colonies; and such is now the necessity which constrains them to alter their former Systems of Government. The history of the present King of Great Britain is a history of repeated injuries and usurpations, all having in direct object the establishment of an absolute Tyranny over these States. To prove this, let Facts be submitted to a candid world.

Each reason gets own ¶

All ¶s begin with "He"—points finger of blame.

3 He had refused his Assent to Laws, the most wholesome and necessary for the public good.

4 He has forbidden his Governors to pass Laws of immediate and pressing importance, unless suspended in their operation till his Assent should be obtained; and when so suspended, he has utterly neglected to attend to them.

5 He has refused to pass other laws for the accommodation of large districts of people, unless those people would relinquish the right of Representation in the Legislature, a right inestimable to them and formidable to tyrants only.

give up

6 He has called together legislative bodies at places unusual, uncomfortable, and distant from the depository of their Public Records, for the sole purpose of fatiguing them into compliance with his measures.

7 He has dissolved Representative Houses repeatedly, for opposing with manly firmness his invasions on the rights of the people.

8 He has refused for a long time, after such dissolutions, to cause others to be elected; whereby the Legislative Powers, incapable of Annihilation, have returned to the People at large for their exercise; the State remaining in the mean time exposed to all the dangers of invasion from without, and convulsions within.

9 He has endeavoured to prevent the population of these States, for that purpose obstructing the Laws for Naturalization of Foreigners; refusing to pass others to encourage their migration hither, and raising the conditions of new Appropriations of Lands.

What does this mean? Trying to keep them small and powerless?

Legal system and army under king's power

10 He has obstructed the Administration of Justice, by refusing his Assent to Laws for establishing Judiciary Powers.

11 He has made Judges dependent on his Will alone, for the tenure of their offices, and the amount and payment of their salaries.

12 He has erected a multitude of New Offices, and sent hither swarms of Officers to harass our People, and eat out their substance.

Wear them down? Vivid image.

13 He has kept among us, in times of peace, Standing Armies without the Consent of our legislature.

14 He has affected to render the Military independent of and superior to the Civil Power.

King has allowed corrupt laws to be imposed over laws of colonies. These laws —force troops on colonies (16)—

15 He has combined with others to subject us to a jurisdiction foreign to our constitution, and unacknowledged by our laws; giving his Assent to their acts of pretended Legislation:

16 For quartering large bodies of armed troops among us:

Now ¶s begin with "For"—why?

—protect troops, even from murder charges (17)
—cut off trade and impose taxes (18–19)
—impede fair, rightful trials (20–21)
—interfere with colonists' self-governance (22–24)

17 For protecting them, by a mock Trial, from Punishment for any Murders which they should commit on the Inhabitants of these States:

18 For cutting off our Trade with all parts of the world:

19 For imposing taxes on us without our Consent:

20 For depriving us in many cases, of the benefits of Trial by Jury:

21 For transporting us beyond Seas to be tried for pretended offences:

22 For abolishing the free System of English Laws in a neighbouring Province, establishing therein an Arbitrary government, and enlarging its Boundaries so as to render it at once an example and fit instrument for introducing the same absolute rule into these Colonies:

Colonies should have same laws as British.

23 For taking away our Charters, abolishing our most valuable Laws, and altering fundamentally the Forms of our Governments:

24 For suspending our own Legislatures, and declaring themselves invested with Power to legislate for us in all cases whatsoever.

King has given up his right to rule colonists by declaring war on them.
He's declared war by:
—invading colonists at sea and on land (26)
—using foreign troops against them (27)

25 He has abdicated Government here, by declaring us out of his Protection and waging War against us.

Back to ¶s beginning with "He"—why?

26 He has plundered our seas, ravaged our Coasts, burnt our towns, and destroyed the lives of our people.

27 He is at this time transporting large armies of foreign mercenaries to compleat the works of death, desolation and tyranny, already begun with circumstances of Cruelty & perfidy scarcely paralleled in the most barbarous ages, and totally unworthy the Head of a civilized nation.

Paid soldiers

Calculated violation of trust

28 He has constrained our fellow Citizens taken Captive on the high Seas to bear Arms against their

—capturing Americans at sea and forcing them to fight or die (28)
—creating violence and unrest in the colonies (29)

Country, to become the executioners of their friends and Brethren, or to fall themselves by their Hands.

29 He has excited domestic insurrections amongst us, and has endeavoured to bring on the inhabitants of our frontiers, the merciless Indian Savages, whose known rule of warfare, is an undistinguished destruction of all ages, sexes and conditions.

On what basis does Jefferson make these claims?

King hasn't listened to colonists' pleas for relief; thus he's unfit to rule them.

30 In every stage of these Oppressions We have Petitioned for Redress in the most humble terms: Our repeated Petitions have been answered only by repeated injury. A Prince, whose character is thus marked by every act which may define a Tyrant, is unfit to be the ruler of a free People.

31 Nor have We been wanting in attention to our British brethren. We have warned them from time to time of attempts by their legislature to extend an unwarrantable jurisdiction over us. We have reminded them of the circumstances of our emigration and settlement here. We have appealed to their native justice and magnanimity, and we have conjured them by the ties of our common kindred to disavow these usurpations, which, would inevitably interrupt our connections and correspondence. They too have been deaf to the voice of justice and of consanguinity. We must, therefore, acquiesce in the necessity, which denounces our Separation, and hold them, as we hold the rest of mankind, Enemies in War, in Peace Friends.

Still calls British brothers; why?

generosity

British people have also ignored pleas for justice.

close relationship

32 We, therefore, the Representatives of the United States of America, in General Congress, Assembled, appealing to the Supreme Judge of the world for the rectitude of our intentions, do, in the Name, and by Authority of the good People of these Colonies, solemnly publish and declare, That these United Colonies are, and of Right ought to be Free and Independ-

Appeals to God

uprightness

Colonies declare themselves free; they have all powers of independent states.

ent States, that they are Absolved from all Allegiance to the British Crown, and that all political connection between them and the State of Great Britain, is and ought to be totally dissolved; and that as Free and Independent States, they have full Power to levy War, conclude Peace, contract Alliances, establish Commerce, and to do all other Acts and Things which Independent States may of right do. And for the support of this Declaration, with a firm reliance on the Protection of Divine Providence, we mutually pledge to each other our Lives, our Fortunes and our sacred Honor.

Claims full rights of an independent nation.

Assumes God approves

12b Outline the reading to clarify its content and structure.

Outlining is an especially helpful strategy for understanding the content and structure of a reading. The key to outlining is distinguishing between the main ideas and supporting material, such as reasons, examples, factual evidence, and explanations. The main ideas form the backbone, which holds the various parts and pieces of the text together. Outlining the main ideas helps you uncover this structure.

If you jot down the main idea of each paragraph as you annotate a reading, you have made a good start on an outline. In fact, you may want to list these main ideas—putting some of them in your own words, if necessary—to form a *scratch outline* like the following:

—When it becomes necessary for political bonds to be broken, the reasons should be declared and explained.

—If a government interferes with basic human rights, people have a right to abolish it and set up a new government.

—The king of England has shown a history of repeated abuses.

—The king has allowed corrupt laws to be imposed over the laws of the colonies.

—He has given up his right to rule the colonists by declaring war on them.
—He has not listened to the colonists' pleas for relief; thus, he is unfit to rule them.
—The colonies declare themselves free. They have all the powers of independent states.

A *formal outline* is generally longer and more detailed than a scratch outline. It also shows the relationship between the text's main ideas and supporting material. Therefore, making a formal outline requires considerable planning.

The following outline of the Declaration of Independence uses a formal structure, with roman numerals indicating main ideas or claims, capital letters indicating the reasons, and arabic numerals indicating the supporting evidence and explanation. (The numbers following the supporting statements correspond to the evidence numbered in the annotated Declaration on pp. 185–190.)

I. When it becomes necessary for one people to separate from another, the reasons for this separation should be declared.
   A. The English government has become destructive of basic rights of colonists; therefore, colonists have a right to abolish that government and form a new one.
      1. Governments derive their power from the consent of the ruled.
      2. Because of the long-time abuses of the British government, colonists can no longer consent to British rule.
   B. The King of England has shown a history of repeated injuries and abuses of power.
      1. He has refused/neglected to pass laws that help colonists (3–4).
      2. He has obstructed colonists' efforts to be represented fairly in the legislature (5–8).
      3. He has obstructed colonial systems of justice (10–11).
      4. He has used officers to harass colonists (12).
      5. He has used military power unjustly (13–14).
   C. The king has allowed corrupt laws to be imposed over the laws of the colonists.

1. He has allowed laws that force troops on the colonies and protect troops, even from murder charges (16–17).
2. He has allowed laws that cut off trade to the colonies and that impose taxes on them (18–19).
3. He has allowed laws that impede fair, rightful trials (20–21).
4. He has allowed laws that interfere with colonies' self-governance (22–24).

D. The king has essentially declared war on the colonies.

1. He has invaded colonists at sea and on land (26).
2. He has used foreign troops against them (27).
3. He has captured Americans at sea and forced them to fight against their fellow Americans (28).
4. He has created violence and unrest in the colonies (29).

E. The king hasn't listened to the colonists' pleas for justice, nor have the British people.

II. Given these reasons, the colonies, under their own authority, declare themselves free and independent states, with all the rights of independent states.

Note: A formal outline may be most helpful when you are doing an in-depth analysis of a reading, but a scratch outline listing the main ideas will be sufficient for most critical reading purposes.

12c Summarize main ideas.

Summarizing helps the reader to understand and remember what is most important in the reading. It also creates a condensed version of the reading that can be referred to or inserted into the reader's own text.

A summary is a relatively brief restatement, mostly in the reader's own words, of the reading's main ideas. Many writers find it helpful to outline the reading prior to writing a summary. But writing a summary requires more than merely stringing together the entries in an outline. A summary has to connect the ideas. To write a summary, you do more than translate the author's meaning into your own words; you have to make decisions about what ideas are most important and how they relate to one another.

In writing a summary, you may quote words or phrases from the original passage, if the author's wording is particularly expressive. You also may cite the title and refer to the author by name, as in the following example showing how one writer summarized the Declaration of Independence.

> Jefferson's careful construction of the Declaration of Independence makes it one of the most forceful public documents of all time. He begins rather blandly, saying simply that when a nation decides to break its ties to another, that nation should declare the reasons for the separation. From then on, however, his argument gains momentum as he lists, in detail, the many reasons that the American colonies should abolish the British government's oppressive rule and establish a new government, one that upholds the rights of "Life, Liberty and the pursuit of Happiness." Among these reasons are King George III's long history of obstructing justice and fair legislative representation in the colonies, his support for corrupt laws that cut off trade to the colonies and impose taxes on them, and his use of military force against Americans.
>
> The sheer number of abuses by the British government, and the way that Jefferson lists them—giving each one its own paragraph for emphasis—prepares readers to accept his powerful, seemingly inevitable conclusion: that the colonies, under their own authority, must declare themselves free and independent states, with all of the rights of independent states.

Like many summaries, this one is directed toward a purpose beyond merely giving the gist. It makes an evaluative argument about the way Jefferson constructed the Declaration of Independence. Notice, for example, the evaluative language throughout this summary: "careful construction," "most forceful," "begins rather blandly," "gains momentum." Summaries such as this are often used in argumentative as well as in explanatory essays. (See 8a for more on summarizing.)

12d Take inventory of your annotations; look for patterns.

When you take inventory, you make various kinds of lists to explore the patterns of meaning you find in the text. Listing and grouping annotations of a certain type—those that point out, say, recurring ideas, images, aspects of style, or examples—can help you to identify patterns and to determine what those patterns indicate about the reading.

By scanning the annotations of the Declaration of Independence, for instance, you can see that a number of them refer to Jefferson's writing style (his capitalization of certain words, the way he breaks out injustices into separate paragraphs, the way he adds force to his argument by beginning many sentences with "He" or "For"). Grouping observations in this way can help you find a perspective for an interesting interpretive essay.

12e Reflect on the writer's perspective.

You can enrich your analysis of a text by considering the social, cultural, or historical perspective from which it was written. Consider questions like these: What are the author's attitudes, assumptions, or values, and how might they differ from your own? How have the author's views been shaped by the place or time in which the piece was written? (If you have no knowledge of the time or place through other reading or from films, you might want to do some research.)

To give an example, many readers today might take offense at Jefferson's apparent exclusion of women in his Declaration of Independence. He refers to "men," "mankind," and "brethren" and never once mentions women. Do you think Jefferson intends to say that only men are entitled to basic rights, or is he merely using a writing convention of his time? Consider also that the Constitution withheld the right to vote from women and African Americans.

12f Evaluate the writer's logic.

An essential part of critical reading is evaluating the logic of a writer's argument to determine whether the support for the thesis is sound and complete. For an argument to be considered logically acceptable, it must meet three conditions of what we call the ABC test:

A. The reasons and other support (facts, examples, and quotations) must be *appropriate* to the thesis.

B. All of the reasons and support must be *believable.*

C. The reasons and support must be *consistent* with one another as well as *complete.*

Test the argument's support for appropriateness.

As a critical reader, you must decide whether the argument's reasons and support are appropriate and clearly related to the thesis. To test for appropriateness, ask, how does each reason or piece of support relate to the thesis? Is the connection between the reasons and support and the thesis clear and compelling, or are parts of the argument irrelevant or only vaguely related to the thesis?

Readers often question the appropriateness of an argument when it invokes a rule or authority that they do not necessarily accept. In his opening paragraph, for instance, Jefferson implies that the American colonies should be freed from British rule because of an entitlement under the "Laws of Nature" and "Nature's God." You might judge whether it is appropriate to appeal to such authorities in making a political argument.

Here are some of the common flaws, called *logical fallacies,* that can cause an argument to fail the test of appropriateness:

- *False analogy,* when two cases are not sufficiently parallel to lead readers to accept the thesis.
- *False use of authority,* when a writer invokes as an expert in the field being discussed a person or people whose expertise or authority lies not in the given field but in another.
- *Non sequitur* (Latin for "it does not follow"), when one statement is not logically connected to another.
- *Red herring,* when a writer raises an irrelevant issue to draw attention away from the central issue.
- *Post hoc, ergo propter hoc* (Latin for "after this, therefore because of this"), when a writer implies that because one event follows another, the first caused the second. Chronology is not the same as causality.

Test reasons and support for believability.

You must also look critically at each statement, giving reasons or support for the thesis to see whether it is believable. You may find some reasons or support self-evidently true and the truth of others less certain. To test for believability, ask, "On what basis am I being asked to accept this reason or support as true? If it cannot be proved true or false, how much weight does it carry?"

In testing for believability, consider the following points.

Facts are statements that can be proved objectively to be true. The believability of facts depends on their *accuracy* (they should not distort or misrepresent reality), their *completeness* (they should not omit important details), and the *trustworthiness* of their sources (sources should be qualified). Jefferson, for example, refers to "the merciless Indian Savages, whose known rule of warfare, is an indistinguished destruction of all ages, sexes and conditions" (paragraph 29). Critics might question the accuracy of this statement, not to mention the prejudicial word choice.

Statistics, often mistaken as facts, are actually interpretations of numerical data. The believability of statistics depends on the *comparability* of the data (apples cannot be compared to oranges), the *precision* of the methods employed to gather and analyze data (representative samples should be used and variables accounted for), and the *trustworthiness* of the sources (sources should be qualified and unbiased).

Examples and *anecdotes* strengthen argumentative writing by clarifying the meaning and dramatizing the point. The believability of examples depends on their *representativeness* (whether they are truly typical and thus generalizable) and their specificity (whether particular details make them seem true to life). For instance, consider how Jefferson's argument is strengthened by the many examples he provides of King George III's abuses of power (in paragraphs 3–14).

Authorities are people to whom the writer attributes expertise on a given subject. The believability of authorities depends on whether readers accept them as experts.

In addition, you should be aware of the following fallacies in reasoning that undermine the believability of an argument:

- *Begging the question,* when the believability of the reasons and support depends on the believability of the thesis. Another name for this kind of fallacy is *circular reasoning.*
- *Failing to accept the burden of proof,* when a writer asserts a thesis but provides no reasons or support for it.
- *Hasty generalization,* when a writer asserts a thesis on the basis of a single reason or an isolated example.
- *Sweeping generalization,* when a writer fails to qualify the thesis and asserts that it applies to *all* instances instead of to *some* instances.
- *Overgeneralization,* when a writer fails to qualify the thesis and asserts that it is *certainly true* rather than that it *may be true.*

Test reasons and support for consistency and completeness.

In looking for consistency, make sure that none of the reasons or support contradict any of the other reasons or support. In addition, the reasons and support, taken together, should be sufficient to convince readers to accept the thesis or at least take it seriously. To test for consistency and completeness, ask, are any of the reasons and support contradictory? Do they provide sufficient grounds for accepting the thesis? Has the writer failed to counterargue by refuting any opposing arguments or important objections?

Reading critically, you might ask why Jefferson lists so many of the king's abuses of power instead of supporting his argument with more details about the most serious abuses, or how a slaveowner like Jefferson could speak of God-given rights.

In evaluating the consistency and completeness of an argument, you should also be aware of the following types of fallacies:

- *Slippery slope,* when a writer argues that taking one step will lead inevitably to a next step, one that is undesirable.
- *Equivocation,* when a writer uses the same term in two different senses.
- *Oversimplification,* when an argument obscures or denies the complexity of the issue.

- *Either-or reasoning,* when a writer reduces the issue to only two alternatives that are polar opposites.
- *Double standard,* when comparable things are judged according to different standards; for example, holding the opposing argument to a higher standard than one's own.

12g Consider collecting your reactions to readings in a journal.

You may find it helpful to record in a journal your reactions to readings, as well as to lectures and other course material. Writing in a journal can not only help you find essay ideas that connect or draw on several readings, but also open up new ways of exploring and expressing ideas.

To develop the habit of keeping a journal, start by writing one brief entry every day, just a few sentences. Jot down any questions or reactions that occur to you. Quote or paraphrase passages you think are important or you do not understand.

Some writers keep a double-entry journal, in which they write summaries of or excerpts from a text on one side of a notebook and record comments about this material on the other side. Others prefer a more free-form mix of excerpts from and reactions to readings. Experiment with these and other approaches to find one that works well for you.

PART 3 DESIGNING DOCUMENTS

PART

3 DESIGNING DOCUMENTS

13 PREPARING A FINAL DOCUMENT

Always turn in a clean, error-free text. Use 8½- by 11-inch sheets of plain, white, nonerasable paper; type or print on one side only. Most instructors require typed or word-processed documents; however, if you are submitting a handwritten document, write clearly and neatly in blue or black ink, again using only one side of the page. If you use a typewriter, use a fresh ribbon to ensure legibility; if erasures and smudges mar your document, hand in a photocopy. If you work on a computer, use the best printer available.

Keep a back-up copy, and save outlines and preliminary drafts until the course is over in case you need to reconstruct a lost project, to defend yourself against a charge of plagiarism, or to complete a subsequent assignment.

13a Place the heading and title of your essay on the first page if you are using MLA style.

Double-space the heading at the left margin, one inch from the top of the page. On separate lines, type your name, your instructor's name, the course name and number, and the date. Double-space again and center your title, taking care to follow the rules for capitalizing titles (see 47d).

Double-space everything in the body of your essay (including source citations and block quotations), and begin each paragraph by indenting five spaces or one-half inch. Use one-inch margins throughout, except for the running head, which is placed one-half inch below the top edge of the page. Align (justify) your text at the left margin only.

For a sample student essay formatted in the MLA style, see 9d.

13b Create an informative running head to number pages.

For MLA style, create a *running head* or *header* aligned with the right margin, consisting of your last name and the current page number. (Word processing software can insert the running head automatically.) For APA style, the running head includes a shortened version of the title and the page number. (For examples of running heads, see the sample student essays in 9d [MLA] and 10d [APA].)

13c If necessary, create a title page.

Create a title page only if title pages are commonly used in your discipline or if your instructor has requested a title page. Center your title about one-third of the way down the page, taking care to follow the rules for capitalizing titles (see 47d). Type your name in centered text about three inches from the bottom of the page. On separate lines below your name, type your instructor's name, the course name and number, and the date. Double-space and center these lines. (For a description of a title page in APA style, see 10d.)

13d Use text headings to forecast the content and organization of your essay or report.

In some disciplines, essays are formatted according to established conventions. In the sciences, for instance, research reports consist of an introduction, a methods section, a results section, and a conclusions section. Each of these sections is labeled with a text heading indicating its content (see the sample lab report in 15f).

Consider using headings in any report longer than a few pages. To be effective, they must be visually distinct from the body of the text—with a different type font for headings or such font attributes as boldface or italics (see 14b). Likewise, headings for major sections (level-one headings) must be visually distinct from subheadings that subdivide major sections (level-two headings).

LEVEL-ONE HEADING

Level-Two Heading

Be consistent in where you place your headings and with all other aspects of heading design: type font and size, boldface, italics, capitalization, and so on. Consistency helps readers to distinguish among major sections (and subsections).

Finally, in drafting headings, try to be as informative as possible. Headings should help your reader understand the content and organization of the material that follows.

Vague:	Critical Responses
Informative:	Critical Responses to the Language Poets

14 SPECIAL DESIGN FEATURES

Computers make it easy for you to design and extensively format documents, using various type fonts, text attributes such as boldface and italics, columns, and vertical and horizontal lines. But what you *can* do with a computer is not necessarily what you *should* do.

14a Find out what formatting conventions your instructor expects you to follow.

Your instructor may require students to format essays according to a particular style. For an example of an essay formatted in MLA style, see 9d; for APA style, see 10d. If your instructor has no specific requirements, you could use the MLA style as a model.

14b Be conservative in your use of type styles and text attributes.

For most word processed papers, use a 12-point type font such as Courier or Times New Roman. Avoid using more than one or two fonts, and avoid unusual fonts within the same essay, such as **casual fonts** and *fonts that* mimic cursive writing; both are difficult to read and inappropriate for most academic essays. Also avoid setting long passages of text in **boldface** or *italics*; such long passages are difficult to read.

14c Use icons, symbols, and other atypical features appropriately.

Check with your instructor to be sure you understand what he or she expects before using icons, symbols, and other atypical features. If you are preparing tables, charts, or other visuals in which these atypical features may be appropriate, ask for your instructor's advice on incorporating these features into your visuals. For more information on visuals, see 14d.

Inappropriate: Originally, the theater was shaped like ∩.

Appropriate: Originally, the theater was shaped like a horseshoe.

14d Use visuals to add interest and convey information.

Charts, graphs, tables, diagrams, drawings, maps, and photographs add visual interest and are often more effective at conveying information than prose alone. Be certain, however, that each visual has a role to play in the document; if a visual would be mere decoration, leave it out.

You can create visuals on a computer, using the drawing tools of a word processing program, the charting tools of a spreadsheet program, or software specifically designed for creating visuals. You can also download visuals from the World Wide Web (see 7d), or photocopy visuals from print materials. (See p. 206 on citing the source of a borrowed visual or a visual based on borrowed information.)

Choose the appropriate visual.

Choose the visual best suited to your purpose. The following list shows the purpose to which different visuals are best suited.

- *Table:* Displays numerical data and other types of information for one or more items, usually including variables for each item (for example, the number of soldiers listed as dead, missing, or wounded following six different Civil War battles: six items, three variables). See Table 1 on page 206.

- *Bar graph:* Compares the values of two or more items (for example, the median salaries of psychologists and counselors). Figure 1, on page 206, is an example of a bar graph.
- *Line graph:* Shows change over time (for example, the change in reading comprehension as students progress from fourth to fifth grade). The student essay in 9d contains an example of a line graph (see p. 147).
- *Pie chart:* Shows the percentage of parts making up a whole. Figure 2 on page 207 is an example of a pie chart.
- *Flowchart:* Shows the stages in a process and their relationships.
- *Organization chart:* Shows the lines of authority within an organization (who reports to whom).
- *Diagram:* Depicts an item or its properties, often using symbols. Diagrams are usually used to show relationships or how things function. Figure 3 on page 207 is an example of a diagram.
- *Drawing:* Shows a simplified version of an object.
- *Map:* Shows geographical areas and spatial relationships of objects.
- *Photograph:* Duplicates what the eye sees.
- *Screen Shot:* Duplicates the appearance of a computer screen.

Create titles, label the parts, and cite your sources.

Number your visuals in sequential order, and create a title for each visual. Refer to tables as Table 1, Table 2, and so on, and other types of visuals as Figure 1, Figure 2, and so on. Make your title reflect both the subject of the visual (unemployment rates) and its purpose (to illustrate changes in those unemployment rates: *Figure 1. Changes in Unemployment Rates for Owyhee County: 1990–1995*). Generally, in student essays the title for a table is placed above the table; titles for figures are placed below the figure.

Table 1
Changes in the Number (in millions) and Percentage of U.S. Households in Three Income Ranges, 1970–1994.[a]

	Less than $25,000		$25,000 to $74,999		$75,000 or more	
Year	Number	Percent	Number	Percent	Number	Percent
1970	25.3	39.1%	35.0	54.1%	4.4	6.8%
1975	29.4	40.3	38.0	52.1	5.5	7.5
1980	32.5	39.4	42.1	51.1	7.8	9.5
1985	34.4	38.9	43.9	49.6	10.2	11.5
1990	35.3	37.4	46.5	49.3	12.5	13.3
1994	39.0	39.4	46.5	47.0	13.5	13.6

[a]Income is reported in 1994 CPI-U-XI adjusted U.S. dollars.
Source: U.S. Census Bureau.

To help readers understand the visual, clearly label all of its parts. In a table, for instance, give each column a heading; likewise, label each section of a pie chart with the percentage and item it represents.

Finally, cite the source of the visual or the source of the information it contains. If you borrow a visual from another document, or create a visual

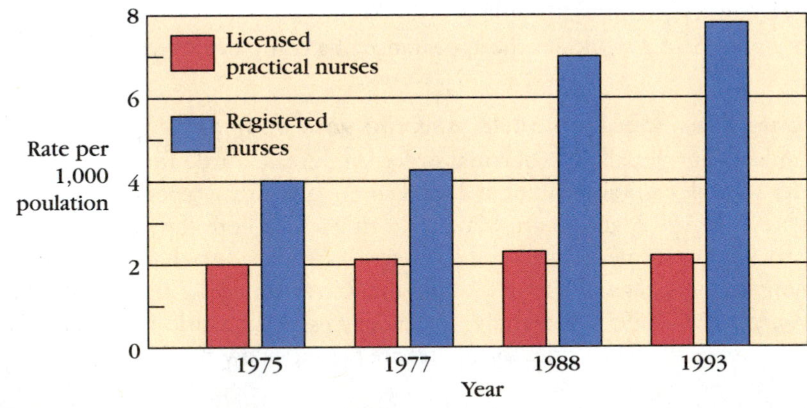

Figure 1. Active Michigan Nurses per 1,000 Population, Selected Years
Source: Michigan Department of the State Registrar and Division of Health Statistics, Michigan Department of Community Health.

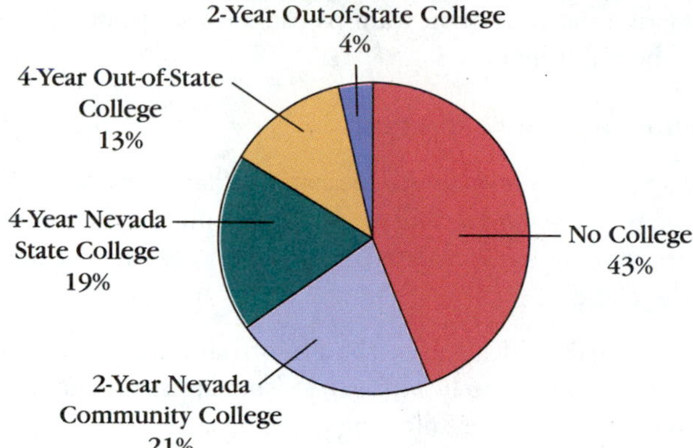

Figure 2. College Choice of All Respondents.

from borrowed information, cite your source in a note as shown in Table 1 and Figure 1 on page 206.

Note: If your essay containing a borrowed visual is to be published (for instance, on a Web page or in the campus newspaper), you must obtain written permission from the author, publisher, or organization holding the copyright. Write a letter asking permission to use the visual: Identify

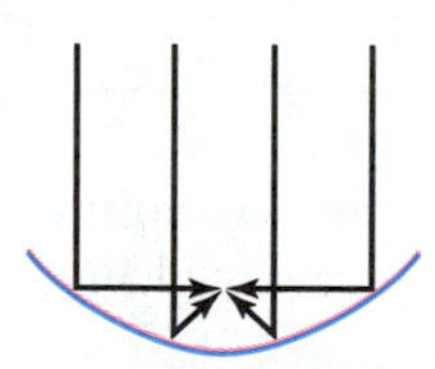

Parabolic: Perfectly focuses parallel rays, but from one direction only; must be aimed.

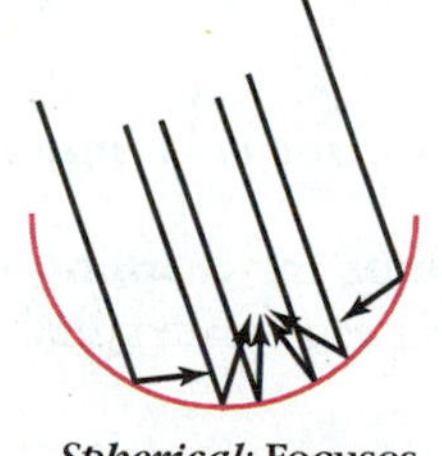

Spherical: Focuses imperfectly, but equally well from any direction; does not need to be aimed.

Together: The circle of curvature nearly coincides with the parabola near the vertex.

Figure 3. A Liquid Reflector Telescope.
Source: Mare Frantz, Indiana University, Purdue University Indianapolis

yourself, describe the visual you want to use, how you intend to use it, and where it will be published.

Integrate the visual into the text.

Place the visual in an appropriate location. Place a visual in the body of your document if the reader will need to consult it. Place a visual in an appendix if it contains supplemental information that may or may not be of interest to the reader.

Introduce the visual. Ideally, you should introduce each visual by referring to it in your text, immediately *before* the visual appears. The most effective textual references answer the following questions.

- What is the number of the visual?
- Where is the visual located?
- What kind of information does it contain?
- What important point (if any) does the visual make or support?

Here is what an effective introduction looks like:

> Unemployment rates for Owyhee County (1990-1995) are shown in Figure 1, page 8. Note the sharp increase in unemployment beginning in the first quarter of 1994. This increase coincides with the closure of the Pioneer Silver Mine.

If the visual is on the same page, use *below* instead of the page number.

Use the following guidelines for creating visuals on a computer.

If you use a computer program to create visuals, keep several guidelines in mind.

- **Make the decisions that your computer cannot make for you.** A computer can automatically turn spreadsheet data into a pie chart or a bar graph, but only you can decide which visual is most appropriate.

- **Avoid "chart junk."** Many computer programs provide an array of special effects that can be used to alter visuals, including three-dimensional renderings, textured backgrounds, and shadowed text. Such special effects often detract from the message of the visual.
- **Use clip art sparingly.** Clip art consists of icons, symbols, and other simple drawings you can use to identify recurring topics. Because clip art simplifies ideas, it is of limited use in conveying complex information.
- **Design the visual with its final use in mind.** If you plan to incorporate a computer-generated visual into an overhead transparency, try to envision what you see on the computer screen as it would appear enlarged on a projection screen. Similarly, if you are designing the visual for use on a Web page, consider how the visual will appear when displayed by Web-browsing software (see 15g).

15 DIFFERENT KINDS OF DOCUMENTS

The following sections offer examples of documents that are commonly written in college or the workplace.

15a Use memos and email messages to communicate with associates.

A memorandum (or memo) is used within an organization for various purposes, including announcements, proposals, and inquiries. Email is an electronic memo sent over a computer network from one user of the network to one or more other users. In many organizations, email messages are replacing handwritten or typed memos, and in some classes, students and instructors rely on email to exchange information about assignments and scheduling as well as to follow up on class discussions. Email messages are usually concise, direct, and informal. They are usually formatted like paper memos and limited to a single subject. Effective memos include a clear subject line.

Begin by stating the main point, with additional information provided in subsequent paragraphs. Consider using headings to organize your material and bulleted or numbered lists to make your points stand out.

In anything other than quick emails to friends, you should maintain a professional tone. Avoid sarcasm and humor, which may not come across as you intend, and be sure to proofread and spell-check your message before sending it. Finally, since email messages are accessible to many people other than the person to whom you are writing, be careful about what you write in an email message. The memo and email messages on pages 211–212 are typical examples. Note the more formal tone of the memo.

15b Compose business letters that represent you and your organization effectively.

The business letter is the document most often used for correspondence between representatives of one organization and representatives of another (though email messages are increasingly being used in place of business letters). Like most other workplace documents, a business letter is written to obtain information about a company's products, to register a complaint, to respond to a complaint, or to introduce other documents (such as a proposal) that accompany the letter.

State the purpose of your letter in the first few lines, and provide supporting information in the paragraphs that follow. Maintain a courteous and professional tone throughout the letter. Avoid using such stilted clichés as *enclosed herewith* or *as per your letter of Wednesday last.* Use a standard format, such as the full-block format shown on page 213.

15c Prepare a resumé that effectively represents you and your accomplishments.

A resumé is used to acquaint a prospective employer with your work experience, education, and accomplishments. All resumés contain such information

A Sample Memo

SMITH AND KLEIN ASSOCIATES
MEMORANDUM

TO: Mary Reynolds, Vice President
FROM: Fred Rivera, Account Manager
DATE: February 25, 1997
SUBJECT: The Staley Pharmaceutical Presentation

The president and advertising director for Staley Pharmaceutical will be in on Tuesday, March 4, to review ideas and preliminary sketches. The presentation will be held in the ninth floor conference room from 9:30 a.m. until noon. We have prepared a complete campaign for their new cold tablet, including television and radio spots and print advertisements. We can expect them to raise the following issues during the meeting.

- **Budget:** Our proposed budget is significantly higher than the original estimate (see the figures attached). The higher numbers reflect their additional requests after the estimate was prepared.
- **Schedule:** Staley plans to bring the product to market on November 1. The advertising campaign is scheduled to begin in mid-October. This schedule will be tight, and we may not be able to meet our deadlines without increasing our costs.

Please let me know if you will be available to attend all or part of the meeting on March 4.

cc: Greg Miller, Senior Designer
Nora Katz, Sales Manager

Subject line states clearly what the memo is about.

Main point stated in the first sentence.

Formal, businesslike tone.

Bulleted list.

Request for action.

A Sample Email Message

Identifying information, formatted like a paper memo.

Accurate, informative subject line.

From: Paula_Garrison@varnay.idbsu.edu
Date: Mon, 5 May 1997 16:00:45-0600
Subject: Suggested Questions for the Panelists Visiting SW-312
To: "Kevin S. Manderino" <kmand@varnay.idbsu.edu>
CC: "Kay Warner" <kwarn@varnay.idbsu.edu>, "Renee Peña" <rpena@varnay.idbsu.edu>

Casual but professional tone.

Hello, everyone.
Just a reminder that Professor Haberer asked our group to come up with some questions for the three social workers who will be visiting SW-312. Since the next class is only a couple of days away, I thought I would get the discussion going by sending you some suggested questions. I took a quick look at the chapter on career opportunities and came up with the following questions:

Numbered list.

1. What education and experience is necessary for the work you do?
2. What is a typical day on the job like for you?
3. What do you like best about the work you do? What do you like least?
4. What projects are you currently working on? What challenges or problems do those projects pose?
5. How has the work you do changed over the last few years? How do you expect it to change in the next few years?

That's about all I can come up with. Feel free to add to the list or change these questions. Email me your suggestions, and I'll put together a final list. I think we'll need at least ten questions, but that's just a guess.

See you in class.

A Sample Business Letter

METROTYPE
409 South 8th Street
Pawkett, KY 45397
Phone: 502.555.1234 Fax: 502.555.4321 Email: type@micran.net

January 23, 1997

Mr. Carl Boyer
Boyer Advertising Co.
1714 North 20th Street, Suite 16
Pawkett, KY 45397

Dear Mr. Boyer:

Thank you for your letter of January 20, 1997. You asked whether MetroType could provide one of your clients with mail-merged letters after first converting your client's files from WordPerfect to Microsoft Word. We certainly can. As I mentioned on the phone earlier today, creating mail-merge documents is one of our key services, and we frequently convert word processing files for customers who are moving from one program to another.

Much of the file conversion is done automatically; however, we have noticed that some parts of a file (such as accented characters and graphics) aren't always converted accurately. For this reason, we will compare a printout of your client's original files to a printout of the converted files and then make whatever corrections are necessary. For an additional fee, we can also proofread the final documents. If your client is interested in having us proofread the documents, I would be happy to furnish you with a quote.

If you have any other questions, please call me at (502) 555-1234. In the meantime, I'll look forward to hearing from you again.

Sincerely yours,

Trudy L. Philips

Trudy L. Philips
Owner/Director
TLP/dmp

A letterhead providing information the recipient will need to communicate with the sender.

Full-block format: Everything is lined up with the left margin.

Letter is single-spaced, with double-spacing between paragraphs and other major parts.

The author refers to earlier correspondence to state purpose of the letter, a common and effective way to begin a business letter.

Elaboration, support, and detail

Signature block

Author's and typist's initials if typist is not author.

as your name, address, phone number, and email address (if you have one). A sample resumé is shown on page 215.

Tailor your resumé to the job for which you are applying. If you have extensive, relevant work experience, consider a chronological resumé, which lists the jobs you have held (beginning with the most recent job) and describes the duties, responsibilities, and accomplishments associated with each one. If you have little work experience, focus your resumé on your grade-point average, the courses you have taken, the projects you have completed, and the applicable skills and abilities you have acquired in college.

Do not include personal information such as height and weight. Mention personal interests or hobbies only if they are relevant to the position. Finally, proofread your resumé carefully; it must be error-free.

15d Compose job-application letters that highlight your education, experience, and achievements.

A job-application letter (sometimes called a *cover letter*) accompanies your resumé when you apply for a job. One purpose of a job-application letter is to tell your reader why you have sent your resumé. However, the primary purpose of a job-application letter is to persuade your reader that you are a qualified candidate for employment.

Most job-application letters consist of four paragraphs.

- The first paragraph identifies which position you are applying for and how you became aware of its availability. (If you are not applying for a particular position, the first paragraph should express your desire to work for that particular organization.)
- The second paragraph briefly describes your education, focusing on specific achievements, projects, and relevant course work.
- The third paragraph briefly describes your work experience, focusing on relevant responsibilities and accomplishments. (The second and third paragraphs should not simply restate what is in your resumé; rather, they should help persuade your reader that you are qualified for the job.)
- The fourth paragraph expresses your willingness to provide additional information and to be interviewed at the employer's convenience.

A Sample Resumé

Kim Hua
Current Address: MS 1789, Union College, Union, PA 55342
Permanent Address: 702 Good Street, Borah, ID 83702
Phone: (412) 555-1234 Email: khua@mailer.union.edu

Ample margins.

Contact information.

EDUCATION

Union College Union, PA	Bachelor of Arts, Child Development	Anticipated May 1998 GPA: 3.7

Relevant Courses: Lifespan Human Development, Infancy and Early Childhood, Parent-Child Relations, Fundamentals of Nutrition, Education of the Preschool Child

---

CHILD DEVELOPMENT WORK EXPERIENCE

Summer 1997, Union College Child-Care Center, Union College, Union, PA

Work experience begins with most current employment.

Child Care Provider: Provided educational experiences and daily care for three 2-year-olds and four 3-year-olds.

Summer 1996, St. Alphonsus Day Care Center, St. Alphonsus Hospital, Union, PA

Child Care Provider: Provided educational experiences and daily care for a group of nine children ages six through ten.

Fall 1995, Governor's Commission for the Prevention of Child Abuse, Union, PA

Intern: Located online resources relevant to the prevention of child abuse. Recommended which resources to include in the Web site of the Governor's Commission.

Relevant volunteer work.

OTHER WORK EXPERIENCE

1996 to present, Union Falls Bed & Breakfast, Union, PA

Payroll Manager: Maintained daily payroll records for all employees, compiled daily and weekly reports of payroll costs for the manager, and ensured compliance with all applicable state and federal laws governing payroll matters.

Other experience showing dependability and responsibility.

(continued)

Professional Affiliations

Past President, Union College Child and Family Studies Club Student Member, American Society of Child Care Professionals Member, National Child Care Providers

The sample job-application letter on page 217 illustrates this four-paragraph format.

15e Use overhead transparencies to enhance your oral presentations.

An overhead transparency consists of text, graphics, or both printed on clear sheets of transparency film. When illuminated by an overhead projector, the enlarged material appears on a screen. Overhead transparencies can help your audience follow and remember your presentation. Think of them as integral to your presentation, not just decorative. They should be concise, easy to read, and uncluttered. You may use an overhead transparency to list the main points of your presentation, to signal transitions from one topic to another, and to summarize information you have presented. (See the sample overhead transparency on page 218.) For more information on oral presentations, see Chapter 5, and for more on using visuals, see 14d.

15f Document research and experiments in a lab report.

A lab report generally consists of the following five sections:

- The *Introduction* provides background information: the hypothesis of the experiment, the question to be answered, how the question arose.
- The *Methods* section describes how you conducted the research or performed the experiment.
- The *Results* section describes what happened as a result of your research or experiment.

A Sample Job-Application Letter

308 Fairmont Street
Warren, CA 07812
June 9, 1997

Ms. Ronda Green
Software Engineer
Santa Clara Technology
P.O. Box 679
Santa Clara, CA 09145

Dear Ms. Green:

I am responding to your February 11 post in the Usenet newsgroup comp .software.testing announcing that Santa Clara Technology is accepting resumés for an entry-level engineer position in the Quality Assurance Department. I think that my experience in quality assurance and my educational background qualify me for this position.

As my resumé states, I graduated this past May from the University of Southern California (USC) with a Bachelor of Science degree in Interdisciplinary Studies. The Interdisciplinary Studies program at USC allows students to develop a degree plan spanning at least two disciplines. My degree plan included courses in computer science, marketing, and technical communication. In addition to university courses, I have completed courses in team dynamics, project management, and C and C++ programing offered by the training department at PrintCom, a manufacturer of high-end laser printers.

Throughout last summer, I worked as an intern in the quality-assurance department of PrintCom. I assisted quality-assurance engineers in testing printer drivers, installers, and utilities. In addition, I maintained a database containing the results of these tests and summarized the results in weekly reports. This experience gave me valuable knowledge of the principles of quality assurance and of the techniques used in testing software.

I would appreciate the opportunity to discuss further the education, skills, and abilities I could bring to Santa Clara Technology. You can reach me any workday after 3 p.m. (PST) at (907) 555-1234 or by email at sstur17@axl.com.

Sincerely yours,

Shelley Sturman

Shelley Sturman

Enclosure: resumé

Modified-block format: Your address, the date, and the signature block begin at the center of the page.

Purpose of the letter.

Education paragraph.

Work-experience paragraph.

Concluding paragraph.

Sample Overhead Transparency

Simple design.

Bulleted list defines main points.

Large, easy-to-read font.

Ample space around text and graphics.

Illustration clarifies text and adds visual interest.

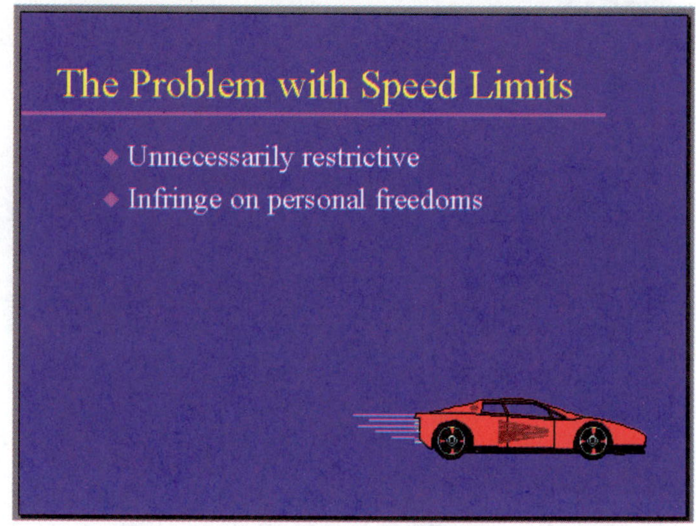

- The *Discussion* section consists of your reasoning about your results.
- The *References* section cites any sources you used in conducting the research, performing the experiment, or writing the lab report.

The content and format of a lab report may vary from discipline to discipline or from course to course. Before writing a lab report, be certain that you understand your instructor's requirements. The following sample lab report was written by two students in a soils science course. It uses the documentation format advocated by the Council of Biology Editors (CBE).

A Sample Lab Report

[Title page: Your instructor may prefer that you use a separate title page. If so, center the title on the page, with your name, course information, and date aligned at the left margin below the title. If not, begin your report as shown here, with two spaces below your name, the course name, and the date.]

Bulk Density and Total Pore Space

Joe Aquino and Sheila Norris
Soils 101
Lab Section 1
February 21, 1996

Introduction

Soil is an arrangement of solids and voids. The voids, called pore spaces, are important for root growth, water movement, water storage, and gas exchange between the soil and atmosphere. A medium-textured soil good for plant growth will have a pore-space content of about 0.50 (half solids, half pore space). The total pore space is the space between sand, silt, and clay particles (micropore space) plus the space between soil aggregates (macropore space).[1]

Background information that the reader will need to understand the experiment.

[The Introduction continues with a discussion of the formulas used to calculate bulk density, particle density, and porosity.]

Methods

To determine the bulk density[2] and total pore space of two soil samples, we hammered cans into the wall of a soil pit (Hagerstown silt loam). We collected samples from the Ap horizon and a Bt horizon. We then placed a block of wood over the cans so that the hammer did not smash them. After hammering the cans into the soil, we dug the cans, now full of soil, out of the horizons; we trimmed off any excess soil. The samples were dried in an oven at 105°C for two days and weighed. We then determined the volume of the cans by measuring the height and radius, as follows:

Detailed explanation of the methods used.

$$\text{volume} = \frac{1}{4}r^2h$$

We used the formulas noted in the Introduction to determine bulk density and porosity of the samples. Particle density was assumed to be 2.65 g/cm^3. The textural class of each horizon was determined by feel; that is, we squeezed and kneaded each sample and assigned it to a particular textural class.

Results

We found both soils to have relatively light bulk densities and large porosities, but the Bt horizon had greater porosity than the Ap. Furthermore, we determined that the Ap horizon was a silt loam, while the Bt was a clay (see Table 1).

Presents the results of the experiment, with a table showing quantitative data.

Table 1 Textural class, bulk density, and porosity of two Hagerstown soil horizons

Textural Class	Ap Silt Loam	Bt Clay
Bulk density (g/cm^3)	1.20	1.08
Porosity	0.55	0.59

[The Results section continues with sample calculations.]

Discussion

Both soils had bulk densities and porosities in the range we would have expected from the discussions in the lab manual and textbook. The Ap horizon is a medium-textured soil and is considered a good topsoil for plant growth, so a porosity around 0.5 is consistent with those facts. The

Explains what was significant about the results of the research.

```
Bt horizon is a fine-textured horizon (containing
a large amount of clay), and the bulk density is
in the predicted range.
```

[The Discussion section continues with further discussion of the results.]

[The References section begins on a new page.]

References

1. Brady NC, Weil RR. The nature and properties of soils. 11th ed. New York: Prentice-Hall; 1996. 291 p.
2. Blake GR, Hartge KH. Bulk density. In: Klute A, editor. Methods of soil analysis. Part 1. 2nd ed. Agronomy 1986;9:363-376.

The references are in the format recommended by the Council of Biology Editors (CBE).

15g Create a World Wide Web page to reach a global audience in a unique, innovative way.

A World Wide Web page is an electronic document stored on a *Web server*, a computer running special software and connected to the network of computers that makes up the World Wide Web. A Web server displays Web pages at the command of computer users accessing the server. Web pages differ from other electronic documents (such as email messages) and from paper documents. What accounts for most of this difference is *hypertext*, a system of codes that enables Web-page authors to link text or graphics on a particular section of the Web page to additional text or graphics, to other Web pages, or to short clips of video, animation, or sound. Readers navigate a Web page in a nonlinear fashion, starting almost anywhere they like and branching off whenever a hypertext link piques their curiosity.

The other unique aspect of a Web page is its global audience. When you publish a Web page, you are literally writing to the world (or at least to those

World Wide Web Page

Link leading to the home page of the Web site maintained by the history department at the University of California, Irvine.

Highly readable font against a muted, neutral background.

Text link leading to a page containing links to other Web pages.

Site map containing links to the main pages of the Web site and to the parent Web site.

Email link to the author of the Web site.

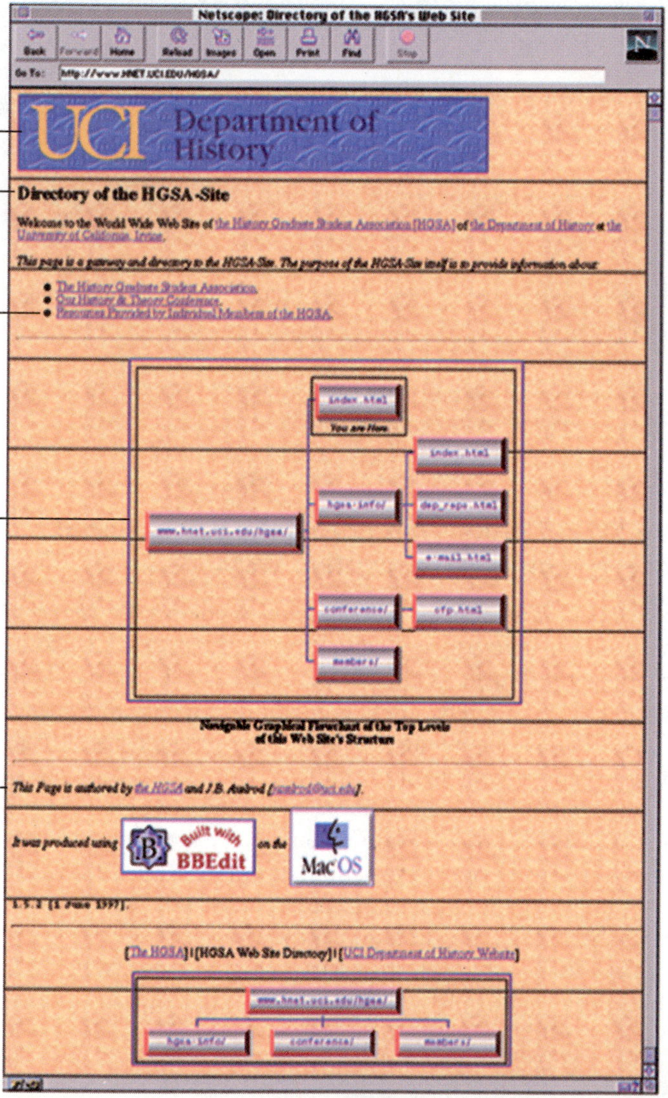

people who have access to the Web). Among other things, having a global audience means that you are writing to culturally diverse readers, many of whom may be unfamiliar with things you take for granted. For instance, if you refer to football on your Web page, many South American readers might first think of the sport that Americans call soccer. Likewise, a graphic that you find mildly humorous might strike readers from other cultures as blasphemous, insulting, or obscene. To design an effective Web page, consider carefully who will be reading your Web page and what you want them to know. A sample Web page is shown on page 222.

PART 4

SENTENCE BOUNDARIES

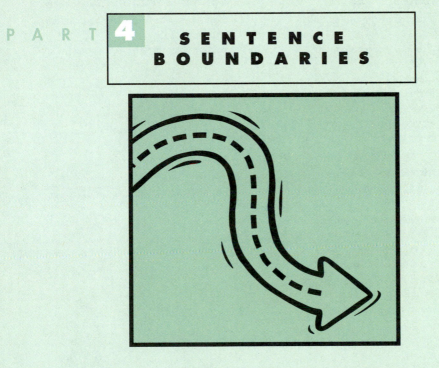

PART

4 SENTENCE BOUNDARIES

16 COMMA SPLICES

In a comma splice, two **independent clauses** are improperly joined by a comma. In the following example, the comma does not provide enough separation between the ideas expressed in the two independent clauses.

Comma splice The voice tells the character to build something or go somewhere, it dictates his actions and makes viewers tense and anxious. [independent clause] [independent clause]

Because a comma splice can be edited in many ways, first consider how the ideas in the two independent clauses relate. For example, are they equally important, or does one depend on or explain the other? Then select the strategy in this chapter that will best clarify this relationship for a reader. In the preceding example, the writer decided to change the comma to a semicolon, which provides a stronger separation between the independent clauses while also suggesting a connection between the clauses.

➤ **The voice tells the character to build something or go somewhere; it dictates his actions and makes viewers tense and anxious.**

See 16c and 39a for more on using a semicolon to link independent clauses.

16a Add a subordinating conjunction to one of the clauses, rewording as necessary.

By beginning a clause with a subordinating conjunction, you indicate that the clause is subordinate to—and dependent on—the main clause. Usually, the **dependent clause** explains or qualifies the main clause.

independent (main) clause A word group with a subject and a predicate that can stand alone as a separate sentence. (A predicate is the part of a clause that includes a complete verb and says something about the subject: At the checkpoint, we *unloaded the canoes.*)

subordinating conjunction A word or phrase (such as *although, because, since,* or *as soon as*) that introduces a dependent clause and relates it to an independent clause.

dependent (subordinate) clause A word group with a subject, a predicate, and a subordinating word (such as *because*) at the beginning. It cannot stand by itself as a sentence but must be connected to an independent (main) clause: *Although it was raining,* we loaded our gear onto the buses.

Each of the following sentences originally consisted of independent clauses separated by a comma. The revisions, by making the first clause subordinate to the second clause, express a clearer and more meaningful relationship between the clauses.

➤ **~~Drug~~ [Because drug] traffickers kill to protect or seize drug turf, almost half of the murders in Baltimore in 1992 were drug related.**

➤ **[Though] *Midnight Cowboy*, ~~was~~ rated X in the early 1970s, ~~it~~ contained one scene that was considered "sexually explicit," ~~yet~~ the movie was tastefully done and could not be considered pornographic by today's standards.**

coordinating conjunction A word that joins comparable and equally important sentence elements: *for, and, or, but, nor, yet,* or *so.*

16b Separate the independent clauses with a comma and a coordinating conjunction.

A coordinating conjunction tells the reader that the ideas in the two clauses are closely related and equally important. Usually, the coordinating conjunction is preceded by a comma, as in these examples.

➤ **On recent albums such as *Two-Ring Circus,* Erasure has been writing more ballads as well as dance tunes, [and] the band's songs have become more vivid, straightforward, and forceful.**

➤ **In 1973 the average American car achieved less than 14 mpg, a figure that remained constant for years, [but] in 1983 that figure jumped to 24.6 mpg.**

Of course, whether you decide to use a coordinating conjunction or subordinating conjunction depends on context. If, in the second example, the writer wanted to emphasize the 1983 mileage, it might be more appropriate to begin the first clause with a subordinating conjunction. The sentence could be rewritten as follows.

➤ **Although ~~In 1973~~ the average American car achieved less than 14 mpg, in 1973, a figure that remained constant for years, ~~in 1983~~ that figure jumped to 24.6 mpg in 1983.**

16c Separate the independent clauses with a semicolon.

A semicolon tells readers that the ideas in the two clauses are closely connected, but it implies a connection rather than stating it.

➤ **The tattoo needle appeared to be like an extension of his arm,; the needle was his brush, and the human body, his canvas.**

➤ **Nate was very lucky,; he lived to see his hundredth birthday.**

Note: Occasionally, a colon may be used to introduce a second independent clause (see 40a).

16d Separate the independent clauses with a semicolon or period, and add a conjunctive adverb or transition.

The semicolon tells the reader that the ideas in the two clauses are closely connected, and the conjunctive adverb or transition (such as *consequently* or *for example*) describes the connection.

conjunctive adverb A word or phrase (such as *finally, however,* or *therefore*) that tells how the ideas in two sentences or independent clauses are connected.

➤ **He doesn't need the map right now,; instead, he just follows the direction Kiem pointed out to him before and checks it with the compass.**

A period provides a stronger break than a semicolon does.

➤ **He doesn't need the map right now, he just follows the direction Kiem pointed out to him before and checks it with the compass.** [edit: ", he" → "; instead, he"]

subordinating conjunction A word or phrase (such as *although, because, since,* or *as soon as*) that introduces a dependent clause and relates it to an independent clause.

Note: A **subordinating conjunction** always begins a dependent clause, but a conjunctive adverb can appear in other positions within a clause. If the conjunctive adverb appears in the middle of one clause rather than between two clauses, the semicolon is still placed between the clauses, not before the adverb.

➤ **The importance of English as a link between those who have little else in common is clear, the true controversy lies in other issues.** [edit: "clear," → "clear;"; "controversy lies" → "controversy, in fact, lies"]

16e Turn the independent clauses into separate sentences.

When the independent clauses in a comma splice express loosely related ideas, consider turning each of the clauses into a separate sentence by inserting a period at the end of the first clause and beginning the second with a capital letter.

➤ **At high noon we were off, paddling down the Potomac River, we were two to a canoe with space in the middle for our gear.** [edit: "River, we" → "River. We"]

➤ **Unfortunately, not many people realize how much scientific research with animals means to the medical world, only the scientists themselves and the diseased patients who suffer and hope for new cures can fully understand the importance of animal testing.** [edit: "world, only" → "world. Only"]

16f Turn one independent clause into a phrase that modifies the other.

In the following example, the writer corrects the comma splice by eliminating the subject and verb in the second clause, turning this clause into a **modifying phrase.**

modifying phrase A word group that serves as an adjective or adverb.

➤ **At high noon we were off, paddling down the Potomac River, ~~we were~~ two to a canoe with space in the middle for our gear.**

See 33b for further help with turning clauses into phrases.

17 FUSED SENTENCES

A fused or run-on sentence consists of two **independent clauses** run together with no punctuation.

independent (main) clause A word group with a subject and a predicate that can stand alone as a separate sentence. (A predicate is the part of a clause that includes a complete verb and says something about the subject: At the checkpoint, we *unloaded the canoes.*)

[independent clause] [independent clause]

Fused sentence Her mood was good I took the opportunity to ask if she had a few minutes to answer some questions.

Because a fused sentence can be edited in many ways, first consider how the ideas in the two independent clauses are related, and then select the most appropriate strategy discussed in this chapter. For example, the writer edited the example just given to emphasize the causal relationship between the clauses.

➤ **Because her ~~Her~~ mood was good, I took the opportunity to ask if she had a few minutes to answer some questions.**

subordinating conjunction A word or phrase (such as *although, because, since,* or *as soon as*) that introduces a dependent clause and relates it to an independent clause.

dependent (subordinate) clause A word group with a subject, predicate, and a subordinating word (such as *because*) at the beginning. It cannot stand by itself as a sentence but must be connected to an independent (main) clause. *Although it was raining,* we loaded our gear onto the buses.

coordinating conjunction A word that joins comparable and equally important sentence elements: *for, and, or, but, nor, yet,* or *so.*

17a Make one of the clauses subordinate to the other by adding a subordinating conjunction and rewording as necessary.

By beginning a clause with a subordinating conjunction, you indicate that the clause is subordinate to—and dependent on—the main clause. Usually, the **subordinate clause** explains or qualifies the main clause.

In the following revisions of the same sentence, punctuation and subordination are used to separate the fused clauses and to express a clear, meaningful relationship between them.

➤ **Kids can be so cruel to each other** [that] **it is a wonder we all make it through childhood.**

➤ [Although kids can be extremely] ~~**Kids can be so**~~ **cruel to each other,** [amazingly,] ~~**it is a wonder**~~ **we all make it through childhood.**

17b Add a comma and a coordinating conjunction to separate the independent clause.

A coordinating conjunction preceded by a comma tells the reader that the ideas in the two clauses are closely related and equally important.

➤ **The beast was upon me**[, and] **I could feel his paws pressing down on my chest.**

If you want to emphasize the feeling of the beast's paws, you could subordinate the first clause to the second.

➤ [Once the] ~~**The**~~ **beast was upon me,** **I could feel his paws pressing down on my chest.**

17c Separate the independent clauses with a semicolon.

The semicolon tells the reader that the ideas in the two clauses are closely connected, but it implies the connection rather than stating it.

➤ **I looked around at the different monitors, most were large color monitors, many of which were connected to the supercomputer.** [handwritten edit: ; inserted after "monitors"]

Note: Occasionally, a colon may be used to introduce a second independent clause (see 40a).

17d Separate the independent clauses with a semicolon or period, and add a conjunctive adverb or transition.

conjunctive adverb A word or phrase (such as *finally, however,* or *therefore*) that tells how the ideas in two sentences or independent clauses are connected.

The semicolon indicates that the ideas in the two clauses are closely connected, and the conjunctive adverb or transition (such as *consequently* or *for example*) explains the connection.

➤ **Most students do not do their homework during the day, they do it in the evening.** [handwritten edit: ; instead, inserted after "day"]

A period provides a stronger break than a semicolon does.

➤ **Most students do not do their homework during the day, they do it in the evening.** [handwritten edit: . Instead, inserted after "day"]

subordinating conjunction A word or phrase (such as *although, because, since,* or *as soon as*) that introduces a dependent clause and relates it to an independent clause.

Note: A **subordinating conjunction** always introduces a dependent clause, but a conjunctive adverb can occupy different positions within a clause. If the conjunctive adverb appears in the middle of one clause rather than between two clauses, the semicolon is still placed between the clauses, not before the adverb.

➤ **Most students do not do their homework during the day, they do it in the evening.** [handwritten edit: ; inserted after "day"; , instead, inserted before "in the evening"]

17e Turn the independent clauses into separate sentences.

When the independent clauses in a fused sentence express loosely related ideas, consider turning each of the clauses into a separate sentence.

➤ **He was only eight. ~~his~~ His life hadn't even started.**

➤ **I couldn't believe it. I had fallen in a puddle of mud.**

modifying phrase A word group that serves as an adjective or adverb.

17f Turn one independent clause into a phrase that modifies the other.

In the following example, the writer corrects the fused sentence by eliminating the subject and verb in the second clause, turning this clause into a **modifying phrase.**

➤ **The beast was upon me, ~~I could feel~~ his paws pressing down on my chest.**

See 33b for further information on turning clauses into phrases.

18 SENTENCE FRAGMENTS

dependent (subordinate) clause A word group with a subject, a predicate, and a subordinating word (such as *because*) at the beginning.

A fragment is a group of words that begins with a capital letter and ends with a period but cannot stand alone as a sentence for one of two reasons.

1. It is a **dependent clause** or phrase that is not attached to a complete sentence. In the following example, the fragment—a dependent clause—is italicized.

   Fragment A transportation system must be established. *Because students have to travel a great distance to school.*

2. It lacks a complete **predicate** (a verb and its object and related words) or **subject** or both. In the following example, the fragment lacks a verb and subject.

   Fragment Establishing a transportation system.

Note: Although *Establishing* in the above example may look like a verb, it is actually part of a **verbal phrase.**

Because a fragment can often be edited in several ways, begin by considering what the fragment lacks and how its ideas relate to those in the sentences before and after it. Then use one of the strategies discussed in this chapter to change the fragment into a complete sentence. To edit a fragment, you can connect it to the preceding sentence, as in this example.

➤ **Tonight it's my turn, ~~A~~ for a ride-along with Sergeant Rob Nether of the Green Valley Police Department.**

Or you can turn the fragment into a separate sentence, as in the following revision, which preserves the punchiness of the short first sentence.

➤ **Tonight it's my turn. ~~A ride-along~~ I am about to ride along with Sergeant Rob Nether of the Green Valley Police Department.**

These strategies are further illustrated in 18a and 18b.

predicate The part of a clause that includes a complete verb and says something about the subject: At the checkpoint, we *unloaded the canoes.*

subject The word or words that identify the topic or theme of the sentence—what is being discussed: *Our defective rubber raft* began to leak air.

verbal phrase A phrase that includes a present participle (*dancing*), a past participle (*frozen*), or an infinitive (*to draw*) as well as modifiers and objects and, depending on its type, can function as a modifier or a noun in a sentence.

18a Connect the fragment to a complete sentence.

Fragments rarely occur in isolation. Rather, they often explain or modify another word group—usually an immediately preceding sentence. Therefore, it is common to attach a fragment to the previous sentence, making it subordinate.

➤ **Frank turned the tarot cards one at a time; ~~Each~~ each time telling me something about my future.**

➤ **The crowd in the lounge is basically young, ~~The~~ consisting of the teenage and early twenties generation.**

18b Add or complete the verb or the subject to change a fragment into a complete sentence.

You may want to turn the fragment into a complete sentence.

➤ **The crowd in the lounge is basically young. The teenage and early twenties generation gathers there.**

➤ **Children are brought up in different ways. Some grow up around violence.**

Sometimes you can turn a fragment into a complete sentence by eliminating the word or words that make a clause dependent.

➤ **The world that I was born into demanded continuous work. ~~Where nobody~~ Nobody got ahead, and everyone came home tired.**

Note: Sometimes writers use fragments intentionally for emphasis or special effect.

> The simplicity of the office startled me. No large desk. No leather chair. No shelves filled with imposing law books.

In general, though, it is best to avoid fragments, especially in academic writing, where many readers may perceive them as errors, regardless of your intentions.

PART 5 GRAMMATICAL SENTENCES

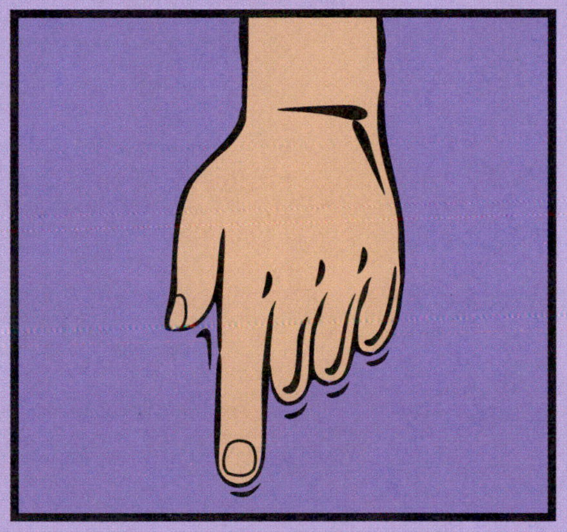

PART

5 GRAMMATICAL SENTENCES

19 PRONOUN REFERENCE

Make sure that each **pronoun** clearly refers to one specific **antecedent,** not to a group of words or a general situation that the reader is assumed to understand.

> *The elderly and children* are victims when no one bothers to check on *them.*

In this example, the pronoun *them* refers to a specific antecedent, *The elderly and children.*

pronoun A word that replaces a specific noun (such as *she, he, it, his, they, them, yours, ours, myself, whose,* or *which*), points out a specific noun (such as *this, these,* or *that*), or refers to an unspecified person or object (such as *each* or *everybody*).

antecedent The word or words that a pronoun replaces and to which it refers.

19a Rewrite to eliminate vague uses of *they, it,* or *you.*

Substitute specific words for *they, it,* or *you* when the antecedent is not clear.

➤ **Lani explained that everything is completely supported by individual contributions. ~~They receive~~ [The organization receives] no tax support.**

Sometimes, when *they* or *them* could refer to more than one plural antecedent, you may have to recast the sentence, perhaps by eliminating a pronoun with no clear antecedent.

➤ **In addition to your tenants' cars, five or six other vehicles are always on and around the property. As a result, not only do ~~they~~ [your tenants] park ~~some of them~~ in front of their neighbors' homes, but their visitors park up and down the street as well.**

➤ **Women have the option of leaving [if] their husbands ~~if they~~ are unfaithful.**

If *it* refers vaguely to a clause or a whole sentence, identify a specific antecedent.

➤ **Often, a guest such as Brooke Shields or Dr. Ruth Westheimer may appear more than once. Although [having the same guest return] ~~it~~ seems repetitious, it actually is not because the guest discusses different topics each time.**

➤ **After the long ride, we reached the place for our expedition at Pine Heaven Forest in western Virginia. At my age, [the trip] ~~it~~ seemed to take forever.**

Like *they, you* often refers broadly to a group of people. To eliminate a vague use of *you,* it may be necessary to recast the sentence.

➤ **Parents argue that beginning the program in the sixth grade is too early. [They say that] ~~By~~ exposing teens to sex education early ~~, you encourage~~ [encourages] them to go out and have sex.**

19b Rewrite to eliminate vague uses of *this, that,* and *which.*

Avoid vague uses of *this, that,* and *which* by adding a noun, by changing the pronoun to a noun, or by recasting the sentence.

➤ **Researchers have noticed that men interrupt women more than women interrupt men. This [finding] may explain why women sometimes find it difficult to start and sustain conversations with men.**

➤ **I was an A student, and I thought** good grades **~~that~~ should have been enough for any teacher.**

➤ **The brevity of the first story prevents the reader from dwelling on the plot and caring about the outcomes.** Because these **~~These~~ faults are not present in "The Soft Voice of the Serpent," ~~which makes~~ it** is **much more fulfilling to read.**

19c Rewrite to eliminate implied references.

A pronoun must refer to a noun. In some sentences, however, the noun the pronoun refers to may be assumed but not actually present. Revise such sentences to give the pronoun an antecedent.

➤ In this **~~This~~ song** the singer **tells about being carefree and going through life without any worries. Years later, though, he starts to remember his past, and things do not seem so problem-free anymore.**

Sometimes the implied noun may be present in another form, such as a possessive (*Mary's* for *Mary*) or as part of another word (*child* in *childhood*).

➤ **Radaker~~'s arguments~~ irritated everyone at the lecture because he failed to support** his arguments **~~them~~ with examples or evidence.**

pronoun A word that replaces a specific noun (such as *she, he, it, his, they, them, yours, ours, myself, whose,* or *which*), points out a specific noun (such as *this, these,* or *that*), or refers to an unspecified person or object (such as *each* or *everybody*).

antecedent The word or words that a pronoun replaces and to which it refers.

number The form of a word that shows whether it refers to one thing (singular) or more than one (plural): *parent, parents; child, children.*

person The form of a word that shows whether it refers to *I* or *we* (first person), to *you* (second person), or to *he, she, it,* or *they* (third person).

gender The form of a word that shows whether it refers to a male *(he)* or a female *(she).*

20 PRONOUN-ANTECEDENT AGREEMENT

A **pronoun** and its **antecedent** must agree in number, in person, and in gender. In other words, the form of the antecedent and the form of the pronoun must correspond. In the following examples, the arrows connect the pronouns and their antecedents.

The *scientists* did not know what *they* were creating.

Because *scientists* is plural in **number,** it takes the plural pronoun *they.*

I thought about Punita's offer while watching the movie. *My* curiosity won.

I is a first- **person** pronoun, so it takes the first-person pronoun *my.*

After we went back to the lab, *Punita* started concentrating on *her* work.

Punita is female, so the pronoun that refers to her must reflect her **gender.**

20a Use either singular or plural forms consistently for both a pronoun and its antecedent.

If the antecedent of a pronoun is singular, the pronoun must be singular so that both agree in number. Likewise, if the antecedent is plural, the pronoun must be plural.

The *shelter* gets most of *its* cats and dogs from *owners* who can't keep *their* pets.

When a pronoun and its antecedent do not agree, you have the following options for eliminating the inconsistency.

Revise the pronoun or antecedent so that both are singular or plural.

➤ The patient is fully aware of the decision that ~~they are~~ he or she is making.

➤ ~~The patient is~~ Patients are fully aware of the decision that they are making.

➤ She points out every obstacle and gives examples of ~~them.~~ it.

Note: As an alternative, you may be able to eliminate the pronoun.

➤ The patient is fully aware of ~~the~~ each decision. ~~that they are making.~~

Revise the sentence to eliminate the inconsistency.

➤ Roommates get agitated at always being told to clean, and the roommate doing the yelling gets tired of ~~hearing their own voice complain~~ complaining.

20b Be aware of tricky situations with singular indefinite pronouns and collective nouns.

Indefinite pronouns and collective nouns cause confusion because they are often, but not always, singular.

Use a singular pronoun to refer to a singular indefinite pronoun such as *each, everyone,* or *somebody.*

The following revision replaces the plural pronoun *their* with the singular pronouns *his or her* so that the pronouns agree with the antecedent *each.*

➤ Whether student, teacher, faculty member, graduate, or parent, each wants ~~their~~ his or her school to be the one that remains open.

indefinite pronoun A pronoun that does not refer to a particular person or object, such as *anybody, anyone, each, everyone, everything, somebody, something, neither, none,* and *nobody* (which take the singular), *few, many,* and *several* (which take the plural), and *all, most,* and *some* (which can take either the singular or plural).

collective noun A noun (such as *class, family, committee,* or *jury*) that refers to a group as a unit and is usually considered singular.

As an alternative, the antecedent could be made plural to agree with *their.*

➤ **~~Whether student, teacher, faculty member, graduate, or parent, each wants~~** All students, teachers, faculty members, graduates, and parents want **their school to be the one that remains open.**

In the following example, the antecedent *everyone* has been replaced with the plural noun *students* to agree with the plural pronoun *themselves.*

➤ **This event would be a good chance for ~~everyone~~** students **to come out, socialize, and enjoy themselves.**

The sentence could also be reworded to eliminate *themselves.*

➤ **This event would be a good chance for everyone to come out, socialize, and enjoy ~~themselves.~~** a relaxing afternoon.

collective noun A noun (such as *class, family, committee,* or *jury*) that refers to a group as a unit and is usually considered singular.

Use a singular pronoun if the antecedent is a collective noun.

➤ **The Santa Barbara School District has a serious problem on ~~their~~** its **agenda.**

Note: A collective noun generally treats a group as a single unit and is therefore considered singular. However, a collective noun may sometimes be considered plural when it refers to the group members as individuals: *The couple decided it was time to consolidate their bank accounts.* (See also 24b.)

20c Use a plural pronoun to refer to most compound nouns joined by *and.*

If *Cinderella and her prince* have worries of divorce or aging, you can't tell by the way *they* ride into "Happily ever after" at the end.

20d Use a pronoun that agrees with the nearer noun if the nouns are joined by *or* or *nor*.

Today, people use cocaine or *other narcotics* because of *their* plummeting street prices.

Because *other narcotics* is closest to the pronoun, the pronoun is plural.

20e Use masculine, feminine, or gender-free forms to match the pronoun with its antecedent.

antecedent The word or words that a pronoun replaces and to which it refers.

Match a masculine pronoun with a masculine antecedent and a feminine pronoun with a feminine antecedent so that the pronoun and its antecedent agree in **gender.**

gender The form of a word that shows whether it refers to a male *(he)* or a female *(she).*

I first met *Mark* the day *he* was hired.

Avoid using a pronoun that stereotypes by gender when an antecedent might be either masculine or feminine.

One way to avoid stereotyping by gender is to use a phrase that includes both masculine and feminine singular pronouns (such as *his or her*) to refer to both sexes.

➤ **Many people believe that a child is better off with a family that is able to provide for all of his** ^or her^ **needs than with a poverty-stricken parent who can barely support the child.**

Note: If repeating a phrase such as *his or her* or *he or she* seems cumbersome or repetitious, try substituting plural forms.

➤ **Many people believe that** ^children are^ **~~a child is~~ better off with** ^families^ **~~a family~~ that** ^are^ **~~is~~ able to provide for all of** ^their^ **~~his~~ needs than with poverty-stricken** ^parents^ **~~mother~~ who can barely support** ^them.^ **~~the children.~~**

Rewrite to eliminate unneeded or awkward pairs of masculine and feminine pronouns when you are referring to both men and women.

> ➤ **This solution, of course, assumes that the bus drivers ~~driver~~ will be where they are ~~he/she is~~ supposed to be; boredom sometimes inspires drivers ~~a driver~~ to make up new and exciting variations on the ~~his or her~~ designated routes.**

Note: Avoid using *he/she* in all but the most informal writing situations.

21 RELATIVE PRONOUNS

relative pronoun A pronoun such as *who, whom, whose, which,* or *that* that introduces an adjective clause (a clause that modifies a noun or pronoun).

Use personal **relative pronouns** to refer to people: *who, whom, whoever, whomever,* and *whose.*

> This reaction is unlike the response of the boys, *who* had trouble focusing on a subject.

Use nonpersonal relative pronouns to refer to things: *which, whichever, whatever,* and *whose.* (Note that *whose* can be used as a nonpersonal relative pronoun as well as a personal one.)

> These interruptions, 75 percent of *which* come solely from males, disrupt conversations.

> The tournament, *which* we had worked for all year, was the most prestigious event of the season.

Use *that* for general references to things and groups of people.

Save Our Sharks tried to promote a bill *that* would forbid the killing of certain sharks.

See also 24f.

21a Change *that* to *who* to refer to a person.

➤ **Illness phobics have countless examinations despite the reassurance of each physician ~~that~~ who examines them.**

➤ **It was his parents ~~that~~ who made him run for student council, play the piano, and go out for sports.**

Note: Simplifying sentence structure sometimes eliminates the problem.

➤ **~~It was his~~ His parents ~~that~~ made him run for student council, play the piano, and go out for sports.**

See 21d for information about the difference between *who* and *whom.*

21b Change *that* to *which* in clauses supplying extra, nondefining information about a thing or group.

A clause that provides extra information is **nonrestrictive** because it does not restrict, or limit, the identity of the word or words it modifies. It is usually set off by a comma or commas.

nonrestrictive clause A clause, set off by commas, that provides extra or nonessential information and could be eliminated without changing the meaning of the noun or pronoun it modifies.

➤ **Caroline had the prettiest jet-black hair, ~~that~~ which went down to the middle of her back.**

restrictive clause A clause, not set off by commas, that provides information essential to defining or identifying the noun or pronoun it modifies.

dependent (subordinate) clause A word group with a subject, a predicate, and a subordinating word (such as *because*) at the beginning. It cannot stand by itself as a sentence but must be connected to an independent (main) clause. *Although it was raining,* we loaded our gear onto the buses.

subjective case The form a pronoun takes when it is a subject: At the checkpoint, *we* unloaded the canoes.

objective case The form a pronoun takes when it is receiving the action of the verb: We helped *him.*

Because *went down to the middle of her back* is extra information about Caroline's hair, it is set off by a comma and the word *which.*

See 37c for more on using commas with nonrestrictive word groups.

21c Change *which* to *that* in clauses supplying essential information about a thing or group.

A clause that provides essential information is **restrictive** because it restricts, or limits, the identity of the word or words it modifies. It is not set off by a comma or commas.

➤ **From the moment we are born, we come into a society ~~which~~ [that] assimilates us into its culture.**

The clause *that assimilates us into its culture* is restrictive because it is essential in defining *society.*

➤ **In addition to the equipment and technology ~~which~~ [that] fill the trauma room, a team of experts assembles before the patient arrives.**

The clause *that fill the trauma room* is an essential description of *equipment and technology.* Therefore, the clause is restrictive.

See 38b on avoiding unnecessary commas with restrictive word groups.

Note: Which is usually used only in nonrestrictive clauses, but you will sometimes find writers using it in restrictive clauses as well.

21d Use *who* as a subject and *whom* as an object in subordinate clauses and questions.

Subordinate clauses

The pronouns *who* (or *whoever*) and *whom* (or *whomever*) are often used to introduce **subordinate clauses.** *Who* is in the **subjective case;** *whom* is in the **objective case.** (See Chapter 22 on pronoun case.) To figure out which case is correct, isolate the clause beginning with *who/whoever* or *whom/whomever* and determine whether the pronoun serves as a subject or an object.

***Who* as Subject.** In the following sentence, the subordinate clauses beginning with *who* are bracketed.

We remember [*who* (subject) tips well] and [*who* (subject) doesn't].

The pronoun is the subject of both clauses, so the pronoun *who* is correct.

***Whom* as Object.** In the following sentence, the subordinate clause beginning with *whom* is bracketed.

Mr. Scott is someone [*whom* I will always admire].

Rewrite the clause as a complete sentence, substituting *him* for *whom.*

I will always admire *him* (object).

Here *I* is the subject of the sentence and *him,* the replacement for *whom,* is the object. Therefore, the pronoun *whom* in the original sentence is correct.

Whom should also be used as the object of a **preposition.**

preposition A word (such as *between, for, from, in, of,* or *to*) that always appears as part of a phrase and indicates the relation between a word in a sentence and the object of the preposition: The water splashed *into* the canoe.

➤ **He also met his wife, ~~who~~ whom he was married to for fifty-two years.**

➤ **He also met his wife, ~~who~~ to whom he was married ~~to~~ for fifty-two years.**

Questions

Who and *whom* are often used at the beginning of questions. As with subordinate clauses, use *who* as a subject and *whom* as an object in questions.

➤ **~~Whom~~ Who is Sinead O'Connor, really?**

Who is the subject of the sentence.

subject The word or words that identify the topic or theme of the sentence—what is being discussed: *Our defective rubber raft* began to leak air.

subject complement A word or word group that follows a linking verb (such as *is* and other forms of *be*) and describes or restates the subject: The tents looked *old and dirty.*

object The part of a clause that receives the action of the verb.

preposition A word (such as *between, for, from, in, of,* or *to*) that always appears as part of a phrase and indicates the relation between a word in a sentence and the object of the preposition: The water splashed *into* the canoe.

➤ ~~Who~~ Whom did the newly elected government fear most?

Whom is the object of the verb *fear.*

22 PRONOUN CASE

A pronoun can take different forms or cases, depending on its role in a sentence—that is, depending on whether it (1) is a **subject** or **subject complement,** (2) is an **object** of a verb or **preposition,** or (3) shows possession or ownership. The following chart shows how pronouns change case depending on their roles.

Singular Pronoun Forms

Subjective	Objective	Possessive
I	me	my, mine
you	you	your, yours
he	him	his
she	her	her, hers
it	it	its

Plural Pronoun Forms

Subjective	Objective	Possessive
we	us	our, ours
you	you	your, yours
they	them	their, theirs

A pronoun functioning as a subject or subject complement should be in the subjective form.

"*You'*d better be careful," *she* said.

Lucy remembered that the most popular eighth-graders were Donna and *she.* [*Donna and she* is a subject complement because it renames the subject *the most popular eighth graders.*]

A pronoun functioning as the object of a verb or preposition should be in the objective form.

This realization spurred *me* to hasten the search.

Her dog, Peter the Great, went with *her* on the excavation in Siberia.

A pronoun showing possession or ownership should be in the possessive form.

I trusted *his* driving.

I finished putting *my* gear on and rolled over backward into the ocean.

See 57a for more on pronoun forms.

22a Change a pronoun to the subjective case if it is part of a compound subject.

compound subject Two or more words acting as a subject and linked by *and.*

➤ **Even though Annie and ~~me~~ I went through the motions, we didn't understand the customs of our host.**

If the pronoun *me* were the only pronoun in the original, the sentence would be ungrammatical: *Even though me went through the motions. . . .*

22b Change a pronoun to the objective case if it is an object (or part of a compound object) of a preposition or a verb.

compound object Two or more words acting as an object and linked by *and.*

➤ **There was an invisible wall between ~~she~~ her and ~~I~~ me.**

In this example, the objective form is correct because the two pronouns are the compound object of the preposition *between.*

reflexive pronoun A pronoun such as *myself* or *ourselves* that refers to a noun or a personal pronoun in the same clause.

22c Replace a reflexive pronoun that does not refer to another noun or pronoun in the clause.

➤ **Kyle and** I ~~**myself**~~ **went upstairs to see how she was doing.**

The reflexive pronoun *myself* is not appropriate in this sentence because it does not refer to a preceding *I*. In contrast, a reflexive pronoun is appropriate in the following sentence because *myself* refers to *I*.

I cleaned the apartment *myself*.

gerund A verb form that is used as a noun and ends with *-ing*: *arguing, throwing.*

gerund phrase A phrase that functions as a noun and includes a gerund plus complements and modifiers.

22d Change a pronoun to the possessive case when it modifies a gerund or a gerund phrase.

➤ **One of the main reasons for** my ~~**me**~~ **wanting to stay home with my children is that I would miss so much if I didn't.**

In this example, the whole gerund phrase *wanting to stay home with my children* is modified by *my*.

22e Change the case of a pronoun to fit the implied or understood wording of a comparison using *than* or *as*.

➤ **I was still faster than** she ~~**her**~~.

In sentences such as this one, you can test whether a pronoun form is correct by filling in the implied wording.

Incorrect pronoun	I was still faster than *her* [was fast].
Correct pronoun	I was still faster than *she* [was fast].

22f Select *we* to precede a subject or *us* to precede an object.

We is the subjective form, and *us* is the objective form. Select the form that matches the role of the noun in the sentence.

➤ **Whenever ~~us~~ [we] neighborhood kids would play, I would always be goalie.**

22g Use the same form for appositives and the words they rename or to which they refer.

> **appositive** A word or word group that identifies or gives more information about a noun or pronoun that precedes it: I called the mayor's office and asked for Jane Kite, *the mayor's assistant.*

➤ **Only two passengers, Jed and ~~me~~ [I], were left on the train.**

Because the appositive *Jed and I* renames the subject, *passengers,* the subjective form *I* is correct.

➤ **The conductor cast an impatient look at the only two passengers left on the train, Jed and ~~I~~ [me].**

In this example, *passengers* is the object of the preposition *at.* Because *Jed and me* renames the object, the objective form *me* is correct.

23 VERBS

Because of the importance of verbs to your meaning, take extra care in choosing the correct tense, form, mood, and voice. The first three sections in this chapter explain the different verb tenses. Section 23d lists the five basic verb forms and provides advice on correcting common verb-form errors. Section 23e explains the concept of mood. Finally, 23f provides advice on choosing between the active and passive voice.

Note: For help with subject-verb agreement, see Chapter 24.

For ESL Writers

See Chapter 54 for advice on using the correct verb tense in conditional clauses, two-word verbs, and helping verbs, and whether to use a gerund or infinitive form after a verb.

23a Use the appropriate verb tense to place events in past, present, and future time.

To get a general idea of how—and when—various tenses are used, see the table below. It shows the past, present, and future tenses of the regular verb *talk* and the irregular verb *speak.*

Past, Present, and Future Tenses, Simple and Perfect Forms

Simple present indicates an action happening now, a truth or fact, or an ongoing principle.

I, you, we, they	talk/speak
he, she, it	talks/speaks

Simple past indicates an action that occurred in the past.

I, you, he, she, it, we, they	talked/spoke

Simple future indicates an action that will take place in the future.

I, you, he, she, it, we, they	will talk/will speak

Present perfect indicates an action that started at some point in the past or that started in the past and is continuing in the present.

I, you, we, they	have talked/have spoken
he, she, it	has talked/has spoken

Past perfect indicates an action that was completed before another began.

I, you, he, she, it, we, they	had talked/had spoken

Future perfect indicates an action that will be completed by the time another action starts.

I, you, he, she, it, we, they	will have talked/will have spoken

Simple and perfect tenses also have progressive forms, which indicate actions that are continuing or in progress. The table below shows the progressive forms of the verbs *talk* and *speak*. To construct a progressive verb, use a form of the verb *be* followed by the **present participle.** (See 23d for more on participles.)

Note: See the list of irregular verbs in 57a for the forms of the irregular verb *be*.

present participle A verb form ending in *-ing* that combines with forms of *be (was going, is freezing)*. Present participles can also function as adjectives.

Progressive Tenses

Present progressive indicates an action that is occurring now.

I	am talking/am speaking
he, she, it	is talking/is speaking
you, we, they	are talking/are speaking

Past progressive indicates actions that were ongoing before now.

I, he, she, it	was talking/was speaking
you, we, they	were talking/were speaking

Future progressive indicates actions that will be ongoing in the future.

I, you, he, she, it, we, they	will be talking/will be speaking

Present perfect progressive indicates actions that started in the past and are continuing now.

I, you, we, they	have been talking/have been speaking
he, she, it	has been talking/has been speaking

Past perfect progressive indicates an ongoing action that ended before another event in the past.

I, you, he, she, it, we, they	had been talking/had been speaking

Future perfect progressive indicates an ongoing action in the future that ends before another event in the future.

I, you, he, she, it, we, they	will have been talking/will have been speaking

 **For ESL Writers**

Certain verbs that indicate existence, states of mind, and the senses of sight, smell, touch, and so on cannot usually be used in the progressive tense. Such verbs include *appear, be, belong, contain, feel, forget, have, hear, know, mean, prefer, remember, see, smell, taste, think, understand,* and *want.*

➤ **I ~~am remembering~~ remember the park I played in as a child.**

23b Use present-tense verbs when discussing events in a literary work or film, general truths, ongoing principles, and facts.

➤ **In the "Monkey Garden," the girl ~~knew~~ knows it ~~was~~ is time to grow up but still ~~wanted~~ wants to play with the other kids in her make-believe world.**

By convention, events in a literary work or film, as well as truths, principles, and facts are written of in the present tense because they are seen as ongoing or as perpetually existing in the present. (See also 27a.) Here are some further examples.

Event in a literary work/film	In the film, Wyatt Earp (Kurt Russell) *is* a tall, courageous man who *knows* the law well.
General truth	The family *is* the foundation for a child's education.
Ongoing principle	Attaining self-sufficiency *is* one of the most important priorities of our energy policy.
Fact	The earth *is tilted* at an angle of 23 degrees.

Note: Conventions for verb tense vary, depending on the field in which you are writing. For instance, though it is conventional to use the present tense to describe or analyze events in literary works, writers in the social sciences and sciences frequently use the past tense to describe works in their respective fields. The *Publication Manual of the American Psychological Association* (APA), commonly used in the social sciences, recommends using the past tense in discussions of research studies and procedures but using the present tense in discussions of the studies' implications and conclusions.

APA style Davidson (1994) *stated* that father absence *is* more than twice as common now as in our parents' generation.

23c Use the past perfect tense (formed with *had*) to show that one past action already had taken place before another past action occurred.

➤ **The victim's roommate also claimed that she ^had^ called the dorm office two days prior to the suicide attempt.**

23d Use the correct verb forms and endings for regular and irregular verbs.

The five verb forms are shown in the list below. The list includes forms of a regular verb *(talk)* and an irregular verb *(speak)*. For a list of irregular verbs, see 57a.

- **Infinitive or base form**

  Every day I *talk* on the phone and *speak* to my friends.

- **Third-person singular present (*-s/-es* form)**

  He *talks* softly, and she *speaks* slowly.

- **Past (*-d/-ed* form)**

  I *talked* to my parents last week, and I *spoke* to Jed on Tuesday.

- **Present participle (*-ing* form)**

  She is *talking* on the phone now, and he is *speaking* to a friend.

- **Past participle (*-d/-ed* form)**

  I have *talked* to her many times, but she has not *spoken* to him yet.

1. Add an *-s* or *-es* ending to present-tense verbs when the subject is in the third-person singular.

The pronouns *he, she,* and *it* and singular nouns such as *policy* are in the third person.

➤ **The national drug control policy ~~treat~~ treats drug abuse as a law enforcement problem.**

Note: If the subject is not in the third person, omit the *-s* or *-es* ending.

➤ **Because I didn't tell you about the movie, I really ~~suggests~~ suggest that you go see it.**

2. Do not omit the *-d* or *-ed* ending from a regular verb when forming the past tense or the past participle.

Sometimes, people leave off the *-d* or *-ed* endings on past-tense or past-participle verbs in conversation. Be sure to include them in your written work.

➤ **As we walked through the library, she ~~explain~~ explained the meaning of the yellow signs.**

➤ **This movie was filmed in New Orleans because it resembles the city where the story is ~~suppose~~ supposed to take place.**

3. Check to be sure you have used the correct form of an irregular verb.

If you are uncertain about a verb form, refer to the list of irregular verbs in 57a or check your dictionary.

➤ **The hostess greeted us and ~~lead~~ [led] us to our seats.**

➤ **We could tell our food had just ~~came~~ [come] off the grill because it still sizzled.**

Note: Some verbs with different meanings are confusing because they have similar forms. For example, the verb *lie (lie, lay, lain, lying)* means "recline," but the verb *lay (lay, laid, laid, laying)* means "put or place." Check such verbs in the Glossary of Usage or in your dictionary to make sure that you use the correct forms of the words you intend.

➤ **I thought everyone was going to see my car ~~laying~~ [lying] on its side.**

23e Choose the correct form of a verb to show the mood.

The three moods in English show the writer's or speaker's perspective on what he or she is writing or saying. The *indicative mood* is used for statements and questions; the *imperative mood* is used for commands or directions; and the *subjunctive mood* is used for wishes, suggestions, and conditions that are hypothetical, impossible, or unlikely. Because subjunctive verb forms can be tricky, it is helpful to keep some general advice in mind.

Usually, present-tense verbs change form to indicate changes in **person** and **number**—for example, *Annie gives. The boys give.* The present subjunctive, however, often used in clauses with *if* or *that,* always uses the **base form** of the verb regardless of the person and number of the subject.

I suggested that she *bring* everything indoors if it rains.

For the past tense of the verb *be,* the subjunctive form is *were,* not *was.*

person The form of a word that shows whether it refers to *I* or *we* (first person), to *you* (second person), or to *he, she, it,* or *they* (third person).

number The form of a word that shows whether it refers to one thing (singular) or more than one (plural): *parent, parents; child, children.*

base form Generally, the form of a verb without any endings: I *eat;* to *play.*

➤ Even if this claim ~~was~~ *were* true, it would raise a very controversial issue.

➤ It was as if he ~~was~~ *were* stretching his neck to pick leaves or fruit out of a high tree.

Note: That clauses calling for the subjunctive often express wishes: *I wish that I were living in the country.* Or they may express suggestions and requests: *Martin recommended that we take only a change of clothes on our island trip.*

active voice The verb form that shows the subject in action: The cat *caught* the mouse.

passive voice The verb form that shows something happening to the subject: The mouse *was caught* by the cat.

23f Use verbs primarily in the active voice.

The **active voice** calls attention to the actor performing an action. By contrast, the **passive voice** emphasizes the recipient of the action or the action itself while omitting or deemphasizing the actor.

Active The girl *tells* the story as she reflects on her own childhood. [*This sentence emphasizes the girl.*]

Passive The story *is told* by a girl as she reflects on her own childhood. [*This sentence emphasizes the story.*]

Straightforward and direct, the active voice creates graceful, clear writing that emphasizes actors. In most writing situations, you should revise to eliminate awkward, unnecessary passive verbs.

➤ *The* ~~Physicians are attracted by the~~ monetary rewards of high-tech research ~~.~~ *attract physicians.*

➤ The guests cluster like grapes ~~as similar interests are sought.~~ *, seeking others with similar interests.*

Note: The passive voice is sometimes useful if you want to shift information to the end of a sentence. It is also frequently used in impersonal writing that focuses on an action rather than an actor, as in a scientific research report.

> When the generator *is turned on,* water *is forced* down the tunnel, and the animals swim against the current. Their metabolism *is measured.* They have participated in this experiment before, and the results from that run and this new one *will be compared.*

subject The word or words that identify the topic or theme of the sentence—what is being discussed: *Our defective rubber raft* began to leak air.

24 SUBJECT-VERB AGREEMENT

verb A word or phrase that expresses action or being and, along with a subject, is a basic component of a sentence: At the checkpoint, we *unloaded* the canoes.

Use **subjects** and **verbs** that agree in **person** and **number.** For example, the subject and verb in the following sentence agree.

> A proper *funeral* [third-person singular noun] *remains* [third-person singular verb] a measure of respect for the deceased.

person The form of a word that shows whether it refers to *I* or *we* (first person), to *you* (second person), or to *he, she, it,* or *they* (third person).

Agreement problems often occur in the situations detailed in this chapter.

24a Make sure the subject and verb agree even if they are separated by other words.

> The *relationship* between artists and politicians *has become* a controversial issue.

number The form of a word that shows whether it refers to one thing (singular) or more than one (plural): *parent, parents; child, children.*

The singular subject, *relationship,* agrees with the third-person singular verb, *has become* even though the phrase *between artists and politicians* separates them. The following examples show how you can change the verb or subject to fix an agreement problem.

➤ **The pattern of echoes from these sound waves ~~are~~ is converted by computer into a visual image.**

➤ **The ~~pattern of~~ echoes from these sound waves are converted by computer into a visual image.**

collective noun A noun (such as *class, family, committee,* or *jury*) that refers to a group as a unit and is usually considered singular.

24b Use a singular verb with a subject that is a collective noun.

The *association distributes* information on showing bison, selling bison, and marketing bison meat.

Association is a collective noun, so it takes the third-person singular form of the verb *(distributes).*

➤ **If a military team ~~fight~~ fights without spirit and will, it will probably lose.**

Note: A collective noun is generally considered singular because it treats a group as a single unit. However, a collective noun may sometimes be considered plural when it refers to the group members as individuals.

Singular The *staff is* amiable.

Plural The *staff exchange* greetings and small talk as *they begin* putting on *their* surgical garb.

24c Use a verb that agrees with a subject placed after it, as in sentences beginning with *There is* or *There are.*

In most sentences, the subject precedes the verb, but in some sentences the subject and verb are inverted. For example, sentences beginning with *There is* and *There are* reverse the standard order, putting the subject after the verb.

verb — subject

There *are no busy lines and brushstrokes* in the paintings.

The verb *are* agrees with *no busy lines and brushstrokes,* the plural subject.

In inverted sentences, change the verb so that it agrees with the subject that follows it, or rewrite the sentence.

➤ **The next morning, there ~~was~~ [were] Mike and Cindy, acting nonchalant.**

➤ **The next morning, ~~there was~~ Mike and Cindy~~,~~ [were] acting nonchalant.**

Occasionally, you may invert a sentence to emphasize a topic or to begin the sentence with information that will be familiar to readers (see 33d and 33e).

➤ **At the end of the line ~~lurks~~ [lurk] syrupy-sweet cousin Joleen and whiskered Uncle Harry, both aiming to kiss me.**

The verb *lurk* agrees with *syrupy-sweet cousin Joleen and whiskered Uncle Harry,* a compound noun.

24d Use a plural verb with a compound subject.

subject — verb

She and her husband have a partnership with her in-laws.

compound subject Two or more words acting as a subject and linked by *and.*

➤ **Dust and dirt ~~accumulates,~~ accumulate bathrooms get mildewy, and kitchens get greasy.**

Note: Treat two subjects joined by *and* as singular when they are two components of a single item or when they describe the same noun: *Rice and beans is a standard dish in Cuban cuisine. My best friend and roommate was also to be my best man.*

24e If two subjects are joined by *or* or *nor,* the verb should agree with the subject that is closer to it.

Most nights, my daughters or my *son starts* dinner.

➤ **Neither the supervisor nor the staff members ~~was~~ were able to calm the distressed client.**

24f Use a verb that agrees with the antecedent of the pronoun *who, which,* or *that.*

antecedent The word or words that a pronoun replaces and to which it refers.

Its staff consists of nineteen *people* who *drive* to work in any kind of weather to make sure the station comes through for its listeners.

Drive agrees with *people,* the antecedent of the relative pronoun *who.*

➤ **Within the ordered chaos of the trauma room are diagnostic tools, surgical devices, and X-ray equipment, which ~~is~~ are required for Sharp to be a designated trauma center.**

Are agrees with *diagnostic tools, surgical devices, and X-ray equipment,* the plural antecedent of the relative pronoun *which.*

Note: When the phrase *one of the* followed by a plural noun is the antecedent of a relative pronoun, use a verb that agrees with the noun.

➤ **One of the features that ~~makes~~ make the monitor different from the others is that it doubles as a television.**

The antecedent of *that* is *features,* not *one.*

Treat *only one of the* followed by a plural noun as singular.

➤ **The monitor hooked up to the cooling system is the only one of the monitors that ~~double~~ doubles as a television.**

The antecedent of *that* is *one,* not *monitors.* The monitor is the only one that can also be a television. Thus the singular verb *doubles* is correct.

24g Use a singular verb with most indefinite pronouns.

Everything on the playground *is* child friendly.

➤ **There are two alternatives to this solution, and neither ~~seem~~ seems feasible.**

Note: If an indefinite pronoun such as *all, none,* or *some* refers to a plural noun, use a plural form of the verb. If it refers to a singular noun, use a singular form.

Some of the *surfers manage* to find jobs that fit their schedule, the surf schedule.

All of the *money is* missing.

indefinite pronoun A pronoun that does not refer to a particular person or object, such as *anybody, anyone, each, everyone, everything, somebody, something, neither, none,* and *nobody* (which take the singular), *few, many,* and *several* (which take the plural), and *all, most,* and *some* (which can take either the singular or plural).

subject complement A word or word group that follows a linking verb (such as *is* and other forms of *be*) and describes or restates the subject: The tents looked *old and dirty.*

24h Use a verb that agrees with the subject rather than a subject complement.

The shark's favorite *diet is* elephant seals and sea lions.

Elephant seals and sea lions are the shark's favorite diet.

Make sure the verb agrees with the actual subject. If necessary, rewrite the sentence.

➤ **Big blocks of color ~~is~~ [are] his artistic trademark.**

➤ **~~Big~~ [He favors big] blocks of color.**

24i Words such as *mathematics, news,* and *politics* are usually singular, even though they end in *-s.*

➤ **Mathematics ~~was~~ [is] Josie's favorite class.**

Note: When a word such as *athletics* or *statistics* refers to individual items rather than to a field as a whole, treat the word as plural: *The new income statistics baffle economists.*

24j Words referred to as words, as well as titles of books, plays, and other works are singular.

➤ **"Fiends" ~~were~~ [was] my father's favorite insult for aggressive drivers.**

➤ ***The Grapes of Wrath* ~~were~~ [was] the first book by Steinbeck that I ever read.**

25 ADJECTIVES AND ADVERBS

Distinguish **adjectives** from **adverbs** so that you select the correct forms of these **modifiers.** (See also 57a.)

Adjectives Because *angry* drivers are *dangerous* drivers, it is *imperative* that the county implement a solution.

Adverbs He often drove *angrily* and *dangerously.*

adjective A word that modifies a noun or a pronoun, adding information about it.

adverb A word that modifies a verb, an adjective, or another adverb, often telling when, where, why, how, or how often.

modifier A word, phrase, or clause functioning as an adjective or adverb that adds information and detail about a noun, a verb, or another word.

25a Select an adverb, not an adjective, to modify an adjective, another adverb, or a verb.

Often ending in *-ly,* adverbs tell how, when, where, why, and how often. Change an adjective that modifies another adjective, an adverb, or a verb to an adverb form.

➤ **This man yelled at me so ~~loud~~ loudly that I began to cry.**

➤ **The day was going ~~slow~~ slowly, and I repeatedly caught my lure on the riverbed or a tree limb.**

➤ **The muffins came out ~~good.~~ well.**

➤ **I found out that Hector did ~~bad~~ badly on the test.**

In the preceding two examples, the adverbs *well* and *badly* are correct because they modify verbs.

subject complement A word or word group that follows a linking verb (such as *is* and other forms of *be*) and describes or restates the subject: The tents looked *old and dirty.*

linking verb *Be, seem, appear, become, taste,* or another verb that connects a subject with a subject complement that describes or modifies it: The chips *taste* salty.

25b Select an adjective, not an adverb, to modify a noun or a pronoun.

I am enamored of the *cool* motor, the *massive* boulder in the middle of the lake, and the sound of the wake *splashing* against the side of the two-seater.

Change an adverb that modifies a noun or a pronoun to an adjective.

➤ **Working within a ~~traditionally~~ traditional chronological plot, Joyce develops the protagonist's emotional conflict.**

Some adjectives act as **subject complements** following **linking verbs.**

My grandfather is *amazing.*

Note: Some verbs act as linking verbs only in certain contexts. When one of these verbs connects a subject and its complement, use an adjective form: She looked *ill.* When the verb is modified by the word that follows it, however, use an adverb: She looked *quickly.*

For ESL writers

ESL writers sometimes have trouble choosing between past and present participles *(looked, looking)* used as adjectives. See 56d for help in selecting the correct form.

25c Be aware of conventions for comparatives and superlatives.

- *Positive* adjectives and adverbs describe just one thing.

  I am *fast.*

- *Comparative* adjectives and adverbs compare two things.

  I had always been a little *faster* than she was.

- *Superlative* adjectives compare three or more things.

  An elite warrior corps grew that soon gained the respect of even its *most bitter* foes.

Most short adjectives (of one or two syllables) form the comparative with the ending *-er* and the superlative with the ending *-est.* Longer adjectives form the comparative with *more* or *less* and the superlative with *most* or *least.* The following chart shows how two positive adjectives, *quick* and *thoughtful,* change form in the comparative and superlative.

Positive	Comparative	Superlative
quick	quicker	quickest
thoughtful	more thoughtful	most thoughtful

More/less and *most/least* are also used to form the comparative and superlative of most adverbs, including all adverbs ending in *-ly: more/less slowly* and *most/least slowly.*

Note: The following adjectives and adverbs have irregular forms in the comparative and superlative.

Positive	Comparative	Superlative
good	better	best
bad	worse	worst
badly	worse	worst

Remember that absolute modifiers such as *impossible* and *unique* cannot logically have comparative and superlative forms.

absolute modifier A word that expresses a condition that cannot be lessened or exceeded (for example, *impossible, perfect,* or *unique*).

➤ Sheila's routine on the uneven bars was ~~more perfect~~ better than Julia's.

25d Avoid double negatives.

To correct a double negative, omit one of the negative words, for example, either *can't* or *hardly* in the following sentence—or make one word positive.

➤ **I can't ~~hardly~~ make it to the post office these days.**

➤ **I ~~can't~~ [can] hardly make it to the post office these days.**

PART 6 EFFECTIVE SENTENCES

PART

6 EFFECTIVE SENTENCES

26 MISSING WORDS

To write effective prose, take care to supply all necessary words.

26a Supply small words needed for clarity and completeness.

When you forget to include small words such as prepositions, conjunctions, and articles, the reader may be puzzled or have to pause momentarily to figure out what you mean. Proofread your essays carefully, even out loud, to catch omitted words.

For ESL writers

If English is not your native language, you may have special trouble with omitted words. See also 56a.

Insert missing prepositions.

- ➤ The car began to skid ^in^ the other direction.
- ➤ He graduated ^from^ high school at the top of his class.
- ➤ A child his age shouldn't be playing outside ^at^ that time of night.

preposition A word (such as *between, for, from, in, of,* or *to*) that always appears as part of a phrase and indicates the relation between a word in a sentence and the object of the preposition: The water splashed *into* the canoe.

For ESL writers

If you are not a native speaker of American English, prepositions may be especially difficult for you because they are highly idiomatic. In other words, native speakers of English use prepositions in ways that do not translate directly into other languages. The best way to understand when prepositions are needed in English sentences is to read widely and study the work of other writers. (See also Chapter 55.)

conjunction A word that relates sentence parts by coordinating, subordinating, or pairing elements, such as *and, because,* or *either . . . or.*

Insert missing conjunctions.

➤ **Most families and patients will accept the pain, inconvenience, ^and financial and emotional strain as long as the patient can achieve a life worth living.**

Here the conjunction *and* is necessary to indicate that *financial and emotional strain* is the third and final item in the series, following *pain* and *inconvenience.*

➤ **The heads of these golf clubs can be made of metal, wood, ^or graphite and often have special inserts in the part of the club that hits the ball.**

The conjunction *or* is needed in this sentence to indicate that *graphite* is the final option in a series of three possible materials for golf-club heads.

infinitive A verb form consisting of the word *to* plus the base form of the verb: *to run, to do.*

Restore the *to* omitted from an infinitive.

➤ **They decided ^to start the following Monday morning.**

➤ **I noticed how he used his uncanny talent for acting ^to make a dreary subject come alive.**

Insert missing **articles.**

➤ **This incident ruined the party, but it was only ^the^ beginning of the worst.**

➤ **But such ^a^ condition could be resolved by other means.**

> **For ESL writers**
>
> Nonnative speakers of English sometimes have trouble understanding when and when not to use the articles *a, an,* and *the.* For more advice on articles, see Chapter 53.

Insert other missing words to clarify or to complete a sentence.

Sometimes writers omit necessary words such as **pronouns** or **helping verbs.**

➤ **Finally, and I'm embarrassed to admit ^it,^ I shouted angrily at Cindy.**

➤ **Malaria was once a widespread human disease^,^ and ^it may^ become so again.**

In the second example, the revision adds a comma to separate the two independent clauses joined by *and.* See 37a for more information on punctuating independent clauses.

Sometimes writers omit words in sentences that are in the passive **voice,** which emphasizes the recipient of the action or the action itself while omitting or deemphasizing the actor.

➤ **In these scenes, women are often ^shown^ with long, luxurious hair.**

The revision adds the past participle *shown.*

article An adjective that precedes a noun and identifies a definite reference to something specific (*the*) or an indefinite reference to something less specific (*a* or *an*).

pronoun A word that replaces a specific noun (such as *she, his, they, myself,* or *which*), points out a specific noun (such as *this*) or refers to an unspecified person or object (such as *each* or *everybody*).

helping verb The verbs *have, do,* and *be,* which can function as helping verbs (they precede or "help" main verbs) or as main verbs, and modal verbs such as *can, may,* and *should,* which must be used with another (main) verb: I *may go* to the bank.

voice Indicates (active) or deemphasizes (passive) the performer of the verb's action.

26b Insert the word *that* if it is needed to prevent confusion or misreading.

Confusing I would like to point out golf is not just a game for rich old men in ugly pants.

Clearer I would like to point out *that* golf is not just a game for rich old men in ugly pants.

Without *that,* the reader may think at first that the writer is pointing out golf and have to double back to understand the sentence.

➤ **Dryer says, ^that as people grow older, they may find themselves waking up early, usually at dawn.**

➤ **Another problem parents will notice is ^that the child leaves out certain words.**

Note: If the meaning of a sentence is clear without *that,* it may be left out.

26c Make sure to include all words necessary for clear comparisons.

Check any comparisons to make sure that the items being compared are clearly identified and of the same kind.

Add words needed for logical comparisons.

➤ **Five-foot-five-inch Maria finds climbing to be more challenging ~~than~~ ^for her than it is for her six-foot-two-inch companions, who can reach the handholds more easily.**

The original version of this sentence says that climbing is more challenging than companions (illogically comparing an activity to people). The edited sentence says that climbing is more challenging for Maria than it is for her companions (logically comparing one person to other people).

Add words needed for complete comparisons.

In writing, it is important to identify clearly for readers all items being compared: not *This movie is better* but *This movie is better than the one I saw last week.*

➤ **Danziger's article is interesting and lightly laced with facts, definitely more entertaining,** than Solomon's article.

In some types of comparative sentences, standard English requires the conventional use of *as.*

Millie is *as* funny *as,* if not more funny than, Margot.

➤ **Students opting for field experience credits would learn as much, or more, than students who take only classes.** [edits: as inserted after "much"; as inserted after "than"]

26d Supply all words needed to clarify the parts of a compound structure.

compound structure A sentence element, such as a subject or a verb, that consists of two or more items linked by *and* or another conjunction.

Although a word or words may be left out of a compound structure, the omitted word or words must still fit in each part of the compound.

Women tend to express feelings in *the form of* requests, whereas men tend to express them in [*the form of*] commands.

When the same word or words do not fit in each part, you need to supply what is missing.

➤ **Water buffalo meat has been gaining popularity in America and** is **being sold to the public.**

27 SHIFTS

The guidelines in this chapter will help you identify and correct inappropriate shifts in your writing.

tense The form of a verb that shows the time of the action or state of being.

27a Keep verb tenses consistent.

As you draft or revise, establish a predominant tense for the actions or events you are writing about and stick with it, unless logic dictates otherwise.

➤ **The nurse tried to comfort me by telling jokes and explaining that the needle wouldn't hurt. With a slight push, the sharp, long needle ~~pierces~~ pierced through my skin and ~~finds~~ found its way to the vein.**

The revisions correct an illogical shift from the past tense (in the first sentence) to the present tense (in the second sentence).

➤ **I noticed much activity around the base. Sailors and chiefs ~~are~~ were walking all over the place. At 8:00 a.m., all traffic, foot and vehicle, halted. Toward the piers, the flag ~~is rising~~ rose up its pole. After the national anthem ~~ends,~~ ended, salutes ~~are~~ were completed, and people ~~go~~ went on with what they ~~are~~ had been doing.**

Because this passage describes past events, the writer changed all of the verbs to either the past tense or past progressive tense. (See 23a for more information on when to use progressive tenses.)

In certain cases, tense shifts are needed for the sake of logic. Consider this italicized addition to an earlier example.

> The nurse tried to comfort me by telling jokes and explaining that the needle wouldn't hurt. With a slight push, the sharp, long needle pierced through my skin and found its way to the vein. *I still remember the feeling.*

Here the shift to the present tense is acceptable because the writer's memory of getting the shot is ongoing, existing forever in the present. Similarly, general truths, facts, ongoing principles, and events in literary works are also seen as perpetual, and they too should be written of in the present tense.

➤ **The highest court in the land held that discretionary death penalties are unconstitutional because laws that ^give ~~gave~~ unlimited discretion to judges and juries to impose the penalty are "pregnant with discrimination."**

➤ **In the story, when the boy ^dies, ~~died,~~ Kathy ^realizes ~~realized~~ that it ^is ~~was~~ also time for her childhood to die, and so she ^returns ~~returned~~ to her South African home as an adult.**

27b Keep nouns and pronouns in a passage consistent in person and number.

person The form of a word that shows whether it refers to *I* or *we* (first person), to *you* (second person), or to *he, she, it,* or *they* (third person).

number The form of a word that shows whether it refers to one thing (singular) or more than one (plural): *parent, parents; child, children.*

➤ **Lynn informs all the kennel patrons of helpful programs for ^them and ~~you and~~ ^their pets. ~~your pet.~~**

The revision fixes the shift from the third-person plural (*patrons*) to the second-person singular (*you* and *your*) by changing *you* and *your* to the third-person plural. An alternative would be to use the second-person singular throughout.

➤ **Lynn informs ^you ~~all the members~~ of helpful programs for you and your pet.**

mood Shows the writer's attitude toward a statement.

voice Indicates (active) or de-emphasizes (passive) the performer of the verb's action.

27c Establish a consistent mood and voice.

In most cases, the verbs you use in a given sentence or passage should maintain one of the three moods: the indicative mood, used for statements and questions *(I entered . . .);* the imperative mood, used for directions, commands, and advice *(Take the car . . .);* and the subjunctive mood, used to indicate wishes and hypothetical, impossible, or unlikely conditions (*I wish I were president* . . .). If a sentence shifts from, say, a command to a statement, readers may be confused.

> ➤ First, ~~The first thing that can be done is~~ **make the community aware of the problem by writing a letter to the editor in the local newspaper.**

The original sentence shifts from the indicative mood to the imperative *(make the community).* The revision makes the whole sentence imperative.

Unwarranted shifts in voice can also be disorienting for readers.

> ➤ **I stepped out of the car with my training permit, a ~~necessary~~ document** I needed to take the test. ~~for the test to be taken.~~

The original sentence shifts from the active voice *(I stepped out)* to the passive voice *(the test to be taken).* The revision puts the whole sentence in the active voice.

> ➤ **I will judge the song according to the following criteria: the depth with which the lyrics treat each issue and the clarity with which** the music ~~each issue~~ presents each issue. ~~is presented in the music.~~

The original shifts from the active voice *(I will judge)* to the passive voice *(each issue is presented).* The revised sentence is in the active voice.

In most cases, choose the active voice over the passive voice. See also 23e on mood and 23f on voice.

27d Avoid mixing direct and indirect quotation.

Use direct quotation to present statements or questions in a speaker's or writer's own words; use indirect quotation to present the person's words without quoting directly. Avoid mixing the two forms of quotation.

> ➤ "Do whatever ~~they wanted to her,~~ [you want to me,"] she cried, "but don't harm Reza."

The revised sentence directly quotes the speaker's command. Because the speaker is quoted word for word, quotation marks are necessary.

A writer could also fix the sentence by turning it into a restatement of the speaker's words.

> ➤ ~~Do~~ [They could do] whatever they wanted to her, she cried, but ~~don't~~ [they shouldn't] harm Reza.

To avoid shifts between direct and indirect quotation, make sure that your pronouns are consistent in **person** and your verbs are consistent in **mood** (see 23e).

person The form of a word that shows whether it refers to *I* or *we* (first person), to *you* (second person), or to *he, she, it,* or *they* (third person).

mood Shows the writer's attitude toward a statement.

28 NOUN AGREEMENT

In most cases, related **nouns** in a sentence or passage should be consistently singular or plural. If nouns needlessly shift in **number,** readers may become confused.

noun A word that names a specific or general thing, person, place, concept, characteristic, or other idea.

number The form of a word that shows whether it refers to one thing (singular) or more than one (plural): *parent, parents; child, children.*

28a Use nouns that agree in number when they refer to the same topic, person, or object.

When several nouns are used to develop a topic, they may describe and expand the characteristics of a key noun, act as synonyms for one another, or develop related points in the discussion. When a sentence or passage includes such nouns, it will generally be clearer and more effective if these nouns agree in number, as in the following example.

> The treatment consists of *injections* of minimal *doses* of the *allergens* given at regular *intervals.*

All of the italicized nouns relating to the treatment are plural.

Sometimes writers use plural nouns to make it clear that they are referring to general, rather than particular, things.

➤ **Many people tend to "take their jobs to bed" with them and stay awake thinking about what needs to be done the next day. They also worry about ~~a promotion, a layoff, or a shift~~** promotions, layoffs, or shifts **in responsibilities.**

The plural nouns in this sentence are appropriate because the writer is referring to promotions, layoffs, and shifts in responsibilities in general—not to a particular promotion, firing, or shift.

➤ **As soon as immigrants get to the United States, they realize that to get ~~a better job~~** better jobs **and better living conditions, they need to learn English.**

Because the writer is referring to a general situation, the plural *better jobs* is appropriate.

Sometimes, however, the context calls for both singular and plural nouns.

> *Students* who want to make the most of *their* college years should pursue *a major course of study* while choosing *electives* or *a few minor courses of study* from the liberal arts.

> *Minnows* are basically inedible because *they* have very little *meat* on *their bodies.*

In the second example, the writer consistently uses plural forms *(they, their,* and *bodies)* to refer to the minnows but also uses *meat,* which conventionally takes a singular form in a context like this one. (See 53d.)

Some common idiomatic expressions, such as *the error of their ways,* also mix singular and plural forms.

Idiomatic wording The penalties set for offenders might be enough to help them to see *the error of their ways* and eventually help them to reform their social habits.

28b Understand the conventions for nouns following *kind, type, or sort.*

Nouns such as *kind, type,* or *sort* are singular, although they have plural forms *(kinds, types).* When following an expression such as *kind of* or *sort of,* a noun is usually singular.

➤ **RAs are allowed to choose what kind of ~~programs~~ program they want to have.**

Use *this* and *that* instead of *these* and *those* to modify the singular forms of *kind, type,* and similar words.

➤ **To comprehend ~~these~~ this type of ~~articles,~~ article, it helps to have a strong background in statistics.**

29 MODIFIERS

modifier A word, phrase, or clause functioning as an adjective or adverb that adds information and detail about a noun, a verb, or another word.

When revising your work, make sure that you position adjectives and adverbs to reflect your intended meaning. In the following examples, arrows show the clear connections between the bracketed **modifiers** and the words they modify.

My *frozen* smile faltered as my chin quivered.

The flurry *of fins, masks, weights, and wet suits* continued.

Beyond the chairs loomed the object *that I feared most*—*a beautiful black Steinway grand* piano *that gleamed under the bright stage lights.*

29a Place a modifying word, phrase, or clause as close as possible to the word that it modifies.

- The ~~attempted~~ number of ^attempted^ suicides this semester was four.
- The women have to do all the hard work, ^needed to maintain the family,^ especially in rural areas. ~~needed to maintain the family.~~
- He and the other people start to look ^as hard as they can^ for any sign of a boat, an island, or an oil platform. ~~as hard as they can.~~

You may choose to rewrite a sentence to clarify the connection between a modifier and what it modifies.

➤ ~~Community~~ leaders should ~~organize meetings open to all neighbors~~ ~~at~~ convenient times and locations. [When organizing meetings open to all neighbors, community ... select]

➤ We were friends until I [turned eighteen and] became too popular and obnoxious for anyone to stand ~~when I turned eighteen.~~

Place a limiting modifier just before the word it modifies to avoid ambiguity.
When a limiting modifier is misplaced, it creates confusion because it could often modify several words in the same sentence.

➤ The San Diego landfill is going to be filled to capacity by 1998, and some experts ~~even~~ say [even] sooner.

When *even* precedes *say,* the sentence suggests that the experts are "even saying," not that the date will be even sooner.

29b Make sure that a modifier qualifies the meaning of a particular word in the sentence.

A modifying phrase that does not refer specifically to any word is called a *dangling modifier.* A dangling modifier usually occurs at the beginning of a sentence and is likely to be a **participial phrase** or a **prepositional phrase.**

➤ By far the best song on the album, ~~the~~ ["Lambada" has] vocals and melodies ~~of~~ [that] ~~"Lambada"~~ create a perfect harmony.

Readers expect the phrase *By far the best song on the album* to be followed immediately by the name of the song.

Correct dangling modifiers using either of the following two methods.

limiting modifier A modifier such as *almost, just,* or *only* that should directly precede the word or word group it limits.

participial phrase A group of words that begins with a present participle *(dancing, freezing)* or a past participle *(danced, frozen)* and modifies a noun or a pronoun: We boarded the bus, *expecting to leave immediately.*

prepositional phrase A group of words that begins with a preposition and indicates the relation between a word in a sentence and the object following the preposition: Her sunglasses slid *under the seat.*

dependent (subordinate) clause A word group with a subject, a predicate, and a subordinating word (such as *because*) at the beginning. It cannot stand by itself as a sentence but must be connected to an independent (main) clause: *Although it was raining,* we loaded our gear onto the buses.

1. Follow the dangling phrase with a noun that it could logically modify.

➤ Rather than receiving several painful shots in the mouth before a cavity is filled, ^a patient may find that^ hypnosis can work just as effectively.

➤ After surveying the floor on which I live, ^I concluded that^ the residents of my dorm don't care much for floor programs.

2. Change the dangling phrase into a dependent clause.

By changing a phrase to a clause, you can correct a dangling modifier by supplying the information or connection that is missing. Be sure to add words and rewrite so that both the subject and the predicate are clearly stated and the clause fits the rest of the sentence.

➤ ^If the school board decides to close^ ~~By closing~~ Dos Pueblos, the remaining high schools ^will^ ~~would~~ have larger student bodies and increased budgets.

➤ After ^I concluded^ ~~concluding~~ my monologue on the hazards of partying, she smiled broadly and said, "OK, Mom, I'll be more careful next time."

infinitive A verb form consisting of the word *to* plus the base form of the verb: *to run, to do.*

limiting modifier A modifier such as *almost, just,* or *only* that should directly precede the word or word group it limits.

29c Keep the two parts of an infinitive together.

When one or more other words follow the *to,* they "split" the infinitive, separating *to* from the base form of the verb. These other words can usually be moved elsewhere in the sentence. Be especially alert for **limiting modifiers** (see 29a) that split infinitives.

➤ His stomach ^always^ seemed to ~~always~~ hang over his pants.

The revision avoids splitting the infinitive *to hang* with the modifier *always,* which logically describes *seemed.*

Note: Occasionally, moving the intervening words to avoid splitting an infinitive can create a sentence that sounds more awkward than the version with the split infinitive. In such cases, leaving the split infinitive may be the better choice.

30 MIXED CONSTRUCTIONS

A sentence is mixed when it starts with one grammatical pattern then changes course in the middle. Mixed sentences can disorient readers and force them to guess at your intended meaning.

30a Choose one of the grammatical patterns in a mixed sentence, and use it consistently throughout the sentence.

Readers expect sentences to begin and end with the same structural pattern (for example, *The more I waited, the more discouraged I became*). The sentence below violates readers' expectations.

➤ **Mixed** **The more oil that we save now, means much more in the future.**

The following revision fulfills readers' expectations.

➤ **Revised** **The more oil that we save now,** ~~**means much more**~~ the more we will have **in the future.**

Alternately, the sentence could be revised as follows.

➤ **Revised** If we save ~~**The**~~ **more oil** ~~**that we save**~~ **now,** we will have ~~**means**~~ **much more in the future.**

Revise mixed sentences to make the connections clear (for instance, by clarifying that one part is subordinate to the other).

➤ **School, ~~is~~ another resource for children who don't have anyone to talk to, can provide information ~~get educated~~ about the problem of teen pregnancy.**

➤ **School is another place where ~~resource for~~ children who don't have anyone to talk to can get educated about the problem of teen pregnancy.**

If neither part of a mixed sentence supplies a workable pattern for the whole, you may have to restructure the sentence.

➤ **~~This is something the~~ The shelter prides itself on ~~and is~~ always looking for new volunteers and ideas. ~~for the shelter.~~**

➤ **The ~~next part of the~~ essay next detailed ~~was where~~ the results of the study ~~were detailed~~ and concluded with ~~finally included~~ a commentary section. ~~concluding the article.~~**

30b Make sure that subjects and predicates are compatible.

You can solve the problem of a logically mismatched subject and predicate—called *faulty predication*—by rewriting either the subject or the predicate so that the two fit together.

➤ **Students attending schools ~~Schools~~ that prohibited paddling behaved as well as those at schools that permitted corporal punishment.**

To test a sentence for faulty predication, ask yourself whether the subject can do what the predicate says. (For example, do schools behave?) If not, you will need to revise the sentence for clarity.

subject The word or words that identify the topic or theme of the sentence—what is being discussed: *Our defective rubber raft* began to leak air.

predicate The part of a clause that includes a complete verb and says something about the subject: At the checkpoint, we *unloaded the canoes.*

➤ **Bean's service is top notch~~,~~ and ^the staff^ is striving continually to meet student needs.**

Bean's service cannot strive continually, but Bean's staff can.

➤ **Ironically, the main character's memory of Mangan's sister on the porch step ^always includes^ ~~cannot recall the image without~~ the lamplight.**

A memory cannot recall, but a memory can include something.

30c Eliminate illogical phrases such as *is where, is when,* and *the reason is because.*

Often you can replace *is where* or *is when* with a noun specifying a category or type.

➤ **An absolutist position is ^a stance taken by someone who^ ~~when someone~~ strongly opposes any restrictions on speech.**

To eliminate *the reason is because,* rewrite the sentence, or use *the reason . . . is that* or *because* instead.

➤ **^In addition,^ ~~Another reason~~ radio stations should not play songs with sexually explicit lyrics ~~is~~ because children like to sing along.**

➤ **Another reason radio stations should not play songs with sexually explicit lyrics is ^that^ ~~because~~ children like to sing along.**

31 INTEGRATING QUOTATIONS, QUESTIONS, AND THOUGHTS

The following guidelines will help you incorporate quotations of source material, questions, or thoughts into your own writing.

direct quotation A speaker's or writer's exact words, which are enclosed in quotation marks.

31a When integrating a direct quotation from a source, clearly introduce the name of the person you are quoting.

In the words of automotive executive M. Paul Tippitt, "The cardinal rule of the new ballgame is change" (Sobel 259).

If you drop a quotation into your text without clearly introducing the speaker's or writer's name, readers may not be sure whom you are quoting. To avoid confusion, name the person or people you are quoting in the sentence that includes the quotation.

➤ **Most people are not even aware of the extent to which television plays a role in their lives.** As Mitroff and Bennis point out, **"Television defines our problems and shapes our actions; in short, how we define our world"** (xi). ~~**(Mitroff and Bennis xi).**~~

(See 8c for additional information on integrating quotations.)

Note: Readers expect quotations and text to fit together gracefully. Your ideas and the material from supporting sources should be unified and coherent. If your own words do not fit with a quotation from a source, you may have to adjust your text and the quotation. (See also 27d.)

➤ **A person with AIDS has lost "disease-fighting white T-4 lymphocytes**
and has contracted
~~. . . also have~~ one or more of a number of life-threatening opportunistic diseases" (Langone 14).

Note: The examples in this section include parenthetical, or in-text, citations that follow the style recommended by the Modern Language Association (MLA). For further information about this style, see Chapter 9.

31b Follow the conventions for presenting direct and indirect quotations of questions.

direct quotation A speaker's or writer's exact words, which are enclosed in quotation marks.

indirect quotation A reworded statement or question that presents a speaker's or writer's ideas without quoting directly or using quotation marks.

Enclose a direct quotation of a question in quotation marks, identifying the speaker and using his or her exact words. Do not use quotation marks for an indirect quotation or a question that you address to the reader.

Direct quotation	"I have to get this car clean by noon," I told her abruptly. "Can you help me out?"
Indirect quotation	Without much hesitation, I explained my mission to her and asked whether she would help me out.
Question addressed to reader	Should sex education be a required class in public schools?

Avoid mixing direct and indirect quotations of questions, as in *Without much hesitation, I asked could she help me out?*

31c Follow the conventions for presenting direct and indirect quotations of thoughts.

When you directly quote words that you or someone else thinks, the quotation marks are optional.

"Go eighty feet for thirty minutes," she reminded herself.

Go eighty feet for thirty minutes, she reminded herself.

However, do not use quotation marks around indirect quotations of thoughts.

She reminded herself to go eighty feet for thirty minutes.

Typically, direct quotations of thoughts are used in fiction and creative nonfiction, but not in formal academic essays and reports.

32 PARALLELISM

noun A word that names a specific or general thing, person, place, concept, characteristic, or other idea.

infinitive phrase A verb phrase consisting of the word *to* plus the base form of a verb and connected words: *to go to the opera.*

present progressive tense A verb form indicating that an action is continuing in the present: *I am singing.*

When you present items in a series or as a pair, using parallel grammatical form will make your sentence more effective and easier to read.

Series By implementing this proposal, administrators could enhance the reputation of the university with quality *publications, plays, concerts,* and *sports teams.*

The italicized items in this series are all plural **nouns.**

An interruption has the potential *to disrupt turns at talk, to disorganize the topic of conversation,* and *to violate the current speaker's right to talk.*

The italicized items in this series are all **infinitive phrases.**

Pair Imagine that you and your daughter are *walking* in the mall or *eating* in a popular restaurant.

Both of the paired items, *walking* and *eating,* are in the **present progressive tense.**

When the items in a series or pair are similar grammatically, their form strongly signals the reader that they are equally important, similar in meaning, and related in the same way to the rest of the sentence.

32a Make sure all items in a series follow the same grammatical pattern.

Items in a series are usually linked by *and* or *or.* Each item should be parallel to the others and presented in a consistent grammatical form.

➤ **The children must deal with an overprotective parent, sibling rivalry, and ~~living~~ life in a single-parent home.**

➤ **Drivers destined for Coronado can choose to turn left, turn right, or ~~proceeding~~ proceed straight into the city.**

32b Make sure both items in a pair follow the same grammatical pattern.

Paired items linked by *and* or *or,* by **correlative conjunctions,** or in comparisons using *than* or *as* should be in the same grammatical form.

correlative conjunctions Word pairs that link sentence elements; the first word anticipates the second: *both . . . and, either . . . or, neither . . . nor, not only . . . but also.*

Linked by *and* or *or*	While Simba is growing up, he is told of *things he should do* and *things he should not do.*
Linked by correlative conjunction	At that time, the person is surprised not only by *where he is* but also by *what has happened.*
In comparisons using *than* or *as*	They feel that *using force* is more effective than *threatening abstract consequences.*

➤ **The viewer need not be offended by the characters because they are clearly stereotypes rather than ~~realism.~~ realities.**

33 EMPHASIS AND CLARITY

When you write a sentence, you make numerous decisions about arranging its basic elements—words, phrases, and clauses. When you write an essay, arranging sentences in a sequence, you make additional decisions in order to maintain coherence and keep your reader focused on your subject. Two primary strategies can be used to arrange the elements of a sentence: coordination and subordination. These strategies are illustrated in 33a. (See also Chapter 29 for help with placing modifiers, and Chapter 30 for help with avoiding mixed constructions.) Three additional strategies can help you to sequence sentences effectively: using cohesive devices, making your sentence topics visible, and introducing information that will be familiar to your readers ahead of new or unfamiliar information (the old-new contract). These strategies are described in 33c, 33d, and 33e, respectively.

independent (main) clause A word group with a subject and a predicate that can stand alone as a separate sentence. (A predicate is the part of a clause that includes a complete verb and says something about the subject: At the checkpoint, we *unloaded the canoes.*)

33a Use coordination and subordination to indicate the relationships among sentence elements.

Use coordination to join sentence elements that are equally important.

When you use coordination, you bring together in one sentence two or more elements of equal importance to the meaning. These elements can be words, phrases, or clauses. In the following examples, the first sentence coordinates two words and the second sentence coordinates three phrases.

> The sheriff's department lacks both the *officers* and the *equipment* to patrol every road in the county.

> Most of us would agree with the evil queen's magic mirror, that this Disney girl, with her *skin as white as snow, lips as red as blood,* and *hair as black as ebony,* is, indeed, "the fairest one of all."

You can also coordinate ideas of equal importance by joining **independent clauses** within the same sentence.

In the United States there are only 1.3 million windsurfers, but the numbers are increasing 10 to 15 percent a year.

Children like to sing along with songs they hear on the radio; consequently, radio stations should not play songs with language that demeans women.

Use subordination to indicate that one sentence element is more important than other elements.

Writers frequently subordinate information to more important information within a single sentence. The most important information appears in an independent clause, and the less important or subordinate information appears in words, **phrases,** or **dependent clauses** attached to the independent clause or integrated into it. (Often, the most important information in a sentence will be information that is new to a reader. See 33d.) In the following examples, the first sentence begins with a dependent clause. In the second sentence, a dependent clause interrupts the independent clause.

After Dave finished his mutinous speech, the corners of Dan's mouth slowly formed a nearly expressionless grin.

Political liberals, *who trace their American roots to the Declaration of Independence,* insist that the federal government should attempt to reduce inequalities of income and wealth.

33b Combine sentences to make your writing more meaningful, graceful, and efficient.

Often, combining sentences improves the clarity or vividness of your writing. It can also reduce the number of words, making your prose more efficient.

Two sentences People love this café because of its impressive lineup of steaming waffle irons at breakfast. They also appreciate the occasional low-price steak and shrimp nights.

Combined People love this café because of its impressive lineup of steaming waffle irons at breakfast and its occasional low-price steak and shrimp nights.

phrase A group of words that does *not* contain both a subject and a verb and is always part of an independent clause. Some common types of phrases include *prepositional* (*After a flash of lightning,* I saw a tree split in half) and *verbal* (*Blinded by the flash,* I ran into the house).

dependent (subordinate) clause A word group with a subject, a predicate, and a subordinating word (such as *because*) at the beginning. It cannot stand by itself as a sentence but must be connected to an independent (main) clause: *Although it was raining,* we loaded our gear onto the buses.

Combining the two sentences brings the two reasons for loving the café closer together and saves four words. The second sentence is reduced to a phrase, a typical benefit of sentence combining (see 34c).

Two sentences There we sat at our speed trap under the County Road 38 bridge on Cedar Avenue. We were eating McDonald's french fries and talking law enforcement.

Combined Eating MacDonald's french fries and talking law enforcement, we sat at our speed trap under the County Road 38 bridge on Cedar Avenue.

By combining the sentences, the writer brings together the two actions of sitting and eating and emphasizes that they are happening at the same time.

There are several ways to combine sentences. Although any two or three sentences might be combined, combine sentences only if the result is more readable, clear, efficient, and direct than the separated sentences.

coordinating conjunction A word that joins comparable and equally important sentence elements: *for, and, or, but, nor, yet,* or *so.*

1. Combine sentences by connecting them with *and, but,* or another coordinating conjunction.

In each of the following sentence pairs, the second sentence can be combined with the first sentence in order to reveal their logical relationship.

➤ **I have seen more than a few schematic computer diagrams~~.~~, but this ~~This~~ one was easily the most confusing diagram I have ever seen.**

The second sentence presents a contrast. When the sentences are combined, the conjunction *but* signals the relationship explicitly.

➤ **Some historians blame Major Reno for not continuing his charge~~.~~, and other ~~Other~~ historians blame Captain Benteen for not coming to Custer's rescue.**

The second sentence provides additional information; the conjunction *and* indicates that one idea is added to another.

Note: Take care to avoid excessive coordination.

➤ **Contingent workers ^who may work either full time or part time ~~and they~~ have no job security and ~~also~~ they rarely get health insurance or retirement benefits.**

➤ **Skim-boarders ^who toss circles of wood or plastic in the shallowest surf at the water line and then leap on them for a ride along the slick sand, ~~but they~~ are considered dangerous by the rival wave surfers. Nevertheless, ~~and yet~~ skim-boarders ~~they still~~ create a fun show to watch.**

adverb clause A clause that nearly always modifies a verb, indicating time, place, condition, reason, cause, purpose, result, or another logical relationship.

dependent (subordinate) clause A word group with a subject, a predicate, and a subordinating word (such as *because*) at the beginning. It cannot stand by itself as a sentence but must be connected to an independent (main) clause.

subordinating conjunction A word or phrase (such as *although, because, since,* or *as soon as*) that introduces a dependent clause and relates it to an independent clause.

2. Combine sentences by using an adverb clause.

One sentence can be made subordinate to the other by turning it into a **dependent clause.** In this way, the ideas in the two sentences are more precisely related.

➤ **As she ~~She~~ stood there next to the chalkboard, her ~~Her~~ back and her shoulders were bent slightly forward.**

The **subordinating conjunction** *as* indicates a time relationship.

➤ **We could tell our food had just come off the grill, because it ~~It~~ still sizzled and snapped.**

The subordinating conjunction *because* indicates a causal relationship.

relative pronoun A pronoun (such as *who, whom, whose, which,* or *that*) that introduces an adjective clause (a clause that modifies a noun or pronoun).

independent (main) clause A word group with a subject and a predicate that can stand alone as a separate sentence. (A predicate is the part of a clause that includes a complete verb and says something about the subject: At the checkpoint, we *unloaded the canoes.*)

participial phrase A group of words that begins with a present participle *(dancing, freezing)* or a past participle *(danced, frozen)* and modifies a noun or a pronoun: We boarded the bus, *expecting to leave immediately.*

3. Combine sentences by using a relative clause.

In the following examples, one of the sentences can be combined with the other by adding a **relative pronoun** and making it an adjective or a relative clause. These clauses follow the nouns they modify in the **independent clause** and provide information about them.

➤ **Representative of this new generation of cars is the 1981 Chrysler Reliant, which ~~It~~ replaced the Valiant in the company lineup.**

➤ **Most five- to nine-year-old children who have experienced a death in the family~~. They~~ can understand that death is irreversible.**

4. Combine sentences by using an introductory participial phrase.

In the following examples, the first sentence can be transformed into a participial phrase, which modifies the subject of the independent clause in the combined sentence. Reducing a sentence to a phrase nearly always saves words, making your writing more efficient. In these two examples, the action in the first sentence takes place at the same time as the action in the second sentence. Converting the first sentence to a phrase helps to emphasize that the two actions happen simultaneously.

➤ Concluding **~~Mom concluded~~ her monologue on the dangers of partying,** Mom **~~Then she~~ first scowled and then smiled. I said, "Okay, Mom. I'll be more careful next time."**

➤ Clenching **~~I clenched~~ my fist and** shutting **~~shut~~ my eyes as tightly as possible, ~~At the same time,~~ I listened to the nurse prepare the needle and vial to draw my blood.**

5. Combine sentences by using an appositive.

In each of the following examples, one sentence has been reduced to an appositive phrase that modifies a noun in the independent clause. Although the appositive is subordinate to the idea in the independent clause, it adds useful identifying information.

➤ **Albert, ~~is~~ Celie's husband in *The Color Purple*, ~~He~~ is the perfect example of a man who has not mastered the art of being sensitive to the feelings of women.**

➤ **The film's twist is revealed when we find out that Harry works for Omega Sector, ~~This is~~ a covert government agency that specializes in preventing nuclear terrorism.**

appositive A word or word group that identifies or gives more information about a noun or pronoun that precedes it: I called the mayor's office and asked for Jane Kite, *the mayor's assistant.*

6. Combine sentences by using an absolute phrase.

In the following examples, the sentences offer information that, when combined, creates an imagined scene that a viewer might take in all at once. Reducing sentences to absolute phrases can help you to express this "all-at-onceness."

➤ **Clothes ~~His clothes are~~ smeared with chalk dust, ~~and his~~ shirt sleeves ~~are~~ rolled up to his elbows, Professor Pomeroy is ready to throw himself into another lecture.**

➤ **She lay sweating on the beach in an orange bikini, a ~~A~~ large-size Sprite bottle ~~was~~ half buried in the damp sand close by, a ~~A~~ spray bottle of baby oil and two novels ~~were~~ within reach in her big straw bag.**

absolute phrase A word group that modifies the whole clause and often includes a noun or pronoun and a past or present participle *(danced, dancing)* as well as modifiers.

7. Combine sentences by using a colon.

You can also use a colon to combine sentences effectively.

> ➤ **Gates has the support of several City Council members~~.~~: ~~These include~~ Bernson, Milke, Flores, and Ferrano.**

The second sentence provides a list. In the combined sentence, the colon introduces the list.

> ➤ **Convenience food at home and fast food on the road pose a special problem for children~~.~~: ~~This kind of food is~~ high ~~in~~ calories but low ~~in~~ nutritional value.**

The colon signals that an example or definition follows.

In both examples, the material following the colon is more concise and more strongly emphasized in the combined sentence than it was originally.

33c Use cohesive devices to help your reader follow your ideas.

If writing is *cohesive,* it "sticks together." The reader can follow the writer's ideas from clause to clause or sentence to sentence. There are no gaps between sentences. Cohesion contributes to *coherence,* the global connections among parts of a written text.

The most frequently used and important cohesive devices are word repetition and pronoun reference.

1. Repeat a word or phrase or use a synonym.

In the following example, the phrase *sexual harassment* and its synonyms are repeated several times. (A *synonym* is a word that has the same or nearly the same meaning as another word.)

One significant reason for the rise in reported incidents of sexual harassment may be the increased awareness of what constitutes sexual harassment. There are two distinct types of sexual harassment, and although their formal names may be unfamiliar, the situations they describe will almost certainly ring a bell. Hostile environment sexual harassment occurs when a supervisor, coworker, or classmate gives the victim "unwelcome sexual attention" that interferes with the victim's ability to work or creates an intimidating or offensive atmosphere (Stanko and Werner 15). Quid pro quo sexual harassment occurs when "a workplace superior demands some degree of sexual favor" and either threatens or does retaliate in a way that "has a tangible effect on the working conditions of the harassment victim" if he or she refuses to comply (Stanko and Werner 15).

Sarah West, "The Rise in Reported Incidents of Sexual Harassment"

Notice that the phrase *sexual harassment* is repeated five times. In addition, the writer relies on synonyms: *unwelcome sexual attention, intimidating or offensive atmosphere,* and *sexual favor.* These frequently repeated words and synonyms help readers follow the writer's ideas.

If a sequence of sentences seems difficult to follow, consider repeating words or using synonyms. In the following revised sentences from student Drew Long's essay "Bullseye," the word *snipers* has been repeated to increase sentence cohesion and readability.

➤ **Snipers can penetrate hundreds of miles into enemy territory. ~~Isolation~~** Snipers **can be ~~the result~~** isolated **for more than a week. ~~Living~~** Therefore, snipers must be skilled at living **off the land for days at a time. ~~is an important skill.~~**

pronoun A word that replaces a specific noun (such as *she, he, it, his, they, them, yours, ours, myself, whose,* or *which*), points out a specific noun (such as *this, these,* or *that*), or refers to an unspecified person or object (such as *each* or *everybody*).

2. Use pronouns to refer to earlier words.

Because many pronouns refer to nouns or other pronouns, using them can increase the cohesion of a group of sentences. The following example includes two chains of nouns and pronouns. Both chains begin in the first sentence: one begins with *John Wright,* and the other begins with *wife.*

> John Wright never sees beyond his own needs to the needs of his wife. He does not understand her need for a pretty creature to fill the void created by her lonely, childless existence. Not content just to kill Minnie's personality, he kills her canary, leaving her with the deafening silence of the lonesome prairie.
>
> Margaret Tate, "Irony and Intuition in 'A Jury of Her Peers'"

The *John Wright* chain includes four pronouns: *his* and *he* each appear twice. In the *wife* chain, *her* appears four times; the noun *Minnie's* is also part of this chain. In these three sentences, notice how eleven of the words, almost four to a sentence, directly function to increase cohesion.

If a sequence of sentences about people seems difficult to follow, add additional pronoun references. For example, in the following revised sentences from "Differing Worldviews: Mom and Feminism" by student Margaret Zenk, the pronoun *she* has been repeated three more times in order to increase cohesion.

➤ **When it was time for Mom to choose a major in college, [she chose to study] math ~~was the choice of study~~. She took all of her math classes from the most famous professors because, she explained, [she thought she deserved] the best ~~was what was deserved~~.**

33d Make sentence topics visible.

A *sentence topic* is the idea that launches the sentence. Sometimes the topic is the grammatical subject of the sentence.

> subject/topic
> Henrietta serves as the antagonist in this story.

Sometimes it is not the subject of the sentence.

> topic — Showing little regard for Hester's feelings, subject — Henrietta is more concerned that Hester have the right attitude.

A string of sentences, each of which opens with the same sentence topic or with a synonym or pronoun that refers to the same topic, is likely to be highly readable. Here is an example.

> Serial killers are almost always male and 92 percent are white. Most are between the ages of twenty-five and thirty-five and often physically attractive. While serial killers may hold a job, many switch employment frequently as they become easily frustrated when advancement does not come as quickly as expected. These killers tend to believe that they are entitled to whatever they desire but feel that they should have to exert no effort to attain their goals.
>
> La Donna Beaty, "What Makes a Serial Killer"

Notice that every sentence begins with the same topic or a reference to it: *Serial killers, Most,* or *These killers.*

If a sequence of sentences seems difficult to follow, create a consistent string of topics. The following passage from student Scott Hyder's essay "*Poltergeist:* It Knows What Scares You" has been revised so that the title of the film either begins, or appears close to the beginning of, four of the five sentences. The fourth sentence begins with the pronoun *It,* which refers to *Poltergeist.*

➤ ***Poltergeist* reflects a lot of fears that most of us grow up with. Poltergeist surfaces scary ~~Scary~~ shadows from the light in the closet and our worst childhood nightmares. ~~are surfaced by *Poltergeist.*~~ Offering ~~The~~ unique thrills, ~~offered by~~ *Poltergeist* captures ~~capture~~ its audience. It allows viewers to link their most inner-locked fears to those on the screen. *Poltergeist:* It knows what scares you!**

33e Introduce information that will be familiar to your readers ahead of new information.

In many languages, including English, writers predictably place old or familiar information (information known to the reader) first in a sentence and new or unfamiliar information last. This pattern is known as the *old-new contract* writers make with their readers. Just as inconsistent topic strings create problems for readers (see 33d), placing new information ahead of old information in a series of sentences makes writing hard to read.

> Coyote's major problem in his pursuit of the Road Runner never seems to be the plan itself, but the products [new] he uses to carry out the plan. None of the equipment [familiar] he buys from Acme ever works correctly [new]. It may work fine in a test run [familiar], but when the Road Runner actually falls into the trap, everything goes crazy or fails completely [new].
>
> Kirsten Dockendorff, "The Road to Acme Looniversity"

Notice that the sentences after the first one begin with familiar information and end with new information.

If a sequence of sentences seems difficult to follow, consider adjusting the pattern of familiar and new information. The following sentences from student Anna Pride's essay "The Art of Wasting Time" have been revised so that every sentence after the first one opens with familiar information.

> ➤ **For every task and every person there is an optimum level of arousal. ~~A function of~~ [This level is controlled by] our nervous system [by a function] called homeostasis~~ controls this level~~. The nervous system regulates hormone and chemical levels in the body and, when faced with a challenge, attempts to bring us to an appropriate level of functioning. ~~We~~ [If this perfect level of functioning is not reached, we] often do not even feel motivated to attempt a task~~ if this perfect level of functioning is not reached~~.**

Before the revisions, the second and fourth sentences in this passage began with new information, a pattern that often interrupts cohesion. The revisions move the familiar information to the beginning of these two sentences, creating a more predictable pattern that is easy for readers to follow.

PART 

WORD CHOICE

PART

7 WORD CHOICE

34 CONCISE SENTENCES

Effective writing is concise, without unnecessary words or phrases.

> Tears stream down James's face as he sits scrunched up in the corner of the shabby living room, wishing that he had anyone else's life.
>
> We need traffic signals for this dangerous intersection.

Concise sentences convey impressions or claims clearly and convincingly.

By contrast, wordy sentences are tiresome to read and may be difficult to understand. Concentrate on eliminating unnecessary words and simplifying sentence structure in your writing.

34a Eliminate redundancies and repetition.

The phrase *blue in color* is redundant because it is clear that blue is a color. In general, a word is redundant when it conveys a meaning already contained in another word.

Redundant	**Concise**
advance planning	planning
in a reluctant manner	reluctantly
large-sized	large
mix together	mix
past memories	memories

Expressions such as *the fact is true, bisect in half,* and *in my opinion, I believe* are redundant because they contain obvious implications: Truth is implied by fact, *bisect* means "to divide in half," and *in my opinion* says the same thing as *I believe.* Pare down these and any similar expressions.

Eliminate redundant expressions from your writing, rewording sentences if necessary.

- ➤ **Student volunteers will no longer be** exhausted **~~overworked, overburdened, and overexhausted~~ from working ~~continuously at the jobs~~ without ~~any~~ breaks because of the labor shortage.**
- ➤ **All these recommendations are interconnected**. **~~to one another.~~**
- ➤ California **~~The~~ colleges ~~in the state of California~~ rely too much on the annual income of a student's parents and not enough on the parents' true financial situation.**

Repetitive expressions—those that repeat other words exactly or restate them without adding meaning—should also be eliminated.

- ➤ **Many of the drilling machines need to be** modernized. **~~updated to better and more modern equipment.~~**
- ➤ **In addition, there is a** convenient **customer service center**. **~~for the convenience of the customers.~~**

34b Avoid empty expressions.

Expressions such as *due to the fact that* and *at this point in time* are considered "empty" because they add words without adding meaning. They can also make your writing sound stilted. Try to replace empty phrases with more concise alternatives.

➤ **~~In many cases, this~~ This situation may ~~be due to the fact that~~ occur because these women were not given the opportunity to work.**

➤ **Demanding Eldridge's resignation ~~at this point in time~~ now will not solve the problem.**

Here is a list of some common empty phrases and their more concise alternatives.

Empty Phrases	Concise Alternatives
due to the fact that in view of the fact that the reason for for the reason that this is why in light of the fact that on the grounds that	for, because, why, since
despite the fact that regardless of the fact that	although, though
as regards in reference to concerning the matter of where . . . is concerned	concerning, about, regarding
it is necessary that there is a need for it is important that	should, must

Wordy	Concise
has the ability to is able to is in a position to	can
in order to for the purpose of	to
at this point in time	now
on the subject of	on, about
as a matter of fact	actually
aware of the fact that	know
to the effect that	that
the way in which	how
in the event that	if, when

prepositional phrase A group of words that begins with a preposition and indicates the relation between a word in a sentence and the object following the preposition: Her sunglasses slid *under the seat.*

34c Simplify the sentence structure.

To simplify sentence structure, concentrate on turning clauses into phrases or replacing phrases, especially strings of **prepositional phrases,** with words.

> Bo Jackson is an excellent recent example ~~One of the best examples in recent times~~ of an overexposed athlete. ~~being completely overexposed is that of Bo Jackson.~~

Sometimes you can simplify your writing by consolidating a series of sentences into one. (See 33a and b for more on combining sentences.)

> No single alternative will solve the problem of teen pregnancy, and all the possible solutions have disadvantages. ~~There are many other possible alternative solutions to teen pregnancy. One solution is not going to work alone to solve the problem. But there are disadvantages that come along with them.~~

Simplify sentences beginning with *There is* or *It is*.
Sentences that begin with *There is* or *It is* may also be simplified to avoid wordiness. Unless you want to shift the emphasis toward information at the end of the sentence (see 33d), avoid beginning with *There is* or *It is.*

> ~~There are always five~~ [Five] or six seats [are always] open at the ends of the rows.

> ~~It is this~~ [This] exaggeration ~~that~~ provides the [characters'] comic appeal. ~~of the characters.~~

Consider changing sentences from the passive to the active voice.
Because the active voice is more direct and less wordy than the passive voice, turning passive sentences into active ones will often make your writing easier to read. (See also 23f.)

voice Indicates (active) or de-emphasizes (passive) the performer of the verb's action.

> ~~The topic is initiated by a~~ [A] member who has nothing to gain by the discussion [initiates] ~~of~~ the topic.

The strong verb *initiates* introduces an actor, *A member,* into the sentence. Sentences with actors performing actions are often easier to read.

In general, the verb *be* is far less precise than another verb might be. Whenever possible, replace *am, are, is, was,* and other forms of the verb *be* with a stronger verb that clearly defines the action.

Note: The passive voice is sometimes useful if you want to shift information to the end of a sentence. It is also frequently used in impersonal writing that focuses on an action rather than an actor, as in a scientific research report.

34d Eliminate unnecessary intensifiers or hedges.

Although intensifiers such as *very, really, clearly, quite,* and *of course* can strengthen statements, eliminating intensifiers—or substituting more forceful words—is often more effective.

➤ **Your choice could ~~very possibly~~ make the difference between a saved or lost life.**

➤ **The plot of this movie is** thrilling. **~~really great.~~**

Some intensifiers, such as *very* in *very unique,* are unnecessary because the words they modify are already as strong as possible. Something either is or is not unique; it cannot be very or slightly unique. (See also 25c.)

➤ **The** unique **arrangement of the plain blocks ~~is so unique it~~ makes the sculpture seem textured.**

You can also eliminate wordiness by avoiding unnecessary hedges, such as *apparently, seem, perhaps, possibly, to a certain extent, tend,* and *somewhat.* Writers typically use hedges to avoid making claims that they cannot substantiate, and these expressions can add subtlety to prose, lending a sense of thoughtfulness and care and acknowledging the possibility of important exceptions. Too many hedges, however, make writing tentative and uncertain. Notice how the following revision is more assured than the original.

➤ **~~In most cases, realistic~~** Realistic **characters** often **~~tend to~~ undermine comedy's primary function of making us laugh at exaggerated character traits.**

34e Eliminate unnecessary prepositions.

Prepositions indicate the relation between a word in a sentence and the preposition's object. In the following example, *rim* is the object of the preposition *to.* The phrase *to the rim* modifies the word *filled.*

I filled the glass *to* the rim.

If the word following the preposition is the object of a verb, however, the preposition may be unnecessary.

➤ **Nothing happened, and my doctor ordered ~~for~~ them to stop inducing labor.**

➤ **Consequently, student volunteers will not be inclined to leave and seek ~~for~~ smaller hospitals with less intense shifts.**

Note: Another way of revising this sentence would be to change the verb.

➤ **Consequently, student volunteers will not be inclined to leave and ~~seek~~ look for smaller hospitals with less intense shifts.**

In addition, often context or usage makes the relations between words in a sentence clear, and a preposition is not needed.

➤ **More than half ~~of~~ the boat planks were stripped away.**

Finally, delete prepositions that do not have an object.

➤ **I went to the hospital so the clerk could admit me. ~~in.~~**

For ESL writers

Prepositions also combine with verbs to form two- or three-word (or phrasal) verbs whose meaning cannot be understood literally *(handed in, get along).* When a preposition is part of a two- or three-word verb, it is called a *particle.* See 54b.

35 EXACT WORDS

Effective writers choose words carefully, paying attention to meaning, form, idiomatic phrasing, and freshness.

> The central library stands like a giant concrete mushroom, towering above the surrounding eucalyptus groves. The strong, angular lines are softened by a few well-placed, sweeping curves on the stabilizing pylons and the shrouds around the low windows.

denotation The dictionary meaning of a word.

connotation The subtle shades of meaning in a word. For example, *forthright* and *blunt* could both be used to describe a person who speaks his or her mind. But *forthright* has a positive connotation and *blunt* has a negative connotation.

35a Become familiar with the subtleties of words.

You can learn the **denotation** of a word by looking it up in the dictionary—a good first step to understanding its meaning. But understanding the **connotations** of a word allows you to use it vividly and precisely.

The best way to become familiar with the denotations and connotations of words is to read widely and observantly. Consult a dictionary when you are unsure of a word's meaning or refer to a dictionary of synonyms or a thesaurus when you want to determine which synonym of a word expresses your exact intention. Avoid the temptation, however, to use a thesaurus as a source of impressive-sounding words. Use it instead as a tool for precision.

DIGITAL HINT

Many computer programs include a thesaurus. The computer displays synonyms for a word that you select and automatically replaces a word with the synonym you choose. While this feature can be a convenience, the same cautions that apply to using a printed thesaurus apply to computer versions.

35b Try to identify and replace incorrectly used words.

Many writers find it difficult to pinpoint words used imprecisely or incorrectly in their own writing. Two strategies can help you identify such words.

1. As you compose drafts, mark any words you are unsure of with a question mark or check, but do not look them up in a dictionary right away; you do not want to inhibit the flow of your writing. When you have completed your draft, look up the marked words and make any necessary revisions. See also the Glossary of Usage.
2. Ask a friend or your instructor to review a draft of your writing, looking out for misused words or any other problems that may need attention.

The following examples show revisions of errors in word choice.

➤ **How do we stop offshore oil drilling and yet offer an alternative to** alleviate **~~appease~~ the energy crisis?**

➤ **The phrase "you know"** introduces **~~is an introductory to~~ someone's opinion.**

35c Use correct prepositions.

Short as they generally are, prepositions define crucial relationships. For a review of the meanings of some common prepositions, see Chapter 55.

> The levels increase *in* width *from* the scrawny third floor *up to* the immense sixth story (*over* two hundred feet across).

> A building's beauty must be determined *by* the harmony *of* its design.

If prepositions are a problem in your writing, look for them as you read, noticing how other writers use them.

➤ **Unlike many of the other pieces of art** on **~~about~~ campus, the statues seemed to fit well.**

preposition A word (such as *between, for, from, in, of,* or *to*) that always appears as part of a phrase and indicates the relation between a word in a sentence and the object of the preposition: The water splashed *into* the canoe.

35d In certain writing situations, use concrete words instead of abstract ones.

In some writing situations, it is appropriate to use abstract words (such as *authority, justice, temperance,* and *truth*), which describe general concepts and qualities. Concrete words (such as the nouns *shack, cliff,* and *jeans* or the adjectives *rickety, tart,* and *sullen*) are especially useful for conveying specific information or vivid details.

> ➤ The dean and other administrators ~~The authorities~~ should make sure that courses are relevant to the professions that students will enter.

Note: As you revise your work, pay special attention to vague words, such as *aspect, situation,* and *area,* and try to find more specific replacements.

idiom An expression in a particular language whose meaning cannot be determined from its parts but must be learned: *call off* for "cancel"; *look after* for "take care of."

preposition A word (such as *between, for, from, in, of,* or *to*) that always appears as part of a phrase and indicates the relation between a word in a sentence and the object of the preposition: The water splashed *into* the canoe.

cliché An overused expression that has lost its original freshness, such as *hard as a rock.*

35e Use standard idioms of American English.

Read and listen carefully to get a sense of standard idioms, especially the ones that consist of small words, such as **prepositions,** and verb forms.

> ➤ **Public schools will not let teachers discuss morality because our values stem** from ~~**to**~~ **religious teachings.**

For ESL writers

Idiomatic two- and three-word verbs *(put down, set up)* and combinations of verbs or adjectives and prepositions *(look for, afraid of)* can be especially troublesome for writers whose first language is not English. See 54b and 55b for more help with these expressions.

35f Eliminate clichés.

Readers prefer lively, original expressions to familiar, overused phrases. Review your drafts for trite phrases such as *at the end of my rope* and *saved by the bell,* and either delete them or replace them with fresher, more vivid expressions.

➤ **During ~~the thick of~~ the night, he must walk alone with only a flashlight for company.**

➤ **The audience ~~is on pins and needles,~~** erupts in gasps and nervous giggles, **wondering whose plan will falter first.**

35g Use appropriate figures of speech.

Figures of speech, such as **similes** and **metaphors,** are vivid and original means of expressing comparisons. They help a reader to perceive a similarity, often creating a striking image or a surprising but engaging idea.

> Our old dog sinks partway into the warm mud and rests his chin on the mushy surface like a hippo basking in the African sun.

> If you think of the *Journal of the American Medical Association* article as a two-hour documentary on PBS, the *American Health* essay is a thirty-second sound bite.

Note: Avoid inaccurate and **mixed metaphors.**

Inaccurate metaphor The children would jump from car to car *as if they were mushrooms.* [Mushrooms cannot jump.]

Mixed metaphor Karma is an inorganic process of development in which *the soul not only pays the price for its misdeeds but also bears the fruit of the seeds sown in former lives.* [The soul is illogically compared to both a criminal defendant and a plant.]

figures of speech Images such as similes and metaphors that suggest a comparison (or analogy) between objects that are generally unlike each other.

simile A direct comparison that uses *like* or *as: like a tree bending in the strong wind.*

metaphor An indirect comparison that refers to or describes one thing as if it were the other: *The mob sharpened its claws.*

mixed metaphor An inconsistent metaphor, one that mixes several images rather than completing one.

36 APPROPRIATE WORDS

jargon A specialized vocabulary used by members of a group or profession.

slang Informal language that tends to change rapidly.

When you choose words carefully, your writing will have the appropriate level of formality, without **jargon** or **slang,** biased wording, or stuffy, pretentious language. Taken from a profile of a large city's trauma system, the following sentences illustrate how appropriate words can convey a sense of a particular place.

> At 6:50 p.m., the hospital's paging system comes alive.
>
> Lying on the table, the unidentified victim can only groan and move his left leg.
>
> All the components are in place: a countywide trauma system, physicians and staff who care and are willing to sacrifice, and private hospitals serving the community.

36a Use the level of formality expected in your writing situation.

Many problems with appropriate language occur when writers use conversational language in formal writing situations. A phone conversation with or email message to your friend, for example, will be more informal than a memo to your employer or a report for your political science class.

Less formal One cool morning in May, I stood on the edge of Mount Everest, or at least that's what it seemed like to me.

More formal Mistreatment of the elderly is an unusually sensitive problem because it involves such value-laden ideas as *home* and *family.*

Taking into account the kind of essay you are writing, reword as necessary to avoid shifts in the level of formality.

➤ **What makes an excellent church, auditorium, or theater makes a ~~lousy~~ poor library.**

➤ **The average cost to join a gymnasium ~~can run you~~ is around $25 a month~~, and that's only~~ when you sign a membership contract. ~~I bet~~ Even if you thought you ~~couldn't~~ could not afford a membership, ~~Well,~~ you can.**

36b Avoid jargon.

Jargon is "insider talk" typically used by members of a certain profession or interest group: *facilitate, impact on,* and *rectify* are examples. If your audience includes only members of a certain group or profession, some specialized terms may be appropriate and even expected. Sometimes, however, writers who use jargon are more concerned with impressing readers with complicated, obscure language than with conveying information clearly. In general, most readers will understand your message more easily if you eliminate jargon or replace it with more accessible language.

➤ **The consultant promised to ~~grow~~ increase the revenues of Holman Manufacturing by 20 percent each year for the next five years.**

36c Limit the use of slang in formal writing situations.

Although slang may be appropriate to define a character or a situation in an autobiography or in reportage, it is likely to be out of place in most academic writing situations.

Appropriate slang "This weather is *awesome* for *peeling out.* You *oughta* try it sometime." [appropriate for dialogue in an essay about a personal experience]

Inappropriate slang Parties are an excellent way to *blow off steam* and take a break from the pressures of college. [too informal in a proposal addressed to college administrators]

If you come across slang as you revise your own writing, you may want to replace it with more formal words.

➤ **We shouldn't ~~dis~~ these girls.** [revised: disrespect]

➤ **The cast of the movie was ~~awesome.~~** [revised: impressive.]

You can also replace slang with more precise and descriptive words.

➤ **The cast of the movie ~~was awesome.~~** [revised: vividly embodied the historical characters.]

Note: In addition to eliminating slang in most academic and professional writing, you should usually avoid regional expressions, such as *I reckon it's time* [southern dialect].

nonsexist language Language that describes people without using words that make assumptions about gender or imply acceptance of gender-based stereotypes.

36d Use nonsexist language that includes rather than excludes.

Avoid using masculine pronouns (such as *he* or *his*) to refer to people who might be either men or women.

➤ **A doctor who did not keep up with his colleagues would be forced to ~~update his~~ procedures.** [revised: his or her colleagues; learn new procedures]

If you find the expression *his or her* too wordy, you can eliminate it by substituting plural nouns and pronouns.

➤ ~~A doctor~~ Doctors who ~~did~~ do not keep up with ~~his~~ their colleagues would be forced to ~~update his~~ learn new procedures.

➤ ~~A student's~~ Students' eligibility for alternative loans is based on whether or not ~~his~~ their school decides ~~he is~~ they are entitled to financial aid.

Replace masculine nouns used to represent people in general with more inclusive words.

➤ Oligarchies have existed throughout ~~the history of man.~~ human history.

Note: Sexist language is not the only type of exclusionary language that you should look out for. In general, you should avoid any expressions that demean various groups in a society.

➤ Oligarchies were left to ~~barbaric tribesmen~~ the tribes and herders ~~who were beyond the reach of civilization.~~ outside the empire.

36e Replace pretentious language and euphemisms with more direct wording.

Using impressive words is sometimes part of the pleasure of writing, but such words may be too elaborate for the situation or may seem to be included for their own sake rather than for the reader's understanding. In this case, they may be considered pretentious. Use words that best express your idea, and balance or replace such unusual words with simpler, more familiar choices.

pretentious language Excessively fancy or wordy language used primarily to impress.

euphemisms Inoffensive but evasive alternatives to words or phrases that are thought to be unpleasant. (*Pre-owned* is sometimes a euphemism for *used*—as in *used car*—and *final resting place* is a euphemism for *grave*.)

euphemisms Inoffensive but evasive alternatives to words or phrases that are thought to be unpleasant. (*Preowned* is sometimes a euphemism for *used*—as in *used car*—and *final resting place* is a euphemism for *grave.*)

➤ **Perhaps ~~apprehension toward instigating~~ fear of these changes stems from financial concern.**

➤ **Expanded oil exploration may seem relatively innocuous, but this proposal is a deplorable suggestion to all but the most ~~pernicious, specious~~ deceptive, destructive ~~entities~~ groups.**

As with pretentious language, **euphemisms** should be used sparingly if at all in academic writing. Often, readers see through and resent writers' attempts to sugar-coat or deemphasize unpleasant things or ideas.

PART 8 PUNCTUATION

PART

8 PUNCTUATION

37 COMMAS

A comma is used to set off or separate sentence elements. Commas organize sentences for readers—for example, telling them that a word, phrase, or clause is introducing the sentence (see 37b) or that information is supplementary rather than essential (see 37c). In the following example, notice how the addition of a few commas makes the sentence easier to read.

Hard to read Situated at the end of the hall as if forgotten by time this elevator with its scratched dingy doors was a remnant of the early 1940s.

Easier to read Situated at the end of the hall, as if forgotten by time, this elevator, with its scratched, dingy doors, was a remnant of the early 1940s.

The sections in this chapter tell you when commas are needed in a sentence. Chapter 38 tells you when commas are not needed in sentences.

Note: The comma is not the only punctuation mark that sets off or separates sentence elements. The semicolon (Chapter 39), colon (Chapter 40), and dash (Chapter 41) are also used to organize sentences for readers.

independent (main) clause A word group with a subject and a predicate that can stand alone as a separate sentence. (A predicate is the part of a clause that includes a complete verb and says something about the subject: At the checkpoint, we *unloaded the canoes.*)

37a Add a comma between independent clauses joined by a coordinating conjunction.

When two independent clauses are joined by a coordinating conjunction such as *and,* a comma is required to tell the reader that another independent clause follows the first one.

independent clause — c.c. — independent clause
My father had the same dream, and perhaps my grandfather did as well.

coordinating conjunction A word that joins comparable and equally important sentence elements: *for, and, or, but, nor, yet,* or *so.*

When you proofread your writing, watch out for coordinating conjunctions, and add a comma in front of a conjunction when it joins two independent clauses.

➤ **In 2002, women's ice hockey will be a full Olympic medal sport, and Lynn plans on bringing home the gold.**

➤ **Researchers have studied many aspects of autism, but they readily acknowledge that they have much more to learn.**

When the independent clauses are brief and unambiguous, a comma is optional.

The attempt fails and Batman must let go.

When one or both of the sentence elements joined by a coordinating conjunction are not independent clauses, a comma is not needed. See 38a.

phrase A group of words that does *not* contain both a subject and a verb and is always part of an independent clause.

clause A group of at least two words that both names a topic and makes a point about the topic; every clause includes a subject and a complete verb (the predicate).

independent (main) clause A word group with a subject and a predicate that can stand alone as a separate sentence.

37b Place a comma after an introductory word, phrase, or clause.

Sentences often begin with words, phrases, or clauses that precede the **independent clause** and modify the whole clause or an element within it. In most cases, these introductory elements should be set off with a comma.

Naturally, this result didn't help him any.

With a jerk, I lifted the lure in a desperate attempt to catch a fish and please my dad.

When we entered the honeymoon suite, the room smelled of burnt plastic and was the color of Pepto Bismol.

The comma following each introductory element lets the reader know where the modifying word or phrase ends and where the main clause begins.

➤ **Unfortunately, violence was a problem among young men before stories about drugs and gangs started hitting the front page.**

➤ **Forgetting my mission for a moment, I took time to look around.**

➤ **When I picked up the receiver, I heard an unfamiliar voice.**

Note: If an introductory phrase or clause is brief—four words or fewer—the comma may be omitted unless it is needed to prevent misreading.

Without hesitation I dived into the lake.

37c Use commas to set off nonrestrictive elements, including appositives and trailing participial phrases.

A nonrestrictive word or word group supplies additional information, but it is not essential to the sentence's meaning. To test whether a word or word group is *nonrestrictive* (nondefining and thus nonessential) or *restrictive* (defining and thus essential), read the sentence with and without it. If the sentence is essentially unchanged in meaning without the word or word group, it is nonrestrictive. Use a comma or commas to set it off. If omitting the word or word group changes the meaning of the sentence by removing a definition or limitation, it is restrictive. Do *not* use a comma or commas.

Nonrestrictive The oldest fishermen, *grizzly sea salts wrapped in an aura of experience,* led the way.

The description of the fishermen tells readers what they look like, but the meaning of the sentence does not change significantly without it: *The oldest fishermen led the way.*

Restrictive Blood and violence can give video games a sense of realism *that was not previously available.*

The restrictive word group provides essential information about the realism of video games. The sentence would not have the same meaning without it.

appositive A word or word group that identifies or gives more information about a noun or pronoun that precedes it: I called the mayor's office and asked for Jane Kite, *the mayor's assistant.*

participial phrase A group of words that begins with a present participle *(dancing, freezing)* or a past participle *(danced, frozen)* and modifies a noun or a pronoun: We boarded the bus, *expecting to leave immediately.*

1. Insert a comma or a pair of commas to set off a nonrestrictive (nonessential) word group.

Insert a comma when the nonrestrictive word or word group appears at the end of the sentence.

➤ **The next period is the preoperational stage, which begins at age two and lasts until age seven.**

➤ **We all stood, anxious and prepared for what he was about to say.**

➤ **As we headed down the trail, I noticed all the dark green needles on the pine trees and heard all types of sounds, such as the rustle of the grass and animal noises from up in the mountains.**

When the nonrestrictive word or word group appears in the middle of a sentence, enclose it in a pair of commas.

➤ **The most common moods are happiness, when the music is in a major key, or sadness, when the music is in a minor key.**

Note: The relative pronoun *that* is often used to introduce restrictive clauses. *Which* is usually used only in nonrestrictive clauses, but writers sometimes use it in restrictive clauses as well. See 21b and 21c for more on the relative pronouns *that* and *which.*

appositive A word or word group that identifies or gives more information about a noun or pronoun that precedes it: I called the mayor's office and asked for Jane Kite, *the mayor's assistant.*

2. Use a comma or a pair of commas to set off a nonrestrictive appositive.

➤ **Laura, our neighbor and best friend, appeared at the kitchen window.**

The gist of this sentence—that Laura appeared at the window—would be the same without the information that she is a neighbor and a friend.

The following example illustrates the importance of context for deciding what is essential in a sentence.

➤ **My oldest dog, Shogun, was lying on the floor doing what he does best, sleeping.**

Here, the dog's name is nonrestrictive (nonessential) information and is placed between commas. If the dog were not specified, however, the name would be essential and would not be set off by commas.

My dog Tracey is the largest of my three dogs.

3. Use a comma before a trailing nonrestrictive participial phrase.

Participial phrases are generally nonrestrictive. Usually, a participial phrase supplies additional information about a noun in the **independent clause.** When it follows the main clause in a sentence, it should usually be set off with a comma.

Participial phrase He opened the package, *expecting to find cookies and a mushy love letter.*

The comma sets off the participial phrase, which modifies the pronoun *He.*

➤ **Every so often, a pelican agilely arcs high over the water, twisting downward gracefully to catch an unsuspecting mackerel.**

➤ **I sat down, confused and distraught.**

Note: If the phrase is restrictive, do not use a comma. (See also 38b.)

Next to the kitchen we found a pantry *stocked with food.*

Here, *stocked with food* is restrictive because it defines or limits *pantry.*

participial phrase A group of words that begins with a present participle *(dancing, freezing)* or a past participle *(danced, frozen)* and modifies a noun or a pronoun: We boarded the bus, *expecting to leave immediately.*

independent (main) clause A word group with a subject and a predicate that can stand alone as a separate sentence. (A predicate is the part of a clause that includes a complete verb and says something about the subject: At the checkpoint, we *unloaded the canoes.*)

participle A verb form showing the present tense *(dancing, freezing)* or the past tense *(danced, frozen)* that can also act as an adjective.

37d Use commas to set off a transitional, parenthetical, or contrasting expression or an absolute phrase.

Like nonrestrictive word groups (see 37c), transitional, parenthetical, or contrasting expressions and absolute phrases supply additional information but are not necessary to the meaning of the sentence. Often used to begin sentences, transitional expressions help the reader to follow a writer's movement from point to point, showing how one sentence is related to the next.

Transitional expression *Besides,* it is summer.

Parenthetical comments interrupt a sentence with a brief aside.

Parenthetical expression These are all indications, *I think,* of Jan's drive for power and control.

Contrasting phrases generally come at the end of a sentence, introduced by *not, no,* or *nothing.*

Contrasting expression Nick is the perfect example of a young, hungry manager trying to climb to the top, *not bothered by the feelings of others.*

Absolute phrases, which can appear anywhere within a sentence, modify the whole clause and often include a noun or pronoun and a past or present **participle** as well as modifiers.

Absolute phrase "Did I ever tell you about the time I worked with Danny Kaye at Radio City Music Hall?" she asked, *her eyes focusing dreamily into the distance.*

1. Insert a comma or commas to set off a transitional phrase.

➤ **For example, in our society a wedding gown is worn by the bride only once, on her wedding day.**

➤ **Students, therefore, frequently complain about their TA's office hours.**

Note: When a transitional element links two **independent clauses** within one sentence, add a semicolon between the clauses to avoid a **comma splice** (see Chapter 16).

➤ One can see how delicate he is, yet this fragility does not detract from his masculinity; instead, it greatly enhances it.

independent (main) clause A word group with a subject and a predicate that can stand alone as a separate sentence. (A predicate is the part of a clause that includes a complete verb and says something about the subject: At the checkpoint, we *unloaded the canoes.*)

comma splice The improper joining of two independent clauses with only a comma.

2. Set off a parenthetical expression with a comma or pair of commas.

➤ We had an advantage, thanks to Patsy's knowledge.

➤ At every response, I defended those innocent people and emphasized that no one, absolutely no one, can decide whether or not a person is worthy of living.

3. Use a comma or commas to set off a contrasting expression.

➤ My uncle talked to me as if I were a person, not a child.

➤ He uttered his famous phrase, "If you don't have time to do something right, you definitely don't have time to do it over," for the first, but not the last, time.

4. Insert a comma or pair of commas to set off an absolute phrase.

➤ "Well, well," he'd grin, his crooked mouth revealing his perfect white teeth.

➤ I followed her, both of us barefoot and breathing white mist, out the door into the snow.

coordinating conjunction A word that joins comparable and equally important sentence elements: *for, and, or, but, nor, yet,* or *so.*

37e Use commas to separate three or more items in a series, placing the final comma before the coordinating conjunction.

The commas in a series separate the items for the reader.

> He was wearing a camouflage hat, a yellow sweatshirt, and a pair of blue shorts.

A series can consist of three or more single words, phrases, or clauses. Sometimes a series will mix words and phrases. All items in a series should be grammatically parallel (see 32a).

➤ **He always tells me about the loyalty, honor, and pride he feels as a Marine.**

➤ **Our communities would get relief from the fear and despair that comes from having unremitting violence, addiction, and open-air drug markets in their midst.**

Note: Some writers omit the final comma preceding a conjunction when the items are brief and the relationship is clear. However, including the final comma prevents possible misreading.

Possible option	She was beautiful, smart and popular.
Preferred	She was beautiful, smart, and popular.

direct quotation A speaker's or writer's exact words, which are enclosed in quotation marks.

37f Place a comma between a complete direct quotation and the text identifying the speaker.

The comma, along with the quotation marks, helps the reader determine where a quotation begins and ends.

I answered, "OK, let me grab the ladder."

"Discipline is effective if you get the students to adopt your values," explained Fathman.

➤ **So I asked her, "Momma, who you talkin' to?"**

➤ **Dr. Carolyn Baily asserts, "I view spanking as an aggressive act."**

Be especially alert for errors in punctuating quotations if you include dialogue or direct quotations from experts in your essay. (See 42a for more information on punctuating quotations.)

When a quotation would ordinarily end with a period—that is, when it is an **independent clause**—a comma is still used to separate it from a phrase such as *she said.*

independent (main) clause A word group with a subject and a predicate that can stand alone as a separate sentence. (A predicate is the part of a clause that includes a complete verb and says something about the subject: At the checkpoint, we *unloaded the canoes.*)

➤ **"It will be OK," Coach reassured me as he motioned for the emergency medical technicians to bring a board.**

When a quotation ends with an exclamation point or a question mark, however, the comma is not needed.

➤ **"My God, what if I'm paralyzed!," I said out loud.**

Note: When the phrase identifying the speaker comes between main clauses, use a period or a semicolon after the phrase. If the quotation is from a written source, choose the punctuation mark used in the original.

➤ **"You can't be a rapper forever," my aunt always told me, ~~"what~~ "What are you going to do to further your studies?"**

direct address Words that are spoken directly to someone else who is named.

interjection An exclamatory word that indicates strong feeling or attempts to command attention: *Shhh! Oh! Ouch!*

37g Add a comma or a pair of commas to set off expressions commonly included in dialogue.

Use commas to set off the name of a person **directly addressed** by a speaker, words such as *yes* or *no,* and mild **interjections.** Also use a comma to set off a question added to the end of a sentence.

"Chadan, you're just too compassionate."

"Yes, sir," replied Danny.

Boy, did we underestimate her.

That's not very efficient, is it?

A comma sets off the comment that precedes or follows it from the rest of the sentence.

➤ **"Well, son, what are you doing?"**

➤ **"No, I won't be going."**

➤ **"So, this is to be a battle of wills, is it? Fine, I'll play."**

➤ **"Besides, it'll be good for me."**

coordinate adjectives Two or more adjectives that modify a noun equally and independently: the *large, red hat.*

37h Use a comma between coordinate adjectives.

If you can change the order of a series of adjectives or add *and* between them without changing the meaning, they are coordinate and should be separated with a comma. The comma signals that the adjectives are equal, related in the same way to the word they modify.

There are reasons for her *erratic, irrational* behavior.

Whether you reversed the order of *erratic* and *irrational* in the sentence *(There are reasons for her irrational, erratic behavior)* or inserted *and* between these words *(erratic and irrational behavior),* the meaning of the sentence would remain unchanged.

If the adjectives closest to the noun cannot logically be rearranged or linked by *and,* they are **noncoordinate adjectives** (also called *cumulative adjectives*) and should not be separated by commas (see 38e).

I pictured myself as a *professional race car* driver.

Once you have determined that adjectives are coordinate, add a comma between them.

➤ **Professionals who use this five-step, systematic approach are less likely to be injured during an assault.**

Note: Coordinate adjectives that follow the noun they modify or that are otherwise separated from it in the sentence should also be separated by a comma or commas.

Skippy was a good-looking guy, *tall, blond,* and *lean.*

noncoordinate adjectives Two or more adjectives that do not modify a noun equally. One or two of the adjectives closest to the noun form a noun phrase that the remaining adjectives modify: *colorful hot-air balloons.*

37i Add commas where needed to set off dates, numbers, addresses, and titles.

Dates. When you include a full date (month, day, and year), use a pair of commas to set off the year.

➤ **According to Robert Boman in the October 21, 1994, issue of *The Optimist,* "When you treat students as adults, you gain their respect."**

If you present a date in reverse order (day, month, and year), do not add commas.

➤ **According to Robert Boman in the ~~October 21,~~ 21 October 1994 issue of *The Optimist,* "When you treat students as adults, you gain their respect."**

If a date is partial (month and year only), do not add commas.

This article appeared in the April 1990 issue of *Personnel Journal.*

Numbers. In large numbers, separate groups of three digits (thousands, millions, and so forth) with commas. Begin counting from the right.

➤ **As of 1985, there were about 630,000 speakers of Chinese in the United States.**

Note: In four-digit numbers, the comma is not required: *1,672* or *1672.*

Addresses. When you write out an address, add commas between the parts, setting off the street address, the city, and the state with the zip code. When an address or place name appears in the middle of a complete sentence, add a comma after the last element.

➤ **Mrs. Wilson relocated to Bowie, Maryland, after moving from Delaware.**

➤ **One of the most famous addresses in the world is 1600 Pennsylvania Avenue, Washington, D.C. 20500.**

Note: Do not put a comma between the name or abbreviation of the state and the zip code.

Titles. When a title (such as *Ph.D.*) appears after a name in a sentence, enclose it with a pair of commas.

➤ **Martha Jansen, M.D., has grouped the most common forms of household environmental hazards into a number of broad categories.**

37j Add a comma if needed for clarity.

When a word is omitted, is repeated twice, or might be grouped incorrectly with the next words, use a comma to make your meaning clear. Such instances are rare. Check the guidelines in Chapter 38 so that you do not add unnecessary or incorrect commas.

> To poison the pike in Lake Davis risks Portola's water supply; to not poison the pike, our state's sports and commercial fisheries.
>
> Politicians who can, collect large amounts of money.
>
> Three dangerous-looking guys settled in, in a booth near the jukebox.

38 UNNECESSARY COMMAS

Because commas are appropriate in so many instances, it is easy to use them where they are not needed.

38a Omit the comma when items in a pair joined by *and* or another coordinating conjunction are not independent clauses.

Many word pairs can be joined by *and* or another coordinating conjunction, including **compound predicates, compound objects,** and **compound subjects.** None of these pairs should be interrupted by a comma.

Compound predicate	I *grabbed my lunchbox* and *headed out to the tree.*
Compound object	As for me, I wore *a pink short set with ruffles* and *a pair of sneakers.*
Compound subject	My *father* and *brother* wore big hiking boots.

coordinating conjunction A word that joins comparable and equally important sentence elements: *for, and, or, but, nor, yet,* or *so.*

independent (main) clause A word group with a subject and a predicate that can stand alone as a separate sentence.

compound predicate Two or more verbs or verb phrases linked by *and.*

compound object Two or more words acting as an object and linked by *and.*

compound subject Two or more words acting as a subject and linked by *and.*

When you proofread your writing, watch out for the conjunction *and* as well as the other coordinating conjunctions. If one or both of the sentence elements it joins are not independent clauses, a comma is not needed.

➤ **According to Ward, many Custer fans believe that Custer was a "hero," and "represents certain endangered manly virtues."**

➤ **She raced through the thirty-seven barbecue specials like an auctioneer, and popped her gum at the same time.**

➤ **I was running out of time, and patience.**

Note: Two independent clauses joined by a coordinating conjunction require a comma. In this case, the comma shows the reader where one independent clause ends and the other begins. (See 37a.)

38b Omit any comma that sets off a restrictive word group.

Use commas to set off a nonrestrictive word group but not a restrictive word group. A *restrictive word group* defines or limits the noun it modifies. A *nonrestrictive word group* provides extra or nonessential information.

Restrictive She demonstrates this shortcoming in her story *"Is There Nowhere Else We Can Meet?"*

The context helps to determine which information is necessary and which is extra. In the preceding example, *"Is There Nowhere Else We Can Meet?"* is restrictive because it identifies a specific story, distinguishing it from other stories by the same writer.

Nonrestrictive The supercomputer center, *which I had seen hundreds of times,* still held many mysteries for me.

In this sentence, *which I had seen hundreds of times* is nonrestrictive because it adds supplementary information to the sentence. The reference to the mysteries of the computer center would be the same without the addition.

A comma signals that a word group is not essential to the meaning of the sentence. If a comma incorrectly sets off a restrictive word group, it suggests that essential information is not important. (See also 37c.)

➤ **The ten people from the community would consist of three retired people, over the age of sixty, three middle-aged people, between the ages of twenty-five and sixty, and four teenagers.**

➤ **Although divorce is obviously a cause of the psychological problems, a child will face, the parents need to support their child through the anxieties and turmoil.**

Note: The relative pronoun *that* is often used to introduce restrictive clauses. *Which* is usually used only in nonrestrictive clauses, but writers sometimes use it in restrictive clauses as well. See 21b and 21c for more on the relative pronouns *that* and *which.*

38c Omit any commas that separate the main elements of the sentence—subject and verb, verb and object, preposition and object.

Even in a complicated sentence, a reader expects the core elements—subject, verb, and object—to lead directly from one to the other.

1. Delete a comma that separates a subject and its verb.

➤ ***Bilateral,*** **means that both the left and the right sides of the brain are involved in processing a stimulus.**

Bilateral is the subject; *means* is the verb.

subject The word or words that identify the topic or theme of the sentence—what is being discussed.

verb A word or phrase that expresses action or being and, along with a subject, is a basic component of a sentence: At the checkpoint, we *unloaded* the canoes.

preposition A word (such as *between* or *for*) that is always part of a phrase and that indicates the relation between a word in a sentence and the object of the preposition: The water splashed *into* the canoe.

object The part of a clause that receives the action of the verb (At the checkpoint, we unloaded *the canoes*) or the part of a phrase that follows a preposition (We dragged them to *the river*).

adverb clause A clause that nearly always modifies a verb, indicating time, place, condition, reason, cause, purpose, result, or another logical relationship.

➤ **This movie's only fault, is that it does not set a good example.**

This movie's only fault is the subject; *is* is the verb.

2. Delete a comma that unnecessarily separates a verb or a preposition from its object.

➤ **Now the voters must decide, the issue of term limits.**

➤ **In the absence of supplementary criteria, financial aid officers could place more weight on, the essay part of the application.**

38d Omit a comma that separates the main part of the sentence from a trailing adverb clause.

When an adverb clause appears at the beginning of a sentence, it is usually set off by a comma because it is an introductory element. When the clause appears at the end of a sentence, however, a comma is ordinarily not needed.

When the film finally reaches its climax, it's a doozy of an ending.

Nicholson demonstrates his talent *when the Joker removes his bandages.*

Omitting an unnecessary comma before an adverb clause makes the sentence flow more smoothly.

➤ **Basically, I liked everything that made Arturo look different, because he was more than a special cousin.**

Note: If the clause presents a contrast or is not essential to the meaning, set it off with a comma.

No-fault automobile insurance is common, although support for it is decreasing.

38e Leave out any comma that separates noncoordinate adjectives.

noncoordinate adjectives Two or more adjectives that do not modify a noun equally. One or two of the adjectives closest to the noun form a noun phrase that the remaining adjectives modify: *colorful hot-air balloons.*

If you cannot logically rearrange the adjectives before a noun or add *and* between them, they are probably noncoordinate adjectives (sometimes called *cumulative adjectives*). Such adjectives are not equal elements; do not separate them with a comma. In contrast, **coordinate adjectives** should be separated by commas (see 37h).

coordinate adjectives Two or more adjectives that modify a noun equally and independently: the *large, red hat.*

> Wearing a pair of jeans, *cutoff, bleached,* and *torn,* [coordinate adjectives] with an embroidered blouse and *soft leather* [noncoordinate adjectives] sandals, she looked older and more foreign than Julie.

Here, *leather* modifies *sandals,* and *soft* modifies *leather sandals* as a unit. Thus, the meaning is cumulative, and a comma would interrupt the connection between the adjectives and the noun.

➤ **Huge~~,~~ neighborhood parties could bring the people in our community together.**

38f Omit any comma that appears before or after a series of items.

Although commas should be used to separate three or more items in a list, they should not be used before the first item or after the final one. (See also 37e.)

➤ **Race, sex, religion, financial situation, or any other circumstance beyond the control of the applicant~~,~~ should not be considered.**

coordinating conjunction A word that joins comparable and equally important sentence elements: *for, and, or, but, nor, yet,* or *so.*

dependent (subordinate) clause A word group with a subject, a predicate, and a subordinating word at the beginning. It cannot stand by itself as a sentence but must be connected to an independent (main) clause. *Although it was raining,* we loaded our gear onto the buses.

subordinating conjunction A word or phrase that introduces a dependent clause and relates it to an independent clause.

indirect quotation A reworded statement or question that presents a speaker's or writer's ideas without quoting directly or using quotation marks.

38g Omit or correct any other unnecessary or incorrect commas.

Check your essays carefully for the following typical comma problems.

1. Omit a comma that follows a coordinating conjunction.

A comma is never needed *after* a coordinating conjunction even if the coordinating conjunction is followed by a transitional or introductory expression.

➤ **I had finally felt the music deep in my soul, and, when I sang, I had a great feeling of relief knowing that everything was going to be all right.**

Be especially alert to this unnecessary comma when *but* or *yet* appears at the beginning of a sentence.

➤ **But, since sharks are not yet classified as endangered species, the members of Congress were not very sympathetic, and the bill was not passed.**

2. Omit a comma after the word that introduces a dependent clause.

Watch for words such as *who, which, that, whom, whose, where, when, although, because, since, though,* and other **subordinating conjunctions.**

➤ **The drinking age should be raised because, drunk driving has become the leading cause of death among young people between the ages of fifteen and twenty-five.**

3. Omit a comma preceding *that* when it introduces an indirect quotation.

Unlike a direct quotation, an indirect quotation is not set off by a comma or quotation marks.

➤ After looking at my tests, the doctor said, that I had calcification.

4. Omit a comma immediately following a preposition.

A comma may follow a complete **prepositional phrase** at the beginning of a sentence, but a comma should not follow the preposition or interrupt the phrase.

➤ Despite, a brief oversupply of teachers in the 1970s, the number of students seeking a career in teaching has been steadily decreasing.

5. Omit unnecessary commas that set off a prepositional phrase in the middle or at the end of a sentence.

When a prepositional phrase appears in the middle of a sentence or at the end, it is usually not set off by commas. When it acts as an introductory element, however, it is generally followed by a comma.

➤ "I've seen the devil b'fore," he grumbled, in a serious tone, as his dark eyes peered into mine.

➤ The children's trauma team gathers in the Resuscitation Room, at the same time that John Doe is being treated.

6. Omit a comma that precedes a parenthesis.

➤ The AIDS virus has three initial stages: the infected stage, the intermediate stage, (called the AIDS-related complex), and full-blown AIDS (Langone 10).

preposition A word (such as *between, for, from, in, of,* or *to*) that always appears as part of a phrase and indicates the relation between a word in a sentence and the object of the preposition: The water splashed *into* the canoe.

prepositional phrase A group of words that begins with a preposition and indicates the relation between a word in a sentence and the object following the preposition: Her sunglasses slid *under the seat.*

7. Omit a comma that directly follows *such as* or *like.*

➤ Old-fashioned clothing, such as~~,~~ antique wedding gowns and Victorian dresses, can connect us to the past.

8. Rewrite a sentence that is full of phrases and commas to simplify both the sentence structure and the punctuation.

➤ ~~The researchers could monitor, by~~ [By] looking through a porthole window, [the researchers could monitor] how much time ~~was spent, by Noah,~~ [Noah spent] in the dome.

39 SEMICOLONS

independent (main) clause A word group with a subject and a predicate that can stand alone as a separate sentence. (A predicate is the part of a clause that includes a complete verb and says something about the subject: At the checkpoint, we *unloaded the canoes.*)

comma splice The improper joining of two independent clauses with only a comma.

Use semicolons to separate parts of a sentence that are equal, usually closely related independent clauses, and to make long sentences with commas easier to read.

39a Use a semicolon to join independent clauses if the second clause restates or sets up a contrast to the first.

In fact, she always had been special; we just never noticed.

Changing a comma to a semicolon is one strategy for correcting a **comma splice** (see 16c).

➤ David was not an angel~~,~~[;] he was always getting into trouble with the teachers.

Note: If the independent clauses are linked by *and, but,* or another coordinating conjunction, use a comma rather than a semicolon (see 37a), unless the independent clauses include internal punctuation (see 39c).

39b Use semicolons to separate items in a series when they include internal commas.

Studies of gender differences in conversational interaction include an Elizabeth Aries article titled "Interaction Patterns and Themes of Male, Female, and Mixed Groups," a study conducted in a research laboratory setting**;** a Pamela Fishman article titled "Interaction: The Work Women Do," a study researched by naturalistic observation**;** and an article by Candace West and Don Zimmerman titled "Small Insults: A Study of Interruptions in Cross-Sex Conversation between Unacquainted Persons," a study conducted in a research laboratory setting.

Because the reader expects items in a series to be separated with commas, other commas within items can be confusing. The solution is to leave the internal commas as they are but to use a stronger mark, the semicolon, to signal the divisions between items.

➤ **Appliances that use freon include air conditioners, small models as well as central systems, ; refrigerators, ; and freezers, both home and industrial types.**

39c Use a semicolon to connect a pair or series of independent clauses when they include other punctuation that might confuse a reader.

Sometimes independent clauses joined by a **coordinating conjunction** include elements set off by internal punctuation. In such cases, use semicolons between the independent clauses if the other punctuation is likely to confuse a reader or make the sentence parts difficult to identify.

➤ **He was the guide, ; he was driving us in this old Ford, just the two of us and him, ; and I had noticed early on that the car didn't have a gas cap.**

independent (main) clause A word group with a subject and a predicate that can stand alone as a separate sentence. (A predicate is the part of a clause that includes a complete verb and says something about the subject: At the checkpoint, we *unloaded the canoes.*)

coordinating conjunction A word that joins comparable and equally important sentence elements: *for, and, or, but, nor, yet,* or *so.*

conjunctive adverb A word or phrase (such as *finally* or *however*) that tells how the ideas in two sentences or independent clauses are connected.

transitional expression A word or group of words (such as *for example*) that expresses the relationship between two or more sentences.

independent (main) clause A word group with a subject and a predicate that can stand alone as a separate sentence.

appositive A word or word group that identifies or gives more information about a noun or pronoun that precedes it.

coordinating conjunction A word that joins equally important sentence elements: *for, and, or, but, nor, yet,* or *so.*

39d Use a semicolon to join two independent clauses when the second clause contains a conjunctive adverb or a transitional expression.

Always place the semicolon between the two clauses, no matter where the conjunctive adverb or transitional expression appears. Place the semicolon *before* the conjunctive adverb or transition if it begins the second independent clause. (See also 37d.)

> ➤ **Ninety-five percent of Americans recognize the components of a healthy diet, ; however, they fail to apply their knowledge when selecting foods.**

39e Omit or correct a semicolon used incorrectly to replace a comma or other punctuation mark.

Be careful not to use semicolons in place of other punctuation.

1. Replace a semicolon with a comma to link an independent clause to a phrase or to set off an appositive.

> ➤ **The threat of a potentially devastating malpractice suit promotes the practice of defensive medicine; , doctors' ordering excessive and expensive tests to confirm a diagnosis.**

See also 37c.

2. Replace a semicolon with a comma to join two independent clauses linked by a coordinating conjunction.

> ➤ **The ashtrays would need to be relocated to that area; , and it could then become an outdoor smoking lounge.**

See also 37a.

3. Replace a semicolon with a colon to introduce a list.

➤ Our county ditches fill up with old items that are hard to get rid of~~;~~: old refrigerators, mattresses, couches, and chairs.

4. Replace a semicolon with a comma to link a dependent clause to a main clause.

➤ He was dressed in white cotton pants that were obviously hitched up a little too high~~;~~, as if he expected a flood.

dependent (subordinate) clause A word group with a subject, a predicate, and a subordinating word (such as *because*) at the beginning. It cannot stand by itself as a sentence but must be connected to an independent (main) clause: *Although it was raining*, we loaded our gear onto the buses.

40 COLONS

Besides introducing specific sentence elements, colons conventionally appear in bibliography entries, introduce subtitles, express ratios and times, and follow the salutations in letters.

40a Use a colon to introduce a list, an appositive, a quotation, a question, or a statement.

appositive A word or word group that identifies or gives more information about a noun or pronoun that precedes it.

Usually, a colon follows an **independent clause** that makes a general statement; after the colon, the rest of the sentence often supplies specifics—a definition, a quotation or question, or a list (generally in grammatically parallel form).

> Society's hatred, violence, and bigotry take root here: the elementary school playground.

Use the colon selectively to alert readers to closely connected ideas, a significant point, a crucial definition, or a dramatic revelation.

1. Consider using a colon to introduce a list.

Most young law graduates become trial lawyers in one of three ways: by going to work for a government prosecutor's office, by working for a private law firm, or by opening private offices of their own.

2. Consider using a colon to emphasize an appositive.

The oldest fishermen are followed by the middle-aged fathers, excited by the chance to show their sons what their fathers once taught them. Last to arrive are the novices: the thrill seekers.

3. Consider using a colon to introduce a formal quotation, a question, a statement, or another independent clause.

Quotation	We learn that the narrator is a troublemaker in paragraph 12: "I got thrown out of the center for playing pool when I should've been sewing."
Questions	I ran around the office in constant fear of his questions: What do you have planned for the day? How many demonstrations are scheduled this week? How many contacts have you made?
Statement	Both authors are clearly of the same opinion: Recycling scrap tires is no longer an option.
Another independent clause	I guess the saying is true: Absence does make the heart grow fonder.

Note: The first word that introduces a complete sentence following a colon can either be capitalized or not, depending on your preference. Whichever choice you prefer, use it consistently within an essay. Always capitalize a word that begins a quotation.

40b Use a colon after the salutation in a business letter, to indicate a subtitle, to separate hours and minutes, to show ratios, and in bibliographic citations.

Salutation	Dear Ms. Klein:
Between title and subtitle	*Blue Sky Dream: A Memoir of America's Fall from Grace*
Time	1:10 P.M. *or* 1:10 p.m.
Ratio	3:1
Bibliographic entry	New York: St. Martin's, 1998

Note: In references to books of the Judeo-Christian Bible, a colon is traditionally inserted between the numbers for chapter and verse: *John 1:5.* Recently, style manuals such as that published by the Modern Language Association recommend using a period instead: *John 1.5.* Both forms are acceptable, but you should choose one style and use it consistently throughout an essay.

40c Delete or correct an unnecessary or incorrect colon.

As you proofread your writing, watch out for the following incorrect uses of the colon.

1. Omit a colon that interrupts an independent clause, especially after words such as *is, are, include, including, composed of, consists of, such as, for instance,* and *for example.*

➤ The tenets include: courtesy, integrity, perseverence, self-control, indomitable spirit, and modesty.

independent (main clause) A word group with a subject and a predicate that can stand alone as a separate sentence. (A predicate is the part of a clause that includes a complete verb and says something about the subject: At the checkpoint, we *unloaded the canoes.*)

2. Replace an inappropriate colon with the correct punctuation mark.

➤ As I was touring the different areas of the shop, I ran into Christy, one of the owners. "Hi, Kim," she said with a smile on her face.

41 DASHES

A dash breaks the rhythm or interrupts the meaning of a sentence, setting off information with greater emphasis than another punctuation mark could supply. In many kinds of published writing, dashes are an option used sparingly—but often to good effect.

41a Type, space, and position a dash correctly.

Type a dash (—) as two hyphens (--) with no space before or after. Use one dash before a word or words set off at the end of the sentence. Use two dashes—one at the beginning and one at the end—if the word or words are in the middle of the sentence.

```
The rigid, asymmetrical structure of the sculpture
blends well with three different surroundings--the
trees, the library building, and the parking lots.
```

Retype a dash using two hyphens and no spaces.

```
➤ And of course, the trees in the sculpture were more
than just imitation--they spoke!
```

Note: Most word processing programs allow you to insert a solid dash (—) instead of two hyphens (--).

Use a pair of dashes, not just one, to mark the beginning and end of a word group that needs emphasis.

➤ **I could tell that the people in the room work in uncomfortable conditions—they all wear white lab coats, caps, and gloves, but they joke or laugh while building the guns.**

If the word group includes commas or other internal punctuation, dashes tell the reader exactly where words that are being set off begin and end.

41b Consider using a dash to set off material from the rest of the sentence.

Because the dash marks a strong break, it emphasizes the material that follows it.

That smell completely cut off the outside world—the smell of the ocean.

Insert a dash or pair of dashes to emphasize a definition, a dramatic statement, a personal comment, or an explanation.

Definition	Binge eating—larger than normal consumption of high-calorie foods—is caused by emotional distress and depression.
Dramatic statement	But unlike the boys, the girls often turn to something other than violence—motherhood.
Personal comment	In many cases it may be more humane—and I personally believe it is much more humane—to practice euthanasia than to cause the patient prolonged suffering and pain.

Explanation The college should adopt a card such as those used in automatic teller machines—with students simply making their deposits and withdrawals at machines located throughout campus.

Consider inserting a dash or pair of dashes to emphasize a list. If the list appears in the middle of the sentence, use one dash at the beginning and another at the end of the list.

Another problem is that certain toy figures—He-Man, Bugs Bunny, and Robocop, just to name a few—are characters from violent cartoon shows.

41c Rewrite a sentence that uses dashes inappropriately or excessively.

Use dashes purposefully; avoid relying on them when another punctuation mark or a different sentence structure would be more appropriate or effective.

➤ **Finally, the TV people were finished with their interviewing~~—now they~~ and wanted to do a shot of the entrance to the restaurant.**

If you are not sure whether you have used a dash or pair of dashes appropriately, try removing the word or word group that the dashes set off. If the sentence does not make logical and grammatical sense, one or both of the dashes are misused or misplaced.

➤ **That's a tall order—and a reason to start~~—~~amassing some serious capital soon.**

42 QUOTATION MARKS

Use double quotation marks, always in pairs, to indicate direct quotations, to set off special uses of words, and to mark some types of titles.

42a Set off direct quotations with quotation marks.

A direct quotation is set off by a pair of quotation marks.

"Mary," I finally said, "I can't keep coming in every weekend."

Field Marshall Viscount Montgomery stated, "A good beating with a cane can have a remarkable sense of awakening on the mind and conscience of a boy" (James, 1963, p. 13).

Note: When a phrase such as *she said* interrupts the quotation, do not capitalize the first word after the phrase unless the word actually begins a new quoted sentence.

Indirect quotations do not need to be enclosed in quotation marks or begin with capital letters.

Ms. Goldman is saying that it's time to face the real issues.

Proofread carefully to be sure that you have added quotation marks at both the beginning and the end of each quotation.

➤ **The commissioners came to the conclusion that alcohol prohibition was, in the words of Walter Lippman," a helpless failure."**

In dialogue, enclose each speaker's words in quotation marks, and begin a new paragraph every time the speaker changes.

"Come on, James," Toby said. "Let's climb over the fence."
"I don't think it's a good idea!" I replied.

direct quotation A speaker's or writer's exact words, which are enclosed in quotation marks.

indirect quotation A reworded statement or question that presents a speaker's or writer's ideas without quoting directly or using quotation marks.

If a quotation from a speaker or writer continues from one paragraph to the next, omit the closing quotation mark at the end of the first paragraph, but begin the next paragraph with a quotation mark to show that the quote continues.

Note: In a research paper, indent a long quotation as a block, double spaced, and omit the quotation marks. If you are following the MLA style, indent prose quotations of five or more typed lines ten spaces or an inch from the left margin (see Chapter 9). If you are following the APA style, indent prose quotations of forty words or more five spaces from the left margin (see Chapter 10).

MLA Style for a Block Quotation

The mother points out the social changes over Dee's and her lifetime, contrasting the two time periods.

> Who can even imagine me looking a strange white man in the eye? It seems to me I have talked to them always with one foot raised in flight, with my head turned in whichever way is farthest from them. Dee, though. She would always look anyone in the eye. (Walker 49)

The parenthetical citation follows the MLA style for in-text citations (see Chapter 9).

If you are quoting four or more lines of poetry, indent the lines ten spaces and follow the line breaks in the poem as much as possible. Use the poet's punctuation; do not insert your own.

42b Follow convention in using punctuation at the end of a quotation, after a phrase such as *he said* or *she said,* and with other punctuation in the same sentence.

Using other punctuation with quotation marks can be tricky at times. The following rules will help you deal with almost any situation.

1. Place a comma or a period inside the closing quotation mark.

➤ **Fishman also discusses utterances such as "umm"*,* "oh"*,* and "yeah."**

➤ **Grandpa then said, "I guess you haven't heard what happened".**

Note: Place a colon or semicolon outside the closing quotation mark.

The doctor who tells the story says that the girl is "furious"; she shrieks "terrifyingly, hysterically" as he approaches her.

In a research paper following either the MLA style or the APA style, the closing quotation mark should follow the last quoted word, but the period at the end of the sentence should follow the parentheses enclosing the in-text citation. (See Chapters 9 and 10.)

➤ **Senator Gabriel Ambrosio added that "an override would send a terrible message, particularly to the young people" (Schwaneberg 60)."**

2. Follow an introductory phrase such as *he said* with a comma or the word *that* and no punctuation.

➤ **I looked down and said, "I was trying on your dress blues."**

➤ **Eberts and Schwirian bluntly point out that: "control attempts which focus upon constraint or rehabilitation of individual criminals . . . are treating the symptoms or results of social conditions" (98).**

If you are introducing a formal quotation with an independent clause, you can also follow the clause with a colon. See 40a. For more on integrating quotations into your essay, see 8c and 31a.

3. Place a question mark, an exclamation point, or a dash inside the closing quotation mark if it is part of the quotation or outside if it is part of your own sentence.

➤ How is it possible that he could have kept repeating to our class, "You are too dumb to learn anything?"?

➤ My father replied, "What have I ever done to you"??

You do not need to add a period if a question mark or an exclamation point concludes a quotation at the end of the sentence.

➤ Miriam produces a highlighter from her bookbag with an enthusiastic Voilà!".

42c Consider using double quotation marks to set off words being defined.

Set off words sparingly (see 42f), using quotation marks only for those you define or use with a special meaning. You may also use underlining or italics rather than quotation marks to set off words (see 50b).

> The two most popular words in the state statutes are "reasonable" and "appropriate," used to describe the manner of administration.

> Men and women use "minimal response terms"—words such as "umm" that indicate that the listener is paying attention—in different ways.

Note: Occasionally, quotation marks identify words used ironically. In general, keep such use to a minimum. (See 42f.)

42d Enclose titles of short works (such as articles, chapters, essays, short stories, short poems, and songs) in quotation marks.

Titles of longer works, such as books and films, are underlined (or italicized). (See 50a.)

Titles of Short Works

Article in a periodical	“The Buzz about Firefly”
Chapter in a book	“The Father from China” (from *China Men* by Maxine Hong Kingston)
Essay	“‘But a Watch in the Night’: A Scientific Fable”
Short story	“Young Goodman Brown”
Short poem	“Sailing to Byzantium”
Song	“What Is This Thing Called Love?”
Television or radio program (individual episode)	“Chuckles Bites the Dust” (from *The Mary Tyler Moore Show*)

If the title ends with punctuation, the mark appears inside the closing quotation mark (see the song title above). If a title includes a quotation, enclose it in single quotation marks (see the essay title).

42e Use single quotation marks inside double quotation marks to show a quotation within a quotation.

Single quotation marks indicate that the quoted words come from another source or that the source added quotation marks for emphasis.

➤ **Flanagan and McMenamin say, “Housing values across the United States have acted more like a fluctuating stock market than the “sure” investment they once were.”**

42f Omit or correct quotation marks used excessively or incorrectly.

Avoid using quotation marks unnecessarily to set off words or incorrectly with direct or indirect quotations.

slang Informal language that tends to change rapidly.

cliché An overused expression that has lost its original freshness, such as *hard as a rock.*

1. Omit unneeded quotation marks used for emphasis.

Avoid using quotation marks to show irony or to distance yourself from **slang, clichés,** or trite expressions. Reserve quotation marks for words that you define or need to mark so that the reader notes a special meaning (see 42c).

➤ **Environmental groups can wage war in the hallways of Washington and Sacramento and drive oil companies away from our virginal stretch of "beach."**

direct quotation A speaker's or writer's exact words, which are enclosed in quotation marks.

indirect quotation A reworded statement or question that presents a speaker's or writer's ideas without quoting directly or using quotation marks.

2. Add quotation marks to show direct quotations, and omit them from indirect quotations, rewording as necessary to present material accurately.

that "while

➤ **To start things off, he said, ~~"While~~ I was farming in Liberty, Texas, at the age of eighteen, the spirit of God ~~came to him to go to Houston."~~**

" inspired him to move to Houston.

In the revised sentence, quotation marks enclose only the direct quotation.

Whenever you quote a written source or a person you have interviewed, check your notes to make sure that you use quotation marks to enclose only the speaker's or writer's exact words.

3. Do not enclose the title of your own essay in quotation marks.

Unnecessary "Auto Liberation"

Appropriate Auto Liberation

4. Omit quotation marks around a nickname.

Unnecessary "Tiger" Woods

Appropriate Tiger Woods

43 APOSTROPHES

Use an apostrophe to mark the possessive form of nouns and some pronouns, the omission of letters or figures, and the plural of letters or figures.

43a Use an apostrophe to show the possessive form of a noun.

possessive form The form that shows that a thing belongs to someone or to something.

The form of a possessive noun depends on whether it is singular (one item) or plural (two or more items).

1. Add *-'s* to a singular noun to show possession.

a student's parents

the rabbit's eye

Ward's essay

Apostrophes are easy to forget; missing apostrophes are easy to overlook. Keep an eye out for possessive nouns without apostrophes when you are proofreading an essay.

➤ **The ~~apartments~~ apartment's design lacks softening curves to tame the bare walls.**

Some nouns change their endings when they become plural (see 52a). Be careful to keep singular nouns in their singular form and to add *-'s* when you make them possessive.

➤ **Mrs. Johnson says that 90 percent of the ~~libraries~~ library's material is on the first floor.**

Indicate shared or joint possession by adding -*'s* to the final noun in a list; indicate individual possession by adding -*'s* to each noun.

father and mother's room (joint or shared possession)

father's and mother's patterns of conversation (individual possession)

Indicate possession by adding -*'s* to the last word in a compound.

mother-in-law's

Note: Even when a singular noun ends in *s,* add an apostrophe and -*s*. If the second *s* makes the word hard to pronounce, it is acceptable to add only an apostrophe.

Louis's life — Cisneros's story

Williams's narrator — Sophocles' plays

2. Add only an apostrophe to a plural noun that ends in -*s* but -*'s* if the plural noun does not end in -*s*.

their neighbors' home — the children's faces

other characters' expressions — the women's team

When you proofread, watch out for plural possessives with missing apostrophes.

➤ **Males tend to interrupt ~~females~~ females' conversations.**

Note: Form the plural of a family name by adding -*s* without an apostrophe *(the Harrisons);* add the apostrophe only to show possession *(the Harrisons' house).*

43b Add an apostrophe to show where letters or figures are omitted in a contraction.

Contractions are usually formed by joining two words, with an apostrophe substituting for one or more letters.

it is	it's
you are	you're
cannot	can't

➤ **"~~Lets~~ [Let's] go back inside and see if you can do it my way now."**

An apostrophe also substitutes for the first two numbers in a date.

➤ **Many people had cosmetic surgery in the ~~80s~~ ['80s].**

Note: The possessive forms of **personal pronouns** do not have apostrophes *(yours, its, hers, his, ours, theirs)* but are sometimes confused with contractions (such as *it's* for *it is*). See 43e.

personal pronoun A pronoun that refers to a specific person or object and changes form depending on its function in a sentence, such as *I, me, my, we, us,* and *our.*

43c Add -'s to form the plural of a number, a letter, an abbreviation, or a word referred to as a word.

perfect 10's	training the R.A.'s
marked with *X*'s	no *if* 's, *and*'s, or *but*'s

➤ **The subjects were shown a series of ~~3s~~ [3's] that configured into a large 5.**

Note: Some experts on style, including the Modern Language Association, prefer to add *-s* without the apostrophe when pluralizing numbers and abbreviations: *temperature in the 90s, ATMs.*

To refer to a decade, add *-s* without an apostrophe: *1950s.*

43d Add -'s to form the possessive of an indefinite pronoun.

➤ **Frequent diners know that good service can enhance ~~anyones~~ [anyone's] dining experience.**

indefinite pronoun A pronoun that does not refer to a particular person or object, such as *anybody, anyone, each, everyone, everything, somebody, something, neither, none,* and *nobody* (which take the singular); *few, many,* and *several* (which take the plural); and *all, most,* and *some* (which can take either the singular or plural).

personal pronoun A pronoun that refers to a specific person or object and changes form depending on its function in a sentence, such as *I, me, my, we, us,* and *our.*

Note: The possessive forms of **personal pronouns,** however, do not have apostrophes: *my, mine, your, yours, hers, his, its, our, ours, their, theirs.*

43e Omit unnecessary or incorrect apostrophes.

Watch for an apostrophe incorrectly added to a plural noun ending in *-s* when the noun is not a possessive.

➤ **Autistic ~~patient's~~ patients can either be high, middle, or low functioning.**

Also remove an apostrophe added to a possessive personal pronoun (*yours, its, hers, his, our, theirs*), watching especially for any forms confused with contractions (such as *it's* for *it is*).

➤ **A huge 10- by 4-foot painting of the perfect wave in all ~~it's~~ its glorious detail hangs high up on the wall of the surfing club.**

44 OTHER PUNCTUATION MARKS

Other punctuation marks include ellipsis marks, slashes, parentheses, and brackets.

44a Use ellipsis marks (. . .) to indicate an omission within a quotation or to mark a dramatic pause.

Type an ellipsis mark as three periods with a single space between each period.

> Aries also noticed this reaction in her research: "The mixed group setting seems to benefit men more than women . . . allowing men more variation in the ways they participate in discussions."

1. Use ellipsis marks to show where you have omitted words from a quotation.

Notice how a student used ellipsis marks in a quotation to indicate the omission of several words from a sentence in James Joyce's short story "Araby."

Original Passage

North Richmond Street, being blind, was a quiet street except at the hour when the Christian Brothers' School set the boys free. An uninhabited house of two storeys stood at the blind end, detached from its neighbours in a square ground. The other houses of the street, conscious of decent lives within them, gazed at one another with brown imperturbable faces.

Quotation with Ellipsis Marks

The street is "blind," with an "uninhabited house . . . at the blind end."

There are a few rules to remember about using ellipsis marks. Several of the rules are illustrated by quotations from the passage above.

- When you omit the end of a quoted sentence or when you omit a sentence or more from the middle of a quoted passage, add a period before the ellipsis to mark the end of the sentence that precedes the omission. No space intervenes between the last word in the quoted sentence and the period.

  "North Richmond Street, being blind, was a quiet street. . . . An uninhabited house of two storeys stood at the blind end."

- If a quotation ends with a complete sentence, it is not necessary to add ellipsis marks following the quotation. If the sentence is grammatically complete but was only part of a sentence in the original, however, add an ellipsis mark. If the last words you are quoting do not form a complete sentence, ellipsis marks are usually needed. Include another punctuation mark such as a comma either before or after the ellipsis points if it will help you to integrate the quotation into your sentence.

  "Conscious of decent lives within them, . . ." the houses, and by implication the people, are complacent and drab.

- Single words and brief phrases can be quoted without ellipsis marks.

  The houses on Richmond Street have "brown imperturbable faces."

- Delete opening or closing ellipsis marks if the quotation is clearly only part of the original sentence.

➤ **The United States ". . . has already exploited its oil reserves and has a reserves-to-production ratio of just nine years" (Flavin 30).**

- In cases where the ellipsis mark is followed by a parenthetical citation, place the period after the parentheses.

  The United States "has already exploited its oil reserves . . ." (Flavin 30).

Note: The rules for quoting poetry are the same as the rules for prose, except that the omission of one line or more is indicated with a complete line of ellipsis points.

See 8c for more on ellipsis marks.

2. Use an ellipsis mark to indicate a pause in a sentence.

I called out, "What in the world . . ."

44b Use a slash (/) to separate quoted lines of poetry and to separate word pairs.

When you quote two or three lines of poetry within the text of your essay, use slashes to separate the lines. Leave a space before and after each slash.

In "A Poison Tree," William Blake gives the same advice: "I was angry with my friend: / I told my wrath, my wrath did end."

Note: A poetry quotation of four lines or more should be presented in the block format: Omit quotation marks and slashes, double-space between lines, and indent each line ten spaces or an inch from the left margin. (See also 42a.)

Slashes are also used to separate word pairs. Do not insert a space before or after the slash.

either/or

actor/manager

44c Add parentheses to enclose additions to a sentence.

Parentheses are useful for enclosing material—a word, a phrase, or even a complete sentence—that would otherwise interrupt a sentence. Place words in parentheses anywhere after the first word of the sentence, as long as the placement is appropriate and relevant and the sentence remains easy to read. Parentheses are used to enclose the following elements.

Citations of research sources

Americans are not utilizing their knowledge, and as a result, their children are not benefiting (American Dietetic Association, 1990, p. 582).

Note: The example above shows the APA style of documentation. When citing sources, follow the documentation format required by your style guide. See Chapters 9, 10, and 11.

An acronym or abbreviation at first mention

People for the Ethical Treatment of Animals (PETA) is a radical animal liberation group.

acronym A word formed from the first letters of the phrase that it abbreviates, such as *BART* for *Bay Area Rapid Transit.*

Added dates, definitions, illustrations, or other elaborations

The bill (S-2232) was introduced to protect people who smoke off the job against employment discrimination.

Mixed breed puppies start at $45, and purebred puppies start at $350 (including the $20 refundable deposit).

Note: When enclosed in parentheses, a word or word group receives less emphasis than it would if it were enclosed by commas or dashes.

Numbers or letters in a list within the text of an essay

Signals would (1) prevent life-threatening collisions, (2) provide more efficient and speedy movement of traffic, and (3) decrease driver frustration.

Note: Always use a pair of parenthesis marks. Use commas to separate the items in a numbered list. If one or more items include internal commas, use semicolons to separate all of the items in the list (see 39b).

Watch out for the following misuses of parentheses.

1. Punctuation used incorrectly with parentheses

When you add information in parentheses, the basic pattern of the sentence should remain logical and complete, and the punctuation should be the same as it would be if the parenthetical addition were removed. Never include a comma *before* a parenthesis mark.

➤ **As I stood at the salad bar, a young lady asked if the kitchen had any cream cheese, (normally served only at breakfast,).**

2. Material within parentheses that could simply be integrated into the sentence

➤ **He didn't exhibit the uncontrollable temper and the high-velocity swearing (typical of many high school coaches).**

44d Use brackets to insert editorial notes into a quotation and to enclose parenthetical material within text that is already in parentheses.

In a quotation, use brackets to indicate where you have added a word or words to the original passage to avoid possible misreading.

"The gang is your family, he [Hagan] explains."

If the original quotation includes a misspelled word or other error, follow it with *[sic],* the Latin word for "so," in brackets to tell the reader that the error occurs in the source. Do not overuse this option, however. Often you can omit the error by rewording your sentence.

Use brackets as well to enclose parenthetical material that is part of a word group already in parentheses.

(The statistics come from the last national census [1990].)

Replace inappropriate brackets with parentheses.

➤ **The report concluded that fossil energy sources (~~[~~mostly petroleum~~]~~) supply 80 percent of the pollution in the United States (Herer 43).**

45 END PUNCTUATION MARKS

The period, question mark, and exclamation point are used to indicate the end of a sentence.

45a Use a period to mark the end of a declarative sentence, an indirect question, or an abbreviation.

declarative sentence A sentence that makes a statement rather than asking a question or exclaiming.

End your declarative sentences and any indirect questions with a period.

➤ **Another use for clinical hypnosis would be to replace anesthesia.**

➤ **She asked her professor why he was so tough on the male students~~?~~.**

In addition, most imperative sentences end in periods.

Think about it before you say it, especially to your mom.

Many, but not all, abbreviations are usually given with periods. Check your dictionary if you are unsure about an abbreviation not listed here.

Abbreviations That Generally Appear with Periods

B.C. *or* BC	e.g.	a.m.	Mr.
A.D. *or* AD	i.e.	p.m.	Ms.
B.C.E. *or* BCE	et al.	A.M. *or* AM	Mrs.
C.E. *or* CE	p., pp.	P.M. *or* PM	Dr.
	etc.	B.A. *or* BA	
		Ph.D.	

Abbreviations That Generally Appear without Periods

IBM	NFL	UNESCO	USA *or* U.S.A.
NCR	NCAA	NOW	NATO

Many specialized fields have their own systems for handling abbreviations.

Note: If a sentence ends with an abbreviation that includes periods, you do not need to add another period: *Plato died in the fourth century* B.C.

45b Add a question mark after a direct question or a series of questions.

➤ **Did they even read my information sheet.?**

When will the federal budget be balanced? By the year 2000? By 2010?

indirect question A statement that tells what a question asked without directly asking the question.

Note: A period is used after an **indirect question:** *I asked if there was any reason we couldn't do business.*

45c Use an exclamation point on rare occasions to show strong emotion or emphasis.

He fell on one knee and exclaimed, "Marry me, my beautiful princess!"

Replace inappropriate or excessive exclamation points with periods.

➤ **If parents know how to discipline, they can protect their children!.**

P A R T 

MECHANICS

PART

MECHANICS

46 HYPHENS

Hyphens are used to form **compound words** and to break words at the end of a line.

46a Use a hyphen to join the parts of a compound adjective when it precedes a noun.

When a compound adjective precedes a noun, the hyphen shows that the compound functions as a unit. A hyphen is not needed, however, if the compound adjective follows the noun.

Before Noun	After Noun
after-school activities	activities after school
well-known athlete	athlete who is well known
fast-growing business	business that is fast growing

➤ **People usually think of locusts as hideous-looking creatures that everyone dislikes and wants to squash.**

➤ **I was a nineteen-year-old, second-semester sophomore.**

➤ **People are becoming increasingly health~~-~~conscious.**

When two different **prefixes** or initial words are meant to go with the same second word, use a hyphen and a space at the end of the first prefix or word.

compound word A word formed from two or more words that function together as a unit. Depending on the word and its position in a sentence, a compound may be written as two separate words with no hyphen between them *(place kick),* one word *(moonshine),* or a hyphenated word *(once-over).*

compound adjective An adjective formed from two or more words that function as a unit.

prefix A word part, such as *pre-, anti-,* or *bi-,* that is attached to the beginning of a word to form another word: *preconceived, unbelievable.*

Over twenty people crowd the small trauma room, an army of green- and blue-hooded medical personnel.

Note: Some compound adjectives are nearly always hyphenated, before or after a noun, including those beginning with *all-* or *self-*.

adverb A word that modifies a verb, an adjective, or another adverb, often telling when, where, why, how, or how often.

all-inclusive fee	fee that is all-inclusive
self-sufficient economy	economy that is self-sufficient

A compound with an **adverb** ending in *-ly* is always left as two words.

brilliantly clever scheme	rapidly growing business

compound noun A noun formed from two or more words that function as a unit.

46b Present a compound noun as one word, as separate words, or as a hyphenated compound.

If you are not certain about a particular compound noun, look it up in your dictionary. If you cannot find it, spell it as separate words.

1. Close up the parts of a compound noun spelled as one word.

➤ **Another road in our county now looks like an appliance grave yard.**

2. Omit hyphens in a compound noun usually treated as separate words.

➤ **First, make the community aware of the problem by writing a letter-to-the-editor.**

3. Add any hyphens needed in a hyphenated compound noun.

➤ **My father in-law is saying that the problems have been so serious that it's time to look at the real issues and deal with them.**

Note: Some compound words have more than one acceptable spelling (*workforce* and *work force,* for example); if you use such a compound, choose one spelling and use it consistently throughout an essay. If you are unsure about whether to use a hyphen, check your dictionary.

46c Hyphenate compound numbers (up to *ninety-nine*) and fractions.

➤ **In 1987, nearly one-third of all health care spending was wasted on unnecessary surgery.**

46d Spell words formed with most prefixes as one word with no hyphen.

Common prefixes include *anti-, mini-, multi-, non-, post-, pre-, re-,* and *un-*.

antismoking	multicultural	postwar	repossess
minicar	nonviolent	predate	unskilled

➤ **This possibility is so rare as to be nonexistent.**

Note: Insert a hyphen in a word beginning with *ex-, great-,* or *self-* (unless it is followed by a suffix, as in *selfish*) or ending in *-elect* or *-in-law.* Check your dictionary in case of a question.

ex-husband   self-motivated   secretary-elect

➤ **Self-sufficiency is not the only motivation.**

Note: Use a hyphen in a word that includes a prefix and a **proper name.**

un-American   anti-American   pro-American

proper name The capitalized name of a specific person, group, place, or thing.

46e Use a hyphen when necessary to avoid ambiguity.

Sometimes a hyphen is necessary to prevent a reader from confusing a word with a prefix *(re-cover* or *re-creation)* with another word *(recover* or *recreation)* or from stumbling over a word in which two vowels occur together *(anti-inflammatory, co-opt).*

46f Insert a hyphen between syllables to divide a word at the end of a line.

If you must divide a word at the end of a line, look for a logical division, such as between syllables, between parts of a compound word, or between the root and a prefix or suffix.

go-ing	height-en	mus-cu-la-ture	back-stage
dis-satisfied	com-mitment	honor-able	philos-ophy

DIGITAL HINT

Although many word processors can automatically divide words at the ends of lines, writing is easier to read without numerous broken words. Check with your instructor or consult the style manual used in a specific field for advice about whether to use the hyphenation function.

47 CAPITALIZATION

proper name The capitalized name of a specific person, group, place, or thing.

common noun The general name of a person, place, idea, or thing.

Capitalize proper names, the first word in a sentence or quotation, and the main words in a title.

47a Capitalize proper names but not common nouns.

Capitalize specific names of people, places, groups, organizations, and other entities (see the accompanying chart). When a reference is general, use a common noun (uncapitalized) rather than a proper one (capitalized). Do not capitalize general names of institutions, seasons, or compass directions or words that you want to emphasize.

Capitalization Guide

People	*Proper name:* Martha Stewart *Common noun:* my sister
Ethnic and tribal groups, races, nationalities, languages	*Proper name:* African American, the Senecas, Caucasian, Irish, Spanish, Mandarin *Common noun:* black, white
Places and geographical locations	*Proper name:* Chicago, Mexico, the Pacific Ocean, the (U.S.) South *Common noun:* the lake, south of the city
Streets and highways	*Proper name:* Old Country Road, U.S. Route 66 (U.S. 66), Interstate 95 (I-95) *Common noun:* the street, the interstate
Events, historical periods, and cultural movements	*Proper name:* the Depression, the Civil War, the Jazz Age *Common noun:* the election, the turn of the century, the twentieth century, the eighties
Monuments and public buildings	*Proper name:* the Washington Monument, the Chrysler Building, the Capitol (national) *Common noun:* the library, the state capitol
Days, months, and holidays	*Proper name:* Wednesday, June, Fourth of July, Yom Kippur, Christmas *Common noun:* spring, the first of the month
Governmental bodies, agencies, and courts of law	*Proper name:* the House of Representatives, the Department of State, the Supreme Court, Circuit Court of Cook County *Common noun:* state legislature, the bureau, traffic court
Organizations, associations, and athletic teams	*Proper name:* Republican Party, the League of Women Voters, Microsoft Corporation, the Teamsters Union, the Buffalo Bills *Common noun:* the association, the corporation, the union, the team

(continued)

Capitalization Guide, *continued*

Documents and legislative acts	*Proper name:* the Declaration of Independence; the Bill of Rights; the Fourteenth Amendment *Common noun:* the amendment, the act
Religions, deities, and sacred texts	*Proper name:* Christianity, the Baptist Church, Judaism, Buddhism, God, Allah; the Bible, the Koran *Common noun:* the church, mass, biblical
Educational institutions and courses	*Proper name:* the University of Nevada, Longview Community College, Chemistry 101 *Common noun:* the university, the college, chemistry

➤ **It is difficult for americans to comprehend the true meaning of freedom.** [A]

➤ **I work in a Law Office that specializes in settling accident cases.** [l, o]

Note: Adjectives derived from proper nouns should be capitalized: *Mexican, Napoleonic.* Common nouns such as *street* and *river* are capitalized only when they are part of a proper name: *Main Street, the Mississippi River.*

independent (main) clause A word group with a subject and a predicate that can stand alone as a separate sentence. (A predicate is the part of a clause that includes a complete verb and says something about the subject: At the checkpoint, we *unloaded the canoes.*)

47b Capitalize the word that begins a sentence.

➤ **the garden was their world.** [T]

Also capitalize the first word of a sentence that appears within parentheses when it is not part of a larger sentence.

Note: When you use a colon to introduce an **independent clause**—usually a dramatic or emphatic statement, a question, or a quotation—you may capitalize the first word of the clause or not capitalize it, using whichever option you choose consistently within an essay. However, when you use a colon to introduce any other type of clause, phrase, or word, as in a list, do not capitalize the first word. (See 40a.)

47c Capitalize the first word in a quotation unless it is integrated into your own wording or continues an interrupted quotation.

Lucy Danziger says, "Forget about the glass ceiling" (81).

Marilyn describes the adult bison as having an "ugly, shaggy, brown coat."

Writers often incorporate short quotations and quotations introduced by *that* into their sentences; neither type of quotation needs an initial capital letter. When a phrase such as *she said* interrupts a quotation, capitalize the first word in the quotation but not the first word after the phrase unless it begins a new sentence. (See also Chapter 42.)

➤ **Toby said, "T trust me—we won't get caught."**

➤ **"R renting," she insists, "deprives you of big tax breaks."**

Note: When you quote from a poem, capitalize the words exactly as the poet does.

47d Capitalize the first and last words in a title and subtitle plus all other words except for articles, coordinating conjunctions, and prepositions.

War and Peace *Stranger in a Strange Land*

The Grand Canyon Suite *Tragedy: Vision and Form*

"How the Waters Closed above Him"

Titles of short works are placed in quotation marks (see 42d), and titles of long works are underlined or italicized (see 50a).

➤ **In her article "The Gun i In t The Closet," Straight writes about violence in booming Riverside, California, a city east of Los Angeles.**

article An adjective that precedes a noun and identifies a definite reference to something specific *(the)* or an indefinite reference to something less specific *(a* or *an).*

coordinating conjunction A word that joins comparable and equally important sentence elements: *for, and, or, but, nor, yet,* or *so.*

preposition A word (such as *between, for, from, in, of,* or *to*) that always appears as part of a phrase and indicates the relation between a word in a sentence and the object of the preposition: The water splashed *into* the canoe.

47e Capitalize a title that precedes a person's name but not one that follows a name or appears without a name.

Professor John Ganim	Aunt Alice
John Ganim, my professor	Alice Jordan, my favorite aunt

➤ **At the state level, Reverend Green is ~~President~~ president of the State Congress of Christian Education and ~~Moderator~~ moderator of the Old Landmark Association.**

Note: References to *the President of the United States* and to other major public figures are sometimes capitalized in all contexts.

47f Use capital letters for certain abbreviations.

Many government agencies and commercial organizations are customarily referred to with abbreviations, which should be capitalized in written text. In addition, capitalize brand names and the call letters of television and radio stations.

CIA NATO ADM Coca-Cola WKBW

47g In general, avoid using capitalization for emphasis.

Although in some writing situations a word that appears entirely in capital letters can create a desired effect, you should limit this use of capital letters to rare occasions.

Acceptable only in some contexts	The powerful SMACK of the ball on the rival's thigh brings an abrupt, anticlimactic end to the rising tension.

In most cases, you should follow the conventions for capitalizing described in this chapter.

➤ **The principles are called the ~~TENETS OF TAI KWON-DO.~~ tenets of Tai Kwon-Do.**

DIGITAL HINT

In an email message, conventional ways of emphasizing words are often not available, and writers are tempted to emphasize words by using capital letters. This strategy should be used cautiously, however. Arlene Rinaldi, in "The Net: User Guidelines and Netiquette" at <http://www.fau.edu/rinaldi/net/index.htm>, notes that this use of capital letters is called *shouting* and suggests enclosing the word or words in asterisks instead.

Not This message is VERY URGENT.

Instead This message is *very urgent.*

48 SPACING

Allow standard spacing between words and punctuation marks.

48a Supply any missing space before or after a punctuation mark.

Proofread carefully for spacing errors around punctuation marks.

➤ **My curiosity got the best of me,so I flipped through the pages to see what would happen.**

➤ **"I found to my horror,"Nadine later wept, "that I was too late!"**

➤ **"I would die without bread! Roberto declared."In my village, the baker made fresh bread every morning."**

48b Close up any unnecessary space between words and punctuation marks.

➤ Karl did not know why this war was considered justifiable by the U.S. government⁀.

➤ The larger florist shops require previous experience⁀, but the smaller⁀, portable wagons require only a general knowledge of flowers.

➤ Do you remember the song "⁀The Wayward Wind"⁀?

NUMBERS

Conventions for the treatment of numbers vary widely. In the humanities, writers tend to spell out numbers as recommended here, but in the sciences and social sciences, writers are far more likely to use numerals.

49a Spell out numbers through *ninety-nine,* numbers that begin sentences, and very large round numbers.

1. Spell out numbers *one* through *ninety-nine* in most nonscientific college writing.

➤ A hefty $125,000 is paid to Wells Fargo Security for ^four ~~4~~ guards who patrol the grounds ^twenty-four ~~24~~ hours a day.

➤ Only ^fifteen ~~15~~ years ago, people seeking plastic surgery wore veils when they visited a plastic surgeon's office.

Be consistent in expressing related numbers. In the following sentence, twenty-five is presented as a numeral because it appears in context with large numbers expressed as numerals.

The dentists examined the mouths of 42,500 children at 970 schools across the nation and 25 schools in Canada.

When two numbers occur in succession, use a combination of spelled-out words and numerals for clarity.

eight 20-cent stamps   ten 3-year-olds

Note: Depending on the type of writing that you do and the conventions of your field, you may decide to spell out only numerals up to ten. Either rule is acceptable. Just be sure to follow it consistently.

2. Spell out a number that begins a sentence, or rewrite so that the number is no longer the first word.

➤ Forty-six thousand ~~46,000~~ women die from breast cancer each year.

➤ As many as 46,000 women die from breast cancer each year.

3. Spell out very large round numbers, or use a combination of numerals and words.

3.5 million people   nearly 14 million
five thousand   a billion

49b Follow convention in using numerals.

Numbers over a hundred	289 envelopes
Fractions and decimals	1/2 *or* one-half; 18.5
Percentages	73 percent *or* 73%
Measurements	65 mph; 100 lbs.

In addresses	175 Fifth Avenue
Volume, page, and chapter numbers	volume 8; page 44; chapter 22
Scenes in plays	*The Tempest,* act 2, scene 1 *or* act II, scene I
Time of day	5 a.m. *or* 5 A.M.; 10:30 p.m. *or* 10:30 P.M.
Dates	October 4, 1954; 36 B.C.; A.D. 54; 1980s
Amounts of money	\$2.50; \$3.5 million
Scores	17 to 8
Statistics	307 individuals

50 ITALICS (UNDERLINING)

When they are set in type, underlined words appear in the slanted type called *italics.* Most word processors now include an italics option, but your instructor may prefer that you continue to underline.

50a Underline or italicize titles of long or self-contained works.

Titles of short works are enclosed in quotation marks (see 42d). Use underlining or italics for the following titles of longer works.

Titles of Long or Self-Contained Works

Books	Hemingway's novel *The Sun Also Rises*
Newspapers	the *Los Angeles Times*
Magazines	*Newsweek;* the *New Yorker*

Scholarly journals	*New England Journal of Medicine*
Pamphlets	*Government Guaranteed Investments*
Long poems	*Beowulf; The Rime of the Ancient Mariner*
Movies and videotapes	*The English Patient; Citizen Kane*
Television and radio programs	*60 Minutes; Car Talk*
Long musical compositions	Bizet's *Carmen*
Works of visual art	Wood's *American Gothic; Autumn Rhythm*
Plays	*Othello; A Streetcar Named Desire*
Comic strips	*Dilbert*
Periodical published on the World Wide Web	*Slate*

I found that the article in the *Journal of the American Medical Association* had more information and stronger scientific proof than the article in *American Health.*

Note: The Bible and its divisions are not underlined or italicized.

50b Underline or italicize words used as words and letters and numbers used as themselves.

the word *committed* a score of *7* a *q* or a *g*

➤ **Rank order is a term that Aries uses to explain the way that some individuals take the role as the leader and the others fall in behind.**

50c Underline or italicize names of vehicles (airplanes, spacecraft, ships, and trains).

Lindbergh's *Spirit of St. Louis* Amtrak's *Silver Star*

➤ **The wreck of the HMS Titanic still fascinates people almost a century after it happened.**

50d Underline or italicize foreign words that are not commonly used in English.

➤ **Upon every table is a vase adorned with a red carnation symbolizing amore.**

Note: Foreign words that have become common in English do not need to be italicized: "laissez-faire," for example. If a word is listed in a standard dictionary, you can assume that it has become part of the English language.

50e On rare occasions, underline or italicize words that need special emphasis.

Underlining or italicizing words for emphasis is a strategy to be used only once in a great while, when the added emphasis makes an idea clearer.

This situation exists because the policy is just that, *reverse* discrimination.

Resist the temptation to emphasize words by putting them in bold type. Usually, underlining (italicizing) provides enough emphasis.

50f Underline or italicize when appropriate but not in place of or in addition to other conventional uses of punctuation and mechanics.

Eliminate any unusual uses of underlining or italics.

Unusual The commissioner of the NFL, Paul Tagliabue, said, *"I do not believe playing [football] in Arizona is in the best interests of the NFL."*

Appropriate The commissioner of the NFL, Paul Tagliabue, said, "I do not believe playing [football] in Arizona is in the best interests of the NFL."

51 ABBREVIATIONS

Although abbreviations are more common in technical and business writing than in academic writing, you may sometimes want to use them to avoid repetition.

Abbreviations that consist of all capital letters are generally written without periods or spaces between the letters. When capital letters are separated by periods, do not insert a space before or after the internal period unless the letters are the initials of a person's name, which are spaced.

USA CNN UPI B.A. Ph.D. W. B. Yeats

51a Use abbreviations that your readers will recognize for names of agencies, organizations, countries, and common technical terms.

Agencies	FBI, IRS
Organizations	CBS, NATO, NOW
Countries	USA *or* U.S.A.
Technical terms	DNA, GNP, CPM or cpm

When an abbreviation may not be familiar to readers, use the full title in your first reference, followed by the abbreviation in parentheses. Then use the abbreviation in subsequent references.

San Diego Humane Society (SDHS)
➤ **The ~~SDHS~~ is an independently run nonprofit organization.**

Note: Spell out geographic names in formal writing *(Tallahassee, Florida)* unless the areas are commonly known by their abbreviations *(Washington, D.C.).*

51b Use *a.m., p.m., No., $, B.C.,* and *A.D.* only with exact numerals or dates.

7:15 a.m. *or* 7:15 A.M.	No. 18 *or* no. 18
10 p.m. *or* 10 P.M.	$172.18, $38
72 B.C. (before Christ)	72 B.C.E. (before the common era)
A.D. 378 *(anno Domini)*	378 C.E. (common era)

Note: A.D., for *anno Domini* ("in the year of our Lord"), is placed before the date, not after it. The alternatives B.C.E. and C.E. are acceptable and may be a better choice, depending on your audience. It is acceptable to write AM, PM, BC, and so on without periods as long as you are consistent.

51c Use commonly accepted abbreviations for titles, degrees, and Latin terms.

Titles and Degrees

Rev. Jesse Jackson	Mr. Roger Smith	Ms. Martina Navratilova
Diana Lee, M.D.	Dr. Diana Lee	James Boyer, D.V.M.
Ann Hajek, Ph.D.	Ring Lardner Jr.	Dr. Albert Einstein

Use a title before a person's name or a degree after the name but not both.

➤ **According to Dr. Ira Chasnoff~~, M.D.,~~ of Northwestern Memorial, cocaine produces a dramatic fluctuation in blood pressure.**

Reserve abbreviations of Latin terms primarily for source citations or comments in parentheses.

Latin Abbreviations

c. *or* ca.	*(circa)* about (used with dates)
cf.	*(confer)* compare
e.g.	*(exempli gratia)* for example
et al.	*(et alia)* and others (used with people)

etc.	*(et cetera)* and so forth
i.e.	*(id est)* that is
N.B. *or* NB	*(nota bene)* note well
P. S. *or* PS	*(postscriptum)* postscript
vs. *or* v.	versus

Some adult rights (e.g., the right to vote) clearly should not be extended to children.

Roe v. Wade is still the law of the land.

51d Use abbreviations when appropriate, but do not use them to replace words in most writing.

In formal writing, avoid abbreviating the following types of words.

Units of measurement	inches (*not* in.)
Technical terms	random access memory (*not* RAM)
Names of months	October (*not* Oct.)
Names of days	Friday (*not* Fri.)
Names of holidays	Christmas (*not* Xmas)
Course titles	English literature (*not* Eng. lit.)
Names of states or countries	Connecticut (*not* Conn. *or* CT); United Kingdom (*not* U.K.)
Names of companies	Parker Brothers (*not* Parker Bros.)
Parts of written works	chapter 7 (*not* ch. 7); page 45 (*not* p. 45)
Names of streets and highways	Hancock Street (*not* Hancock St.)

Note: If you use a term extensively, you may use its abbreviation if you first introduce it in parentheses right after the full term (see 51a).

In formal writing, avoid abbreviating words that you might abbreviate in an informal note to a friend or in your lecture notes, such as *especially, regarding,* and *for example.*

➤ **The Pets for People Program gives older people the companionship they need, ~~esp.~~ especially if they live alone.**

52 SPELLING

Try several (or all) of the following suggestions for catching and correcting your spelling errors.

- Proofread your writing carefully to catch transposed letters (*becuase* for *because*), omitted letters *(becaus),* and other careless errors (*then* for *than*). When you proofread for spelling, read the essay backward, beginning with the last word. (This strategy keeps you from reading for content and lets you focus on each word.)
- Check a good dictionary for any words you are uncertain about. When you are writing and doubt the spelling of a word, put a question mark by the word but wait to check it until you have finished drafting.
- Keep a list of words you often misspell.

DIGITAL HINT

If you use a word processing program, get in the habit of using the spell-checker as one of your final steps before turning in an assignment. Keep in mind, however, that a spell-checker will help you catch many misspelled words, but it will not highlight most proper names, terms not included in the word processor's dictionary, or misspellings that are themselves words (*then* for *than*). You will need to proofread your essay yourself to catch these spelling errors.

52a Study the spelling rules for adding prefixes and suffixes to words and forming plural nouns.

Although English has a large number of words with unusual spellings, many follow patterns described by spelling rules.

ADDING PREFIXES AND SUFFIXES

1. Add a prefix to a root without doubling or dropping letters.

distrust misbehave unable
dissatisfy misspell unnatural

2. Add a suffix beginning with a vowel (such as *-ing*) by following these rules.

- If the word has a single syllable that ends in a single consonant preceded by a single vowel, double the final consonant.

  begging hidden fitting

- If the word has a final stressed syllable that ends in a single consonant preceded by a single vowel, double the final consonant.

  beginning occurrence

- If the word ends in a double consonant or has a double vowel, do not double the final consonant.

  acting parted seeming stooped

- In some cases, the stress shifts to the first syllable when a suffix is added. When it does, do not double the final consonant.

  prefér: preférring, preférred
  préference, préferable

prefix A word part, such as *pre-, anti-,* or *bi-,* that is attached to the beginning of a word to form another word: *preconceived, unbelievable.*

suffix A word part added to the end of a word, such as *-ly, -ment,* or *-ed.* Adding a suffix either changes the word's form *(bright, brightly)* or tense *(call, called)* or forms another word *(govern, government).*

3. Drop a final silent *e* when adding a suffix that begins with *y* or a vowel.

achieving	icy	location
grievance	lovable	continual

Note: Keep the final silent *e* to retain a soft *c* or *g* sound, to prevent mispronunciation, or to prevent confusion with other words.

changeable	courageous	noticeable
eyeing	mileage	canoeist
dyeing	singeing	

4. Keep a final silent *e* when adding a suffix that begins with a consonant.

achievement discouragement sincerely

Exceptions: acknowledgment, argument, awful, judgment, truly, wholly

5. Change *y* to *i* when adding *-es* or *-ed* to a verb that ends in a consonant followed by *y*.

cry, cries, cried

FORMING PLURAL NOUNS

1. Change *y* to *i* when adding *-es* to form the plural of a noun ending in a consonant followed by *y*.

baby, babies

Note: Simply add *-s* to proper names: *her cousin Mary, both Marys.*

2. Add *-s* to form the plural of a singular noun that ends in a vowel followed by *y*.

trolley, trolleys day, days

3. Form the plural of a singular noun that ends in a consonant and *o* by adding *-es;* if it ends in a vowel and *o,* add *-s.*

potato, potatoes echo, echoes veto, vetoes
video, videos rodeo, rodeos radio, radios

Exceptions: autos, dynamos, pianos, sopranos

4. Form the plural of a singular noun that ends in *s, ss, sh, ch, x,* or *z* by adding *-es.*

Jones, Joneses hiss, hisses bush, bushes
match, matches suffix, suffixes buzz, buzzes

Note: The plural of *fish* is *fish;* the plural of *thesis* is *theses.*

5. Check your dictionary to form the plural of terms that were originally Latin, French, or some other language.

For many of these terms, a plural formed according to the rules listed above is acceptable.

criterion, criteria

medium, mediums *or* media

hors d'oeuvre, hors d'ouevres *or* hors d'oeuvre

Note: The term *data* is the plural of *datum.* Often writers use *data* as a singular noun, especially when they are referring to a collection of statistics or other information; this usage is now widely accepted.

The *data* is all in and being processed.

6. Form the plural of a compound word by making the principal word plural, wherever it appears.

brothers-in-law men-of-war foot-pounds
justices of the peace lookers-on

7. Note that some frequently used nouns have irregular plural forms.

child, children   woman, women

Some words have the same singular and plural forms: *moose, sheep.*

52b Study the spelling rules (and the exceptions) that apply to words you routinely misspell.

1. Add *i* before *e* except after *c*.

Most people remember this rule because of the jingle "Write *i* before *e* / Except after *c* / Or when sounded like *ay* / As in *neighbor* and *weigh.*"

Write *i* before *e*	retrieve, belief, siege
Except after *c*	deceive, receipt, conceive
Or when sounded like *ay*	eight, feint, reign

Exceptions: either, foreign, forfeit, height, leisure, neither, seize, weird

2. Spell most words ending in the sound "seed" as *-cede.*

precede   recede   secede   intercede

Exceptions: proceed, succeed, supersede

For ESL writers

If you have learned Canadian or British English, you may have noticed some differences in the way that words are spelled.

U.S. English	Canadian or British English
color	colour
realize	realise (*or* realize in Canadian English)
center	centre
defense	defence

52c Watch for words that are often spelled incorrectly because they sound like other words.

A number of common words sound the same or almost the same as other words but have entirely different meanings. Watch carefully for words such as the following, and check their meanings in the Glossary of Usage.

accept, except
advice, advise
affect, effect
allusion, illusion
already, all ready
an, and
beside, besides
capital, capitol
cite, sight, site
coarse, course
conscience, conscious
everyone, every one
its, it's
knew, new
lead, led
loose, lose
maybe, may be
passed, past
principal, principle
stationary, stationery
than, then
their, there, they're
to, too, two
weather, whether
who's, whose
vary, very
your, you're

Watch for and correct words that are missing word endings or that sound the same as the words you mean but are spelled differently.

➤ **The campfire had ~~burn~~** burned **down to a sizzle.**

➤ **I just ~~new~~** knew **it was a bear, and I was going to be its dinner.**

52d Watch for words that are often misspelled.

Check your written work for the following words, which are often spelled incorrectly. Look up any other questionable words in a dictionary, and keep a personal list of words that you are likely to misspell.

absence
accidentally
accommodate
accomplish
achievement
acknowledge
acquaintance
acquire
against
aggravate
all right
a lot
although
altogether
analyze
apparently
appearance
appropriate
argument
arrangement
attendance
audience
basically
before
beginning
believe
benefited
business
businesses
cannot
categories
changeable
choose
chose
coming
commitment
committed
competitive
conceivable
conscience
conscientious
conscious
convenient
criticism
criticize
curiosity
definitely
dependent
desperate
dictionary
disappear
disappoint
dissatisfied
eighth
eligible
embarrass
emphasize
environment
equivalent
especially
every day
exaggerated
exercise
exercising
experience
explanation
extraordinary
extremely
fascinate
February
finally
foreign
forty
fourth
friend
guidance
harass
heroes
immediately
incidentally
incredible
indefinitely
inevitable
infinite
intelligence
interesting
irrelevant
knowledge
laboratory
legitimate
literature
loose
lose
maintenance
maneuver
mathematics
mischievous
necessary
noticeable
occasion
occur
occurred
occurrences
parallel
particularly
performance
permissible
perseverence
phenomena
phenomenon
physically
playwright
practically
precede
preference
preferred
prejudice
preparation
prevalent
privilege
probably
proceed
professor
quiet
quite
receive
recommend
reference
referred
rhythm
roommate
schedule
separate
similar
sincerely
sophomore
specimen
studying
subtly
succeed
success
successful
therefore
thorough
tragedy
truly
unnecessarily
until
usually
without
whether
woman
women

PART 10 BRIEF GUIDE FOR ESL WRITERS

PART

10 BRIEF GUIDE FOR ESL WRITERS

53 ARTICLES

An article is used before a common noun to indicate whether the noun refers to something specific *(the moon)* or whether it refers to something that is one among many or has not yet been specified *(a planet, an asteroid)*. In addition, for plural count nouns, the absence of an article indicates that the reference is not specific.

Specific I performed the procedure on *the volunteers.*

Nonspecific *Volunteers* for scientific experiments are hard to find.

Note: A is used before a consonant sound *(a bird, a unit)* and *an* before a vowel sound *(an ocean, an hour).*

The rules for using articles *(a, an,* and *the)* are complicated. Your choice depends on the following two factors.

- Whether the article appears before a **count** or **noncount noun**
- Whether this noun is a **common noun** or **proper noun**

The following guidelines will help you to choose the correct article in a given situation and to proofread your written work for incorrect or missing articles. As an added precaution, consider asking a native speaker of English to check your use of articles in an essay.

count noun A noun that names people, things, and ideas that can be counted: one *teacher,* two *teachers;* one *movie,* several *movies;* one *belief,* several *beliefs.*

noncount noun A noun that names things or ideas that are not or cannot be counted: *thunder, happiness.*

common noun The general name of a person, place, idea, or thing.

proper noun The capitalized name of a specific person, group, place, or thing.

53a Use *a* or *an* with nonspecific singular count nouns.

Nonspecific nouns refer to one thing among many or to something that has not been specifically identified.

➤ **As [a] society, the United States must educate young people about avoiding drugs.**

> A darkroom
> ➤ ~~Darkroom~~ is essential for any serious photographer.

53b Use *the* for specific references to a count noun.

Use *the* if the noun has been introduced within the text or if the noun is familiar to most people.

1. After you have used *a* or *an* with a count noun, later references to the noun become specific and take the article *the.* Use *the* with specific singular and plural count nouns.

> When I walked into the doctor's waiting room, *a* woman in her mid-forties was waiting to be called. As I sat down, I looked at *the* woman.

An exception is a second mention followed by a description.

> I was guided to *a* classroom. It was *a* bright room, filled with warm rays of Hawaiian sunlight.

Note: In most situations, use *the* with a count noun modified by a superlative adjective.

> *the* most frightening moment   *the* smallest person
>
> but: He gave *a* most unusual response.

2. Nouns such as *sun* and *sky* refer to unique things: There can be only one sky. Nouns such as *house* and *yard* often refer to things that people own. A writer may talk about *the yard* meaning his or her own yard. In most situations, both types of nouns can be preceded by the definite article *the.*

> Don't look directly at *the sun.* [Only one sun could be meant.]

> I spent Saturday cleaning *the house.* [The reader will infer that the writer is referring to his or her own house.]

You can also introduce count nouns referring to specific entities with possessive nouns or pronouns *(Maya's friends, your friends)* or with demonstrative pronouns *(these friends)*. Indefinite count and noncount nouns can also be introduced by words that indicate amount *(a few friends, some thunder)*.

Count noun She stayed with *her* eight children.

Noncount noun Her family wanted *some* happiness.

53c Do not use an article with nonspecific plural count nouns.

➤ ~~The people~~ People like Dee cannot forget their heritage.

53d Do not use *a, an,* or *the* before a general noncount noun; use *the* before a noncount noun that refers to something specific.

The many kinds of general noncount nouns include the following.

Natural phenomena: thunder, steam, electricity

Natural elements: gold, air, sunlight

Manufacturing materials: steel, wood, cement

Fibers: wool, cotton, rayon

General categories made up of specific items: money, music, furniture

Abstract ideas: happiness, loyalty, adolescence, wealth

Liquids: milk, gasoline, water

Some nouns naming foodstuffs and other commodities are always non-count *(pork, rice, broccoli, furniture)*. Other nouns are noncount when they refer to food or the item as it is eaten or used *(We ate barbecued chicken and fruit)* or count when they refer to individual items or varieties. *(We bought a plump chicken and various fruits)*.

The indefinite article *a* or *an* is not used with noncount nouns. Depending on the meaning of the sentence, a noncount noun takes either no article or the definite article *the*.

count noun A noun that names people, things, and ideas that can be counted: one *teacher,* two *teachers;* one *movie,* several *movies;* one *belief,* several *beliefs.*

noncount noun A noun that names things or ideas that are not or cannot be counted: *thunder, happiness.*

adjective clause A clause that modifies a noun or pronoun and is generally introduced by a relative pronoun (such as *that* or *which*).

prepositional phrase A group of words that begins with a preposition and indicates the relation between a word in a sentence and the object following the preposition: Her sunglasses slid *under the seat.*

proper noun The capitalized name of a specific person, group, place, or thing.

1. Do not use an article before a noncount noun when it refers to something general.

➤ **The destruction of the war drew artists away from ~~the~~ reality and toward ~~the~~ abstract art, a change that allowed them to avoid a sense of despair.**

2. Use *the* before a noncount noun when it refers to something specific or when it is specified by an **adjective clause** or a **prepositional phrase.**

The coffee is probably cold by now.

The water [adjective clause: that we have left] has to be rationed.

The mood [prepositional phrase: of the people] changed from joy to fear.

53e Use *the* with most plural proper nouns; do not use an article before most singular proper nouns.

Most plural proper nouns require *the: the United States, the Philippines, the Black Hills, the Clintons, the Los Angeles Dodgers.* Exceptions include business names *(Hillshire Farms, Miller Auto Sales).*

In general, singular proper nouns are not preceded by an article: *Dr. Livingston, New York City, Hawaii, Disneyland, Mount St. Helens.*

➤ **~~The~~ Campus Security is a powerful deterrent against parties because if you are written up twice, you can lose your housing contract.**

Note: The is used before proper noun phrases that include *of (the Rock of Gibraltar, the Gang of Four, the Commonwealth of Massachusetts). The* is also required before singular proper nouns that name the following things.

1. Bodies of water, except when the generic part of the name precedes the specific name: *the* Atlantic Ocean, *the* Red River, but Lake Erie
2. Geographic regions: *the* West Coast, *the* Sahara, *the* Grand Canyon

3. Vehicles for transportation: *the Concorde*
4. Named buildings and bridges: *the* Pentagon, *the* Golden Gate Bridge
5. National or international churches: *the* Russian Orthodox Church
6. Governing bodies preceded by a proper adjective: *the* British Parliament
7. Titles of religious and political leaders: *the* Dalai Lama, *the* Speaker of the House
8. Religious and historical documents: *the* Bible, *the* Magna Carta
9. Historical periods and events: *the* Gilded Age, *the* Civil War
10. Highways: *the* New York State Thruway, *the* Pacific Coast Highway, but I-95 or Interstate 95

54 PROBLEMS WITH VERBS

In addition to this chapter on **verbs,** see 57a for a review of the basic English verb forms, including a list of common irregular verbs. For help with verb problems that all writers of English are likely to experience, see Chapter 23 on verb tense, form, mood, and voice, and Chapter 24 on agreement between subjects and verbs.

verb A word or phrase that expresses action or being and, along with a subject, is a basic component of a sentence: At the checkpoint, we *unloaded* the canoes.

As you proofread your writing, pay particular attention to the four problem areas for ESL writers discussed in this chapter: using the appropriate verb tenses in conditional clauses, two-word verbs, helping verbs, and using gerunds or infinitive forms after verbs.

54a Select verb tenses carefully in main clauses and conditional clauses.

independent (main) clause A word group with a subject and a predicate that can stand alone as a separate sentence. (A predicate is the part of a clause that includes a complete verb and says something about the subject: At the checkpoint, *we unloaded the canoes.*)

Conditional clauses beginning with *if* or *unless* generally indicate that one thing causes another (a factual relationship); predict future outcomes or possibilities; or speculate about the past, present, future, or impossible events or circumstances.

Factual relationship — [conditional clause] If we *use* television correctly, [main clause] it *gives* us information and entertainment.

Prediction — [conditional clause] If television *merges* with the Internet, [main clause] it *will control* our families and our community.

Speculation — [conditional clause] If programming *were controlled* by the government, [main clause] television *would be* less entertaining.

Each type of conditional sentence requires a different verb tense and form.

1. To express factual relationships or actions that happen together habitually, use the same tense for both verbs. Use the present tense for general truths or actions that are connected in the present.

> If an owner *maintains* a car, it *lasts* longer.

For actions that were connected in the past, use the past tense.

> In the nineteenth century, if people *immigrated* to the United States, they generally *improved* their lives.

Note: When is also used to introduce clauses expressing factual relationships.

> *When* we moved to America, my family had little money.

2. To express predictions or future possibilities, use the present tense for the verb in the conditional clause and the future tense for the verb in the main clause.

> If you *inspect* any of her restaurants, you *will find* an immaculate kitchen.

base form Generally, the form of a verb without any endings: I *eat;* to *play.*

3. To speculate about improbable events in the present or future, or events or circumstances that are contrary to fact, use the past tense in the *if* conditional clause and use *would, could,* or *might* plus the **base form** of the verb in the main clause.

Improprobable Some people believe that if the Health Department *distributed* clean needles, the number of people using drugs *would increase.*

Contrary to fact If women *controlled* the U.S. Congress, day care *would be* a priority.

In formal writing, use *were* rather than *was* in an *if* clause.

If Andrew *were* a more sociable person, he *would have* an easier time.

To speculate about events in the past that did not occur, change the verb in the *if* clause to the past perfect, and change the verb in the main clause to *would have, might have, could have,* or *should have* plus the **past participle.**

past participle A verb form usually ending in *-ed* that combines with a form of *be* or *have* (*is needed, had stayed*). Past participles can also function as adjectives.

If the computer lab *had added* more hours during finals week, students *would* not *have had* to wait to use a computer.

Note: Do not add *would have* to the *if* clause.

➤ **If slavery ~~would have~~ [had] been abolished by the Constitution, the Civil War would have been avoided.**

54b Learn the meanings of the idiomatic two- and three-word verbs used in English.

Idiomatic two- or three-word (or phrasal) verbs usually combine a verb with a word that appears to be a preposition or an adverb (called a *particle*). The combined meaning cannot be understood literally, and similar expressions often have very different meanings.

hand in means "submit"
hand out means "distribute"
look into means "investigate"
look out for means "watch carefully"

When you are unsure of the meaning or usage of such verbs, consult a dictionary designed for nonnative speakers of English or ask a native speaker.

In addition to verifying the meaning of these two- and three-word verbs, you will need to determine which verbs can be separated from their particles by other words and which are inseparable.

1. The following phrasal verbs are inseparable.

Inseparable Two- and Three-Word Verbs

come across	go over	run into	stay away
get along	grow up	run out of	stay up
give in	keep on	speak up	take care of

➤ **I knew I had to ~~speak loudly up~~ against the proposition.** [inserted: speak up loudly]

2. Other phrasal verbs can be separated by a direct object.

Did you *make up* that story?

Did you *make* that story *up?*

If the direct object of a separable phrasal verb is a pronoun, it must appear between the verb and the particle.

➤ **I was reluctant to turn [inserted: her] down ~~her.~~**

The following list will help you identify common two- and three-word verbs that are separable.

Separable Two- and Three-Word Verbs

ask out	do over	give away	hang up
bring up	drop off	give back	help out
call off	fill out	hand in	leave out
call up	fill up	hand out	make up

pick out	put off	take out	try on
pick up	put on	take over	try out
point out	put out	think over	turn down
put away	put together	throw away	turn on
put back	shut off	throw out	wake up

54c Use the correct verb forms after helping verbs.

1. After the helping verbs *do, does,* and *did,* always use the **base form** of the main verb.

➤ **They do not ~~cooperated~~ [cooperate] with the police.**

The forms of *do (do, does,* and *did)* can be used in the following situations.

- To form a question: *Do you know why Helene tried to swim from Caribou Island to the coast?*
- To add emphasis to the main verb: *She did reach the mainland.*
- To make the main verb negative: *I did not understand why she attempted this feat.*

2. After the helping verbs *have, has,* and *had,* always use the **past participle** form of the main verb to form one of the perfect tenses. (See 23a and 57a.)

➤ **They have [been] doing these things for a long time.**

Note: A modal such as *will* sometimes precedes *have, has,* or *had: By Friday I will have finished this project.*

3. Following the helping verbs *be, am, is, are, was, were,* and *been* (forms of *be*), the **present participle** is used to show ongoing action (progressive tense).

➤ **The president is ~~given~~ [giving] a speech on all major networks.**

helping verbs The verbs *have, do,* and *be,* which can function as helping verbs (they precede or "help" main verbs) or as main verbs, and *modals* such as *can, may, could, will, shall,* and *should,* which must be used in conjunction with another (main) verb.

base form Generally, the form of a verb without any endings: I *eat;* to *play.*

past participle A verb form usually ending in *-ed* that combines with a form of *be* or *have (is needed, had stayed).* Past participles can also function as adjectives.

present participle A verb form ending in *-ing* that combines with forms of *be (was going, is freezing).* Present participles can also function as adjectives.

past participle A verb form usually ending in *-ed* that combines with a form of *be* or *have* (*is needed, had stayed*). Past participles can also function as adjectives.

passive voice The verb form that shows something happening to the subject: The mouse *was caught* by the cat.

modals The helping verbs *can, could, may, might, must, shall, should, will,* and *would,* which must be used in conjunction with another (main) verb: I *may go* to the bank.

base form Generally, the form of a verb without any endings, or the verb as it appears after *to* in its infinitive form: I *eat;* to *play.*

Note: Use one of the modal verbs with *be: Terence could be making some calls while I go out.* Use *have, has,* or *had* with *been: I have been working hard.*

4. After the helping verbs *am, is, are, was,* and *were* (forms of *be*), use the **past participle** to form the **passive voice.**

> ➤ **Regular programming is ~~cancel~~ [canceled] for tonight.**

To form the passive, *be, being,* and *been* need another helping verb in addition to the past participle.

Be Tonya *will be challenged* in graduate school this fall. [preceded by *will* or any other modal verb]

Being She *is being taken* by her sister Sophie. [preceded by another form of *be,* in this case *is*]

Been She *has been accepted* into the master's program in history. [preceded by *have, has,* or *had*]

5. After a **modal,** the **base form** is used.

The Senate *might* vote on this bill next week.

Common meanings of the modal verbs are listed below.

Meaning	*Modal Verb(s)*	*Example*
Ability	*can* (present and future tenses)	Pets *can* respond to their owners' moods.
	could (past tense)	Eli *could* walk when he was ten months old.
Permission	*may, might, can, could* (present and future tenses)	*May* I come in? I *can* submit my assignment a day late.
	could, might (past tense)	My instructor told me I *could* take the test a day later.

Meaning	*Modal Verb(s)*	*Example*
Polite request	*would, could* (present and future tenses)	*Would* you pass the bread? *Could* I see your ticket, please?
Possibility	*may, might* (present and future tenses)	I *might* take a vacation in Mexico.
	may have, might have + past participle (past)	I *might have lost* my wallet.
Necessity	*must* or *have to* (present and future tenses)	Kim *must* find a good doctor.
	had to (past tense)	She *had to* go to the emergency room.
Probability	*must* (present and future tenses)	Joe *must* be home by now.
	must have + past participle (past tense)	The furnace *must have stopped* working.
Intention	*will, shall* (present and future tenses)	Maria *will* plan the party. *Shall* I go to the bank?
	would (past tense)	I promised I *would* go to the bank.
Expectation	*should* (present and future tenses)	It *should* rain tomorrow.
	should have + past participle (past tense)	We *should have received* the package by now.
Advisability	*should, ought to* (present and future tenses)	Juan *should* get his car repaired.
	should have, ought to have + past participle (past tense)	You *should have eaten* the burritos.

Meaning	*Modal Verb(s)*	*Example*
Speculation	*would* (present and future tenses)	If Olga were here, she *would* know what to do.
	would have + past participle (past tense)	If Angel had planned more carefully, he *would have had* enough supplies.
Prohibition	*must not*	You *must not* leave a child near a pool unsupervised.

gerund A verb form that is used as a noun and ends with *-ing: arguing, throwing.*

infinitive A verb form consisting of the word *to* plus the base form of the verb: *to run, to do.*

54d Learn which verbs are followed by gerunds, which are followed by infinitives, and which can be followed by either.

Some verbs may be followed by either the gerund or the infinitive form of a verb without changing their meaning. For other verbs, the meaning changes, and still others can be followed only by a gerund or by an infinitive. The following lists will help you to sort out this complex situation.

1. Verbs that can be followed by either a gerund or an infinitive with no change in meaning

begin	continue	like	prefer
can't stand	hate	love	start

The roof *began leaking.*

The roof *began to leak.*

2. Verbs that change their meaning, depending on whether a gerund or an infinitive follows

forget remember stop try

Salam *remembered going* to the park on Saturday. [Salam recalled a weekend visit to a park.]

Salam *remembered to go* to the park on Saturday. [Salam remembered that he had to go to the park on Saturday.]

3. Verbs that can be followed by a gerund but not an infinitive

admit	deny	keep	recall
appreciate	discuss	miss	resist
avoid	dislike	postpone	risk
can't help	enjoy	practice	suggest
consider	finish	put off	tolerate
delay	imagine	quit	

➤ **I recall ~~to see~~ [seeing] Michel there.**

Note: Not or *never* can separate the verb and the gerund.

We discussed *not* having a party this year.

4. Verbs that can be followed by an infinitive but not a gerund

agree	expect	need	refuse
ask	fail	offer	venture
beg	have	plan	wait
choose	hope	pretend	want
claim	manage	promise	wish
decide	mean		

➤ **Children often only pretend ~~eating~~ [to eat] food they dislike.**

Note: In a sentence with a verb followed by an infinitive, the meaning changes depending on the placement of a negative word such as *not* or *never.*

I *never* promised to eat liver. [I did not make the promise.]

I promised *never* to eat candy. [I promised not to do it.]

5. Verbs that must be followed by a noun or pronoun and an infinitive

Magda taught *her parrot to say* a few words.

advise	encourage	order	teach
allow	force	persuade	tell
cause	instruct	remind	urge
command	invite	require	warn
convince	need		

Note: Use an infinitive, not *that,* following a verb such as *want* or *need.*

➤ **José wants ~~that~~ his new car ^to stay^ ~~stays~~ in good condition.**

6. The verbs *let, make* ("force"), and *have* ("cause")
Use a noun or pronoun and the **base form** of the verb (not the infinitive) after these verbs.

base form Generally, the form of a verb without any endings: I *eat;* to *play.*

He *let me borrow* the car.

The drill sergeant *makes the recruits stand* at attention.

I *had the children draw* in their notebooks.

55 PREPOSITIONS

This chapter deals with three common **prepositions**—*in, on,* and *at*—and verb-preposition and adjective-preposition combinations. See page 429 for a list of common prepositions.

preposition A word (such as *between, for, from, in, of,* or *to*) that always appears as part of a phrase and indicates the relation between a word in a sentence and the object of the preposition. The water splashed *into* the canoe.

55a Use *in, on,* and *at* to indicate location and time.

Location

- *In* usually means "within a geographic place or enclosed area" *(in Mexico, in a small town, in the park, in my bedroom, in a car).*
- *On* means "on top of" *(on the shelf, on a hill, on a bicycle);* it is also used with modes of mass transportation *(on a train, on the subway),* streets *(on Broadway),* pages *(on page 5),* floors of buildings *(on the tenth floor),* and tracts of private land *(on a farm, on the lawn).*
- *At* refers to specific addresses and named locations *(at 1153 Grand Street, at Nana's house, at Macy's),* to general locations *(at work, at home, at the beach),* and to locations that involve a specific activity *(at the mall, at the gym, at a party, at a restaurant).*

Time

- *In* is used with months *(in May),* years *(in 1998),* and seasons *(in the fall),* as well as with *morning, afternoon,* and *evening (in the morning).*
- *On* is used with days of the week *(on Monday)* and dates *(on June 2).*
- *At* is used with times *(at 7:30, at noon)* and with *night (at night).*

As you proofread your written work, make sure that *in, on,* and *at* convey time and location correctly in your sentences.

➤ **People are driving at 55 or 60 miles per hour ~~in~~ [on] the highway.**

55b Develop a personal list of verb or adjective + preposition combinations.

In English, prepositions combine with verbs or adjectives in sometimes arbitrary ways. Some combinations of verbs and prepositions create meanings that cannot be understood literally, such as *run into* for "meet" (see 54b). In other cases, readers will expect a writer to use certain prepositions with certain verbs or adjectives to express a particular shade of meaning. Note the differences in meaning in the verb + preposition combinations listed here.

look *for* a parking space	look *toward* the future
look *at* a new apartment	look *up* a quotation
talk *with* a person (suggests a two-way conversation)	talk *about* a subject
talk *to* a person (suggests a one-sided conversation)	talk *among* yourselves

Similarly, the following adjective + preposition combinations display subtle differences in meaning.

afraid *for* people in danger	inspired *by* a work of art
afraid *of* crime	inspired *to* give generously

Many more combinations exist in English. The *Longman Dictionary of Contemporary English* can help you with these combinations as well as other idiomatic usages. As you proofread your writing, look for these combinations, and check in a dictionary or with a native speaker of English if you are not sure about a particular one.

gerund A verb form that is used as a noun and ends with *-ing: arguing, throwing.*

infinitive A verb form consisting of the word *to* plus the base form of the verb: *to run, to do.*

55c When a noun or gerund follows the preposition *to,* do not mistake the preposition for the *to* in an infinitive.

Nouns and gerunds often function as objects of prepositions, including the preposition *to.*

I threw my hiking boots *into the tent.*

I won ten dollars *for guessing* the number of beans in a jar.

Mr. Singh is dedicated *to building* his business.

When *to* functions as a preposition, do not mistake it for the *to* in an infinitive.

➤ **Scientists are looking forward to ~~learn~~ learning more about Mars.**

Note: The difference in meaning between *used to* followed by the **base form** of the verb and *get used to* followed by a gerund can be confusing for ESL writers.

In the United States, most people *used to live* in rural areas. [This situation existed in the past but has changed.]

My daughter *is getting used to going* to school every day. [She is getting in the habit of attending school.]

base form Generally, the form of a verb without any endings: I *eat,* to *play.*

56 PROBLEMS WITH OMITTED OR REPEATED WORDS AND ADJECTIVES

As you edit and proofread your written work, watch out for the following common errors in sentence structure and the use of adjectives.

56a Check for omitted subjects and verbs.

In English, every sentence, with rare exceptions, should have both a **subject** and a **verb.** If your native language allows you to omit either sub-

subject The word or words that identify the topic or theme of the sentence—what is being discussed: *Our defective rubber raft* began to leak air.

verb A word or phrase that expresses action or being and, along with a subject, is a basic component of a sentence: At the checkpoint, we *unloaded* the canoes.

ject or verb, check your drafts carefully to be sure that you supply both a subject and a verb in each sentence.

> subject: My brother — verb: has been
>
> My brother has been very successful in his job.

Add a missing subject.

➤ **On the contrary, the compliments increase his irritability.**

Add a missing verb.

➤ **Mr. Yang is a man who owns a butcher shop.**

Supply a missing expletive (*there* or *it*) if the subject follows the verb.

➤ **There are ~~Are~~ many ways to help poor people to get off welfare.**

Note: In questions, subjects can follow verbs without an expletive.

> verb subj.
>
> Is she leaving now?

56b Do not repeat the subject.

➤ **The poor woman on the sofa ~~she~~ must have an eye infection.**

When the sentence includes a relative clause (beginning with *which, that,* or *who*), the relative pronoun replaces the subject of the clause. It is not necessary to add another pronoun.

➤ **Only a few people who are very wealthy ~~they~~ live in that neighborhood.**

56c Use the accepted order for adjectives that precede a noun.

Adjectives generally appear in the following order in English sentences.

1. Article, possessive, demonstrative, or other determiner: *a, an, the, his, their, Janine's, that*
2. Evaluation or judgment: *elegant, magnificent, impressive*
3. Size or dimension: *short, tall, long, large, small, big, little*
4. Shape: *round, rectangular, square, baggy, circular, octagonal*
5. Age: *new, young, old, aged, antique*
6. Color: *pink, turquoise, gray, orange*
7. History or origin (country and religion): *German, Buddhist*
8. Material: *copper, cotton, plastic, oak, linen*
9. Noun used as a descriptive adjective: *kitchen* (sink), *bedroom* (lamp)

Arrange adjectives in the order expected in English.

1	2	4	6	
a	*magnificent*	*round*	*turquoise*	stone

1	3	5	
her	*skinny,*	*young*	cousin

56d Use present participles for adjectives with active meanings; use past participles for adjectives with passive meanings.

Use the present form of the participle *(-ing)* if it describes someone or something causing or producing a mental state (active meaning). Use the past form *(-ed)* if it describes someone or something experiencing the mental state (passive meaning). Problem participles include the following pairs.

> **present participle** A verb form ending in *-ing* that combines with forms of *be (was going, is freezing)*. Present participles can also function as adjectives.

> **past participle** A verb form usually ending in *-ed* that combines with a form of *be* or *have (is needed, had stayed)*. Past participles can also function as adjectives.

annoying/annoyed	exhausting/exhausted
boring/bored	pleasing/pleased
confusing/confused	surprising/surprised
disappointing/disappointed	taking/taken
exciting/excited	tiring/tired

The students were *confused* by the directions.

Something happened to the students in the class. They were confused.

The directions were *confusing.*

The directions caused a mental state—confusion— among the students.

Use the present participle to describe someone or something causing or producing a situation.

➤ **Parents must not accept the ~~frightened~~ [frightening] behavior that their children learn.**

Use the past participle to describe someone or something experiencing a situation.

➤ **I was not ~~pleasing~~ [pleased] with the information about religion in this article.**

quantifier An adjective that indicates the amount of the noun it modifies: *four* friends; *some* peaches.

56e Watch out for common problems with quantifiers.

1. Differentiating among *most, most of,* and *the most*

Most and *most of* mean "in nearly every case."

Most novels include a character readers care about.

Most of the time my dorm room is a mess.

The most is used in comparisons.

Muhammad Ali is *the most* famous boxer in the world.

2. Differentiating *few* from *a few*

Few means "only a small number" and suggests that there is not enough of something; *a few* means "some."

We have *few* songbirds left in our area. [There are not enough songbirds—negative connotation.]

A few songbirds are nesting in our tree. [Some songbirds are living in the tree—positive connotation.]

Note: Another pair of words with a comparable difference in meaning is *little* and *a little.*

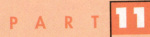

PART 11 A BRIEF REVIEW OF SENTENCE STRUCTURE

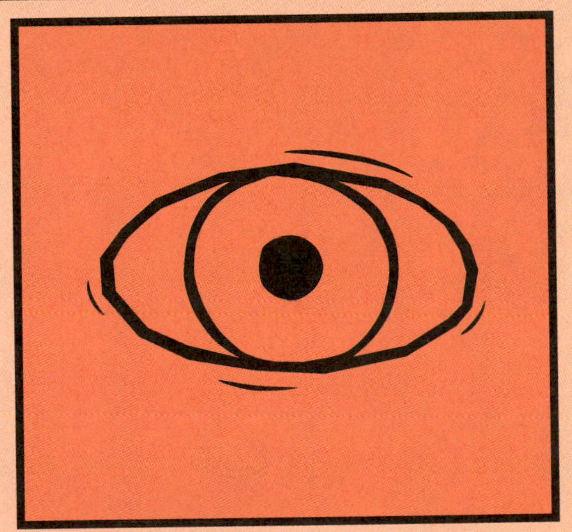

PART 11 A BRIEF REVIEW OF SENTENCE STRUCTURE

57 BASIC SENTENCE ELEMENTS

This chapter reviews the parts of speech and the types of clauses and phrases. Chapter 58 describes basic sentence structure.

As you practice your writing, your primary concern will be with rhetoric, not parts of speech or sentence structure. You will focus on learning how to develop ideas, illustrate general statements, organize an argument, and integrate information. However, it is also important to have a basic understanding of sentence elements and structure. After all, writing clear and correct sentences is part of being a competent writer.*

57a Parts of speech

There are nine parts of speech: nouns, pronouns, verbs, adjectives, adverbs, prepositions, conjunctions, articles, and interjections.

Nouns

Nouns are names. Everything and everyone surrounding you has a name, as do the ideas in your textbooks and lecture notes and the feelings and sensations you have experienced since you woke up this morning.

- *Proper nouns:* Burger King, Julia Child, General Foods
- *Common nouns:* tomato, food, lunch, café, waffle, gluttony
  - *Abstract:* hunger, satiation, indulgence, appetite
  - *Concrete:* spareribs, soup, radish, champagne, gravy

Nouns can be singular *(biscuit)* or plural *(biscuits);* they may also be collective *(kitchen staff)*. They can be marked to show possession *(gourmet's*

*English sentence structure has been described with scientific precision by linguists. This brief review is based on an extraordinary sentence grammar, *A Grammar of Contemporary English* (New York: Harcourt, 1972).

choice, lambs' kidneys). Nouns take determiners *(that lobster, those clams),* quantifiers *(many hotcakes, several sausages),* and articles *(a milkshake, the eggnog).* They can be modified by adjectives *(fried chicken),* adjective phrases *(chicken in a basket),* and adjective clauses *(chicken that is finger-licking good).*

Nouns function in sentences or clauses as **subjects, objects,** and **complements.** They also serve as objects of various kinds of **phrases** and as **appositives.**

subject The word or words that identify the topic or theme of the sentence—what is being discussed: *Our defective rubber raft* began to leak air.

object The part of a clause that receives the action of the verb (At the checkpoint, we unloaded *the canoes*) or the part of a phrase that follows a preposition (We dragged them to *the river*).

subject complement A word or word group that follows a linking verb and describes or restates the subject: The tents looked *old and dirty.*

phrase A group of words that does *not* contain both a subject and a verb and is always part of an independent clause.

appositive A word or word group that identifies or gives more information about a noun or pronoun that precedes it.

Pronouns

Pronouns come in many different forms and have a variety of functions.

Personal pronouns replace nouns and come in three case forms.

1. *Subjective* (for use as subjects or subject complements): I, we, you, he, she, it, they.
2. *Objective* (for use as objects of verbs and prepositions): me, us, you, him, her, it, them.
3. *Possessive:* mine, ours, yours, his, hers, theirs. Possessive pronouns also have a form used before nouns: my, our, your, his, her, its, their.

   Calvin Trillin says the best barbecued beef can be eaten in Kansas City, but *he* was born there, so I'm not sure I trust *him.*

   Your memory of that lunch at Bryant's is clearer than *mine.*

Personal pronouns also come in three persons.

- *First person:* I, me, we, us
- *Second person:* you
- *Third person:* he, him, she, her, it, they, them

A personal pronoun can be in one of three genders: masculine *(he, him),* feminine *(she, her),* or neuter *(it).* It can be one of two numbers: singular *(I, me, you, he, him, she, her, it)* or plural *(we, us, you, they, them).*

Reflexive pronouns, like personal pronouns, function as replacements for nouns, nearly always replacing nouns or personal pronouns in the same clause. Reflexive pronouns include *myself, ourselves, yourself, yourselves, himself, herself, oneself, itself, themselves.*

Aunt Odessa prided *herself* on her chocolate sponge cake.

Reflexive pronouns may also be used for emphasis.

Barry baked the fudge cake *himself.*

Indefinite pronouns do not refer to a specific person or object: *each, all, everyone, everybody, everything, everywhere, both, some, someone, somebody, something, somewhere, any, anyone, anybody, anything, anywhere, either, neither, none, nobody, many, few, much, most, several, enough.*

Not *everybody* was enthusiastic about William Laird's 1698 improvement on apple cider—Jersey lightning applejack.

In the Colonies, *most* preferred rum.

Relative pronouns introduce **adjective (or relative) clauses** and come in three forms.

adjective clause A clause that modifies a noun or pronoun and is generally introduced by a relative pronoun (such as *that* or *which*).

- *Personal* (to refer to people): who, whom, whose, whoever, whomever
- *Nonpersonal:* which, whose, whichever, whatever
- *General:* that

It was Jacob Fussell of Baltimore *who* established the first wholesale ice-cream business in 1851.

In 1846, Nancy Johnson invented a small hand-operated machine, *which* was the forerunner of today's portable ice-cream freezer.

Interrogative pronouns have the same forms as relative pronouns but have a different function. They serve to introduce questions.

Who invented the ice-cream sundae?

The waiter asked, "*Whose* chocolate walnut sundae is this?"

Demonstrative pronouns point out particular persons or things: *this, that, these, those.*

This dish is what Mandy likes best for brunch: pecan waffles with blueberry syrup.

Of everything on the menu, *these* must be most fattening.

transitive verb A verb that needs an object—something that receives the action of the verb—to make its meaning complete.

intransitive verb A verb that does not need an object to make its meaning complete.

subject complement A word or word group that follows a linking verb (such as *is* and other forms of *be*) and describes or restates the subject: The tents looked *old and dirty.*

linking verb *Be, seem, appear, become, taste,* or another verb that connects a subject with a subject complement that describes or modifies it: The chips *taste* salty.

Verbs

Verbs tell what is happening in a sentence by expressing action *(cook, stir)* or a state of being *(be, stay).* Depending on the structure of the sentence, a verb can be **transitive** *(Jerry bakes cookies)* or **intransitive** *(Jerry bakes for a living);* an intransitive verb that is followed by a **subject complement** *(Jerry is a fine baker, and his cookies always taste heavenly)* is often called a **linking verb.**

Nearly all verbs have several forms (or principal parts), many of which may be irregular rather than follow a standard pattern. In addition, verbs have various forms to indicate *tense* (time of action or state of being), *voice* (performer of action), and *mood* (statement, command, or possibility).

Verb Phrases. Verbs divide into two groups: (1) *main verbs* and (2) *helping (auxiliary) verbs.* Helping verbs combine with main verbs to create verb phrases. The three primary helping verbs are *do, be,* and *have,* in all their forms.

> *do:* does, did, doing, done
>
> *be:* am, is, are, was, were, being, been
>
> *have:* has, had, having

These primary helping verbs can also act as main verbs in sentences. However, other common helping verbs, or modals *(can, could, may, might, shall, should, will, would, must, ought to, used to),* cannot be the main verb in a sentence but are used in combination with main verbs in verb phrases. The helping verb works with the main verb to indicate tense, mood, and voice.

> A favorite cheese in the United States *has* always been cheddar.
>
> After cheddar cheese is shaped into a block, it *should be aged* for at least several months.

Principal Parts of Verbs. All main verbs (as well as the primary auxiliary verbs *do, be,* and *have*) have five forms. The forms of a large number of verbs are regular, but many verbs have irregular forms.

Form	**Regular**	**Irregular**
Infinitive or base	sip	drink
Third-person singular present (*-s* form)	sips	drinks
Past	sipped	drank
Present participle (*-ing* form)	sipping	drinking
Past participle (*-ed* form)	sipped	drunk

The past tense and past participle for most verbs in English are formed by simply adding *-d* or *-ed (posed, walked, pretended, unveiled).* However, a number of verbs have irregular forms, most of which are different for the past and the past participle.

For regular verbs, the past and past participle forms are the same: for example, *sipped.* All new verbs coming into English have regular forms: *format, formats, formatted, formatting.*

Irregular verbs have unpredictable forms. (Dictionaries list the forms of irregular verbs under the base form.) Their *-s* and *-ing* forms are generally predictable, just like those of regular verbs, but their past and past participle forms are not. In particular, be careful to use the correct past participle forms of irregular verbs.

Listed here are the principal parts for fifty-one commonly troublesome irregular verbs. Check your dictionary for a more complete listing.

Irregular Verbs

Base	**Past Tense**	**Past Participle**
be: am, is, are	was, were	been
beat	beat	beaten
begin	began	begun
bite	bit	bitten
blow	blew	blown
break	broke	broken

Base	**Past Tense**	**Past Participle**
bring	brought	brought
burst	burst	burst
choose	chose	chosen
come	came	come
cut	cut	cut
deal	dealt	dealt
do	did	done
draw	drew	drawn
drink	drank	drunk
drive	drove	driven
eat	ate	eaten
fall	fell	fallen
fly	flew	flown
freeze	froze	frozen
get	got	got (gotten)
give	gave	given
go	went	gone
grow	grew	grown
have	had	had
know	knew	known
lay	laid	laid
lead	led	led
lie	lay	lain
lose	lost	lost
ride	rode	ridden
ring	rang	rung
rise	rose	risen

Base	Past Tense	Past Participle
run	ran	run
say	said	said
see	saw	seen
set	set	set
shake	shook	shaken
sit	sat	sat
speak	spoke	spoken
spring	sprang (sprung)	sprung
steal	stole	stolen
swear	swore	sworn
swim	swam	swum
take	took	taken
teach	taught	taught
tear	tore	torn
throw	threw	thrown
wear	wore	worn
win	won	won
write	wrote	written

Tense. Native speakers of English know the tense system and use it confidently. They comprehend time as listeners and readers. As talkers, they use the system in combination with adverbs of time to identify the times of actions. As writers, however, even native speakers may find it difficult to put together sentences that express time clearly through verbs: Time has to be expressed consistently from sentence to sentence, and shifts in time perspective must be managed smoothly. In addition, certain conventions permit time to be expressed in unusual ways: History can be written in present time to dramatize events, or characters in novels may be presented as though their actions are in present time. See 23a for a listing of verb tenses in English.

tense The form of a verb that shows the time of the action or state of being.

Voice. A verb is in the *active voice* when it expresses an action taken by the subject. A verb is in the *passive voice* when it expresses something that happens to the subject.

In sentences with active verbs, it is apparent who is performing the action expressed in the verb.

The chef *disguised* the tasteless broccoli with a rich cheese sauce.

In sentences with passive verbs, it may not be clear who is performing the action.

The tasteless broccoli *was disguised* with a rich cheese sauce.

The writer could reveal the performer by adding a phrase *(by the chef),* but such a revision would create a clumsy sentence. Graceful, clear writing relies on active, rather than passive, verbs. Passive forms do fulfill certain purposes, however, such as expressing the state of something.

The restaurant *was closed.*

Passives can give prominence to certain information by shifting it to the end of the sentence.

Who closed this restaurant? It was closed by *the Board of Health.*

noun clauses Like nouns, noun clauses can function as subjects, objects, or complements in independent clauses.

Writers also use passives to make sentences more readable by shifting long **noun clauses** to the end.

Active *That the chef disguised the tasteless broccoli* disgusted Elvira.

Passive Elvira was disgusted *that the chef disguised the tasteless broccoli.*

Mood. Mood refers to the writer's attitude toward a statement. There are three moods: indicative, imperative, and subjunctive. Most statements or questions are in the *indicative mood.*

The chuck wagon *fed* cowboys on the trail.

Did cowboys ever *tire* of steak and beans?

Commands or directions are given in the *imperative mood.*

Eat those beans!

Writers use the *subjunctive mood* mainly to indicate hypothetical, impossible, or unlikely conditions.

If I *were* you, I'd compliment the cook.

Had they *been* here yesterday, they would have had hot camp bread.

Adjectives

Adjectives modify nouns and pronouns. Adjectives occur immediately before or after the nouns they modify.

Creole cooking can be found in *many* diners along the Gulf of Mexico.

As **subject complements** (sometimes called *predicate adjectives*), adjectives are separated by the verb from the nouns or pronouns they modify.

subject complement A word or word group that follows a linking verb (such as *is* and other forms of *be*) and describes or restates the subject: The tents looked *old and dirty*.

Subject complement Jambalaya tastes *delicious*, and it is *cheap*.

Some adjectives change form in comparisons.

Gumbo is *spicier* than crawfish pie.

Gumbo is the *spiciest* Creole soup.

Some words can be used as both pronouns and adjectives; nouns are also sometimes used as adjectives.

Many (adj.) people love *crawfish* (adj.) pie, and *many* (pron.) prefer gumbo.

Adverbs

Adverbs modify verbs *(eat well)*, adjectives *(very big appetite)*, and other adverbs *(extremely well done)*. They often tell when, how, where, why, and how often. A number of adverbs are formed by adding *-ly* to an adjective *(hearty appetite, eat heartily)*.

Walter Jetton started the charcoal fires *early*. [when]

He basted the sizzling ribs *liberally* with marinade. [how]

Pots of beans simmered *nearby.* [where]

The cooking utensils are placed *conveniently* near the grill. [why]

The barbecue takes place *annually.* [how often]

Like adjectives, adverbs can change form for comparison.

He ate the buttermilk biscuits *fast.*

He ate them *faster* than Bucky ate his biscuits.

He ate the biscuits *fastest* of all the hungry diners.

With adverbs that end in *-ly,* use the word *more* or *most* when making comparisons.

Junior drank the first cold lemonade *quickly.* He drank it *more quickly* than Billy Joe and *most quickly* of all those at the table.

The *sentence adverb* (or simply the *connective*) is a special kind of adverb used to connect the ideas in two sentences or independent clauses. Familiar connectives include *consequently, however, therefore, besides,* and *nevertheless.*

The inspiration for Tex-Mex food came from Mexico. *Nevertheless,* it is considered a native American cuisine.

Finally, adverbs may evaluate or qualify the information in a sentence.

"Barbecue" comes from *barbacoa,* a word the Spaniards *probably* picked up from the Arawak Indians.

phrase A group of words that does *not* contain both a subject and a verb and is always part of an independent clause. Some common types of phrases include *prepositional* (*After a flash of lightning,* I saw a tree split in half) and *verbal* (*Blinded by the flash,* I ran into the house).

object The part of a clause that receives the action of the verb (At the checkpoint, we unloaded *the canoes*) or the part of a phrase that follows a preposition (We dragged them to *the river*).

Prepositions

Prepositions occur in **phrases,** followed by **objects.** (See 57c for more on prepositional phrases.) Most prepositions are single words, but some consist of two or three words. They are used to indicate relations—usually of place, time, cause, purpose, or means—between their objects and some other word in the sentence.

Single-Word Prepositions

about	before	except	on	to
above	behind	for	onto	toward
across	below	from	out	under
after	beneath	in	outside	unlike
against	beside	inside	over	until
along	between	into	past	up
among	by	like	regarding	upon
around	despite	near	since	with
as	down	of	than	within
at	during	off	through	without

Two- or Three-Word Prepositions

according to	because of	in comparison with	instead of
along with	except for	in front of	on account of
away from	in addition to	in spite of	out of

I'll meet you *at* El Ranchero *for* lunch.

You can split an order *with* Georgette and me.

Objects of prepositions can be single or compound nouns or pronouns in the **objective case** (as in the preceding examples), or they may be phrases or clauses that act as nouns.

objective case The form a pronoun takes when it is an object (receiving the action of the verb): We helped *him.*

Herman began making nachos *by* grating the cheese.

His guests were happy *with* what he served.

Conjunctions

Like prepositions, conjunctions show relations between sentence elements. There are coordinating, subordinating, and correlative conjunctions.

Coordinating conjunctions join logically comparable sentence elements.

Coordinating Conjunctions

and but for nor or so yet

Guacamole is made with avocados, tomatoes, onions, *and* chilies.

Add a little lemon or lime juice, *but* be careful not to add too much.

Subordinating conjunctions introduce **dependent clauses.**

dependent (subordinate) clause A word group with a subject, a predicate, and a subordinating word (such as *because*) at the beginning. It cannot stand by itself as a sentence but must be connected to an independent (main) clause.

Subordinating Conjunctions

after	because	once	unless
although	before	rather than	until
as	even if	since	when
as if	even though	so that	where
as soon as	if	than	whereas
as though	in order that	though	while

As soon as the waiter came, Susanna ordered an iced tea.

She dived into the salsa and chips *because* she was too hungry to wait for her combination plate.

Correlative conjunctions come in pairs, with the first element anticipating the second.

Correlative Conjunctions

both . . . and	not . . . but
either . . . or	not only . . . but also
neither . . . nor	whether . . . or

Charley wanted to order *both* the chile relleno *and* the enchiladas verdes.

Articles

There are only three articles in English: *the, a,* and *an. The* is used for definite references to something specific; *a* and *an* are used for indefinite references to something less specific. *The Mexican restaurant in Westbury* is different from *a Mexican restaurant in Westbury.* See Chapter 53 for more help with using articles.

Interjections

Interjections indicate strong feeling or an attempt to command attention: *phew, shhh, damn, oh, yea, yikes, ouch, boo.*

57b Dependent clauses

Like independent clauses, all dependent clauses have a **subject** and a **predicate.** Unlike independent clauses, however, dependent clauses cannot stand by themselves as complete sentences; they always occur with independent clauses as part of either the subject or the predicate.

subject The word or words that identify the topic or theme of the sentence—what is being discussed: *Our defective rubber raft* began to leak air.

predicate The part of a clause that includes a complete verb and says something about the subject: At the checkpoint, we *unloaded the canoes.*

Independent Ribbon-shaped pasta is popular in northern Italy.

Dependent . . . , while tubular-shaped pasta is popular in southern Italy.
. . . , which is generally made by hand, . . .
Although it originally comes from China, . . .

There are three types of dependent clauses: *adjective, adverb,* and *noun.*

Adjective clauses

Also known as *relative clauses,* adjective clauses modify nouns and pronouns in independent clauses. They are introduced by relative pronouns *(who, whom, which, that, whose)* or adverbs *(where, when),* and most often they immediately follow the noun or pronoun they modify.

Vincent bought a package of agnolotti, *which is a pasta used in soup.*

We went back to the restaurant *where they serve that delicious veal.*

subject The word or words that identify the topic or theme of the sentence—what is being discussed: *Our defective rubber raft* began to leak air.

object The part of a clause that receives the action of the verb (At the checkpoint, we unloaded *the canoes*) or the part of a phrase that follows a preposition (We dragged them to *the river*).

subject complement A word or word group that follows a linking verb (such as *is* and other forms of *be*) and describes or restates the subject: The tents looked *old and dirty*.

independent (main) clause A word group with a subject and a predicate that can stand alone as a separate sentence. (A predicate is the part of a clause that includes a complete verb and says something about the subject: At the checkpoint, we *unloaded the canoes*.)

Adverb clauses

Introduced by a subordinating conjunction (such as *although, because,* or *since*), adverb clauses nearly always modify verbs in independent clauses, although they may occasionally modify other elements (except nouns). Adverb clauses are used to indicate a great variety of logical relations with their independent clauses: time, place, condition, concession, reason, cause, circumstance, purpose, result, and so on. (See 38d for help with punctuating adverb clauses.)

Concession *Although the finest olive oil in Italy comes from Lucca,* good-quality olive oil is produced in other regions of the country.

Condition *If you know mushrooms,* you probably prefer them fresh.

Reason Ken carefully watches the spaghetti *because he does not like it to be overcooked.*

Noun clauses

Like nouns, noun clauses can function as **subjects, objects,** or **complements** in independent clauses. They are thus essential to the structure of the **independent clause** in which they occur and so are not set off by commas (see 38b). A noun clause usually begins with a relative pronoun *(who, whom, which, that, whose),* but the introductory word may sometimes be omitted.

subject
That we preferred the sausage surprised us.

object
Harold did not know for sure *whether baloney came from Bologna.*

subject complement
His assumption was *that it did.*

direct object
Hillary claims *no one eats pizza in Italy.* [relative pronoun *that* dropped]

prep. direct object
Gnocchi may be flavored with *whatever fresh herbs are available.*

57c Phrases

Like **dependent clauses,** phrases can function as either nouns, adjectives, or adverbs in sentences. However, unlike clauses, phrases do not contain both a subject and a verb. (A phrase, of course, cannot stand on its own as a sentence but occurs as part of an **independent clause.**) The six most common types of grammatical phrases are *prepositional, appositive, participial, gerund, infinitive,* and *absolute.*

Prepositional phrases

Prepositional phrases always begin with a **preposition** and include an object. They function as either adjectives or adverbs.

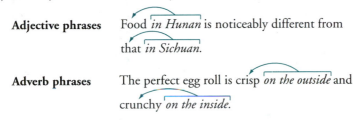

Adjective phrases Food *in Hunan* is noticeably different from that *in Sichuan.*

Adverb phrases The perfect egg roll is crisp *on the outside* and crunchy *on the inside.*

Appositive phrases

Appositive phrases identify or give more information about a noun or pronoun just preceding. They take several forms. A single noun may also serve as an appositive.

The baguette, *the most popular bread in France,* is about two feet long.

The baker *Marguerite* makes superb croissants.

Participial phrases

Participles are verb forms used to indicate certain tenses (present: *sipping;* past: *sipped*). They can also be used as verbals—words derived from verbs—and function as adjectives.

At breakfast, we were first served *steaming* coffee and a simple *buttered* roll.

dependent (subordinate) clause A word group with a subject, a predicate, and a subordinating word (such as *because*) at the beginning. It cannot stand by itself as a sentence but must be connected to an independent (main) clause: *Although it was raining,* we loaded our gear onto the buses.

independent (main) clause A word group with a subject and a predicate that can stand alone as a separate sentence.

preposition A word (such as *between, for, from, in, of,* or *to*) that always appears as part of a phrase and indicates the relation between a word in a sentence and the object of the preposition: The water splashed *into* the canoe.

A participial phrase is an adjective phrase made up of a participle and any complements or modifiers it might have. Like participles, participial phrases modify nouns and pronouns in sentences.

Two-thirds of the breakfasts *consumed in the diner* included eggs.

Prepared in the chef's personal style, the vegetable omelets are served with a cheese sauce *flavored with garlic and herbs.*

Mopping up the cheese sauce with the last of his roll, Mickey thought to himself, I could get used to this.

complement A word or word group that describes or restates a subject or an object.

Gerund phrases

Like a participle, a *gerund* is a verbal. Ending in *-ing,* it even looks like a present participle, but it functions as a noun, filling any noun slot in a clause. Gerund phrases include **complements** and any modifiers of the gerund.

subject
Roasting is the quickest way to cook a turkey.

subject
Preparing a stuffed turkey takes several hours.

You begin by *mixing the dressing.*
object of preposition

Infinitive phrases

Like participles and gerunds, *infinitives* are verbals. The infinitive is the base form of the verb, preceded by *to: to simmer, to broil, to fry.* Infinitives and infinitive phrases can function as nouns, adjectives, or adverbs.

To assemble tamales, begin by cutting the kernels off the corncobs.
adverb

Remembering *to save the corn husks* is important.
object of gerund phrase

Anyone's first tamale dinner is a meal *to remember for a long time.*
adjective

Absolute phrases

The absolute phrase does not modify or replace any particular part of a clause; it modifies the whole clause. An absolute phrase includes a noun or pronoun and often includes a past or present participle as well as modifiers. Nearly all modern prose writers rely on absolute phrases. Some style historians consider them a hallmark of modern prose.

> *Her eyes glistening,* Lucy checked out the cases of doughnuts at Dunkin' Donuts.
>
> She walked slowly to a table, *each hand bearing a sugar-glazed treasure.*

58 BASIC SENTENCE STRUCTURE

This review of basic sentence structure looks first at the elements that make up simple sentences and then at how simple sentences produce compound and complex sentences.

58a Words, phrases, and clauses

The basic building blocks of sentences are, of course, words, which can be combined into discrete groupings or *phrases.*

Words and phrases are further combined to create clauses. A *clause* is a group of at least two words that both names a topic and makes some point about that topic; every clause, then, can be divided into a subject and a predicate. The *subject* identifies the topic or theme of the sentence—what the clause is concerned with—while the *predicate* says something about the subject and is the focus of information in the clause. A clause can be either *independent* (a complete idea in itself) or *dependent* (combined with an independent clause to create a complete idea). Dependent (subordinate) clauses are discussed in 57b.

58b Sentence units

To introduce the principles of sentence structure, it is useful to consider *simple sentences,* those with only a single independent clause made up of a subject and a predicate.

Subject	**Predicate**
Native Americans	introduced baked beans to the New England settlers.
The Native Americans	were a source of many new dishes.

object The part of a clause that receives the action of the verb (At the checkpoint, we unloaded *the canoes*) or the part of a phrase that follows a preposition (We dragged them to *the river*).

complement A word or word group that describes or restates a subject or an object.

adverbial modifier A word or word group that modifies a verb, an adjective, or another adverb.

The subject and the predicate may each be a single word or a group of words. In addition to its verb, the predicate may include **objects, complements,** and **adverbial modifiers.** Simple sentences are composed of a combination of these basic units: subject, verb, direct object, indirect object, subject complement, object complement, and adverbial modifier.

Of these seven units, two—subject and verb—are required in every sentence. Note that the subject determines whether the verb in the predicate is singular or plural: In the second example, the plural subject *Native Americans* requires the plural verb *were.*

The basic sentence units can be defined as follows.

- *Subjects* The simplest subject can be a single noun or pronoun, but a subject may also consist of a *noun phrase* (including adjectives and other sentence elements) or even a *noun clause.* Subjects may also be *compound* if two or more nouns or pronouns are linked by a conjunction. (See 57b and 57c for definitions and examples of these various elements.)
- *Verbs* A verb can be classified as *transitive,* when it occurs with an object, or *intransitive,* when it occurs without an object. Intransitive verbs that occur with complements are often called *linking verbs.* Like subjects, verbs may be compound.
- *Objects* These include direct and indirect objects, which, like subjects, can be nouns, noun phrases, noun clauses, or pronouns. Objects usually follow the subject and verb in a sentence.
- *Complements* These are either *subject complements,* which refer to the subject, or *object complements,* which refer to an object. Like subjects

and objects, complements can be nouns or pronouns, noun phrases or noun clauses. Complements can also be adjectives or adjective phrases. Like objects, complements usually follow the subject and verb. They also follow any objects.

- *Adverbials* These are modifiers that modify the verb in the sentence. They can be adverbs, adverb phrases, or adverb clauses.

58c Types of simple sentences

The basic sentence units listed in 58b can be put together in various ways to produce seven general types of simple sentences. The basic units are subject (S), verb (V), direct object (DO), indirect object (IO), subject complement (SC), object complement (OC), and adverbial modifier (A).

S	V (intransitive)		
Pizza	bubbles.		

S	V (transitive)	DO	
Americans	love	pizza.	

S	V (transitive)	IO	DO
Some people	serve	their guests	pizza.

S	V (linking)	SC (adjective)	S	V (linking)	SC (noun)
Pizza	is	delicious.	It	is	an inexpensive meal.

S	V (intransitive)	A	
The best pizza	comes	from a local restaurant.	

S	V (transitive)	DO	OC
Vegetarians	consider	pepperoni pizza	unhealthy.

S	V (transitive)	DO	A
They	prefer	cheese pizza	any day.

58d Combinations and transformations

The simple sentence patterns described in 58c can be combined and transformed to produce all of the sentences that writers of English need. Two or more clauses may be combined with a coordinating conjunction (such as *and* or *but*) or a pair of correlative conjunctions (such as *either . . . or*) to create a *compound sentence.*

Compound Pizza is delicious, and it is an inexpensive meal. [independent clause: Pizza is delicious] [independent clause: it is an inexpensive meal]

Either Americans love pizza or they consider it junk food. [independent clause: Americans love pizza] [independent clause: they consider it junk food]

Writers create *complex sentences* by combining independent clauses with a subordinating conjunction (such as *although* or *because*) or by linking two clauses with a relative pronoun (such as *which* or *who*); clauses that contain subordinating conjunctions or relative pronouns are *dependent clauses* and can no longer stand on their own as simple sentences.

Complex Vegetarians consider pepperoni pizza unhealthy because it is high in saturated fat. [dependent clause: because it is high in saturated fat]

People who want to please their guests serve them pizza. [dependent clause: who want to please their guests]

Clauses can be combined to produce *compound-complex sentences*—compound sentences that contain dependent clauses.

Compound-complex Even though pepperoni pizza is unhealthy, it is a delicious meal, and Americans love it. [dependent clause: Even though pepperoni pizza is unhealthy]

All of the sentences listed so far have been *declarative* statements. Simple sentences may also be transformed into *questions, commands,* and *exclamations.* In addition, sentences in the **active voice** can generally be transformed into the **passive voice** if they have **transitive** verbs and objects.

Question Why is pizza popular?

Command Bake the pizza in a brick oven.

Exclamation This pizza is delicious!

Passive Pepperoni pizza is considered unhealthy by vegetarians.

active voice The verb form that shows the subject in action: The cat *caught* the mouse.

passive voice The verb form that shows something happening to the subject: The mouse *was caught* by the cat.

transitive verb A verb that needs an object—something that receives the action of the verb—to make its meaning complete.

GLOSSARY OF USAGE

Writers misuse words or phrases for many reasons. Sometimes the word is incorrect, imprecise in meaning, pronounced the same as the correct word, or used widely even though it is unacceptable in formal writing situations. In addition, problems can arise with idiomatic phrases or with words whose denotations or connotations do not precisely suit the context of the sentence.

a, an Use *a* as the indefinite article before words that begin with a consonant or a consonant sound: *a boy, a house; a ewe, a humanitarian, a one-to-one relationship.* Use *an* before words that begin with a vowel or a vowel sound: *an angel, an edge, an iota, an only child, an umbrella; an hour, an FBI report.*

accept, except *Accept* is a verb meaning "receive with favor." *Except* may be a verb meaning "leave out," but it is more commonly used as a preposition meaning "excluding." *None of the composition instructors will accept late papers, except Mr. Siu.* Other forms: *acceptance, acceptable, exception.*

adapt, adopt *Adapt* means "adjust to make more suitable"; *adopt* means "take as one's own." *To adopt an older child, parents must be willing to adapt themselves to the child's needs.*

adverse, averse *Adverse* means "contrary" or "unfavorable" and has the noun form *adversity. Averse,* often used with *to,* means "reluctant" or "opposed" and has the noun form *aversion. Averse* implies emotion; *adverse* usually does not. *She is averse to taking the drug because of adverse effects reported in the media.*

advice, advise *Advice* is a noun; *advise* is a verb. *Everyone advised him to heed the expert's advice.* Other forms: *advisable, adviser.*

affect, effect *Affect* is commonly used as a verb, most often meaning "influence"; in psychology the noun *affect* means an emotional state. *Effect* is gener-

This glossary includes several computer-related terms. Advice in those entries generally follows the preferences stated in *Wired Style: Principles of English Usage in the Digital Age* (San Francisco: HardWired, 1996).

ally a noun meaning "result or consequence"; it is only occasionally used as a verb, meaning "bring about," although the adjective form *(effective)* is common. *Researchers are studying the effect of stress. How does stress affect the human body?*

agree to, agree with *Agree to* means "consent to" or "say 'yes' to"; *agree with* means "share an opinion" or "be in agreement with." *I agreed to the terms of employment because the company agreed with my views on training the sales force.*

all ready, already *All ready* means "completely prepared"; *already* is an adverb meaning "previously" or "by now." *Is your friend all ready to join us for the hike, or is he already looking for an excuse to drop out?*

all right *All right* is the preferred spelling rather than *alright,* which many people regard as unacceptable.

all together, altogether *All together* suggests "all at the same place at the same time"; *altogether* is an adverb meaning "completely." *The sisters were all together at their parents' anniversary party but not altogether happy to see one another.*

allude, refer Use *refer,* not *allude,* when you directly mention someone or something. Reserve *allude* for casual or indirect mentions by hint, figure of speech, or quotation. *The novelist refers to one of literature's great love affairs when his protagonist writes in an email, "Our love is as hopeless as that between Romeo and Juliet." The novelist alludes to Romeo and Juliet's romance when he has the protagonist write, "Parting is such sweet sorrow. . . ."* Other forms: *allusion, reference.*

allusion, illusion An *allusion* is an indirect reference; an *illusion* is a false or deceptive appearance. *Do his allusions to Romantic poetry mean he has seriously studied it, or is he merely creating the illusion of being well read?*

almost, most *Almost* means "not quite"; *most* means "the larger number of." You can write *most of the students* or *almost all the students,* but you should not write *most all the students.*

a lot A common expression meaning "a large number," *a lot* is always written as two words. Because it is vague and informal, avoid it in college writing.

among, between Use *among* to refer to more than two objects; limit *between* to references to only two objects. *It is hard to choose one winner among so many highly qualified candidates. Between the two positions lies a vast middle ground.*

amoral, immoral *Amoral* means "neither moral nor immoral" and "not caring about right and wrong." *Immoral* means "objectionable." *The amoral athlete took steroids to increase her strength. Cheating on exams is immoral.*

amount, number *Amount* refers to the quantity of a unit *(amount of water, amount of discussion)*; *number* refers to the quantity of individual items *(number of papers, number of times)*. In general, use *amount* only with a singular noun.

and/or The conjunction *and/or* in business or legal writing tells the reader that "one or the other or both" (that is, one of three options) apply. In formal writing, try to avoid this conjunction.

ante-, anti- *Ante-* means "earlier" or "in front of" *(antedate, anteroom); anti-* means "against" or "opposed to" *(antiwar, anti-intellectual, anti-British).* Note that before an *i* or a capital letter, *anti-* is followed by a hyphen.

anxious, eager *Anxious* means "nervous" or "worried"; *eager* means "looking forward (impatiently)." Avoid using *anxious* to mean "eager." *The students were eager to learn their grades. They were anxious they wouldn't pass.*

anybody, anyone These are singular indefinite pronouns. Do not confuse *anybody* with *any body (any body of water),* or *anyone* with *any one (Any one of these novels is worth reading).* See also *everybody, everyone; somebody, someone.*

anyplace, anywhere *Anywhere* is the preferred one-word form in writing. Write *I have never lived anywhere with a basement* or *I have never lived in any place with a basement.*

anyways, anywheres Use *anyway* and *anywhere* (no *s*).

as Avoid using *as* in a way that may confuse your reader. In *As he is leaving, he sees Daisy for a moment,* it is not clear whether he sees Daisy *because* he is leaving or simply *when* he is leaving. See also *since* and *while.*

as, like In writing, do not use *like* (a **preposition**) to introduce a **dependent clause.** Use *as* or *as if* instead: *She writes in free verse, as* [not *like*] *you would expect from a disciple of Whitman's. She writes as if she grew up in another era.* Use *like* as a preposition meaning "in the same way as" or "similar to": *The vice president, like the president, turns down many invitations. She is like a barracuda.*

as, than When you use *as* or *than* in a comparison, carefully select the personal pronoun that follows. If the pronoun functions as a **subject,** use *I, he, she, they,* or *we*. If the pronoun functions as an **object,** use *me, him, her, them,* or *us. My mother is as eager to learn French as I [am]. The teacher praises her more than [she praises] me.* See Chapter 22.

preposition A word (such as *between, for, from, in, of,* or *to*) that always appears as part of a phrase and indicates the relation between a word in a sentence and the object of the preposition: The water splashed *into* the canoe.

dependent (subordinate) clause A word group with a subject, a predicate, and a subordinating word (such as *because*) at the beginning.

subject The word or words that identify the topic or theme of the sentence—what is being discussed: *Our defective rubber raft* began to leak air.

object The part of a clause that receives the action of the verb (At the checkpoint, we unloaded *the canoes*) or the part of a phrase that follows a preposition (We dragged them to *the river*).

preposition A word (such as *between, for, from, in, of,* or *to*) that always appears as part of a phrase and indicates the relation between a word in a sentence and the object of the preposition: The water splashed *into* the canoe.

linking verb *Be, seem, appear, become, taste,* or another verb that connects a subject with a subject complement that describes or modifies it: The chips *taste* salty.

adjective A word that modifies a noun or a pronoun, adding information about it.

adverb A word that modifies a verb, an adjective, or another adverb, often telling when, where, why, how, or how often.

assure, ensure, insure *Assure* means "promise," "convince," "guarantee"—with the sense of "setting the mind at rest." *Ensure* and *insure* both mean "make certain" or "guarantee against risk," but in American English *insure* suggests financial protection. *The attorney assured the client that he was sufficiently insured to ensure a good income for his wife if he died first.*

averse, adverse See *adverse, averse.*

awful Do not use *awful* (or the adverb *awfully*) to mean "bad" or "very."

awhile, a while Both *Stay awhile* and *Stay a while* are acceptable. *A while* can be the object of a **preposition;** *awhile* cannot. *Stay for a while* [not *awhile*].

bad, badly Use *bad* after a **linking verb** to describe the subject; use *badly* to modify an action verb, an **adjective,** or another **adverb.** *I feel bad. The toast is badly burned. I play tennis badly.*

being as, being that Instead of these expressions, use *because* or *since. Because* [not *Being that*] *she is bilingual, she is eligible for the position.*

beside, besides *Beside* is a **preposition** meaning "next to," "at the side of," or "in comparison with." *Besides* is a preposition meaning "except" or "in addition to"; *besides* is also an **adverb** meaning "in addition" or "moreover." *All the professors besides Dr. Herman work with a computer beside them. Computers are convenient; besides, they are affordable now.*

between, among See *among, between.*

bring, take *Bring* (like *come*) refers to movement from a farther place to a nearer place; *take* (like *go*) refers to movement from nearer to farther away. *You can take this book home with you tonight, but bring it back in the morning.*

can, may Conventionally, *can* refers to ability or capacity, whereas *may* refers to permission or possibility. *Can you say, "May I leave the table" in Spanish?*

capital, capitol *Capital* is the more common word and has a variety of meanings, among them the principal city in a state or country; *capitol* refers only to a government building.

censor, censure *Censor* means "remove or suppress material that is offensive or objectionable"; *censor* is also a noun that identifies the person who removes the material. *Censure* means "scold, reprimand, or criticize formally." *The politician was censured because she tried to censor the official record.*

cite, sight, site *Cite* is a verb meaning "refer to as proof" or "summon to appear in court": *Can you cite your sources for these figures? Sight,* which may be a verb or a noun, always refers to seeing or what is seen: *The desert in moonlight is a sight I will never forget. Site* is a noun meaning "place or location": *A new dormitory will be built on this site.*

compare to, compare with *Compare to* suggests a similarity between objects: *"Shall I compare thee to a summer's day?" Compare with* is the preferred expression when measuring size or examining another specific quality: *Compare his grades with yours.*

complement, compliment *Complement* refers to completion, the making of a satisfactory whole, whereas *compliment* indicates admiration or praise; both can be used as either nouns or verbs. *Complementary* means "serving to complete"; *complimentary* means "given free." *The designer received many compliments on the way the elements of the room complemented one another. Buy a new refrigerator, and receive a complimentary ice maker.*

compose, comprise Traditionally, *compose* means "make up": *The fifty states compose the nation. Comprise* means "contain": *The nation comprises fifty states.*

conscience, conscious *Conscience* means "a sense of morality or ethics," and *conscientious* means "guided by conscience" or "thoroughness." *Conscious* means "alert or aware," and *consciousness* means "a state of being alert or aware." *I was conscious after the accident. My conscience guides my behavior.*

consensus of opinion The phrase *of opinion* does not add meaning to *consensus: The consensus* [not *consensus of opinion*] *is to abandon the quarter system.*

contact Even though *contact* is frequently used as a verb in casual conversation and informal writing, in formal writing use more specific verbs to mean "get in touch with": *write, telephone, call.*

continual, continuous *Continual* suggests ongoing repetition—with breaks; *continuous* suggests no interruption at all. *The baby's continual wailing made it impossible for me to watch the movie. The car alarm made a continuous racket.*

could care less Do not use *could care less* to mean its opposite, *couldn't care less. I couldn't care less* [not *could care less*] *who wins the Super Bowl.*

could of See *have, of.*

council, counsel *Council* is a noun meaning "an assembly of people who deliberate or govern"; *counsel* is a verb meaning "advise" or a noun meaning "advice." Other forms include *councilor* ("member of a council") and *counselor* ("one who gives advice"). *The council on drug abuse has issued guidelines for counseling addicted students. Before voting on the important fiscal issue, City Councilor Lopez sought the counsel of her constituents.*

criteria This word is the plural of *criterion,* which means "a standard, a rule, a test." *One criterion is employment; another is acceptable references. These criteria for obtaining a mortgage are common.*

cyber Usually, this term appears as a combining form, closed up to another word or word part, as in *cyberspace* and *cyberpunk.* Some writers also use it as a stand-alone adjective *(cyber commercial center).*

data This word is the plural of the Latin word *datum,* meaning "fact." *Data* is often treated as singular, especially when the writer is referring to a collection of information: *The data support* [or *supports*] *my conclusion.*

device, devise *Device* is a noun; *devise* is a verb. *Inventors devise devices that make our lives easier.*

different from, different than Formal writing calls for *different from: Coleridge's poetry is different from Wordsworth's.* Sometimes writers use *different than* to avoid wordiness: *He is a different novelist now than he used to be* rather than *He is a different novelist now from the novelist he used to be.*

differ from, differ with *Differ from* means "be unlike"; *differ with* means "not agree with." *I differ with you on how much the twins differ from each other.*

digital Going well beyond its general meaning—"expressed in digits," as in *digital clock—digital* is a common adjective in computer contexts. Technically, *digital* has to do with the storage of data in bits, but the word also appears as a catch-all adjective in lieu of *computer: digital world, digital hint.*

disc, disk Experts on writing about computers advise using *disc* to refer to a compact disc, a CD-ROM, a laserdisc, or a videodisc, and *disk* to refer to a floppy disk or a hard disk.

disinterested, uninterested *Disinterested* means "impartial, objective"; *uninterested* means "not interested." *The couple needs a disinterested marriage counselor. The husband and wife seem uninterested in a reconciliation.*

don't *Don't,* the contraction of *do not,* agrees with *you, they,* or any other plural subject: *They don't work.* Do not use *don't* with *he, she, it,* or any other singular subject: *He doesn't* [not *don't*] *work.*

due to Remember that *due* is an **adjective.** After a form of *be,* you can use *due to* to describe the subject: *His headache was due to tension.* In other constructions, use the preposition *because of* instead of *due to: His head ached because of tension.*

adjective A word that modifies a noun or a pronoun, adding information about it.

due to the fact that Replace this wordy expression with *because. His head ached because* [not *due to the fact that*] *he felt tense.*

effect, affect See *affect, effect.*

e.g. In most formal writing, replace this Latin abbreviation with *for example* or *for instance.* See also *like, such as.*

elicit, illicit The verb *elicit* means "draw out, call forth"; the adjective *illicit* means "illegal": *The police tried to elicit from the prisoner the hideout for illicit activities.*

email Working as both a noun and a verb, this shorthand for *electronic mail* appears also as *E-mail,* and *e-mail.* Any of these three alternatives is acceptable, as long as you are consistent within an essay.

emigrant, immigrant Use *emigrant* to identify someone moving out of a country; use *immigrant* to identify someone moving into a country. Other forms: *emigration, émigré; immigration.*

emigrate from, immigrate to A person *emigrates from* [leaves] one country and *immigrates to* [moves to and settles in] another country.

ensure See *assure, ensure, insure.*

enthused In formal writing, replace this word with *enthusiastic.* Instead of *She was enthused about the trip,* write *She was enthusiastic about the trip.*

etc. An abbreviation of the Latin words *et cetera* ("and other things"), *etc.* should never be preceded by *and* in English. In general, use *etc.* sparingly, if at all, in formal writing.

everybody, everyone These indefinite pronouns are singular: *Everybody is present and has his or her ticket.* Do not confuse *everybody* with *every body,* as in *every body of water.* Do not confuse *everyone* with *every one,* as in *Every one of the exam questions is challenging.* See also *anybody, anyone; somebody, someone.*

everyday, every day Use *everyday,* an adjective, when you mean "ordinary"; use *every day,* an adjective + noun, when you are pointing out particular days. *I wear everyday clothes every day of the week except Saturday.*

except, accept See *accept, except.*

explicit, implicit *Explicit* means "directly stated" or "definite"; *implicit* means "indirectly stated" or "implied." *The mother's explicit message was "Don't forget to call"; the mother's implicit message was "or I'll be very upset."*

farther, further Use *farther* when you are discussing physical distance; use *further* when discussing other kinds of advancement or progression. *As the athlete makes further progress in her training, she will be able to jump farther.*

fewer, less In formal writing, remember to use *fewer* when referring to **count nouns;** reserve *less* for amounts you cannot count. *The new cookies have fewer calories than the other brand because they contain less sugar.*

count noun A noun that names people, things, and ideas that can be counted: one *teacher,* two *teachers;* one *movie,* several *movies;* one *belief,* several *beliefs.*

finalize Instead of this pompous verb, write *complete, conclude, finish, make final,* or a similar expression. *I will write a final draft of my essay* [not *I will finalize my essay*] *tonight.*

firstly *First, second, third,* and so on are usually preferable. If you use *firstly,* remember to use *secondly* [not *second*] for your next point.

flaunt, flout *Flaunt* means "show off" or "make a public display of"; flout means "to show contempt for." *"If you've got it, flaunt it" is the motto of people who flout dress codes.*

former, latter *Former* refers to the first of two items mentioned, and *latter* refers to the second of two items. *I bought a down coat and a cloth coat—the former for everyday use and the latter for special occasions.*

fortuitous, fortunate Often used incorrectly, the adjective *fortuitous* means "by chance" or "unplanned" and should not be confused with *fortunate* ("lucky"). *Because the antagonistic politicians wished to avoid each other, their fortuitous meeting in the parking lot was not a fortunate event.*

further, farther See *farther, further.*

get In formal writing, avoid expressions such as *it gets to me, get lost, get back at someone, have got to* (a weak substitute for *must*). In other sentences, replace *get* with a more specific verb: *The situation is improving* [rather than *getting bet-*

ter]. Avoid using *get* in passive constructions in academic writing: *The students were penalized* [not *got penalized*] *for being late.*

good, well *Good* is always an **adjective.** Use it after a form of *be* or another **linking verb:** *That color looks good on you. Well* is usually an **adverb;** use it to modify an action verb: *You dress well. Well* is an adjective only when it describes someone's health, as in *You look well,* meaning "You look healthy." (*You look good* means "you are attractive.")

hanged, hung Write *hanged* only if you are referring to an execution. In all other instances, write *hung. The sheriff hanged the murderer. We hung our heads.*

hardly, scarcely Although you may say and hear the expression *can't hardly* or *can't scarcely,* avoid it and other double negatives in formal writing: *The child can hardly* [not *can't hardly*] *wait until his birthday.*

have, of Expressions such as *could of, should of,* and *may of* are too casual. Instead, write *could have, should have, may have,* and so on.

he/she, him/her, his/her To avoid these awkward expressions, use *he or she* and *him or her.* You can also avoid the need for singular pronouns by using plural nouns. Instead of *Everyone must bring his/her passport,* write *Everyone must bring his or her passport* or *All travelers must bring their passports.*

hisself, theirselves In nonstandard speech, *hisself* is sometimes used for *himself* and *theirselves* for *themselves;* such usage is not acceptable in written work.

hopefully The adverb *hopefully,* meaning "full of hope," should always modify a specific verb or adverb: *The candidate inquired hopefully about the results.* In conversation, *hopefully* often is used to suggest that some outcome is generally to be hoped for *(Hopefully, our nominee will win the election)*; however, many people find this usage unacceptable in written work. Substitute *I hope, one hopes, let us hope, everyone hopes,* or *it is to be hoped,* depending on your meaning.

hung, hanged See *hanged, hung.*

i.e. In most formal writing, replace this Latin abbreviation with *that is.*

if, whether Use *if* when writing about conditions; use *whether* when writing about choices. *If it is cloudy, the family will debate whether to go ahead with the outdoor party or cancel it.*

adjective A word that modifies a noun or a pronoun, adding information about it.

linking verb *Be, seem, appear, become, taste,* or another verb that connects a subject with a subject complement that describes or modifies it: The chips *taste* salty.

adverb A word that modifies a verb, an adjective, or another adverb, often telling when, where, why, how, or how often.

illicit, elicit See *elicit, illicit.*

illusion, allusion See *allusion, illusion.*

immigrant, emigrant See *emigrant, immigrant.*

immigrate to, emigrate from See *emigrate from, immigrate to.*

immoral, amoral See *amoral, immoral.*

impact Many people object to the use of *impact* or *impact on* as a verb. Instead of *Demographics impact college enrollment,* write *Demographics have an impact on* [or *affect*] *college enrollment.*

implicit, explicit See *explicit, implicit.*

imply, infer *Imply* means "suggest indirectly"; *infer* means "reach a conclusion." Speakers or writers are impliers, and listeners or readers are inferrers. *The poet implies and critics infer that the woman in the poem represents his mother.*

in regards to Use either *in regard to* or *as regards,* not *in regards to. In regard to* [or *As regards*] *stage design, he has no peer.*

insure See *assure, ensure, insure.*

interface In its computer context, the noun *interface* refers to the point of communication between a computer and a user or a computer and another device—say, a printer. As a verb, *interface* often expresses an action involving a computer but also is used to mean "to interact or coordinate smoothly." Readers may consider *interface* to be jargon (see 36b).

Internet Capitalize *Internet* and precede it with *the,* unless you are using it as an adjective. When referring to the Internet, also capitalize *Net.*

irregardless This word is an improper blend of *irrespective* and *regardless. A two-parent family has advantages regardless* [not *irregardless*] *of arguments to the contrary.*

is when, is where Avoid these expressions in definitions. *Obsessive compulsive disorder is a condition in which* [not *is when*] *patients dwell on unwanted thoughts.* See also 30c.

its, it's *Its* is a possessive pronoun; *it's* is the contraction of *it is. It's true that this job has its advantages.* See also 43b.

kind(s) Write either *This kind of mirror distorts* or *These kinds of mirrors distort.* Do not write *These kind of mirrors distort.* Consider also whether you can omit *kind of,* often used as filler: *These mirrors distort.* See also 28b.

kind of, sort of Do not use these expressions as modifiers in writing. *Book reviewers have been somewhat* [not *kind of*] *generous to the author.*

latter, former See *former, latter.*

lay, lie The verb *lay,* meaning "put, place," is **transitive** (forms of *lay* are *lay, laid, laid*). The verb *lie,* meaning "recline," is **intransitive** (forms of *lie* are *lie, lay, lain*). Writers may incorrectly use *laid* as the past tense of *lie,* or *lay* as the present tense of *lie. The lion lies* [not *lays*] *in wait for the approach of its prey. Joseph laid down his shovel, took a shower, and lay* [not *laid*] *down for a nap.* Other forms: *laying, lying.*

transitive verb A verb that needs an object—something that receives the action of the verb—to make its meaning complete.

intransitive verb A verb that does not need an object to make its meaning complete.

lead, led *Lead* (pronounced "led") is a metal or refers to a metal; *led* is the past tense of the verb *lead* (pronounced "leed"), meaning "show the way." *The parent led the inspector to the child's room, where the lead paint was peeling.*

leave, let Avoid using *leave* in writing to mean "permit." *The candidate should let* [not *leave*] *the vote count stand, not challenge it. Leave alone* and *let alone* are interchangeable.

less, fewer See *fewer, less.*

lie, lay See *lay, lie.*

like, as See *as, like.*

like, such as Write *such as* to introduce examples of a general class, as you would use *for example.* Write *like* when you mean to suggest a comparison. *He praises the early social theorists, such as* [not *like*] *Durkheim and Weber. Sociologists, like psychologists, study human behavior.*

loose, lose *Lose* is a verb meaning "mislay" or "fail to maintain"; *loose* is most often used as an adjective meaning "not fastened tightly." *A loose board may make someone lose his or her balance.*

lots, lots of In formal prose, write *much, many,* or *a great deal of* instead of *lots* or *lots of.*

may, can See *can, may.*

maybe, may be *Maybe* is an adverb that means "possibly" or "perhaps"; *may be* is a verb phrase. *"Maybe" may be replaced by "perhaps."*

may of, might of, must of See *have, of.*

media This word is the plural of the noun *medium* and is gaining acceptance as a **collective noun** (meaning "industry"): *The media has criticized the presi-*

collective noun A noun (such as *class, family, committee,* or *jury*) that refers to a group as a unit and is usually considered singular.

dent. You will, however, always be considered correct if you treat *media* as plural: *The media have criticized the president.*

most See *almost, most.*

myself, herself, himself, yourself Do not use these words in place of the personal pronouns *I, me, she, her, he, him, you,* and *your. An assistant and I* [not *myself*] *conducted the experiment.* Use *-self* pronouns in constructions such as *I pleased myself,* and *The pregnant woman must submit a passport-size photograph of herself for her medical chart.* See also 22d.

nowheres Use *nowhere* instead (no *-s*).

number, amount See *amount, number.*

of See *have, of.*

off of Use only *off,* or use *from: Linguists copied the symbols off* [or *from,* but not *off of*] *the Rosetta Stone.*

OK, O.K., okay While all three spellings are acceptable, avoid this term in formal writing.

online Treat this adjective meaning "logged on to a network" as a closed compound, although you will occasionally see writers use *on-line.*

passed, past *Passed* is a verb; *past* is not. *This past semester 80 percent of the sophomores passed all their classes.*

people, persons In formal writing, use *people* to refer to a whole group and *persons* to refer to particular individuals. *We the people of the United States. The blood bank seeks persons with Type A blood.*

per Except in phrases taken directly from Latin and in technical writing, avoid *per. The per capita income is $75,000. The speed limit is 55 miles an* [not *per*] *hour. Judging by* [not *Per* or *As per*] *the letters to the editor, the townspeople did not share the opinion of the editorial board.*

percent, per cent, percentage Use *percent* (or *per cent*) when you cite a particular number. Use *percentage* when you refer to a share in relation to the whole and when you use a term such as *large* or *small. Only a small percentage of students earned a score of 90 percent or higher on the test.*

persecute, prosecute *Persecute* means "mistreat" or "oppress"; *prosecute* most often means "bring a legal suit or action against." *A biased majority can easily persecute minority groups. The law may prosecute only those who are indicted.*

phenomena This word is the plural of *phenomenon. Those phenomena still puzzle scientists.* Use *phenomenons* as the plural when you mean "extraordinary things, occurrences, or persons" or "marvels." *As child movie stars, they were phenomenons.*

plus Do not use *plus* to mean "besides" or "moreover." *The CD-ROM under review is not multimedia; moreover* [not *plus*], *it contains errors of fact.*

post In computer contexts, *post* means "send a message online." The noun *post* refers to the message itself.

precede, proceed *Precede* means "come or occur before"; *proceed* means "go forward or ahead." *The hospitalization preceded his most creative period. After the hospitalization, he proceeded to paint his most famous works.*

pretty Do not use *pretty* as a substitute for *very, rather, somewhat,* or *quite. Beach erosion has been rather* [not *pretty*] *extensive for the last decade.*

principal, principle *Principal* implies "first in rank, chief," whether it is used as an adjective (*the principal cities of the Midwest)* or a noun *(the principal of a midwestern high school). Principle* is generally a noun meaning "a basic law or truth": *The principle of free speech will be the principal topic of discussion.*

prosecute, persecute See *persecute, prosecute.*

quotation, quote In academic writing, use only *quotation,* not *quote,* when you need a noun. Use *quote* only as a verb. *Fewer and fewer students can quote Shakespeare. I included a handful of quotations in my essay.*

raise, rise *Raise* means "lift" or "cause to move up"; it requires a direct object. *Rise* means "move up" or "wake up"; it does not take a direct object. *The elevator rises* [not *raises*] *quickly.*

real, really Do not use *real* as a substitute for *really,* meaning "truly." *Reading his journal was really* [not *real*] *eye-opening.*

reason is because Avoid this expression. Instead, write *reason is that* or simply *because. The reason children like poetry is that it is predictable in some ways. Children like poetry because it is predictable in some ways.* See also 30c.

reason why This expression is redundant. *The reason* [not *The reason why*] *he stopped writing is far from obvious.*

refer, allude See *allude, refer.*

relation, relationship Both words can refer to family ties. Use only *relation,* not *relationship,* when writing about a connection between things rather than people. *The relation of hyperactivity in childhood to violence in adolescence is under study.*

respectable, respectful, respective *Respectable* means "worthy of respect" or "appropriate to convention"; *respectful* means "polite"; *respective* means "separate" or "individual." *Young adults who want to be considered respectable must appear respectful toward adults. My parents fled repression in their respective native countries.*

rise, raise See *raise, rise.*

scarcely, hardly See *hardly, scarcely.*

sensual, sensuous Both *sensual* and *sensuous* suggest the enjoyment of physical pleasure through the senses. However, *sensual* generally implies self-indulgence, particularly in terms of sexual activity; *sensuous* suggests the ability to appreciate intellectually what is received through the senses. *When drunk, the emperor became only a sensual, not a political, being. Anyone can enjoy a sensuous spring night.* Other forms: *sensuality, sensuousness.*

set, sit *Sit* is generally intransitive and means "having a seat"; *set* is transitive and means "put something in a certain place." *Set* also has a number of uses as a noun. The past-tense and **past-participle** forms of *sit* are both *sat;* these forms for *set* are *set. He set his suitcase on the ground and then sat on it.*

shall, will *Will* can be used as a **helping verb** to mean "intention." You may use *shall* in certain first-person questions and in legal writing: *Shall we banish Shakespeare from the curriculum? The applicant shall submit two passport-size photographs of himself or herself.* See also 54c.

should of See *have, of.*

sight, site, cite See *cite, sight, site.*

since *Since* can mean "from the time that" or "because." Use *since* only when context clarifies whether you want to denote time or cause-effect. *Since the school distributed laptops, seventh graders are doing better* is ambiguous because *since* may have either meaning. See also *as* and *while.*

past participle A verb form usually ending in *-ed* that combines with a form of *be* or *have* *(is needed, had stayed).* Past participles can also function as adjectives.

helping verbs The verbs *have, do,* and *be,* which can function as helping verbs (they precede or "help" main verbs) or as main verbs, and *modals* such as *can, may, could, will, shall,* and *should,* which must be used in conjunction with another (main) verb: I *may go* to the bank.

sit, set See *set, sit.*

so When you use *so* as an intensifier, add *that* and a clause to state an effect or result: *His performance in the role of Hamlet generated so much interest that the play's run was extended.*

somebody, someone These words are singular indefinite pronouns. Do not confuse *somebody* with *some body,* as in *some body like Congress.* Do not confuse *someone* with *some one,* as in *Many Americans select some one charity and remain loyal to it.* See also *anybody, anyone; everybody, everyone.*

sometime, some time, sometimes *Sometime* refers to an indefinite time; *some time* means "a period of time"; *sometimes* means "occasionally." *Sometime the scholar intends to spend some time in London. Sometimes she dreams of studying in the British Museum.*

sort of, kind of See *kind of, sort of.*

stationary, stationery *Stationary* is an adjective meaning "fixed, remaining in one place," as in *Concrete will make the pole stationary. Stationery* refers to writing paper.

such as, like See *like, such as.*

supposed to, used to Write *He was supposed* [not *suppose*] *to be the greatest playwright of his generation* and *He used* [not *use*] *to produce three plays a season.*

take, bring See *bring, take.*

than, as See *as, than.*

than, then Use *than* when stating a comparison; use *then* when remarking on a time sequence. *The reviews praised the young writer's first novel, and then the teacher knew that her student was going to be more famous than she.*

that, which, who Use *that* to refer to nonhumans and groups of humans. Use *which* to refer only to nonhumans and *who* to refer only to humans. Furthermore, use *that* (without commas) to introduce **restrictive** (necessary) **clauses** and *which* (with commas) to introduce **nonrestrictive** (unnecessary) **clauses.** *The news that the executor discovered unpublished manuscripts, which had resided for thirty years in a cardboard box, stunned the critics, who thought they had read all of the writer's work.* See also 21b and 21c.

restrictive clause A clause, not set off by commas, that provides information essential to defining or identifying the noun or pronoun it modifies.

nonrestrictive clause A clause, set off by commas, that provides extra or nonessential information and could be eliminated without changing the meaning of the noun or pronoun it modifies.

their, there, they're *Their* is a possessive pronoun; *there* specifies a place or functions as an expletive; and *they're* is a contraction of *they are. The coauthors say there are no copies of their script in their office, but they're not telling the truth.*

theirselves See *hisself, theirselves.*

to, too, two *To* is a preposition, *too* is an adverb, and *two* is generally an adjective. Be careful not to substitute *to* for *too. It is too early to predict either of the two scores.*

toward, towards American writers tend to use *toward,* and British writers tend to use *towards.* Whichever word you choose to use, use it consistently within an essay.

try and Use *try to* rather than *try and* in formal writing. *Linguists try to* [not *try and*] *avoid labels such as* nonstandard.

uninterested, disinterested See *disinterested, uninterested.*

unique To be precise, *unique* means "one of a kind, like no other." Careful writers do not use it loosely to mean simply "unusual" or "rare," or try to use a comparative form *(most unique),* although advertisers sometimes use *unique* in this way. *This example of Mayan culture is apparently unique; none other like it has so far been discovered.*

usage This word is used as a noun to refer to language conventions; it is not a substitute for the noun *use. The use* [not *usage*] *of the server is off limits to undergraduates.*

use to See *supposed to, used to.*

utilize In most situations, write *use* and avoid the longer verb *utilize,* which is sometimes considered pretentious. *Hospitals are using* [not *utilizing*] *operating rooms around the clock.*

ways Use *way,* not *ways,* when talking about distance or an interval of time. *A paycheck sometimes seems a long way* [not *ways*] *off to the young actor in New York City.*

weather, whether *Weather* refers to climate; *whether* is a conjunction that introduces alternatives. *Whether the weather did or did not affect the artist's color choices is a question worth investigating.* See also *if, whether.*

Web Capitalize this word when using it to refer to the World Wide Web.

well, good See *good, well.*

whether, if See *if, whether.*

which, that, who See *that, which, who.*

while Do not use *while* if ambiguity may result. In *While the writer was institutionalized, she wrote her famous memoir,* the word *while* might mean "although" or "at the time that." See also *as* and *since.*

who, which, that See *that, which, who.*

who, whom To introduce a relative clause, use *who* when the next word is a verb and *whom* when the next word is a noun or pronoun. *The producer, who used to stage only classics, now supports experimental theater. The producer, whom critics laud, now supports experimental theater. He is a producer who, critics say, resembles backers of an earlier age.* In the last example, if the parenthetical expression *critics say* is omitted, the word after *who* is the verb *resembles.* See also 21d.

who's, whose *Who's* is the contraction of *who is* or *who has; whose* is the possessive form of *who. Who's responsible for supporting new playwrights, whose works must be produced?*

will, shall See *shall, will.*

would have This expression is inappropriate in an *if* clause that states a condition contrary to fact. Simply use *had: If Shakespeare had* [not *would have*] *lived longer, what would he have written next?* See also 54a.

would of See *have, of.*

you Do not use *you* in an indefinite sense: *During the Depression, people* [not *you*] *were lucky to be working.*

your, you're *Your* is a possessive form of *you; you're* is a contraction of *you are. You're going to be surprised by your grade.*

Acknowledgments (*continued from page iv*)

Paul Auster. Excerpt from "Why Write." First appeared in *The New Yorker,* December 25, 1995 & January 1, 1996. Copyright © 1995 Paul Auster. Reprinted by permission of the author.

James Baldwin. Excerpt from "Stranger in the Village" is collected in *Notes of A Native Son* by James Baldwin. Copyright © 1955, renewed 1983 by James Baldwin. Reprinted by permission of Beacon Press.

Joseph Berger. Excerpt from "What Produces Outstanding Science Students." Originally titled "Science Education for the Gifted and Talented" from *The American Enterprise* (January/February 1994), pp. 16–18. Reprinted by permission of the American Enterprise Institute.

Janice Castro. Excerpt from "Contingent Workers." Originally titled "Disposable Workers." Published in *Time* magazine, March 29, 1993. © 1993 Time, Inc. Reprinted by permission.

Richard Estrada. Excerpt from "Sticks and Stones and Sports Teams Names." The *Los Angeles Times,* October 29, 1995. Copyright © 1995, The Washington Post Writers Group. Reprinted with permission.

William Least Heat-Moon. Excerpt from *Blue Highways* by William Least Heat-Moon. Copyright © 1982 by William Least Heat-Moon. Reprinted by permission of Little, Brown & Company, Inc.

"Home Schooling." Academic Index database. © 1997 Information Access Company. All rights reserved. Reprinted by permission.

Steven D. Kay. Excerpt from "Hello 75, So Long 55." *U.S. News & World Report,* December 18, 1995, p. 73. Copyright © 1995 U.S. News & World Report. Reprinted by permission.

David Noonan. Excerpt from "Inside the Brain" in *Neuro-Life on the Frontlines of Brain Surgery & Neurological Medicine* by David Noonan. Copyright © 1989 by David Noonan. Reprinted by permission of Simon & Schuster.

Steven Waldman. Excerpt from "The Tyranny of Choice." *The New Republic,* January 27, 1992. Copyright © 1992 The New Republic. Reprinted by permission.

Tobias Wolff. Excerpt from "On Being a Real Westerner" in *This Boy's Life* by Tobias Wolff. Copyright © 1989 by Tobias Wolff. Used by permission of Grove/Atlantic, Inc.

INDEX

INDEX FOR ESL WRITERS

The following index includes topics from Part 10, "Brief Guide for ESL Writers," as well as topics from other parts of *A Writer's Guidebook* that are especially important for ESL writers.

CORRECTION SYMBOLS

Numbers and letters in **bold type** refer to chapters and sections of the book.

ab	Faulty abbreviation **51**
ad	Misuse of adverb or adjective **25**
agr	Agreement **20, 24, 28**
appr	Inappropriate word **36**
art	Error in the use of an article **53**
awk	Awkward
cap	Use a capital letter **47**
case	Error in pronoun case **22**
coh	Coherence needed **33c, d, e**
comb	Combine sentences **33a, b**
coord	Coordination **33a**
cs	Comma splice **16**
dev	Paragraph development needed **3c**
dm	Dangling modifier **29b**
emph	Emphasis **33**
exact	Inexact word **35**
frag	Sentence fragment **18**
fs	Fused sentence **17**
hyph	Error in use of hyphen **46**
inc	Incomplete construction **26**
integ	Question, quotation, or thought has not been integrated smoothly **8c, 31**
ital	Italics (underline) **50**
lc	Use lowercase letter **47**
mixed	Mixed construction **30**
MLA	Error in MLA style **9**
mm	Misplaced modifier **29a**
mood	Error in mood **23e**
ms	Manuscript form **13, 14**
mw	Missing word
no ab	Do not abbreviate **51d**
no cap	Do not capitalize **47g**
no ital	Do not italicize (underline) **50f**
no und	Do not underline (italicize) **50f**
num	Error in use of numbers **49**
p	Punctuation
^,	Comma **37**
no ^,	No comma **38**
;	Semicolon **39**
no ;	No semicolon **39e**
:	Colon **40**
no :	No colon **40c**
—	Dash **41**
no —	No dash **41c**
“ ”	Quotation marks **42**
no “ ”	No quotation marks **42f**
∨'	Apostrophe **43**
no ∨'	No apostrophe **43a**
( )	Parentheses **44c**
[ ]	Brackets **44d**
. . .	Ellipsis marks **44a**
/	Slash **44b**
. ? !	Period, question mark, exclamation point **45**
par, ¶	New paragraph **3d**
pass	Ineffective use of passive voice **23f**
ref	Error in pronoun reference **19**
shift	Passage contains a shift in tense, person, number, mood, voice, or from direct to indirect discourse **27**
sp	Spelling **52**
ss	Simplify sentence structure or separate sentences **33, 34**
sub	Subordination **33a**
t	Error in verb tense **23a, b, c**
trans	Transition needed **3d**
und	Underline (italicize) **50**
var	Vary sentence structure **33b**
vb	Error in verb form **23d**
w	Wordy **34**
wc	Ineffective word choice **35, 36**
ww	Wrong word **35a, b, c, Glossary**
//	Faulty parallelism **32**
#	Add a space **48a**
⁀	Close up space **48b**
^	Insert
ℓ	Delete
∩∪	Transpose
X	Obvious error

CONTENTS